THE ENVIRONMENTAL PREDICAMENT

Four Issues for Critical Analysis

THE ENVIRONMENTAL PREDICAMENT

Four Issues for Critical Analysis

CAROL J. VERBURG

Bedford Books *of* **St. Martin's Press**
Boston

For Bedford Books

President and Publisher: Charles H. Christensen
General Manager and Associate Publisher: Joan E. Feinberg
Managing Editor: Elizabeth M. Schaaf
Developmental Editor: Pam Ozaroff
Production Editor: Ann Sweeney
Copyeditor: Barbara G. Flanagan
Text Design: Melinda Grosser for *silk*
Cover Design: Night & Day Design

Acknowledgments

Judd H. Alexander, excerpt from *In Defense of Garbage*. Reprinted with permission of Greenwood
 Publishing Group, Inc., Westport, CT. Copyright © 1993 by Judd H. Alexander.
Frank Edward Allen, "Labs Rely on Computer Models to Predict Changes in Climate." From the
 Wall Street Journal, 3 June 1992. Reprinted by permission of the *Wall Street Journal*, © 1992
 Dow Jones & Company, Inc. All Rights Reserved Worldwide.
Scott Allen, excerpt from "Bay State Ships Out Its Waste Problems." From the *Boston Globe*, 16
 February 1994. Reprinted courtesy of the *Boston Globe*.
Isaac Asimov and Frederik Pohl, excerpt from *Our Angry Earth*. Copyright © 1991 by Isaac Asi-
 mov and Frederik Pohl, and reprinted with permission of Tom Doherty Associates, Inc., New
 York.
Regina Austin and Michael Schill, excerpt from "Black, Brown, Red, and Poisoned," by Regina
 Austin and Michael Schill, from *Unequal Protection*, edited by Robert D. Bullard.
 Copyright © 1994 by Robert D. Bullard. Reprinted with permission of Sierra Club Books.
Bruce Babbitt, "A New Conservation Ethic." Adapted in the *Los Angeles Times*, 1 June 1994,
 from a speech delivered by Bruce Babbitt 23 May 1994 at Independence National Park,
 Philadelphia. Reprinted with permission.

50% TOTAL RECYCLED FIBER
10% POST-CONSUMER

PRINTED WITH
SOY INK™

Preface for Instructors

Give me the liberty to know, to utter, and to argue freely according to conscience, above all liberties.

— John Milton, *Areopagitica* (1644)

The popularity of the argument-based composition course can be seen as tacit recognition that knowing how to argue is an essential skill for participating in human society. A student who can frame an effective argument is one equipped to utilize the knowledge and the freedom of speech offered by his or her college education. For to argue effectively depends on being able to think critically: not only to amass information but also to evaluate it, organize it, and re-present it convincingly to a reader or listener.

Students entering the argument course, however, may or may not appreciate the value of the skills they can sharpen there. Part of the challenge for the instructor is motivating students to try their hand at reading and writing arguments so that they can discover how interesting and useful these activities are. If the topic is an intriguing one, students are more likely to engage with it. Many instructors find it productive to focus the argument course on a single issue so that class members can compare notes, explore various approaches, and probe more deeply into the material than one or two assignments permit.

Whatever students' backgrounds and fields of interest, the relationship between the earth and human beings is a topic in which all share a vital involvement. *The Environmental Predicament* is the first short, inexpensive, single-theme reader on this topic that is specifically designed for the argument course. As the twenty-first century approaches, every one of us is called on to make decisions and take positions on environmental issues. Yet expert opinion is sharply divided as to which problems are the most urgent, let alone which tactics are most likely to solve them. What richer subject for argumentation?

In the interests of brevity and focus, *The Environmental Predicament* comprises only expository writing on contemporary controversies, in contrast to the usual mix of literary, personal, and argumentative writing in longer texts. Its thirty selections represent a wide range of opinions by scientists, policy makers, activists, journalists, and philosophers such as Barry Commoner, Helen Caldicott, Dixy Lee Ray, Dave Foreman, Julian L. Simon, and Donella Meadows. The book is ideal as a supplemental reader to an argument text, as a sourcebook for controlled research papers, or as the core text in a single-theme course.

Each of *The Environmental Predicament*'s four chapters considers a controversial topic at the forefront of current debate: What is our responsibility, as earth's dominant species, to other forms of life? How can we prevent the refuse we generate from fatally fouling our own nest? Is the threat of global warming an authentic crisis or mere hysteria? What actions can we take to ensure the survival of our species and our planet? By opening with a familiar, tangible issue and expanding outward to more global concerns, the book equips students step by step to grapple with questions of increasing complexity and abstraction.

Prefacing the introduction to each chapter are "Points of View": brief, provocative epigraphs that highlight concepts and attitudes related to the chapter's core issue. Within each chapter, six to eight main selections present a range of views as well as a variety of argumentative strategies. Some pieces can serve as models for student writing; others will encourage critical analysis and rebuttal. Following many of the main selections, "In the News" pieces from current newspapers and magazines offer dramatic examples of theory in action.

Both main selections and "In the News" pieces are followed by "Analyzing Issues and Arguments" — questions that encourage students to dissect the writers' theses, tactics, and hidden assumptions. Each main selection is also followed by a "Writing about Issues and Arguments" assignment, which asks students to write an argumentative essay about an issue posed by that selection, to compare and contrast the strategies of different writers within a chapter, or to produce a research paper that draws on a few additional sources. At the end of each chapter, "Making Critical Connections" questions help tie the selections together and encourage students to use the readings as a springboard to further research. At the end of the book, a glossary of environmental terms helps students understand the key scientific concepts in the readings, and an annotated bibliography lets them expand their investigations to additional sources.

Resources for Teaching The Environmental Predicament, written by Nancy Hurrelbrinck, features an introduction to each selection with suggested teaching strategies, sample answers to the discussion questions in the text, and an annotated bibliography that expands on the one in the text. The instructor's manual also includes a useful introduction on teaching environmental issues in an argument course, written by Carole Pfeffer of Bellarmine College. Thanks to both writers for their fine work.

Many people helped to bring this book into existence. Special thanks go to six friends who influenced my thinking and reading about "the environmental predicament" long before Chuck Christensen at Bedford Books raised the possibility of turning that multifaceted issue into a book title: Sara Neustadtl and Peter Molnar, Maria Quintana and Howard Boyer, and Bettyann and Dan Kevles. Thanks also to my friend Nöel Yount for her help with headnote research. At Bedford Books, Karen Henry helped get the project off the ground, and Pam Ozaroff and Ann Sweeney kept it in the air, with invaluable assistance from Mark Reimold, Diane Bernard, Jonathan Burns, Kim Chabot, Alanya Harter, Mary Lou Wilshaw, and Verity Winship, among others. Reviews of the manuscript along the way were contributed by composition instructors Elizabeth Bell, University of South Carolina, Aiken; Carole Pfeffer, Bellarmine College; Don Ulin, Indiana University; and Nan Wishner, Solano Community College, as well as by environmental experts Penelope ReVelle, professor of Geography and Environmental Engineering, Johns Hopkins University; Philip Shabecoff, environmental journalist and publisher of Greenwire news service; and Peter Wehrwein, environmental journalist and journalism fellow at the Harvard School of Public Health. Last but not least, I thank the writers whose commitment and effort have compelled all of us to think — and argue — about the intricate relationship between the earth and human affairs.

Contents

2 *What Should We Do about Our Garbage?* *83*

1

What Is Our Responsibility
to Other Species?

POINTS OF VIEW

The history of life on earth has been a history of interaction between
living things and their surroundings. To a large extent, the physical form
and the habits of the earth's vegetation and its animal life have been
molded by the environment. Considering the whole span of earthly time,
the opposite effect, in which life actually modifies its surroundings, has
been relatively slight. Only within the moment of time represented by
the present century has one species—man—acquired significant power to
alter the nature of his world.

      —Rachel Carson, *Silent Spring* (1962)

Opinions on the human prospect have tended to fall loosely into two
schools. The first, exemptionalism, holds that since humankind is
transcendent in intelligence and spirit, so must our species have been
released from the iron laws of ecology that bind all other species. No
matter how serious the problem, civilized human beings, by ingenuity,
force of will and—who knows — divine dispensation, will find a
solution.

      Population growth? Good for the economy, claim some of the
exemptionalists, and in any case a basic human right, so let it run. Land
shortages? Try fusion energy to power the desalting of sea water, then
reclaim the world's deserts. (The process might be assisted by towing
icebergs to coastal pipelines.) Species going extinct? Not to worry. That is
nature's way. Think of humankind as only the latest in a long line of
exterminating agents in geological time. In any case, because our species
has pulled free of old-style, mindless Nature, we have begun a different
order of life. Evolution should now be allowed to proceed along this new
trajectory. Finally, resources? The planet has more than enough resources
to last indefinitely, if human genius is allowed to address each new
problem in turn, without alarmist and unreasonable restrictions imposed
on economic development. So hold the course, and touch the brakes
lightly.

      The opposing idea of reality is environmentalism, which sees human-
ity as a biological species tightly dependent on the natural world. As
formidable as our intellect may be and as fierce our spirit, the argument
goes, those qualities are not enough to free us from the constraints of the

natural environment in which our human ancestors evolved. We cannot draw confidence from successful solutions to the smaller problems of the past. Many of Earth's vital resources are about to be exhausted, its atmospheric chemistry is deteriorating, and human populations have already grown dangerously large. Natural ecosystems, the wellsprings of a healthful environment, are being irreversibly degraded.

At the heart of the environmentalist world view is the conviction that human physical and spiritual health depends on sustaining the planet in a relatively unaltered state. Earth is our home in the full, genetic sense, where humanity and its ancestors existed for all the millions of years of their evolution. Natural ecosystems—forests, coral reefs, marine blue waters—maintain the world exactly as we would wish it to be maintained. When we debase the global environment and extinguish the variety of life, we are dismantling a support system that is too complex to understand, let alone replace, in the foreseeable future. Space scientists theorize the existence of a virtually unlimited array of other planetary environments, almost all of which are uncongenial to human life. Our own Mother Earth, lately called Gaia, is a specialized conglomerate of organisms and the physical environment they create on a day-to-day basis, which can be destablilized and turned lethal by careless activity. We run the risk, conclude the environmentalists, of beaching ourselves upon alien shores like a great confused pod of pilot whales.

—Edward O. Wilson, "Is Humanity Suicidal?,"
The New York Times Magazine (May 30, 1993)

Children who throw stones at birds and children who feed birds are both responding to what may be an innate tendency to focus their attention on living things. The choice of behavior used to engage the animal in the interaction is different and it is a *learned* behavior. The study of cruelty to animals as well as the study of pet keeping would profit from the recognition that both activities are alternative and learned means of dealing with an innate attraction to animals.

—Aaron Katcher and Gregory Wilkins,
"Dialogue with Animals: Its Nature
and Culture," *The Biophilia Hypothesis,*
edited by Stephen R. Kellert and Edward O. Wilson (1993)

INTRODUCTION

"And God said, Let us make man in our image, after our likeness; and let them have dominion over the fish of the sea, and over the fowl of the air, and over the cattle, and over all the earth, and over every creeping thing that creepeth upon the earth" (Genesis 1:26).

For thousands of years, hardly anyone questioned man's right to rule the earth and its creatures. Recently, however, human dominion has come under fire. That *Homo sapiens* is the most powerful animal on the planet is clear; but what rights does our power give us, and what responsibilities? Are we entitled to exploit the species around us for food, clothing, or recreation as guiltlessly as other animals do? Does our biological kinship with other species mean we should treat them as equals rather than as resources? Does our superior intelligence justify a sense of overall superiority, or does it put the burden on us to manage our common home for the benefit of all its inhabitants? When we do exploit other species, are we acting in our own best interest, or are we endangering their survival and ours?

These are practical as well as philosophical questions. How we answer them affects what laws we make, which products we buy, where we build houses, roads, and businesses, and—as many commentators emphasize—what kind of world we will pass on to our children and grandchildren.

Known for his writing on human responsibility to other species is biologist Edward O. Wilson, whose opening comments identify a core contrast in points of view. As Wilson sees it, *exemptionalists* regard human beings as separate from other animals by virtue of our superior intelligence and technology, while *environmentalists* regard us as living together in mutual dependence with other species. The environmentalist position is advocated in detail by Aldo Leopold in "Toward a Land Ethic"—a radical approach when he proposed it half a century ago.

Wilson also is known for his support of preserving *biodiversity*—the variety of living species on earth. In "The Rivet Poppers," scientists and activists Paul and Anne Ehrlich use the analogy of rivets in an airplane wing to dramatize the dangers of allowing species to become extinct. "A Logger's Lament," by Leila L. Kysar, takes the opposite point of view, contending that human welfare must come before saving animals and plants. Charles C. Mann and Mark L. Plummer's "The Butterfly Problem" shows the difficulty of reconciling such clashing priorities by examining a recent case that pitted an Oregon developer against protectors of the endangered silverspot butterfly. In "The Case for Human Beings," Thomas Palmer offers a defense of human uniqueness and achievements—the exemptionalist position. Does a tropical rainforest contain more information than, say, the Library of Congress? In contrast, storyteller Joseph Bruchac describes the Native American tradition of respect and humility toward the earth and its creatures in "The Circle Is the Way to See." The idea that all species are created equal is taken to an extreme by animal rights advocate Peter Singer in "Ethics and the New Animal Liberation Movement." Carl Cohen rebuts Singer's argument against exploiting animals for human benefit, particularly in medical experiments, in "The Case Against Animal Rights."

ALDO LEOPOLD

Toward a Land Ethic

Aldo Leopold has been called the father of wildlife management. As a conservationist, forester, writer, and teacher, he strongly influenced American attitudes and actions related to what we now call "the environment." Besides founding the Wilderness Society in 1934, Leopold was instrumental in creating the national wildlife refuge system and the first designated wilderness area in the United States, in New Mexico's Gila National Forest. He died in 1948 of a heart attack while fighting a forest fire in Wisconsin. "Toward a Land Ethic" comes from his landmark book *A Sand County Almanac,* published the year after his death. In it Leopold argues for changing the way we think about our surroundings and other living creatures—a proposal that has become a cornerstone of the environmental movement.

When god-like Odysseus returned from the wars in Troy, he hanged all on one rope a dozen slave-girls of his household whom he suspected of misbehavior during his absence.

This hanging involved no question of propriety. The girls were property. The disposal of property was then, as now, a matter of expediency, not of right and wrong.

Concepts of right and wrong were not lacking from Odysseus' Greece: witness the fidelity of his wife through the long years before at last his black-prowed galleys clove the wine-dark seas for home. The ethical structure of that day covered wives, but had not yet been extended to human chattels. During the three thousand years which have since elapsed, ethical criteria have been extended to many fields of conduct, with corresponding shrinkages in those judged by expediency only. . . .

The first ethics dealt with the relation between individuals; the Mosaic Decalogue[1] is an example. Later accretions dealt with the relation between the individual and society. The Golden Rule[2] tries to integrate the individual to society; democracy to integrate social organization to the individual.

There is as yet no ethic dealing with man's relation to land and to 5
the animals and plants which grow upon it. Land, like Odysseus' slave-

[1]**the Mosaic Decalogue:** The Ten Commandments given by God to Moses in the Bible.—Ed.
[2]**The Golden Rule:** "Do unto others as you would have them do unto you."—Ed.

girls, is still property. The land-relation is still strictly economic, entailing privileges but not obligations. . . .

The Community Concept

All ethics so far evolved rest upon a single premise: that the individual is a member of a community of interdependent parts. His instincts prompt him to compete for his place in the community, but his ethics prompt him also to cooperate (perhaps in order that there may be a place to compete for).

The land ethic simply enlarges the boundaries of the community to include soils, waters, plants, and animals, or collectively: the land.

This sounds simple: do we not already sing our love for and obligation to the land of the free and the home of the brave? Yes, but just what and whom do we love? Certainly not the soil, which we are sending helter-skelter downriver. Certainly not the waters, which we assume have no function except to turn turbines, float barges, and carry off sewage. Certainly not the plants, of which we exterminate whole communities without batting an eye. Certainly not the animals, of which we have already extirpated many of the largest and most beautiful species. A land ethic of course cannot prevent the alteration, management, and use of these "resources," but it does affirm their right to continued existence, and, at least in spots, their continued existence in a natural state.

In short, a land ethic changes the role of *Homo sapiens* from conqueror of the land-community to plain member and citizen of it. It implies respect for his fellow members, and also respect for the community as such.

In human history, we have learned (I hope) that the conqueror role 10 is eventually self-defeating. Why? Because it is implicit in such a role that the conqueror knows, *ex cathedra*,[3] just what makes the community clock tick, and just what and who is valuable, and what and who is worthless, in community life. It always turns out that he knows neither, and this is why his conquests eventually defeat themselves. . . .

Substitutes for a Land Ethic

. . . One basic weakness in a conservation system based wholly on economic motives is that most members of the land community have no economic value. Wildflowers and songbirds are examples. Of the 22,000 higher plants and animals native to Wisconsin, it is doubtful whether more than 5 percent can be sold, fed, eaten, or otherwise put

[3]*ex cathedra:* From the seat of authority.—Ed.

to economic use. Yet these creatures are members of the biotic community, and if (as I believe) its stability depends on its integrity, they are entitled to continuance.

When one of these noneconomic categories is threatened, and if we happen to love it, we invent subterfuges to give it economic importance. At the beginning of the century songbirds were supposed to be disappearing. Ornithologists jumped to the rescue with some distinctly shaky evidence to the effect that insects would eat us up if birds failed to control them. The evidence had to be economic in order to be valid.

It is painful to read these circumlocutions today. We have no land ethic yet, but we have at least drawn nearer the point of admitting that birds should continue as a matter of biotic right, regardless of the presence or absence of economic advantage to us.

A parallel situation exists in respect of predatory mammals, raptorial birds, and fish-eating birds. Time was when biologists somewhat overworked the evidence that these creatures preserve the health of game by killing weaklings, or that they control rodents for the farmer, or that they prey only on "worthless" species. Here again, the evidence had to be economic in order to be valid. It is only in recent years that we hear the more honest argument that predators are members of the community, and that no special interest has the right to exterminate them for the sake of a benefit, real or fancied, to itself. Unfortunately this enlightened view is still in the talk stage. In the field the extermination of predators goes merrily on. . . .

Some species of trees have been "read out of the party" by 15 economics-minded foresters because they grow too slowly, or have too low a sale value to pay as timber crops: white cedar, tamarack, cypress, beech, and hemlock are examples. In Europe, where forestry is ecologically more advanced, the noncommercial tree species are recognized as members of the native forest community, to be preserved as such, within reason. Moreover some (like beech) have been found to have a valuable function in building up soil fertility. The interdependence of the forest and its constituent tree species, ground flora, and fauna is taken for granted.

Lack of economic value is sometimes a character not only of species or groups, but of entire biotic communities: marshes, bogs, dunes, and "deserts" are examples. Our formula in such cases is to relegate their conservation to government as refuges, monuments, or parks. The difficulty is that these communities are usually interspersed with more valuable private lands; the government cannot possibly own or control such scattered parcels. The net effect is that we have relegated some of them to ultimate extinction over large areas. If the private owner were ecologically minded, he would be proud to be the custodian of a reasonable proportion of such areas, which add diversity and beauty to his farm and to his community.

In some instances, the assumed lack of profit in these "waste" areas has proved to be wrong, but only after most of them had been done away with. The present scramble to reflood muskrat marshes is a case in point. . . .

To sum up: a system of conservation based solely on economic self-interest is hopelessly lopsided. It tends to ignore, and thus eventually to eliminate, many elements in the land community that lack commercial value, but that are (as far as we know) essential to its healthy functioning. It assumes, falsely, I think, that the economic parts of the biotic clock will function without the uneconomic parts. It tends to relegate to government many functions eventually too large, too complex, or too widely dispersed to be performed by government.

An ethical obligation on the part of the private owner is the only visible remedy for these situations.

The Land Pyramid

An ethic to supplement and guide the economic relation to land pre- 20 supposes the existence of some mental image of land as a biotic mechanism. We can be ethical only in relation to something we can see, feel, understand, love, or otherwise have faith in.

The image commonly employed in conservation education is "the balance of nature." For reasons too lengthy to detail here, this figure of speech fails to describe accurately what little we know about the land mechanism. A much truer image is the one employed in ecology: the biotic pyramid. I shall first sketch the pyramid as a symbol of land, and later develop some of its implications in terms of land-use.

Plants absorb energy from the sun. This energy flows through a circuit called the biota, which may be represented by a pyramid consisting of layers. The bottom layer is the soil. A plant layer rests on the soil, an insect layer on the plants, a bird and rodent layer on the insects, and so on up through various animal groups to the apex layer, which consists of the larger carnivores.

The species of a layer are alike not in where they came from, or in what they look like, but rather in what they eat. Each successive layer depends on those below it for food and often for other services, and each in turn furnishes food and services to those above. Proceeding upward, each successive layer decreases in numerical abundance. Thus, for every carnivore there are hundreds of his prey, thousands of their prey, millions of insects, uncountable plants. The pyramidal form of the system reflects this numerical progression from apex to base. Man shares an intermediate layer with the bears, raccoons, and squirrels which eat both meat and vegetables.

The lines of dependency for food and other services are called food chains. Thus soil-oak-deer-Indian is a chain that has now been largely converted to soil-corn-cow-farmer. Each species, including ourselves, is a link in many chains. The deer eats a hundred plants other than oak, and the cow a hundred plants other than corn. Both, then, are links in a hundred chains. The pyramid is a tangle of chains so complex as to seem disorderly, yet the stability of the system proves it to be a highly organized structure. Its functioning depends on the cooperation and competition of its diverse parts.

In the beginning, the pyramid of life was low and squat; the food 25 chains short and simple. Evolution has added layer after layer, link after link. Man is one of thousands of accretions to the height and complexity of the pyramid. Science has given us many doubts, but it has given us at least one certainty: the trend of evolution is to elaborate and diversify the biota.

Land, then, is not merely soil; it is a fountain of energy flowing through a circuit of soils, plants, and animals. Food chains are the living channels which conduct energy upward; death and decay return it to the soil. The circuit is not closed; some energy is dissipated in decay, some is added by absorption from the air, some is stored in soils, peats, and long-lived forests; but it is a sustained circuit, like a slowly augmented revolving fund of life. There is always a net loss by downhill wash, but this is normally small and offset by the decay of rocks. It is deposited in the ocean and, in the course of geological time, raised to form new lands and new pyramids.

The velocity and character of the upward flow of energy depend on the complex structure of the plant and animal community, much as the upward flow of sap in a tree depends on its complex cellular organization. Without this complexity, normal circulation would presumably not occur. Structure means the characteristic numbers, as well as the characteristic kinds and functions, of the component species. This interdependence between the complex structure of the land and its smooth functioning as an energy unit is one of its basic attributes.

When a change occurs in one part of the circuit, many other parts must adjust themselves to it. Change does not necessarily obstruct or divert the flow of energy; evolution is a long series of self-induced changes, the net result of which has been to elaborate the flow mechanism and to lengthen the circuit. Evolutionary changes, however, are usually slow and local. Man's invention of tools has enabled him to make changes of unprecedented violence, rapidity, and scope.

One change is in the composition of floras and faunas. The larger predators are lopped off the apex of the pyramid; food chains, for the first time in history, become shorter rather than longer. Domesticated species from other lands are substituted for wild ones, and wild ones are moved to new habitats. In this world-wide pooling of faunas and floras, some species get out of bounds as pests and diseases, others are extinguished. Such effects are seldom intended or foreseen; they represent unpredicted and often untraceable readjustments in the structure. Agricultural science is largely a race between the emergence of new pests and the emergence of new techniques for their control.

Another change touches the flow of energy through plants and ani- 30 mals and its return to the soil. Fertility is the ability of soil to receive, store, and release energy. Agriculture, by overdrafts on the soil, or by too radical a substitution of domestic for native species in the superstructure, may derange the channels of flow or deplete storage. Soils depleted of their storage, or of the organic matter which anchors it, wash away faster than they form. This is erosion.

Waters, like soil, are part of the energy circuit. Industry, by polluting waters or obstructing them with dams, may exclude the plants and animals necessary to keep energy in circulation.

Transportation brings about another basic change: the plants or animals grown in one region are now consumed and returned to the soil in another. Transportation taps the energy stored in rocks, and in the air, and uses it elsewhere; thus we fertilize the garden with nitrogen gleaned by the guano birds from the fishes of seas on the other side of the equator. Thus the formerly localized and self-contained circuits are pooled on a world-wide scale.

The process of altering the pyramid for human occupation releases stored energy, and this often gives rise, during the pioneering period, to a deceptive exuberance of plant and animal life, both wild and tame. These releases of biotic capital tend to becloud or postpone the penalties of violence.

This thumbnail sketch of land as an energy circuit conveys three basic ideas:

1. That land is not merely soil.
2. That the native plants and animals kept the energy circuit open; others may or may not.
3. That man-made changes are of a different order than evolutionary changes, and have effects more comprehensive than is intended or foreseen. . . .

Land Health and the A–B Cleavage

A land ethic, then, reflects the existence of an ecological conscience, 35 and this in turn reflects a conviction of individual responsibility for the health of the land. Health is the capacity of the land for self-renewal. Conservation is our effort to understand and preserve this capacity.

Conservationists are notorious for their dissensions. Superficially these seem to add up to mere confusion, but a more careful scrutiny reveals a single plane of cleavage common to many specialized fields. In each field one group (A) regards the land as soil, and its function as commodity-production; another group (B) regards the land as a biota, and its function as something broader. How much broader is admittedly in a state of doubt and confusion.

In my own field, forestry, Group A is quite content to grow trees like cabbages, with cellulose as the basic forest commodity. It feels no inhibition against violence; its ideology is agronomic. Group B, on the other hand, sees forestry as fundamentally different from agronomy because it employs natural species, and manages a natural environment rather than creating an artificial one. Group B prefers natural reproduction on principle. It worries on biotic as well as economic grounds about the loss of species like chestnut, and the threatened loss of the white pines. It worries about a whole series of secondary forest functions: wildlife, recreation, watersheds, wilderness areas. To my mind, Group B feels the stirrings of an ecological conscience.

In the wildlife field, a parallel cleavage exists. For Group A the basic commodities are sport and meat; the yardsticks of production are ciphers of take[4] in pheasants and trout. Artificial propagation is acceptable as a permanent as well as a temporary recourse—if its unit costs permit. Group B, on the other hand, worries about a whole series of biotic side-issues. What is the cost in predators of producing a game crop? Should we have further recourse to exotics? How can management restore the shrinking species, like prairie grouse, already hopeless as shootable game? How can management restore the threatened rarities, like trumpeter swan and whooping crane? Can management principles be extended to wildflowers? Here again it is clear to me that we have the same A-B cleavage as in forestry. . . .

In all of these cleavages, we see repeated the same basic paradoxes: man the conqueror versus man the biotic citizen; science the sharpener of his sword versus science the searchlight on his universe; land the slave and servant versus land the collective organism. . . .

The Outlook

It is inconceivable to me that an ethical relation to land can exist without love, respect, and admiration for land, and a high regard for its value. By value, I of course mean something far broader than mere economic value; I mean value in the philosophical sense. 40

[4]*ciphers of take:* The number caught.—Ed.

Perhaps the most serious obstacle impeding the evolution of a land ethic is the fact that our educational and economic system is headed away from, rather than toward, an intense consciousness of land. Your true modern is separated from the land by many middlemen, and by innumerable physical gadgets. He has no vital relation to it; to him it is the space between cities on which crops grow. Turn him loose for a day on the land, and if the spot does not happen to be a golf links or a "scenic" area, he is bored stiff. If crops could be raised by hydroponics[5] instead of farming, it would suit him very well. Synthetic substitutes for wood, leather, wool, and other natural land products suit him better than the originals. In short, land is something he has "outgrown."

Almost equally serious as an obstacle to a land ethic is the attitude of the farmer for whom the land is still an adversary, or a taskmaster that keeps him in slavery. Theoretically, the mechanization of farming ought to cut the farmer's chains, but whether it really does is debatable. . . .

The "key-log"[6] which must be moved to release the evolutionary process for an ethic is simply this: quit thinking about decent land-use as solely an economic problem. Examine each question in terms of what is ethically and esthetically right, as well as what is economically expedient. A thing is right when it tends to preserve the integrity, stability, and beauty of the biotic community. It is wrong when it tends otherwise.

It of course goes without saying that economic feasibility limits the tether of what can or cannot be done for land. It always has and it always will. The fallacy the economic determinists have tied around our collective neck, and which we now need to cast off, is the belief that economics determines *all* land-use. This is simply not true. An innumerable host of actions and attitudes, comprising perhaps the bulk of all land relations, is determined by the land-users' tastes and predilections, rather than by his purse. The bulk of all land relations hinges on investments of time, forethought, skill, and faith rather than on investments of cash. As a land-user thinketh, so is he. . . .

The evolution of a land ethic is an intellectual as well as emotional 45 process. Conservation is paved with good intentions which prove to be futile, or even dangerous, because they are devoid of critical understanding either of the land, or of economic land-use. I think it is a truism that as the ethical frontier advances from the individual to the community, its intellectual content increases.

The mechanism of operation is the same for any ethic: social approbation for right actions: social disapproval for wrong actions.

---

[5]**hydroponics:** Greenhouse cultivation of plants in water.—Ed.
[6]**"key-log":** The log that causes a logjam.—Ed.

By and large, our present problem is one of attitudes and implements. We are remodeling the Alhambra[7] with a steam shovel, and we are proud of our yardage. We shall hardly relinquish the shovel, which after all has many good points, but we are in need of gentler and more objective criteria for its successful use.

Analyzing Issues and Arguments

1. In paragraph 22 Aldo Leopold refers to "a circuit called the biota." What does he mean? After rereading paragraphs 22 and 26, how would you define *biota?*
2. What is a food chain (para. 24)? How does energy flow through it? Give two examples of food chains that include human beings.
3. Compare Leopold's description of the A–B cleavage (paras. 36–39) with Edward O. Wilson's description of exemptionalists versus environmentalists (p. 1). What are the similarities between the two pairings? In what ways are Leopold's and Wilson's concerns different?

Writing about Issues and Arguments

Which of Leopold's ideas are central to debates about the environment today? What specific current controversies reflect his concerns? Choose one such issue that interests you. Write a research paper describing both sides of the conflict, or arguing in favor of your position on it, or both. (See, for example, Leopold's comments in paragraph 16 on protecting biotic communities with no economic value, such as "marshes, bogs, dunes, and 'deserts.'")

[7]**Alhambra:** The palace of the Moorish kings in Granada, Spain, known for its intricate architectural detail.—Ed.

PAUL AND ANNE EHRLICH

The Rivet Poppers

Among the books coauthored by husband and wife Paul and Anne Ehrlich are *Population, Resources, Environment: Issues in Human Ecology* (1970), *The Population Explosion* (1990), and *Healing the Planet* (1991). "The Rivet Poppers" is the preface to *Extinction: The Causes and Consequences of the Disappearance of Species* (1981). Anne Ehrlich is associate director of the Center for Conservation Biology at Stanford University. She has served as a consultant to the White House Council on Environmental Quality and on the board of the Center for Innovative Diplomacy. Paul Ehrlich is Bing Professor of Population Studies at Stanford University. His first best-seller was *The Population Bomb* (1968). A recent recipient of a MacArthur Fellowship, he is currently president of the American Institute of Biological Sciences. In "The Rivet Poppers," the Ehrlichs use the analogy of rivets in an airplane wing to press the case for preserving all species on Spaceship Earth.

As you walk from the terminal toward your airliner, you notice a man on a ladder busily prying rivets out of its wing. Somewhat concerned, you saunter over to the rivet popper and ask him just what the hell he's doing.

"I work for the airline—Growthmania Intercontinental," the man informs you, "and the airline has discovered that it can sell these rivets for two dollars apiece."

"But how do you know you won't fatally weaken the wing doing that?" you inquire.

"Don't worry," he assures you. "I'm certain the manufacturer made this plane much stronger than it needs to be, so no harm's done. Besides, I've taken lots of rivets from this wing and it hasn't fallen off yet. Growthmania Airlines needs the money; if we didn't pop the rivets, Growthmania wouldn't be able to continue expanding. And I need the commission they pay me—fifty cents a rivet!"

"You must be out of your mind!"

"I told you not to worry; I know what I'm doing. As a matter of fact, I'm going to fly on this flight also, so you can see there's absolutely nothing to be concerned about."

Any sane person would, of course, go back into the terminal, report the gibbering idiot and Growthmania Airlines to the FAA, and

5

make reservations on another carrier. You never *have* to fly on an airliner. But unfortunately all of us are passengers on a very large spacecraft—one on which we have no option but to fly. And, frighteningly, it is swarming with rivet poppers behaving in ways analogous to that just described.

The rivet poppers on Spaceship Earth include such people as the President of the United States, the Chairman of the Soviet Communist Party, and most other politicians and decision makers; many big businessmen and small businessmen; and, inadvertently, most other people on the planet, including you and us. Philip Handler, the president of the United States National Academy of Sciences, is an important rivet popper, and so are industrialist Daniel Ludwig (who is energetically chopping down the Amazon rainforest), Senator Howard Baker, enemy of the Snail Darter [see p. 31], and Vice President George Bush, friend of nuclear war. Others prominent on the rivet-popper roster include Japanese whalers and woodchippers, many utility executives, the auto moguls of Detroit, the folks who run the AMAX corporation, almost all economists, the Brazilian government, Secretary of the Interior James Watt, the editors of *Science, Scientific American,* and the *Wall Street Journal,* the bosses of the pesticide industry, some of the top bureaucrats of the U.S. Department of Agriculture and some of those in the Department of the Interior, the officers of the Entomological Society of America, the faculties of every engineering school in the world, the Army Corps of Engineers, and the hierarchy of the Roman Catholic Church.

Now all of these people (and especially you and we) are certainly not crazy or malign. Most of them are in fact simply uninformed— which is one reason for writing a book on the processes and consequences of rivet-popping.

Rivet-popping on Spaceship Earth consists of aiding and abetting 10 the extermination of species and populations of nonhuman organisms. The European Lion, the Passenger Pigeon, the Carolina Parakeet, and the Sthenele Brown Butterfly are some of the numerous rivets that are now irretrievably gone; the Chimpanzee, Mountain Gorilla, Siberian Tiger, Right Whale, and California Condor are prominent among the many rivets that are already loosened. The rest of the perhaps ten million species and billions of distinct populations still more or less hold firm. Some of these species supply or could supply important direct benefits to humanity, and all of them are involved in providing free public services without which society could not persist.

The natural ecological systems of earth, which supply these vital services, are analogous to the parts of an airplane that make it a suitable vehicle for human beings. But ecosystems are much more complex than wings or engines. Ecosystems, like well-made airplanes, tend to have redundant subsystems and other "design" features that permit them to continue functioning after absorbing a certain amount of abuse. A dozen rivets, or a dozen species, might never be missed. On the other hand, a thirteenth rivet popped from a wing flap, or the extinction of a key species involved in the cycling of nitrogen, could lead to a serious accident.

In most cases an ecologist can no more predict the consequences of the extinction of a given species than an airline passenger can assess the loss of a single rivet. But both can easily foresee the long-term results of continually forcing species to extinction or of removing rivet after rivet. No sensible airline passenger today would accept a continuous loss of rivets from jet transports. Before much more time has passed, attitudes must be changed so that no sane passenger on Spaceship Earth will accept a continuous loss of populations or species of nonhuman organisms.

Over most of the several billion years during which life has flourished on this planet, its ecological systems have been under what would be described by the airline industry as "progressive maintenance." Rivets have dropped out or gradually worn out, but they were continuously being replaced; in fact, over much of the time our spacecraft was being strengthened by the insertion of more rivets than were being lost. Only since about ten thousand years ago has there been any sign that that process might be more or less permanently reversed. That was when a single species, *Homo sapiens,* began its meteoric rise to planetary dominance. And only in about the last half-century has it become clear that humanity has been forcing species and populations to extinction at a rate greatly exceeding that of natural attrition and far beyond the rate at which natural processes can replace them. In the last twenty-five years or so, the disparity between the rate of loss and the rate of replacement has become alarming; in the next twenty-five years, unless something is done, it promises to become catastrophic for humanity.

The form of the catastrophe is, unfortunately, difficult to predict. Perhaps the most likely event will be an end of civilization in T. S. Eliot's whimper.[1] As nature is progressively impoverished, its ability to provide a moderate climate, cleanse air and water, recycle wastes, protect crops from pests, replenish soils, and so on will be increasingly degraded. The human population will be growing as the capacity of earth to support people is shrinking. Rising death rates and a falling quality of life will lead to a crumbling of postindustrial civilization. The end may come so gradually that the hour of its arrival may not be recognizable, but the familiar world of today will disappear within the life span of many people now alive.

Of course, the "bang" is always possible. For example, it is likely 15 that destruction of the rich complex of species in the Amazon basin would trigger rapid changes in global climatic patterns. Agriculture remains heavily dependent on stable climate, and human beings remain heavily dependent on food. By the end of the century the extinction of perhaps a million species in the Amazon basin could have entrained famines in which a billion human beings perished. And if our species is very unlucky, the famines could lead to a thermonuclear war, which could extinguish civilization.

Fortunately, the accelerating rate of extinctions can be arrested. It will not be easy; it will require both the education of, and concerted action by, hundreds of millions of people. But no tasks are more important, because extinctions of other organisms must be stopped before the

---

[1]**Eliot's whimper:** "This is the way the world ends/Not with a bang but a whimper." T. S. Eliot, "The Hollow Men," v, 1925.—Ed.

living structure of our spacecraft is so weakened that at a moment of stress it fails and civilization is destroyed.

Analyzing Issues and Arguments

1. What is the thesis of Paul and Anne Ehrlich's essay? Where and how do they state it?
2. What parallels do the authors suggest in "The Rivet Poppers" between an airplane and the earth? Without this analogy, what point or points about the earth and its species would the Ehrlichs have a harder time establishing?
3. What factual evidence do the Ehrlichs present in support of their ideas? How would the essay's impact change if they included more data?

Writing about Issues and Arguments

Compare and contrast the views of Edward O. Wilson (p. 1), Aldo Leopold (p. 4), and the Ehrlichs on the reasons for preserving biodiversity—that is, the full range of species that now inhabit the earth. What ideas and assumptions do all these writers share? How do their priorities differ? Which arguments do you find most and least persuasive? Write an essay summarizing the reasons human beings should (or should not) act to protect biodiversity.

IN THE NEWS

Biodiversity vs. Bioengineering?

Peter Huber

The following column appeared in longer form in the October 26, 1992, issue of *Forbes* magazine. Peter Huber is a lawyer and writer specializing in telecommunications and liability issues. A senior fellow of the Manhattan Institute for Policy Research, a conservative think tank, Huber writes a monthly "Science and Technology" column for *Forbes*. He is the author and editor of many books, including *Galileo's Revenge: Junk Science in the Courtroom* (1991) and *Phantom Risk: Scientific Inference and the Law* (1993).

It's the new pinnacle of environmental chic. Biodiversity, we are told, is much like oil in the ground: We should conserve it for good, solid, old-fashioned economic reasons. The rainforest probably contains cures for cancer or disease-resistant food crops. A decade or two from now, when we desperately need new genetic stock for some reason or another, it won't be there if the forests are gone. Curiously, these arguments are often pressed by the same crew who hate biodiversity when it comes out of the bioengineer's bottle. What we see here, once again, is an important environmental objective getting all tangled up in arguments that don't really wash.

Begin with the basics. Species are defined by genes, and genes are just complex chemicals. We can mine those genetic chemicals from the canopies of the rainforest. Or we can replicate and modify them in kennels, stables, and experimental farms, which have given us such biodiverse beasts as Chihuahuas and St. Bernards. Or, as we've recently learned, we can dice, slice, and splice genes in laboratories and fermentation tanks, to create transgenic pigs and mice, disease-resistant corn, or bacteria that keep the frost off strawberries.

So, from a strictly economic perspective, where's the best place to explore for useful new genes? Probably not in any equatorial jungle. . . . We used to need forests for rubber, then we learned how to make rubber out of oil. We used to get salicylates from willow bark, but the synthetic version, aspirin, works better. We used to rely on sick cows to provide a crude smallpox vaccine (*vacca* is Latin for cow), but we don't anymore.

. . . To be sure, Nature has been doing gene chemistry for billions of years, whereas we've been at it only for a short while. But we don't have to rely on blind luck and natural selection, either. On balance, it seems to me, we are far more likely to find economically valuable biodiversity in a laboratory at Genentech than to stumble across it in the upper reaches of the Amazon. Our days as hunter-gatherers of wild genes are coming to a close. . . .

This doesn't mean, however, that we should slash and burn with impunity. We don't preserve the pyramids because they contain some magical mathematical formula about the stars, nor do we preserve Niagara just because it generates megawatts. The economic case for biodiversity is weak, but there are still transcendentally important esthetic reasons for treating life on earth with gentle respect. The genetic code of life is a gigantic biological manuscript that we have scarcely yet begun to examine or decode. It is a record as ancient as life on earth, encrypted in molecules scattered across the vast, delicate, shining abundance of the canopies, trunks, stems, and soil of the rainforest. We should revere life on earth not because we expect it will profit us economically, nor because it is very likely to cure cancer, but because life is a good that requires no further justification.

I suspect many rabid greens [environmentalists] believe that, too, but peddle the economic rationalization for biodiversity because they think that's the only thing they can sell to American business or politicians in Brazil. Perhaps they're right. But it's a risky strategy to promise an economic boom that will never come. When the economic case for biodiversity collapses, when it becomes crystal clear that orchids can't cure cancer, the more fundamental truth about the beauty and spiritual qualities of nature may be swept away as well. ■

Analyzing Issues and Arguments

1. What are Peter Huber's reasons for and against preserving biodiversity? How convincing do you find them?
2. How would you characterize Huber's tone? In what ways does his tone help his argument, hurt it, or both?

LEILA L. KYSAR

A Logger's Lament

> Leila L. Kysar grew up among loggers and for twenty years was the busi-
> ness manager of a tree farm management company in Washington State.
> Recently retired, she now lives in eastern Oregon, where she and her
> husband own a tree farm. "A Logger's Lament" originally appeared as a
> "My Turn" column in *Newsweek* magazine on October 22, 1990. In her
> essay Kysar strikes back at environmental groups who oppose two contro-
> versial logging practices carried out in the Pacific Northwest: cutting
> down old-growth forests (trees that are hundreds of years old) and clear-
> cutting (leveling entire forests without leaving any trees standing).

My father was a logger. My husband is a logger. My sons will not be
loggers. Loggers are an endangered species, but the environmental
groups, which so righteously protect endangered species in the animal
kingdom, have no concern for their fellow human beings under siege.
Loggers are a much misunderstood people, pictured as brutal rapists of
our planet, out to denude it of trees and, as a result, of wildlife.

It is time to set the record straight. Loggers take great pride in the
old-growth trees, the dinosaurs of the forests, and would be sorry to
see them all cut. There are in the national forests in Washington and
Oregon (not to mention other states) approximately 8.5 million acres
of forested land, mostly old growth, set aside, never to be used for timber production. In order to see it all, a man would have to spend every
weekend and holiday for sixty years looking at timber at a rate of more
than 1,000 acres per day. This does not include acreage to be set aside
for spotted owl protection.

In addition to this huge amount of forested land never to be
logged, the State of Washington Forest Practices Act, established in
1973, specifies that all land that is clear-cut of trees must be replanted
unless converted to some other use. As a tree farmer generally plants
more trees per acre than he removes, more trees are being planted than
are being cut. In the last twenty years in Clark County, Washington,
alone, the Department of Natural Resources has overseen the planting
of at least 15,000 acres of previously unforested private lands.

The term *logger* applies to the person harvesting trees. A tree
farmer is the one who owns the land and determines what is to be
done with it. To a tree farmer, clear-cutting is no more than the final
harvest of that generation of trees. The next spring, he reforests the

land. To the public, clear-cutting is a bad word. Does the public cry shame when a wheat farmer harvests his crop and leaves a field of stubble in place of the beautiful wheat?

In the Pacific Northwest, in five years, the newly planted trees will 5
grow taller than the farmer's head; in ten years, more than fifteen feet tall; and in twenty to thirty years, the trees will be ready for the first commercial harvest. The farmer then thins the trees to make room for better growth. In forty to fifty years, he will be ready to clear-cut his farm and replant again. Contrary to public opinion, it does *not* take three hundred to four hundred years to grow a Douglas fir tree to harvestable age.

Tree farming keeps us in wood products. We build with wood, write on paper, and even use the unmentionable in the bathroom. But in order to keep this flow of wood products available, we need to keep it economically feasible to grow trees. If we restrict the tree-farming practices because we do not like clear-cuts or because some animal might (and probably might not) become extinct, or we restrict markets for the timber by banning log exports or overtax the farmer, we are creating a situation where the farmer will no longer grow trees. If he cannot make money, he will not tree-farm. He will sell his tree farm so that it can grow houses. The *land* that grows trees is the natural resource; the *trees* are just a crop.

Legislation is constantly being introduced to take away the private-property rights of tree farmers. They are beleaguered by the public, who believe that any forest belongs to the public. Who, after all, buys the land and pays the taxes? Who invests money in property that will yield them an income only once every twenty to thirty years? Would John Q. Public picnic in a farmer's wheat field?

The tree farmer must have a diversified market. When there is a building slump in this country, it is vital to the industry to have an export market. Earlier recessions were devastating to tree farmers until markets were developed overseas. Some trees have little market value in the United States. The logs China and Korea bought in the late 1980s could not be sold here to cover the cost of delivery.

As to the wildlife becoming extinct, that is a joke that is not very funny. Animals thrive in clear-cuts better than in old-growth timber. Look at the Mount St. Helens blast area. Nature created an immense clearing and now deer, elk, and other wildlife are returning in numbers. Why? Because there is more food growing in an open area than under the tall trees. And as for the spotted owl, surely the 8.5 million acres set aside is enough to maintain quite a respectable owl population. Numerous recent observations show that the owl lives in second-growth timber as well as in old growth. In the Wenatchie National Forest there are more than two hundred fifty examples of spotted owls

living in other than old-growth timber. The owl is a tool of the environmentalist groups to get what they want: the complete eradication of the species *Logger.*

Consider the scenic value of a preserved old-growth forest versus a   10
managed stand of timber. In Glacier National Park, Montana, for example, which is totally untouched, one sees the old trees, the dead and dying trees, the windfalls crisscrossing the forest. In a managed forest, one sees the older stands with the forest floor cleared of the dead windfalls, leaving a more parklike setting. In the younger stands, one sees the beautiful new trees with their brilliant greens thrusting their tops to the sky and, in the clear-cuts, before the new trees obscure the view, one sees the huckleberry bushes with their luscious-tasting berries, the bright pink of fireweed, and deer and elk feeding. True environmentalists husband the land; they do not let the crops stagnate and rot. Tree farming regenerates the trees *and* utilizes the product.

A tree farmer from Sweden (where they are fined if they do *not* tree-farm their forests) asked me recently why we do not just explain these facts to the environmental groups so that they will work *with* us instead of *against* us. Well, do you know the difference between a terrorist and an environmentalist? It is easier to reason with the terrorist.

Analyzing Issues and Arguments

1. What course of action does Leila L. Kysar advocate in this essay, and why? What course of action does she oppose, and why?
2. What does Kysar imply about old-growth trees by calling them "dinosaurs" in paragraph 2?
3. At what points in her essay does Kysar use hyperbole (exaggeration for the sake of emphasis)? Do her uses of hyperbole make you more sympathetic to her position or less sympathetic?

Writing about Issues and Arguments

Write an essay comparing and contrasting Kysar's views on tree farming in "A Logger's Lament" with Aldo Leopold's views in "Toward a Land Ethic" (see p. 1, especially paras. 34 and 37).

IN THE NEWS

Businesses Are Battling Environmentalism with Its Own Laws

Charles McCoy

> The following article is excerpted from a news story that appeared in the *Wall Street Journal* on April 28, 1994. Charles McCoy, a San Francisco-based staff reporter for the *Journal,* covers environmental and natural resources issues.

In courtrooms across the country, industry and landowners—including some renowned polluters—are trying to turn the tables on their environmental foes with the novel argument that strengthened environmental protections run afoul of environmental laws. They are using the Endangered Species Act, the National Environmental Policy Act, and a host of other federal and state laws—the very laws used by environmentalists to win their most cherished victories, such as logging curbs on behalf of the spotted owl. . . .

An Oregon federal judge last year ruled that the U.S. Fish and Wildlife

Service broke environmental laws by not properly evaluating various possible impacts of its owl-protection zones on people. (The case is on appeal.). . .

Just last month, the U.S. Court of Appeals in Washington, D.C., threw out a key Interior Department interpretation of wildlife law under which regulators have slapped broad restrictions on private landowners whose property is home to protected species. The court held that regulators had read meaning into the law that didn't exist.

Even when the suits fail in court, simply filing them often succeeds in slowing environmental efforts in the same way that environmentalists have stalled countless dams, freeways, and shopping malls. Moreover, the recent victories have muddled environmental matters so much that the Supreme Court ultimately will have to wade in, many environmental-law experts believe.

"Now you've got some contradictory rulings and some real confusion" 5 surrounding application of environmental laws, says David Price, a conservative legal expert. Many environmental lawyers fear that, given the chance, the high court would significantly water down the laws. Moreover, congressional critics of environmental laws are using the rulings as more ammunition in their fight to weaken the statutes, especially the Endangered Species Act, which is up for reauthorization this year.

Environmentalists, naturally, find all this galling. Indeed, some of those involved in the suits are high on their list of alleged eco-villains: ranchers whose heavy grazing has damaged rangeland and rivers; aluminum companies whose voracious need for hydropower has contributed much to the decline of Northwestern salmon; loggers who have ravaged Western forests; giant mining concerns; dirt bikers whose motocross rallies have trashed miles of desert habitat.

"These abuses are the very things these laws were designed to prevent," says Todd True, a Sierra Club Legal Defense Fund attorney who helped argue many of the spotted owl cases. "They're turning the laws on their heads."

Advocates of the strategy say they are merely mimicking the tactics and tools that environmentalists mastered in recent years. "Environmental lawyers have made these laws into neutron bombs for opponents of development," asserts James Burling of the Pacific Legal Foundation. "They obstruct or destroy everything in their path and leave the environment intact. To think that you can create a weapon that powerful and have exclusive dominion over it is foolish."

Simply filing such a suit permits lawyers to exploit environmental laws' elaborate procedural requirements: strict timetables for endangered-species filings, requirements for painstaking environmental reviews and the like. The result is delay.

In another tactic, lawyers deconstruct the science behind the regulation, 10 arguing that it doesn't meet the laws' strict scientific standards.

The objective: to go about farming, mining, logging, or other business without the added and sometimes heavy cost of complying with new environmental protections. Thus, aluminum companies have sued the National Marine Fisheries Service, alleging that federal efforts to save the endangered salmon in the Columbia River basin are scientifically lame and violate the Endangered Species Act. The nation's biggest aluminum producers—such as Aluminum Company of America and Kaiser Aluminum Corporation—have plants that take advantage of the cheap power generated by the towering dams along the Columbia and its tributaries. Those dams, however, are blamed by environmentalists and federal regulators for much—some say most—of the dizzying decline of salmon.

In their suit, the aluminum companies argue that the dams aren't so bad after all. They say their scientific studies show the real culprits to be overfishing and fish hatcheries, which introduce diseases and dilute the wild-salmon gene pool. They contend it is the companies that are endangered by the service's plan to make alterations in dam operations that would reduce power generation (and, regulators contend, fish deaths). . . .   ▪

Analyzing Issues and Arguments

1. On what grounds have traditional enemies of environmentalism begun to challenge the legality of environmental protections?
2. How can an unsuccessful lawsuit against environmental protections succeed in thwarting those protections?

CHARLES C. MANN AND
MARK L. PLUMMER

The Butterfly Problem

Charles C. Mann and Mark L. Plummer have coauthored two books and a number of articles. Plummer is an economic consultant specializing in environmental regulation and a senior fellow at the Discovery Institute in Seattle. Mann, a science writer who lives in western Massachusetts, is a contributing editor for the *Atlantic Monthly,* where "The Butterfly Problem" appeared in longer form in January 1992. Their article looks at the tangle of issues stirred up when developers' plans clash with the Endangered Species Act.

Richard Schroeder was five when he moved into the new house. It had a big backyard that opened up into the tall grass of the dunes—his own private slice of the Oregon coast. He played there almost every day until he was ten or eleven. Then his father began taking him to play golf. Richard loved the game, and was soon working as a caddy at the country club. In college he won several regional amateur tournaments. After graduation he went into the securities business, but he still played whenever he could. And he kept thinking about the land behind his parents' house. The rippling dunes, the smell of the surf—he could create a world-class golf course, eighteen holes as good as Pebble Beach, right there in Gearhart, Oregon. People would come from thousands of miles away just to play on his course.

Dropping out of securities, he spent the mid-1970s working as a club pro, learning the golf trade. He also learned the development business. For the scheme to be profitable, the course had to be built in conjunction with a destination resort—a mixture of hotel and residential space. Schroeder was looking at a $100 million project. The acreage was split into a dozen parcels, each with a separate owner. Schroeder got them all behind the scheme and found a backer who would build it and a famous golf-course designer who would lay it out. All this took ten years—a long time, but Schroeder knew that dreams do not come true easily. Only in 1986, he says, did he learn about the "butterfly problem."

Schroeder was hardly planning to build on pristine wilderness. Part of the site is fenced off for cow pasture; the rest, to his annoyance, is strewn with beer cans and the tracks of four-wheel-drive vehicles. But the land is also one of the few remaining habitats for the rare Oregon silverspot butterfly (*Speyeria zerene hippolyta*). A finger-sized reddish-brown insect, *S.z. hippolyta* is registered as a threatened species under the Endangered Species Act of 1973, which directs the U.S. Fish and Wildlife Service, a branch of the Department of the Interior, to maintain a list of species that are either endangered (in imminent peril of becoming extinct) or threatened (likely to become endangered in the near future) and to fine or imprison people who "harass, harm, pursue, hunt, shoot, wound, kill, trap, capture, or collect" species on the list. Fines, jail—all at once Schroeder was in different territory. In addition to the usual obstacles facing developers (lawsuits, permits, bonding agents), he would now have to guarantee that his golf course could be built without killing a single Oregon silverspot butterfly.

The Endangered Species Act first gained notoriety in 1978, when the Supreme Court stopped work on an almost finished dam in Tennessee because it menaced a little-known fish. Since then the act has reached its long fingers into many aspects of American life. The Fish and Wildlife Service has forced the cancellation of one dam, in Colorado, because it put whooping cranes at risk; pushed the Bureau of Reclamation to postpone expanding another, because it jeopardized the humpbacked chub; induced Massachusetts to close beaches just north of Boston at the height of summer, to protect the piping plover; started a lengthy political battle by proposing to settle packs of gray wolves in western states; sent a warning to six hundred landowners in Polk and Highlands counties, Florida, spelling out the consequences if the development of their property harms the Florida scrub jay; and hauled the town of Ranchos Palos Verdes, California, into criminal court for inadvertently driving the endangered Palos Verdes butterfly into apparent extinction, in part by turning one of its major breeding grounds into a baseball field (the suit was thrown out on a technicality).

None of this comes cheap. Buying land for the Mississippi sandhill crane has cost more than $20 million. Riverside County, California, is spending an equal sum on the Stephens' kangaroo rat, and would have authorized an additional $100 million had voters not rejected the idea. Voters will not get the chance to refuse in the Pacific Northwest, where the Fish and Wildlife Service plans to save the northern spotted owl, a native of forests in Washington, Oregon, and California, by halting most logging on 8.2 million acres, an area nearly the size of Massachusetts and Connecticut combined. Some estimates of the cost of locking up the timber reach into the tens of billions of dollars. In the case of the California gnat-catcher, now proposed for the endangered-species list, the costs may rise even higher, for the bird lives in Los Angeles, and efforts to save it will require clamping down on the most powerful real-estate market in the nation.

Richard Schroeder worked diligently to accommodate *S.z. hippolyta*. He met with the silverspot recovery team, the group of scientists and Fish and Wildlife Service staffers in charge of the butterfly's future. He hired the world's expert on the insect, Paul Hammond, of Oregon State University, to put together an official lepidopterist-certified conservation plan for the Fish and Wildlife Service. But all came to naught. Last March, Hammond found an additional patch of butterfly habitat. Exasperated, Schroeder's financial backers pulled the plug—it seemed they would never know where the butterfly might turn up next. When we visited Schroeder last summer, he was a deeply frustrated man. "The whole thing's crazy," he said, shaking his head. He seemed to be trying to control his anger. Society had chosen an insect over the dream of a human being, and for the life of him Schroeder couldn't see the logic in it, or how anyone was better off for it.

The Noah Principle

The Endangered Species Act is up for reauthorization this year,[1] and tales like Schroeder's are why a political brawl has already begun. Most Americans would be appalled if a shopping center wiped out the last bald eagle. And it is likely that they would be dismayed to learn the fate of the obscure Tecopa pupfish, which lost its sole habitat, a hot springs in Death Valley, to a bathhouse that could easily have been redesigned to save the fish. Instead, it became the first species to be removed from the endangered list by reason of extinction. But feelings are much less certain when it comes to canceling a $100 million golf course to save a bug nobody has ever heard of.

Perhaps fifty silverspots live on the land for Schroeder's project. How can anyone imagine that they are worth keeping in place of a multimillion-dollar resort? On the other hand, how can anyone sanction the elimination of a species from this earth to profit a few people? Would the decision be different if the land housed five insects, rather than fifty? Or if it held not butterflies but bald eagles? What if chemicals within butterflies turn out to have medical benefits, whereas eagles are useful only as a national symbol? And what if saving the eagle required canceling not one but ten resorts?

Until recent decades Americans were untroubled by such questions. The nation was still empty. It didn't seem possible that preserving a few animals could impose real hardship. There seemed no need to choose between a species and economic growth. But now the country's

[1]The Endangered Species Act was reauthorized in 1992 and is up for reauthorization again in 1995. (For more information on the act, see "Administration Moves to Ease Opposition to Endangered Species Act," p. 52.)—Ed.

empty corners are filling up, and biologists warn that in the next decade or two the fate of thousands of species will be decided. In making those decisions, ordinary notions of balancing the benefits against the costs may seem inappropriate, inapplicable, or even immoral. Yet any time we decide that a course of action makes some entity "better off"—butterfly, golf-course builder, or society as a whole—we are perforce judging that whatever the benefits, they are greater than the costs. At present these decisions are governed by the Endangered Species Act. Unfortunately, the act fails to balance costs and benefits meaningfully. Indeed, it is put together in such a way that it explicitly avoids the terrible choices that must be faced.

Federal wildlife-protection laws go back to the end of the past cen- 10
tury, when a famous poacher named Ed Howell slaughtered bison in Yellowstone National Park with impunity because no statute forbade it; public outrage at Howell's cheeky remarks to the newspapers pushed Congress into passing the Yellowstone Park Protection Act of 1894. Other laws followed. Mostly aimed at poachers, they cost society little, and roused little opposition. In 1964 the Bureau of Sports Fisheries and Wildlife, the bureaucratic ancestor of today's Fish and Wildlife Service, compiled a "redbook" of sixty-three endangered species. Assembled informally by a panel of nine biologists, the redbook was the government's first endangered-species list. Laws passed in 1966 and 1969 directed the Department of the Interior to formalize the list and to protect the species on it by acquiring their habitats. These statutes were weak—they did not actually ban killing members of endangered species except in national wildlife refuges. When President Richard M. Nixon called for stringent legislation in 1972, the bid fell on receptive ears. Congress passed the Endangered Species Act by a large majority in December of 1973, and Nixon quickly signed it. Neither seems to have had a clue about what they were setting in motion.

"They thought they were writing a law about saving bald eagles and elk—what I call the 'charismatic megafauna,'" says Dennis Murphy, the director of the Center for Conservation Biology at Stanford. "Instead, they got a law protecting *species*"—a difference with unexpected implications. According to Edward O. Wilson, a renowned entomologist at Harvard, there are only a few thousand types of the mammals and birds that people like to anthropomorphize, but there may be something on the order of 100 million species, of which only about 1.4 million have been named. Creatures such as fungi, insects, and bacteria form the vast majority of this horde; mammals, birds, and other vertebrates are little but colorful epiphenomena. (Asked what years of research had taught him about God, J. B. S. Haldane, one of the founders of evolutionary biology, replied that the Creator had an "inordinate fondness for beetles.") Those not initiated into the ways of biological thought may equate "preserving global biodiversity" with saving whales and whooping cranes, but scientists who use the phrase are concerned with protecting organisms that most people wouldn't hesitate to step on.

Because the majority of species are unknown, no one can say with certainty how many are going extinct. Moreover, extinction itself is hard to observe—one can never be certain that a few specimens somewhere have not been overlooked. Thought for more than a decade to be extinct, the Shoshone pupfish, a cousin of the Tecopa pupfish, turned up in its native hot springs in 1986. The long-lost black-footed ferret was rediscovered accidentally a decade ago, when a ranch dog near Meeteetse, Wyoming, returned home with a dead one in its mouth; excited conservationists then found a small colony of the weasel-like creatures. But no one doubts that extinction occurs, and most biologists believe that it is now taking place at an accelerating rate. Worldwide, Wilson guesses, the rate may be 50,000 species a year. Figures for the United States are surprisingly uncertain, but Peter Hoch, of the Missouri Botanical Garden, has calculated what he calls a "rough but defensible approximation": some 4,000 domestic species are at risk of extinction within five to ten years.

Biologists advance three arguments for avoiding this prospect. On a utilitarian level, living creatures are the source of almost all foods and many medicines; wiping out even the humblest mold might deprive humanity of the genes for a future penicillin. Wilson has calculated that the genetic information encoded in the DNA from the common mouse, if represented as ordinary-size letters, would almost fill the fifteen editions of the *Encyclopaedia Britannica* printed since 1768. Who, conservationists ask, would like to see that information vanish, along with its potential benefit to humanity?

More generally, the web of species around us helps generate soil, regulate freshwater supplies, dispose of waste, and maintain the quality of the atmosphere. Pillaging nature to the point where it cannot perform these functions is dangerously foolish. Simple self-protection is thus a second motive for preserving biodiversity. When DDT was sprayed in Borneo, the biologists Paul and Anne Ehrlich relate in their book *Extinction* (1981), it killed all the houseflies. The gecko lizards that preyed on the flies ate their pesticide-filled corpses and died. House cats consumed the dying lizards; they died too. Rats descended on the villages, bringing bubonic plague. Incredibly, the housefly in this case was part of an intricate system that controlled human disease. To make up for its absence, the government was forced to parachute cats into the area.

These reasons for protecting biodiversity are practical and anthro- 15 pocentric. But the "foremost argument for the preservation of all non-human species," the Ehrlichs argue in *Extinction,* is neither. It is the "religious" belief "that our fellow passengers on Spaceship Earth . . . *have a right to exist.*" Far from being extreme, the "Noah Principle," as this argument was named by the biologist David Ehrenfeld, is shared by many scientists and conservationists. As a species, the Noah Principle says, the smallest grub has the same right to exist as the biggest whale; so does every species of cockroach, every species of stinging nettle (all plants are included in these arguments), and even the microorganisms that cause malaria and syphilis. Anthropologists refuse to categorize cultures as "higher" and "lower" civilizations, because all have intrinsic worth; biologists believe that there is no inherent difference in value between "higher" and "lower" organisms. All are precious, and human beings have a moral responsibility to each and every one. "It's a matter of stewardship," Wilson says.

The practical and moral costs of losing the nation's biological endowment may be enormous. But so may be the cost of saving it. To halt the spasm of extinction, Wilson and Paul Ehrlich wrote in a special biodiversity issue of *Science* last August,

> the first step . . . would be to cease "developing" any more relatively undisturbed land. Every new shopping center built in the California chaparral, every hectare of tropical forest cut and burned, every swamp converted into a rice paddy or shrimp farm means less biodiversity. . . . [Even so,] ending direct human incursions into remaining relatively undisturbed habitats would be only a start. . . . The indispensable strategy for saving our fellow living creatures and ourselves in the long run is . . . to reduce the scale of human activities.

"To reduce the scale of human activities" implies telling people to make do with less: nations must choose between their natural heritage and the economic well-being of their citizens.

The Endangered Species Act is this country's response to that choice. It strongly favors preserving biodiversity—more strongly, conservationists say, than any other environmental law in the world. "Quite frankly," Murphy says, "it is the best weapon we have." It didn't start out that way. Indeed, few grasped the act's implications until its first test before the Supreme Court. On one side was the Tellico Dam, a Tennessee Valley Authority project frequently described as a boondoggle. On the other was the snail darter, a three-inch snail-eating fish that was first observed in 1973, six years after Tellico began construction and shortly before the act became law. Handed this unexpected weapon, Tellico's opponents petitioned the Fish and Wildlife Service to list the fish on an emergency basis in 1975. The amazed TVA complained that Tellico's environmental-impact statement had passed two federal court reviews, that $50 million in taxpayers' money had already been spent, that the dam would provide flood control, hydroelectric power, and recreational facilities (a lake). It claimed that the snail darter was found elsewhere, and thus was not endangered. Nonetheless the service listed the darter, and a civil action ensued, based on the Endangered Species Act. By 1978 the suit had wound its way up the legal trellis to the Supreme Court.

Attorney General Griffin Bell personally argued the case, attempting to demonstrate the snail darter's insignificance by displaying one to the justices. The tactic failed. In June of 1978 the Court ruled that "the plain intent of Congress" was to stop extinction *no matter what the cost.* The language of the act, the Court said, "shows clearly that Congress viewed the value of endangered species as 'incalculable' "—in practical terms, infinite. Obviously, a $100 million dam was worth less than an infinitely valuable fish. Simple logic dictated halting Tellico.

The decision had a "bombshell impact on Capitol Hill," says Donald Barry, of the World Wildlife Fund, who was then a staff attorney in the solicitor's office of the Department of the Interior. Even some of the law's most ardent congressional supporters were alarmed by its inflexibility, although that inflexibility, of course, endeared the act to environmentalists. Tellico's principal sponsor, Senate minority leader Howard H. Baker, Jr., of Tennessee, set out to change the act. The ensuing political maneuvering led to the establishment of a small escape hatch: a committee that could be convened when all other attempts had failed to resolve conflicts between protecting a species and building a project requiring federal funds or permits. Because it included several Cabinet members, the committee could not be summoned every time an endangered species was threatened. On the other hand, it could authorize the extinction of a species, as long as the benefits of the project strongly outweighed the benefits of actions aimed at saving the species. In its first meeting the "God Committee," as it was soon nicknamed, unanimously found in favor of the snail darter, though mostly because the group regarded Tellico as a waste of money.

Baker rammed through legislation exempting Tellico from the Endangered Species Act. The dam was built and, as predicted, proved to be less than an economic dynamo; a few years later more snail darters turned up in other rivers nearby. (The fish was downgraded to "threatened" in 1984.) But the whole affair set a pattern that has continued to the present. People who care little about the endangered species frequently invoke them as an excuse to stop projects; the science used to justify the actions of one side or another is often rushed, as it was for Tellico, and can be so incomplete that it verges on the fraudulent; and, 20 most important, the law still insists that species must be saved no matter what the cost.

For the Fish and Wildlife Service, this set of circumstances has turned the Endangered Species Act into a bureaucratic horror. The agency, formerly a haven for guys who liked to work outdoors, is now a hot spot of sophisticated partisan arm-twisting. Hundreds of petitions flow in every year, and the service must evaluate them all, with litigious interest groups scrutinizing every move. Consequently, listing moves at a crawl. As of November, the most recent date for which official figures are available, 668 domestic species, more than half of which are plants and invertebrates, clung to their places on the list. Another 100 had been accepted for the list, but the service had not yet published a final notice about them in the *Federal Register,* the last step in listing. Some 500 species resided in a curious state of limbo called Category I: the Fish and Wildlife Service agreed that they merited listing but had not got around to accepting them officially. A further 3,000 occupied a *second* limbo, Category II: the service thought they might merit listing but had not yet investigated fully. At the current rate of progress, according to a 1990 report by the Department of the Interior's own Office of Inspector General, clearing today's backlog may take up to forty-eight years, during which time many more species will be menaced. Already, several species have vanished while the government was trying to decide whether they were endangered.

After listing a species, the Fish and Wildlife Service puts together a "recovery plan" for it. And here, too, the agency is behind, though the reasons are as much budgetary as political. It has approved 364 recovery plans, covering about half the listed species, but few have been implemented. In its 1990 report the Office of Inspector General estimated the recovery cost for all species currently listed or expected to be at $4.6 billion, spread over ten years. The service's 1990 budget for recovering species was $10.6 million. Other agencies pitch in, but even so, in 1990 the total state and federal budget for all aspects of endangered species—listing, research, land acquisition, and so on—was just $102 million, less than a fourth of the annual amount needed for recovery alone.

In reading these figures, one conclusion is inescapable: more species—many more—will be driven, like the Tecopa pupfish, to extinction. Few species are unsavable today; concerted human effort can save most of them. But we are unlikely to have the means to save them all. In this deficit-ridden age Fish and Wildlife Service budgets will not climb to the altitude necessary to save the few hundred species on the list, let alone the thousands upon thousands of unlisted species that biologists regard as endangered. Like cost-conscious Noahs, Americans will pick which creatures to bring with them and which to leave behind. The choice is inescapable—but the Endangered Species Act, in its insistence that we save every species, implicitly rejects this responsibility. As a result, the government is left with little guidance. It moves almost at random, with dismaying consequences. . . .

The Butterfly Solution

Richard Schroeder is not the only person in Clatsop County, Oregon, with a butterfly problem. A few miles up the coast Northwest Conference Resorts, of San Carlos, California, is trying to build another golf course and housing complex in another patch of silverspot butterflies. Northwest Conference is run by Frank Hildreth and Donald Wudtke, two developers who would like people to know that they are not the sort of rapacious individuals one sees in the movies. "We're not fighting the system," Wudtke says. "We really believe in it." After the two men began thinking about the Oregon coast, Wudtke attended meetings of the butterfly recovery team, the group of scientists and bureaucrats set up by the Fish and Wildlife Service to guide the agency's efforts to restore the silverspot. Twenty-five professionals for a butterfly! He thought it astonishing. The scientists, Wudtke decided, were frustrated. "After eight years they hadn't established anything," he says. "They just talked and talked." In March of 1990 Northwest Conference signed a contract to buy 276 acres of grassy sand dunes. Like Schroeder, they had a butterfly problem. Hildreth and Wudtke were confident, however, that they had a solution: building a golf course and housing right around *S.z. hippolyta*.

Their notion is more promising than it might seem at first glance. 25 Silverspots, like many butterflies, are choosy about where they place their eggs. Because their caterpillars eat only the common blue violet, an inconspicuous wildflower that is customarily referred to by its scientific name, *Viola adunca,* they lay eggs exclusively near it. Because *V. adunca* grows only on open coastal grassland, that is where *S.z. hippolyta* lives. As it happens, the silverspot tied its fortunes to the wrong flower, because such grassland is, in ecologists' terms, at a low "successional state," which means that it is inevitably overrun by brush—especially Scotch broom, a tall shrub with brilliant yellow flowers—and then by lodgepole pine. Luckily for the butterfly, it is also linked to a second species: *Homo sapiens.* Preferring to hunt in open fields, Native Americans periodically set fire to the grasslands, stopping the natural succession to brush and pine. The violets, a pioneering species, sprang up again after each burn, and in this way the butterfly flourished for centuries. Only in the 1930s did the silverspot meet its nemesis: Smokey Bear. The U.S. Forest Service campaigned against fires, and the ecological succession from grasslands to forest began anew. Scotch broom overwhelmed the six-inch violets, and with them the butterfly. Although development has joined ecological succession in shrinking the silverspot's habitat along the coast, more than nine-tenths of the loss has been natural, according to Paul Hammond, the lepidopterist who is the principal expert on *S.z. hippolyta*. Eight small populations have managed to hang on, two of which are in Clatsop County. Without human intervention, Hammond told us, Mother Nature will expunge the butterfly from the Clatsop plains by the year 2000.

Options are limited. Because the land is far more valuable than the butterfly, no market will save *S.z. hippolyta*. It is unlikely to be the key to a new cancer cure, and it isn't nutritious. No nationwide group of amateur lepidopterists will pay admission to a silverspot park. Without the Endangered Species Act, the last silverspots in Clatsop County would already have been bulldozed out of existence. But with the act the butterfly has a slim chance. The law prevents private-property owners from acting to destroy a species. Where the threat is of natural origin, as it is for the silverspot, nothing compels the landowners to act to reverse the course of nature. They can twiddle their thumbs and wait for Scotch broom to annihilate the insect. With a recovery priority of 9, the silverspot is tied for 456th place on the Fish and Wildlife Service's priority list. Hence no federal wildlife refuge will be established on the site of either of the two proposed resorts.

The butterfly's existence in Clatsop County depends on finding a compromise that will allow the insect to be saved by its apparent enemy: developers. Such a compromise is one of the many solutions that Schroeder, working with Hammond, tried without success; it is also what Hildreth and Wudtke hope to devise. The notion is far from foolish. "Golf courses and resorts are a perfect match for the butterfly's management needs," Hammond says. Although the habitat would have to remain separate from the golf course, putting them together could still be "a win-win situation."

Before 1982 such compromises were nearly impossible. Initially aimed mainly at poachers, the act's prohibition against killing endangered species gradually expanded to encompass the destruction of their habitat as well. People were almost completely barred from altering the territory of a listed species, no matter how low its numbers. (On the land belonging to Hildreth and Wudtke, the last survey found exactly one butterfly.) Developers had no reason to cooperate with the law. Recognizing the problem, Congress altered the Endangered Species Act to create what it called an opportunity for a "unique partnership between the public and private sectors in the interest of endangered species and habitat conservation." The amendment authorized the Fish and Wildlife Service to perform what are in effect swaps. People like

Hildreth and Wudtke create a "habitat conservation plan," which ensures that private development will not hurt a species's chances of survival. If the plan is acceptable, the service issues an "incidental take permit," which promises that nobody will go to jail if a bulldozer operator inadvertently flattens a butterfly. The permit does not allow anyone to wipe out a species; only a few individuals of the species, if that, may be taken, and then just by accident. But it gives developers legal protection—provided that their plans do not imperil the species. . . .

. . . Last summer the two men showed us a color map depicting their preliminary habitat-conservation plan. It set aside twenty-five acres, a tenth of the resort, for the butterfly. Hildreth said they had spent more than $50,000 determining the right area; another $200,000 was destined for environmental studies. "We'd like to think we're doing it as just part of good planning," Wudtke explained. Construction would be starting soon, and when the complex was finished the butterfly land would be managed properly instead of being overgrown by Scotch broom.

A few weeks later Hammond listened politely to our description of 30 their plan. He sat in an office full of wide wooden trays, each of which contained dozens of spotted butterflies mounted on pins. He was, he stressed, not opposed to such projects. But he thought that the area the two men had set aside was probably too small. They would need to add more land. "And then," he said, "it will get expensive."

No doubt Hildreth and Wudtke will add as little as possible, and the Fish and Wildlife Service will find some reason to nitpick. One might call the resultant paralysis the silverspot syndrome: no resort, no butterfly, a lose-lose situation that combines the worst of both worlds.

Such an outcome may not be rare. The two butterfly plans were created by the developers alone. A likelier route to success . . . is to enlist the aid of local governments and environmental groups, all parties investing time and money in drafting the plan. (Among other things, this makes the plan less litigation-prone.) But that drives up costs substantially, and sometimes drives them beyond the $250,000 spent by Hildreth and Wudtke. Ultimately, preparation of the plan becomes so expensive that it is worthwhile only when the stakes are high—that is, when the value of the land in question is high. If land is expensive, so is setting it aside for the species, as many habitat-conservation plans require. . . .

More important, the plans are only a means of choosing *how* to save a species. They do not decide *whether* to save it. In the eyes of the law, listing a species is equivalent to making that decision; if human plans threaten the species, they must be set aside. Conservationists often claim that such stark conflicts will be uncommon. (Peter Raven, the director of the Missouri Botanical Garden, has argued that trade-offs are "truly necessary" only in "rare cases.") But the United States has thousands of people like Richard Schroeder and it has thousands of endangered species. Inevitably, they will collide—everywhere and often. In these fights, according to the law, only one side is supposed to win.

Technically, losers do have one hope: the God Committee. But it can be convened only when the controversy involves the federal government; if private developers do not need federal permits, there is no avenue of appeal. In practice even this limited way out is rarely used, because making the appeal places the appellant in the unenviable position of going on record as wanting to do in a species. Few wish to be seen that way—one reason that the God Committee has been called on only three times in the fourteen years of its existence. . . .

As a practical matter, endangered species almost always win in con- 35 flicts with development—an outcome that flows from the act's grounding in the Noah Principle. Yet the Noah Principle makes choices next to impossible, and in this regard the Endangered Species Act must be changed. In the eyes of the law all species are equal, because each is of incalculable worth. Americans are willing to set aside some human concerns to save the bald eagle and the grizzly bear. But no one has demonstrated that they will give their informed consent to laws that grant the same privileges to the Kretschmarr Cave mold beetle. Indeed, a casual glance through the magazines of the environmental movement reveals a marked preference for charismatic megafauna over creepy-crawlies; the pages of *Sierra* and *National Wildlife* are devoted to lush color photographs of mammals and birds. As a result, funding for species preservation is awarded with blithe disregard for the principle of equality. On the infrequent occasions when the Noah Principle is invoked, it creates contempt for the law. If society prefers charismatic megafauna, priority should be given to them without apology. If biologists think otherwise, it should fall to them to change public preferences.

More important, the claim of incalculable value forces all sides into acting as if cost meant nothing. Powerful interests don't want endangered species anywhere near them, yet the law states with great specificity that their wishes are not to be heeded. The situation invites hypocrisy. Thousands of jobs and billions of dollars are at stake, and economic considerations *will* be heard. Unable to get in the front door legitimately, money and influence sneak in through the back. (The same Congress that declared endangered species to be of "incalculable" value evaded the intent of the act by allocating little for their welfare, and subsequent Congresses have not done much better.) Many species never make it onto the list for fear of the consequences—not to the species but to the economic and political forces that may be crimped if they are listed. And little wonder, for those who cannot prevent listing are forced, actively or passively, to restore the species for the enjoyment of the rest of society. Compensating them for their costs may not, as some economists claim, be the easiest resolution. But it would stop the law from turning property owners into the enemies of the endangered species on their land. Without the support of property owners, the "incalculable" value of species will eventually become a chimera.

The thought of deliberately consigning any species to extinction, let alone thousands of them, is repugnant, and no one we spoke to liked it. (Asked if he would like to see the silverspot vanish, Schroeder looked surprised. "Of course not," he said.) But we will inevitably cause extinctions; we cannot hide from it. Taking responsibility for our actions is a better course than letting species die of our indecision. To pretend that we are acting to save everything is intellectually dishonest. It turns the hard choices over to the forces of litigation and bureaucratic inertia. Clinging to the Noah Principle may make us feel good, but it ensures that the nation's biological heritage will be managed, as Lewis Carroll would have had it, by Helter and Skelter.

Last June we drove down the coastal highway to Richard Schroeder's proposed golf course. We found it just north of a gas station and across from a driving range, as Schroeder had said. A dirt road led into the property; we took it, rocking through the ruts left by four-wheel-drive vehicles. In a moment we came to a cow pasture: prime butterfly territory. Dotted with the bright-yellow blossoms of Scotch broom, the field was a sad sight—if you were interested in butterflies. The owner, one of Schroeder's neighbors, wants to retire after decades on the farm. He is waiting for the shrub to take over. Then, maybe, the land can be sold for condominiums.

It was too early in the season to see silverspots. We looked anyway —but of course we didn't find them.

Analyzing Issues and Arguments

1. What are the two main opposing positions presented in "The Butterfly Problem"? Who holds each position?
2. At what points in their essay do Charles C. Mann and Mark L. Plummer appeal to readers' emotions? What other methods do they use, and what kinds of evidence do they present, to support the arguments in "The Butterfly Problem"?
3. Reread paragraph 16. The concluding sentence, which interprets remarks by Edward O. Wilson and Paul Ehrlich, is: "'To reduce the scale of human activities' implies telling people to make do with less: nations must choose between their natural heritage and the economic well-being of their citizens." What elements in Wilson and Ehrlich's remarks represent nations' "natural heritage"? What

elements represent the "economic well-being of their citizens"? What elements are the basis for Mann and Plummer's statement that "nations must choose"?

Writing about Issues and Arguments

Write an argument supporting one or the other of the opposing points of view presented in "The Butterfly Problem."

IN THE NEWS

Letter to the Editor in Response to "The Butterfly Problem"

William Robert Irvin

> William Robert Irvin's letter to the editor was one of several that appeared in response to "The Butterfly Problem" in the April 1992 issue of the *Atlantic Monthly*. Irvin is counsel to the National Wildlife Federation in Washington, D.C.

In "The Butterfly Problem," by Charles C. Mann and Mark L. Plummer . . . , the authors conclude that the Endangered Species Act is imposing unfair burdens on private-property owners and threatening to undermine the political consensus necessary for continued efforts to preserve endangered species. The centerpiece of their article is the saga of Richard Schroeder, whose failure to realize his lifelong dream of carving fairways on the Oregon coast is attributed entirely to unbending implementation of the act's protection of the threatened Oregon silverspot butterfly. Schroeder's story is hardly that simple.

In building his resort, Schroeder faced hurdles imposed by Oregon's stringent state land-use planning laws, completely unrelated to protection of the silverspot butterfly. His application for permission to alter the coastal dune line in order to construct three holes of his planned golf course was denied by the local planning commission. That denial was overturned by the county Board of Commissioners, a decision that has been appealed to the state's Land Use Board of Appeals, where it is pending.

In addition, Schroeder was never denied an incidental-take permit under the Endangered Species Act. Indeed, according to Doug Smithey, of the Portland office of the U.S. Fish and Wildlife Service, the service believed that it was possible for Schroeder to develop his golf course and protect the silverspot. Neil Maine, a member of the silverspot advisory committee, says the service "bent over backwards" to encourage Schroeder to develop a habitat-conservation plan, recognizing the importance of such a plan to perpetuation of the silverspot's preferred habitat. Rather than seeing that process through, however, Schroeder gave up.

Application of the Endangered Species Act will not always be painless. However, to damn the entire act, as the authors have done, on the basis of isolated and incomplete anecdotal evidence does a great disservice to what should be an informed public debate on the act's merits.   ∎

Analyzing Issues and Arguments

1. What is William Robert Irvin's argumentative strategy? In other words, how does he attempt to refute Charles C. Mann and Mark L. Plummer (p. 26)?
2. Do you find Irvin's letter convincing? Why or why not?

IN THE NEWS

Rare Butterfly Consigned to Extinction

Carol Kaesuk Yoon

> The following article is excerpted from a longer news story that appeared in the *New York Times* on April 26, 1994. Carol Kaesuk Yoon holds a Ph.D. in biology and evolutionary biology from Cornell University. She is a regular contributor to the *Times,* the *Washington Post,* the *Los Angeles Times,* and the journal *Science,* and she has recently written on biodiversity for *Garbage* magazine.

Scientists say the country's most recently discovered species of butterfly is about to become extinct. But rather than taking what they call "heroic measures" to save it, they are advocating a more hands-off policy that they predict will soon have biologists counting one less species among North America's butterflies.

Like concerned family members gathered around a loved one's death bed, the biologists who studied this small alpine insect, the Uncompahgre fritillary butterfly, have begun the mourning process, already sadly shaking their heads. They say there is no clear way to save the butterfly, so rather than spending precious conservation dollars to try to resuscitate the species, they suggest letting it go.

"This is probably a fairly heretical stance to some people," said Dr. Hugh Britten, a conservation biologist at the Nevada Biodiversity Research Center in Reno who is an author of a paper about the species. "It's not very easy for me to say I am presiding over the extinction of this species. But in the world of science, so what? Your personal feelings are not relevant and they shouldn't be."

While Dr. Britten and his coauthors, Dr. Peter Brussard, president of the Society for Conservation Biology, and Dr. Dennis Murphy, a conservation biologist at Stanford University, recommend continued monitoring and guarding of the survivors, their ominously titled study, "The Pending Extinction of the Uncompahgre Fritillary Butterfly," makes clear their vision of the future.

"Remember that the whole funding for endangered species is one pie,"   5
Dr. Britten said. "We're saying there's not much we can do that's sure to work and we ought to leave those funds in there to be applied somewhere else where they can work."

Among conservationists, the recommendation on this butterfly, which measures barely an inch across its wings, has already elicited everything from hearty approval to anger. Some say the researchers are making exactly the kind of hard decision they need to make and have been promising to make, forgoing expensive last-ditch efforts to conserve doomed single species.

"I think they're right on target with no heroic measures," said Dr. Paul R. Ehrlich, the Bing Professor of Population Studies and president of the Center for Conservation Biology at Stanford. "I can't get excited about captive breeding of an alpine arctic ecosystem species that may go extinct on its own. It'd be much better to work much harder to save the species of the Northwest—to save whole huge habitats."

But others warn that the recommendation may be typical of many examples to come in which biologists subscribe to a triage mentality, too quickly writing off one species in favor of others in the name of economic prudence.

"Personally, I find the triage idea ethically repugnant," said Dr. Reed Noss, editor of *Conservation Biology,* the journal in which the butterfly report was published. "We too readily assign species to the category of hopeless. It's too easy for political reasons to say we can't do anything about that species, that it would put too much of a burden on our economy. I probably wouldn't have concluded the same thing." . . .

Ann Swengel, international coeditor for the annual July 4 butterfly count   10
run by the Xerces Society and the North American Butterfly Association, said: "When is it O.K. not to try to save a species? I think conservationists are groping with this now.

In the end, it's an opinion, a judgment call just like everything in conservation. You never know what would have happened if you'd done something else." ▪

Analyzing Issues and Arguments

1. Which speakers quoted in this article indicate that their position on saving the Uncompahgre fritillary butterfly is based partly or completely on economic considerations?

2. Reread Hugh Britten's remarks in the third paragraph. In your opinion, should conservation biologists deem their feelings irrelevant when their decisions involve not only scientific issues, but also economic and political ones? Explain your response.

THOMAS PALMER

The Case for Human Beings

> Thomas Palmer published two novels before writing the nonfictional *Landscape with Reptile: Rattlesnakes in an Urban World* (1992), a study of the timber rattler population near Palmer's home in the Blue Hills south of Boston, Massachusetts. "The Case for Human Beings" was excerpted from that book in the January 1992 issue of the *Atlantic Monthly* and was included in *Best American Essays 1993.* Rebutting the argument that we should give top priority to protecting biodiversity, Palmer contends that human beings and their contributions to life on earth are unique.

An argument, a human argument, maintains that we ought to be concerned about the disappearance of individual animal species. If it could be directed at the objects of its solicitude, it would go approximately as follows: "You lesser beasts had better watch your step—*we'll* decide when you can leave." It recognizes that once chromosome patterns combine at the species level, they become unique and irreplaceable—one cannot make a rattlesnake, for instance, out of anything but more rattlesnakes. It looks at the speed at which such patterns are disappearing and shudders to think how empty our grandchildren's world might become, pattern-wise.

In the past twenty years this argument has conquered much of the world; it may soon become part of the thinking of nearly every school child.

Perhaps because we ourselves are a species, we regard the species level as that at which deaths become truly irreversible. Populations, for instance, can and do fade in and out; when a species dies, however, we call it extinct and retire its name forever, being reasonably certain that it will not reappear in its old form.

Students of evolution have shown that species death, or extinction, is going on all the time, and that it is an essential feature of life history. Species are adapted to their environments; as environments change, some species find themselves in the position of islanders whose islands are washing away, and they go under. Similarly, new islands (or environments) are appearing all the time, and they almost invariably produce new species.

What alarms so many life historians is not that extinctions are oc- 5
curring but that they appear to be occurring at a greater rate than they have at all but a few times in the past, raising the specter of the sort of

wholesale die-offs that ended the reign of the dinosaurs. Do we want, they ask, to exile most of our neighbors to posterity? Exactly how much of our planet's resources do we mean to funnel into people-making? Such questions are serious; they involve choosing among futures, and some of these futures are already with us, in the form of collapsing international fisheries, rich grasslands gnawed and trampled into deserts, forests skeletonized by windborne acids, and so forth. Thus high rates of extinction are seen as a symptom of major problems in the way our species operates—problems that may, if we're not careful, be solved for us. A new word has been coined to define the value most threatened by these overheated rates: "biodiversity." As species disappear, biodiversity declines, and our planet's not-quite-limitless fund of native complexities—so some argue—declines with it.

The process described above is indeed occurring. Human beings tend to change environments; when they do, species vanish. The Puritans, for example, though famous for their efforts to discipline sexuality, imposed upon Massachusetts an orgy of ecological licentiousness: they introduced dozens of microbes, weeds, and pests foreign to the region, some of which played havoc with the natives. Human beings tend to travel everywhere, and to bring their cats, rats, and fleas with them, so that hardly any environment is truly isolated today, and creatures that evolved in isolated environments have paid a high price. Of the 171 species and subspecies of birds that have become extinct in the past 300 years, for example, 155 were island forms.

Since extinction is a particularly final and comprehensive form of death, species preservation and its corollary, habitat protection, are now seen as the most important means available to stem the erosion of biodiversity. So far, so good—but I wonder if these ideas, which emphasize diversity at the species level, fail to give an adequate picture of recent biological history. If, for instance, biodiversity is regarded as the chief measure of a landscape's richness, then the American continents reached their peak of splendor on the day after the first Siberian spearmen arrived, and have been deteriorating ever since. More recent developments—such as the domestication of maize, the rise of civilizations in Mexico and Peru, and the passage of the U.S. Bill of Rights—are neutral at best, and are essentially invisible, since they are the work of a single species, a species no more or less weighty than any other, and already present at the start of the interval. But what kind of yardstick measures a handful of skin-clad hunters against Chicago, Los Angeles, and Caracas, and finds one group no more "diverse" than the other?

A considerable amount of pessimism is built into this species-based notion of diversity. Nearly all change on such a scale is change for the worse—especially human-mediated change. Change involves stress, and stress causes extinctions; each extinction is another pock in the skin of an edenic original. This original is frozen in time; more often than not, it is defined as the blissful instant just prior to the arrival of the first human being. In fact, the only way to re-create this instant, and restore biodiversity to its greatest possible richness, would be to arrange for every human being on earth to drop dead tomorrow.

This is not to say that cities are better than coral reefs, or that binary codes are an improvement on genetic ones, but only that "biodiversity" cannot adequately account for the phenomenon of *Homo sapiens.*

Maybe it's time to give up the notion of human beings as intruders, 10 tramplers, and destroyers. We are all of these, there's no doubt about it, but they are not all we are. And yet the same mind-set that interprets human history as little more than a string of increasingly lurid ecological crimes also insists that our species represents the last, best hope of "saving" the planet. Is it any wonder that the future looks bleak?

Here we have the essential Puritan outlook disguised as science — human beings, the sinners, occupy center stage, and cannot move a muscle without risking the direst consequences in a cosmic drama. At stake is the fate of the world; thousands of innocents (other species) rely on the shaky powers of human foresight. One false step — and our ancestors, as we know, have taken almost nothing but false steps — and our dwelling place may be mutilated beyond redemption.

This outlook is realistic in its recognition that our species is different in kind from all others, as any visitor from outer space would admit; it is obnoxious in the limits it places on the organic experiment. Human consciousness — whether in the form of Bach chorales, three-masted schooners, or microwave communications — cannot, in this view, contribute to biodiversity, except by staying as far out of the picture as possible, so as to avoid tainting still-intact landscapes with unnatural influences. The possibility that chorales and schooners might represent positive contributions to biotic richness — that they might, just as much as any rainforest orchid, embody the special genius of this planet — is never admitted. Somehow an agreement has been reached to exclude whatever is human from the sum of biodiversity — as if the Apollo landings, for example, do not represent an astonishing breakthrough *in strictly biological terms.*

This view has a certain legitimacy as long as its definition of diversity is narrowly chromosomal, or species-based. Those environments richest in species — the tropical forests and the warmwater seas — are, from its perspective, the most diverse and complex. But I would argue that this definition, though accurate enough for most of the history of life, became obsolete about a half million years ago, when *Homo sapiens* came on the scene. This creature released organic change from its age-old dependence on genetic recombination and harnessed it to new energies—culture, symbolic language, and imagination. As is becoming more and more evident, nothing has been the same since.

Being reluctant to acknowledge this fact, ecologists, biologists, and environmentalists have had fits trying to introduce our species into their models of the natural world. These models are based on the idea of balance, or equilibrium, wherein each variety of plant or animal plays a limited, genetically prescribed role in the cycling of materials and energy. The roles are not absolutely fixed—natural selection, by sorting and resorting chromosomes, can adapt lines of descent to new ones—but change, by and large, is assumed to be gradual, and millions of years can pass without any notable restructuring of communities.

Human beings cannot be worked into such models. One cannot look at human beings and predict what they will eat, or where they will live, or how many of their children a given landscape will support. If they inhabit a forest, they may burn it down and raise vegetables, or flood it and plant rice, or sell it to a pulp-and-paper manufacturer. They may think of anything; the life their parents led is not a reliable blueprint, but merely a box with a thousand exits. Moralists in search of instructive contrasts will sometimes idealize primitive societies, claiming that they deliberately live "in balance" with their environments, but these examples don't stand up to scrutiny. The Massachuset Indians, for instance, though sometimes presented as sterling conservationists, were the descendants of aboriginal American hunters who appear to have pursued a whole constellation of Ice Age mammals to extinction (including several species of horses). When, in historical times, they were offered metal fishhooks, knives, and firearms, they didn't say, "Thanks, but we prefer rock-chipping."

The revelation that we are not like other creatures in certain crucial respects is an ancient one, and may be nearly as old as humanity; it probably contributed to the idea, central to several major religions, that we inhabit a sort of permanent exile. Until recently, however, we could still imagine ourselves encompassed by, if not entirely contained in, landscapes dominated by nonhuman forces—weather, infectious illness, growing seasons, light and darkness, and so forth. This is no longer so; today most human beings live in artificial wildernesses called cities, and don't raise the food they eat, or know where the water they drink fell as rain. A sort of vertigo has set in—a feeling that a rhythm has been upset, and that soon nothing will be left of the worlds that made us. This feeling is substantiated by population curves, ocean pollution, chemical changes in the earth's atmosphere, vanishing wildlife, mountains of garbage, and numerous other signs that anyone can read. The nineteenth-century conservation movement, which sought to preserve landscapes for largely aesthetic reasons, has become absorbed in the twentieth-century environmental movement, which insists that more is at stake than postcard views. We are, it argues, near to exceeding the carrying capacity of our planet's natural systems, systems whose importance to us will become very obvious when they begin to wobble and fail.

These are not empty warnings. Human communities can and occasionally do self-destruct by overstraining their resource bases. Historical examples include the Easter Islanders, the lowland Maya, and some of the classical-era city-dwellers of the Middle East and North Africa. But if we set aside the equilibrium-based models of the ecologists, and do not limit ourselves to species-bound notions of diversity—in other words, if we seek to include human beings in the landscape of nature, rather than make them outcasts—what sort of picture do we get of the phenomenon of life?

The difference between life and nonlife, according to the biologists, is a matter of degree. A glass of seawater, for instance, contains many of the same materials as a condor (or a green turtle). What makes one alive and the other not are the varying chemical pathways those materials follow. The glass of water contains few internal boundaries, and gases diffuse freely across its surface. In the condor, in contrast, a much more complex array of reactions is in progress, reactions that maintain certain molecular-energy potentials in an oddly elevated state, even though the bird as a whole shows a net energy loss. In other words, both the condor and the glass of water cycle energy, but in the condor the energy goes to support a level of complexity not present in the water.

Perhaps the condor is more like a candle flame—both burn energy, and that burning keeps certain patterns intact. The condor, like the candle, can burn out. But although one can relight the candle, one cannot relight the condor—it is too delicately tuned, too dependent on various internal continuities.

As useful as these distinctions are, they tend to blur under increased 20 magnification. A virus, for instance, is more condorlike than flamelike, because the energy and materials it draws from its surroundings reappear not primarily as heat, light, and simple oxides but as viral protein and nucleic acids—complex substances that the flame cannot construct but only disassemble. And yet most students agree that viruses are not alive, because they cannot build these substances without the aid of the machineries inside a living cell. A certain level of independence is necessary—living things, according to this definition, not only must transform simple compounds into more varied and characteristic ones but also must be able to do so in an atmosphere of nonlife.

Life, for the biologists, is an uphill or retrograde process—it adds order and complexity to environments whose overall tendency is toward diffusion and disorder. It captures energies released by decay and exploits them for growth and rebirth. It is startlingly anomalous in this respect: so far as we know, it occurs nowhere but on the surface of this planet, and even here its appearance seems to have been a one-time-only event; though many lifelike substances have been produced inside sterile glassware, none has ever quickened into veritable beasthood.

The evidence suggests that life continued to fructify and elaborate itself for several billion years after its appearance. The milestones along the way—the nucleated cell, photosynthesis, sexual reproduction, multicellularity, the internal skeleton, the invasion of the land and sky, and so forth—are usually interpreted as advances, because they added additional layers of complexity, interconnection, and ordered interaction to existing systems. This drama did not proceed without crises —photosynthesis, for instance, probably wiped out entire ecosystems by loading the atmosphere with a deadly poison, free oxygen—but life as a whole laughed at such insults, and continued on its protean way.

If we believe that all life—in contrast to rocks and gases—shares a certain quality of sensitivity, or self-awareness, then *Homo sapiens* was an astonishing and wholly unpredictable leap forward in this respect, because human beings manifested an idea of personhood never before achieved. The exact moment of this discovery is of course problematic, as are most events in evolution, but I would date it from early summer about 60,000 years ago, when a group of Neanderthals living in present-day Iraq lost one of their members, dug a grave for him in the Shanidar Cave of the Zagros Mountain highlands, placed his body inside, and covered it with yarrow blossoms, cornflowers, hyacinths, and mallows. Here, in a gesture of remarkable grace, a group of living creatures betrayed an awareness that creatureliness is a pose, a pose that can't be held forever.

The poignancy of this moment is profound. Though the idea is startling to consider, all the evidence suggests that most of life's history has unfolded unobserved, so to speak. I would bet that the dinosaurs, for instance, did not know that they were reptiles, or that they had faces like their neighbors, or that they once hatched from eggs like their offspring.

Consciousness. Mind. Insight. Here are qualities that, if not exclu- 25 sively human, seem appallingly rudimentary elsewhere. Primitive peoples distributed them throughout their worlds; we moderns hold to stricter standards of evidence. Does a cloud yearn, for instance, to drop rain? Is a seed eager to sprout?

The irruption of thoughtfulness that our species represents is not inexplicable in Darwinian terms. Once our apelike and erect ancestors began using weapons, hunting large animals, and sharing the spoils, the ability to develop plans and communicate them acquired considerable survival value, and was genetically enhanced. This ability, and the tripling in brain weight that accompanied it, turned out to be one of the most revolutionary experiments in the history of gene-sorting. It was as if Nature, after wearing out several billion years tossing off new creatures like nutshells, looked up to see that one had come back, and was eyeing her strangely.

The distance between that moment and today is barely a hiccup, geologically speaking. We are genetically almost indistinguishable from those bear-roasters and mammoth-stickers. But the world is a different place now. Grad students in ecology, for instance, are expected to do a certain amount of "fieldwork," and many of them have to travel hundreds and even thousands of miles before they consider themselves far enough from classrooms to be in the field.

Plainly, our planet contained vast opportunities for creatures willing to shape it consciously toward their ends. The way was clear; we know of no other species that has divined what we've been up to, or has a mind to object. What seems simple to us is far beyond them; it's almost as if we move so fast that we are invisible, and they are still trying to pretend—without much success—that the world is the same as it was before we arrived.

This speed on the uptake appears to be the chief advantage that cultural adaptation has over genetic. When human beings encounter new circumstances, adaptation rarely depends on which individuals are genetically best suited to adjust, passing on their abilities more successfully than others and producing subsequent generations better adapted to the new order. No, human beings tend to cut the loop short by noticing the new, puzzling over it, telling their friends, and attempting to find out immediately whether it is edible, combustible, domesticable, or whatever. In this way we develop traditions that are immaterial, so to speak, in that they evolve on a track largely disengaged from the double helix.

This talent for endless jabber and experiment, and the pooling of useful knowledge it makes possible, means that human beings, unlike orangutans or condors, operate not primarily as individuals scattered over a landscape but as shareholders in a common fund of acquired skills, many of them the work of previous generations. This fund is extraordinarily deep and sophisticated, even among the most isolated bands of hunter-gatherers; when, as in recent times, it has included experience accumulated by thousands or even millions of forebears, it has enabled our species to become the quickest-acting agent of change in life's history. In fact, we might sensibly think of the human species not as five billion distinct selves but as five billion nodes in a single matrix, just as the human body is more commonly considered a unit than an accumulation of cells.

If life, as before noted, is a paradoxical chemical process by which order arises from disorder, and a movement toward uniformity produces more complex local conditions, then human enterprise, though full of disasters for other species, is clearly not outside the main line of development. Equatorial rainforests, for instance, are probably the most diverse and multifaceted communities of species on earth. But are they more densely stuffed with highly refined codes and labels than, say, the Library of Congress? Long ago certain moths learned to communicate over as much as two miles of thick woods by releasing subtle chemicals that prospective mates could detect at levels measured in parts per million; today a currency broker in Tokyo can pick up a phone and hear accurate copies of sounds vocalized a split second earlier by a counterpart on the other side of the world. Which system of signals is more sensitive and flexible?

I am concerned, as is obvious, with an image—the image of our species as a vast, featureless mob of yahoos mindlessly trampling this planet's most ancient and delicate harmonies. This image, which is on its way to becoming an article of faith, is not a completely inaccurate description of present conditions in some parts of the world, but it portrays the human presence as a sort of monolithic disaster, when in fact *Homo sapiens* is the crown of creation, if by creation we mean the explosion of earthly vitality and particularity long ago ignited by a weak solution of amino acids mixing in sunlit waters. Change—dramatic, wholesale change—is one of the most reliable constants of this story. To say that the changes we have brought, and will continue to bring, are somehow alien to the world, and are within a half inch of making its "natural" continuance impossible, displays some contempt, I think, for the forces at work, along with a large dose of inverted pride. Who are we, for instance, to say what's possible and what isn't? Have we already glimpsed the end? Where exactly did things go awry? It's useful to remember that just yesterday our main concern was finding something to eat.

I prefer to suppose that we will be here awhile, and that such abilities as we have, though unprecedented in certain respects, are not regrettable. The human mind, for instance, could never have set itself the task of preserving rare species if earlier minds had not learned how to distinguish light from darkness, or coordinate limbs, or identify mates. Now that we think we know something about our immediate neighborhood, we are beginning to realize what a rare quality life is, and if we think of its multibillion-year history on earth as a sort of gradual awakening of matter, we must conclude that the dawning of human consciousness represents one of the most extraordinary sunrises on record. Is it any wonder, then, that the world is changing?

Perhaps because we have become so expert at interrogating our surroundings, we tremble a little at our own shadows. God, for in-

"It's made from an endangered species for that one person in a thousand who couldn't care less."

Drawing by Weber; © 1992 The New Yorker Magazine, Inc.

stance, has become almost a fugitive. We have disassembled the atom; we have paced off the galaxies; He doesn't figure in our equations.

Maybe it would be useful at this point to compare our common 35 birthplace to a fertile hen's egg. Nearly everyone has seen the delicate tracery of blood vessels that begins to spread across the yolk of such an egg within a few hours of laying. Before long a tiny pump starts to twitch rhythmically, and it drives a bright scarlet fluid through these vessels. The egg doesn't know that it is on its way to becoming a chicken. Chickens, for the egg, lie somewhere on the far side of the beginning of time. And yet the egg couldn't be better equipped to make a chicken out of itself.

I would argue that our planet, like the egg, is on a mission of sorts. We don't know what that mission is any more than the nascent nerve cells in the egg know why they are forming a network. All we know is that things are changing rapidly and dramatically.

Today many believe that these changes are often for the worse, and represent a fever or virus from which the body of life will emerge crippled and scarred. We look back with longing on a time, only a moment ago, when the human presence barely dimpled the landscape —when the yolk, so to speak, was at its creamiest, and no angry little eye-spots signaled an intent to devour everything.

I'm not persuaded by this picture—I think it arises from a mistaken belief that the outlines of earthly perfection are already evident. It has inspired a small army of doomsayers—if we burn the forests of the Amazon, we are told, our planet's lungs will give out, and we will slowly asphyxiate. Surely we have better, more practical reasons for not burning them than to stave off universal catastrophe. I can easily imagine similar arguments that would have required the interior of North America to remain empty of cities—and yet I don't think this continent is a poorer place now than it was 20,000 years ago. The more convinced we are that our species is a plague, the more we are obliged to yearn for disasters.

Students of historical psychology have noticed that the end of the world is always at hand. For the Puritan preachers it was to take the form of divine wrath, and they warned that the Wampanoag war was only a foretaste. The Yankees saw it coming in the flood of nineteenth-century immigrants, who meant to drown true Americanism. Today we are more likely to glimpse it in canned aerosols, poisoned winds, and melting ice caps.

Curiously enough, the end of the world always *is* at hand—the 40 world dies and is reborn on a daily basis. A fertile hen's egg is never today what it was yesterday, or will be tomorrow. Few would deny that the effort to preserve and protect as many as possible of the millions of species now existing represents a fresh and heartening expansion of human ambitions. But to suppose that earthly diversity is past its prime, and that a strenuous program of self-effacement is the best contribution our species has left to offer, is neither good biology nor good history.

Analyzing Issues and Arguments

1. Where in this essay does Thomas Palmer rebut Paul and Anne Ehrlich's ideas in "The Rivet Poppers" (p. 13)? Where does Palmer agree with the Ehrlichs? What effects does his agreement have on his rebuttal?

2. What shared views appear in Palmer's essay and in Peter Huber's comments on page 17? On what points do these two writers disagree?

3. What actions and attitude changes does Palmer recommend in "The Case for Human Beings"? What reasons does he give for his recommendations?

Writing about Issues and Arguments

According to Edward O. Wilson's definitions on page 1, is Palmer an exemptionalist or an environmentalist? Review the arguments you have read supporting each of these positions. Which do you find more persuasive? Write an essay presenting your view on the relative value of biodiversity (as Aldo Leopold, the Ehrlichs, and others defend it) and human uniqueness (as Palmer, Leila L. Kysar, and others defend it).

IN THE NEWS

Administration Moves to Ease Opposition to Endangered Species Act

Tom Kenworthy

> The following article appeared in the *Washington Post* on June 15, 1994. Tom Kenworthy is a staff writer for the *Post,* covering natural resources issues.

The Clinton administration, moving to soften opposition to the Endangered Species Act before risking a difficult political fight in Congress over reauthorizing the law, yesterday said it will administer the act in a more flexible way to accommodate concerns of business and private-property owners.

Although the 1973 act has been acclaimed throughout the world as a model for protection of biodiversity, it is under increasing attack here as a blunt and expensive regulatory instrument that runs roughshod over the commercial and property rights of individuals in its pursuit of protecting wildlife and plants.

The administrative changes announced by Interior Secretary Bruce Babbitt and Undersecretary of Commerce D. James Baker would broaden public participation in designing recovery plans for species in peril, clarify land-use changes required by listing endangered species, and require independent scientific scrutiny of listing and recovery decisions.

"My feeling is that the Endangered Species Act has a great deal of flexibility and administrative discretion," Babbitt said at a news conference.

But Babbitt conceded many of the policies announced yesterday are al-   5
ready being employed in many cases, and he was seeking a more consistent implementation to build political support for the eventual reauthorization of the act, probably in 1995.

To date, the administration has been unwilling to begin that fight out of fears that rewriting the legislation would serve as a magnet for a burgeoning private-property rights movement that seeks to loosen federal environmental regulations.

Opponents of the act have been adept at highlighting what they charge are abuses, such as the recent seizure of a Taiwanese immigrant's tractor in Kern County, California, after the farmer plowed up some land and killed several endangered kangaroo rats. Opponents have also won recent federal court decisions that, if upheld, could limit aggressive enforcement of the act's provisions protecting habitat.

Since becoming Interior Secretary, Babbitt has rarely missed an opportunity to counter critics by demonstrating the act can be used in a flexible manner to accommodate both a growing population and the nearly nine hundred animals and plants now on the [nation's] list of threatened and endangered species.

Babbitt has encouraged development of so-called habitat conservation plans that allow developers to destroy some prime endangered species habitat in exchange for protecting other areas. And he has instructed subordinates to highlight endangered species success stories, such as the upcoming announcement that the status of the American bald eagle has been changed from endangered to threatened.

The administrative directives announced yesterday will require more peer 10 review of scientific decisions by government agencies, speed up development of recovery plans and give affected parties more of a say in their preparation, provide timely information to citizens on what activities will be allowed or prohibited by endangered species listings, direct the Fish and Wildlife Service and National Marine Fisheries Service to prepare multiple listings and recovery plans for species that share a common ecosystem, and require greater cooperation with state and local governments in carrying out the act.

Industry groups that have frequently been at odds with the government over endangered species praised the administration's announcement. "We support the action taken today by Secretary Babbitt and see it as a sign that problems with the ESA are being recognized," said William R. Murray, an attorney with the American Forest and Paper Association.

Environmental groups were less enthusiastic. Pamela P. Eaton, director of refuges and wildlife programs for the Wilderness Society, called the changes a "good first step," but expressed concern that broadening public participation in recovery plans could put political pressure on government scientists. "We're concerned that the administration, in its desire to make the Endangered Species Act more user-friendly, not make it species-unfriendly."   ▪

Analyzing Issues and Arguments

1. According to this article, what does the Clinton administration hope to gain by changing its application of the Endangered Species Act? What risk is the administration taking by shifting its approach to the act?

2. How do you think Charles C. Mann and Mark L. Plummer (p. 126) would respond to the Clinton administration's plans to make the act more user-friendly? How would Paul and Anne Ehrlich (p. 13) react?

JOSEPH BRUCHAC

The Circle Is the Way to See

Storyteller and writer Joseph Bruchac is a member of the Abenaki Nation; his ancestry is Abenaki, English, and Slovak. The winner of numerous writing awards and fellowships, he lives in the same house in the Adirondack foothills of New York State where he was reared by his Abenaki grandfather. Bruchac's poetry has been published in hundreds of magazines and anthologies. His most recent books include *Turtle Meat* (1992), a collection of short stories; *Dawn Land* (1993), a novel about life among the ancient Abenaki people; and *Keepers of the Night* (1994), a book of Native American stories and activities for children, coauthored with Michael J. Caduto. "The Circle Is the Way to See" appeared in the anthology *Story Earth: Native Voices on the Environment* (1993). Relating traditional Native American observations and prophecies to recent environmental changes, Bruchac argues for a shift in perspective to heal the sick earth.

Waudjoset nudatlokugan bizwakamigwi alnabe. My story was out walking around, a wilderness lodge man. *Wawigit nudatlokugan.* Here lives my story. *Nudatlokugan Gluskabe.* It is a story of Gluskabe.

One day, Gluskabe went out to hunt. He tried hunting in the woods, but the game animals were not to be seen. Hunting is slow, he thought, and he returned to the wigwam where he lived with his grandmother, Woodchuck. He lay down on his bed and began to sing:

> I wish for a game bag
> I wish for a game bag
> I wish for a game bag
> To make it easy to hunt

He sang and sang until his grandmother could stand it no longer. She made him a game bag of deer hair and tossed it to him. But he did not stop singing:

> I wish for a game bag
> I wish for a game bag
> I wish for a game bag
> To make it easy to hunt

So she made him a game bag of caribou hair. She tossed it to him, but still he continued to sing:

I wish for a game bag
I wish for a game bag
I wish for a game bag
To make it easy to hunt

She tried making a game bag of moose hair, but Gluskabe ignored 5
that as well. He sang:

I wish for a game bag
I wish for a game bag
I wish for a game bag
Of woodchuck hair

Then Grandmother Woodchuck plucked the hair from her belly
and made a game bag. Gluskabe sat up and stopped singing. *"Oleohneh,*
nohkemes," he said. "Thank you, Grandmother."

He went into the forest and called the animals. "Come," he said.
"The world is going to end and all of you will die. Get into my game
bag and you will not see the end of the world."

Then all of the animals came out of the forest and into his game
bag. He carried it back to the wigwam of his grandmother and said,
"Grandmother, I have brought game animals. Now we will not have a
hard time hunting."

Grandmother Woodchuck saw all the animals in the game bag.
"You have not done well, Grandson," she said. "In the future, our small
ones, our children's children, will die of hunger. You must not do this.
You must do what will help our children's children."

So Gluskabe went back into the forest with his game bag. He 10
opened it. "Go, the danger is past," he said. Then the animals came out
of the game bag and scattered throughout the forest. *Nedali medabegazu.*

There my story ends.

The story of Gluskabe's game bag has been told many times. A version much like this one was given to the anthropologist Frank Speck in
1918 by an elderly Penobscot man named Newell Lion. This and other
Gluskabe stories that illustrate the relationship of human beings to the
natural order are told to this day among the Penobscot and Sokokl, the
Passamaquoddy and the Mississquoi, the Micmac and the other Wa-
banaki peoples whose place on this continent is called Ndakinna in the
Abenaki language. Ndakinna—Our Land. A land that owns us and a
land we must respect.

Gluskabe's game bag is a story that is central for an understanding
of the native view of the place of human beings in the natural order
and it is a story with many, many meanings. Gluskabe, the Trickster, is
the ultimate human being and also an old one who was here before
human beings came. He contains both the Good Mind, which can

benefit the people and help the earth, and that other Twisted Mind, a mind governed by selfish thoughts that can destroy the natural balance and bring disaster.

He is greater than we are, but his problems and his powers are those of human beings. Because of our cunning and our power—a magical power—to make things, we can affect the lives of all else that lives around us. Yet when we overuse that power, we do not do well.

We must listen to the older and wiser voices of the earth—like the voice of Grandmother Woodchuck—or our descendants will, quite literally, starve. It is not so much a mystical as a practical relationship. Common sense.

Though my own native ancestry is Abenaki, and I regard the teachings and traditions of my Abenaki friends and elders, like the tales of Gluskabe, as a central part of my existence, I have also spent much of the last thirty-two years of my life learning from the elders of the Haudenosaunee nations, the People of the Longhouse—those nations of the Mohawk, Oneida, Onondaga, Cayuga, Seneca, and Tuscarora—commonly referred to today as the Iroquois.

We share this endangered corner of our continent, the area referred to on European-made maps as New York and New England. In fact, I live within a few hours' drive of the place where a man regarded as a messenger from the Creator and known as the Peacemaker joined with Hiawatha—perhaps a thousand years ago—to bring together five warring tribal nations into a League of Peace and plant a great pine tree as the living symbol of that green and growing union of nations.

That Great League is now recognized by many historians as a direct influence on the formation of modern ideas of democracy and on the Constitution of the United States.

I think it right to recall here some of the environmental prophecies of the Haudenosaunee people, not as an official representative of any native nation, but simply as a humble storyteller. I repeat them not as a chief nor as an elder, but as one who has listened and who hopes to convey the messages he has heard with accuracy and honesty.

According to Iroquois traditions, some of which were voiced by the prophet Ganio-dai-yo in the early 1800s, a time would come when the elm trees would die. And then the maple, the leader of all the trees, would also begin to die, from the top down.

In my own early years, I saw the elms begin to die. I worked as a tree surgeon in my early twenties, cutting those great trees in the Finger Lakes area of New York State, the traditional lands of the Cayuga Nation of the Iroquois.

As I cut them, I remembered how their bark had once been used to cover the old longhouses and how the elm was a central tree for the old-time survival of the Iroquois. But an insect, introduced inadvertently, like the flus and measles and smallpox and the other diseases of humans that killed more than 90 percent of the natives of North America in the sixteenth and seventeenth centuries, brought with it Dutch elm disease and spelled the end of the great trees.

Those trees were so beautiful, their limbs so graceful, their small leaves a green fountain in the springtime, a message that it was time to plant the corn as soon as they were the size of a squirrel's ear. And now they are all gone because of the coming of the Europeans. Now, in the last few years, the maple trees of New York and New England have begun to die, from the top down—weakened, some say, by the acid rain that falls, acid blown into the clouds by the smokestacks of the industries of the Ohio Valley, smoke carried across the land to fall as poison.

Is the earth sick? From a purely human perspective, the answer must certainly be yes. Things that humans count on for survival—basic things such as clean water and clean air—have been affected.

The Iroquois prophecies also said a time would come when the air 25 would be harmful to breathe and the water harmful to drink. That time is now. The waters of the St. Lawrence River are so full of chemicals from industries, like Kaiser and Alcoa, on its shores that the turtles are covered with cancers. (In the story of Creation as told by the Haudenosaunee, it was the Great Turtle that floated up from the depths and offered its back as a place to support the earth.)

Tom Porter, a Bear Clan chief of the Mohawks, used to catch fish from that same river to feed his family. The water that flowed around their island, part of the small piece of land still legally in the hands of the Mohawk people and called the St. Regis Reservation, that water brought them life. But a few years ago, he saw that the fish were no longer safe to eat. They would poison his children. He left his nets by the banks of the river. They are still there, rotting.

If we see "the earth" as the web of life that sustains us, then there is no question that the web is weakened, that the earth is sick. But if we look at it from another side, from the view of the living earth itself, then the sickness is not that of the planet, the sickness is embodied in human beings, and, if carried to its illogical conclusion, the sickness will not kill the earth, it will kill us.

Human self-importance is a big part of the problem. It is because we human beings have one power that no other creatures have—the power to upset the natural balance—that we are so dangerous to ourselves. Because we have that great power, we have been given ceremonies and lesson stories (which in many ways are ceremonies in and of themselves) to remind us of our proper place.

We are not the strongest of all the beings in Creation. In many ways, we are the weakest. We were given original instructions by the Creator. Those instructions, to put them as simply as possible, were to be kind to each other and to respect the earth. It is because we human beings tend to forget those instructions that the Creator gave us stories like the tales of Gluskabe and sends teachers like the Peacemaker and Handsome Lake every now and then to help us remember and return us to the path of the Good Mind.

I am speaking now not of Europeans but of native people them- 30 selves. There are many stories in the native traditions of North America —like the Hopi tales of previous worlds being destroyed when human beings forgot those instructions—that explain what can happen when we lose sight of our proper place. Such stories and those teachers exist to keep human beings in balance, to keep our eyes focused, to help us recognize our place as part of the circle of Creation, not above it. When we follow our original instructions, we are equal to the smallest insects and the greatest whales, and if we take the lives of any other being in this circle of Creation it must be for the right reason—to help the survival of our own people, not to threaten the survival of the insect people or the whale people.

If we gather medicinal herbs, we must never take all that we find, only a few. We should give thanks and offer something in exchange, perhaps a bit of tobacco, and we should always loosen the earth and plant seeds so that more will grow.

But we, as humans, are weak and can forget. So the stories and the teachers who have been given the message from Creation come to us and we listen and we find the right path again.

That had been the way on this continent for tens of thousands of years before the coming of the Europeans. Ten thousand years passed after the deaths of the great beasts on this continent—those huge beings like the cave bear and the mammoth and the giant sloth, animals that my Abenaki people remember in some of our stories as monsters that threatened the lives of the people—before another living being on this continent was brought to extinction.

If it was native people who killed off those great animals ten thousand years ago, then it seems they learned something from that experience. The rattlesnake is deadly and dangerous, the grizzly and the polar bear have been known to hunt and kill human beings, but in native traditions those creatures are honored even as they are feared; the great bear is seen as closely related to human beings, and the rattlesnake is sometimes called Grandfather.

Then, with the coming of the Europeans, that changed. In the five 35 hundred years since the arrival of Columbus on the shores of Hispaniola, hundreds of species have been exterminated. It has been done largely for profit, not for survival. And as the count goes higher, not only the survival of other species is in question but also the survival of the human species.

Part of my own blood is European because, like many native Americans today, many of my ancestors liked the new white people and the new black people (some of whom escaped from slavery and formed alliances and even, for a time, African/Indian maroon[1] nations on the soils of the two American continents—such as the republic of Palmares in northeastern Brazil, which lasted most of the seventeenth century). I am not ashamed of any part of my racial ancestry. I was taught that it is not what is in the blood but what is carried in the culture that makes human beings lose their balance and forget their rightful place.

The culture of those human beings from Europe, however, had been at war with nature for a long time. They cut down most of their forests and killed most of the wild animals. For them, wildness was something to be tamed. To the native peoples of North America, wilderness was home, and it was not "wild" until the Europeans made it so. Still, I take heart at the thought that many of those who came to this hemisphere from Europe quickly learned to see with a native eye. So much so that the leaders of the new colonies (which were the first multinational corporations and had the express purpose of making money for the mother country—not seeking true religious freedom, for they forbade any religions but their own) just as quickly passed laws to keep their white colonists from "going native."

If you do not trust my memory, then take a look at the words written by those colonizing Europeans themselves. You will find laws still on the books in Massachusetts that make it illegal for a man to have long hair. Why? Because it was a sign of sympathy with the Indians who wore their hair long. You will find direct references to colonists "consorting with the devil" by living like the "savages."

The native way of life, the native way of looking at the world and the way we humans live in that world, was attractive and meaningful. It was also more enjoyable. It is simple fact that the native people of New England, for example, were better fed, better clothed, and healthier than the European colonists. They also had more fun. European chroniclers of the time often wrote of the way in which the Indians made even work seem like play. They turned their work, such as planting a field or harvesting, into a communal activity with laughter and song.

Also, the lot of native women was drastically different from that of the colonial women. Native women had control over their own lives. 40

---

[1]**maroons:** Fugitive slaves of the West Indies and Guiana in the seventeenth and eighteenth centuries.—Ed.

They could decide who they would or would not marry, they owned their own land, they had true reproductive freedom (including herbal methods of birth control), and they had political power. In New England, women chiefs were not uncommon, and throughout the Northeast there were various arrangements giving women direct control in choosing chiefs. (To this day, among the Haudenosaunee, it is the women of each clan who choose the chiefs to represent them in the Grand Council of the League.)

In virtually every aspect of native life in North America—and I realize this is a huge generalization, for there were more than four hundred different cultures in North America alone in the fifteenth century and great differences between them—the idea of the circle, in one form or another, was a guiding principle. There was no clock time, but cyclical time. The seasons completed a circle, and so too did our human lives.

If we gather berries or hunt game in one place this year, then we may return to that place the following year to do the same. We must take care of that place properly—burning off the dry brush and dead berry bushes so that the ashes will fertilize the ground and new canes will grow, while at the same time ensuring that there will still be a clearing there in the forest with new green growth for the deer to eat.

The whole idea of wildlife conservation and ecology, in fact, was common practice among the native peoples of this continent. (There is also very sound documented evidence of the direct influence of native people and native ideas of a "land ethic" on people such as Henry David Thoreau, George Bird Grinnell, Ernest Thompson Seton, and others who were the founders of organizations like the Audubon Society, the Boy Scouts of America, and the whole modern conservation movement itself.) There was not, therefore, the European idea of devastating your own backyard and then moving on to fresh ground—to a new frontier (the backyard of your weaker neighbor).

If you see things in terms of circles and cycles, and if you care about the survival of your children, then you begin to engage in commonsense practices. By trial and error, over thousands of years, perhaps, you learn how to do things right. You learn to live in a way that keeps in mind, as native elders put it, seven generations. You ask yourself—as an individual and as a nation—how will the actions I take affect the seven generations to come? You do not think in terms of a four-year presidency or a yearly national budget, artificial creations that mean nothing positive in terms of the health of the earth and the people. You say to yourself, what will happen if I cut these trees and the birds can no longer nest there? What will happen if I kill the female deer who has a fawn so that no animals survive to bring a new generation into the world? What will happen if I divert the course of this river or build a dam so that the fish and animals and plants downstream are deprived of water? What will happen if I put all the animals in my game bag?

And then, as the cycles of the seasons pass, you explain in the form 45 of lesson stories what will happen when the wrong actions are taken. Then you will remember and your children's children will remember. There are thousands of such lesson stories still being kept by the native people of North America, and it is time for the world as a whole to listen.

The circle is the way to see. The circle is the way to live, always keeping in mind the seven generations to come, always asking: how will my deeds affect the lives of my children's children's children?

This is the message I have heard again and again. I give that message to you. My own "ethnic heritage" is a mixture of European and native, but the messages I have heard best and learned the most from spring from this native soil.

If someone as small and pitiful as I am can learn from those ancient messages and speak well enough to touch the lives of others, then it seems to me that any human being—native or nonnative—has the ability to listen and to learn. It is because of that belief that I share these words, for all the people of the earth.

Analyzing Issues and Arguments

1. In what ways does the story of Gluskabe's game bag prepare readers for uncommon features in the argument that follows?
2. Where in the Gluskabe story does Joseph Bruchac introduce his essay's central point? Where else in the essay does he make the same point?
3. What is the meaning of Bruchac's title, "The Circle Is the Way to See"? What actions besides seeing does Bruchac recommend?

Writing about Issues and Arguments

Go through "The Circle Is the Way to See" and identify the key points in Bruchac's argument. Rewrite his argument in a more traditional form. (You may either agree or disagree with his position.)

Beyond Spotted Owls:
Saving Ecosystems instead of Species

David Foster

The following is an excerpt from an Associated Press article that ran in newspapers throughout the country on May 15, 1994. Based in Seattle, David Foster is the Northwest regional reporter for the Associated Press, a national newswire service.

Hoping to end a three-year deadlock between wildlife protection and timber production, the Clinton administration last month adopted a plan embracing ecosystem management across 24 million acres of federal forest land in Washington, Oregon, and California. . . .

Environmentalists view the Northwest experiment as a step toward more holistic wildlife conservation, an improvement over the species-by-species approach fostered by the Endangered Species Act, which is up for reauthorization by Congress.

But those who defend the use of natural resources see something more ominous—a government using analysis to create paralysis, enlisting ever more obscure organisms to prevent humans from carving out their own ecological niche. . . .

Late on a Friday afternoon in Portland, Oregon, when most people are making tracks out of the city, Tom Tuchmann is in his office, pursuing the sticky business of turning science into public policy.

"People want more timber, more recreation, more biological diversity," 5 Tuchmann says. "At some point we have to recognize that we have a limited land base, and then start making decisions about how much of each we want."

Tuchmann, head of the Northwest office implementing the government's new forest plan, knows how unpopular those decisions can be.

He must tell unemployed loggers that the region's annual timber harvest will drop to one-fourth of its average during the 1980s. Then he must face lawsuit-prone conservationists and try to convince them it's enough to protect 80 percent of the remaining old growth, not 100 percent.

What Tuchmann sees in ecosystem management is a way to untie the knot of environmental laws and recent court rulings involving the old-growth forest. Protect habitat, he says, and you protect wildlife—including species that may be listed as endangered in years ahead.

"We're trying to get ahead of the Endangered Species Act," he says. "We feel that over time, we will have enough habitat to protect old-growth-related species."

Environmental groups say the government's plan points in the right di- 10 rection but does not go far enough. They're already drawing up new legal challenges.

The plan's net effect can be put simply—more federal land for wildlife and less for loggers.

Thirty-six percent of the 24 million-acre planning area is already pre-served as national park, wilderness, or administratively withdrawn areas. The plan puts an additional 31 percent into old-growth reserves, and 11 percent into riparian reserves that will protect every river and stream with a forested buffer up to 600 feet wide.

Even in the 22 percent open to logging, the region's familiar checker-board of forested and clear-cut squares will give way to a more careful land-scape.

Loggers will have to leave 15 percent of the trees in every watershed they cut. Dozens of rare plants and animals will get special protection wherever they're found—100 acres around spotted-owl nests, 1.5 acres around the roosts of certain bats.

The fuzzy sandoze [a fungus] will fare especially well. Each specimen will 15 get a 600-acre reserve until its needs are better known.

Bat buffers? Fungus reserves?

It's the kind of talk that pushes Myron Ebell's buttons. He works for the American Land Rights Association, which represents private landowners and users of public lands.

Ebell says the forest plan is part of a "criminal conspiracy" to cripple the Northwest timber industry in the name of wildlife protection.

"If they're able to move ahead, we're going to see similar economic dis-locations around the country," he says.

Ecosystem management, by his definition, is a meaningless abstraction in- 20 voked by bureaucrats who want to exercise national land-use controls but lack the authority to do it.

Ebell says the current concern over endangered species is overwrought.

"Nature's not fragile at all," he says. "It's an incredibly resilient thing. There are people who say any loss of genetic variety is a disaster, not admit-ting that any gaps are quickly filled by new species."

But environmentalists, noting threats such as global warming, say humans have made a risky habit of modifying the environment in ignorance. They say that to ensure we're not the gap filled by new species, more intelligent tinker-ing is needed. . . .   ■

Analyzing Issues and Arguments

1. How do you think Joseph Bruchac (p. 54) would respond to the new ecosystem management plan discussed in this article?

2. How does ecosystem management differ from the way the Endangered Species Act has been implemented in the past? Do you think it represents an improvement?

PETER SINGER

Ethics and the New Animal Liberation Movement

Peter Singer is professor of philosophy and director of the Centre for Human Bioethics at Monash University in Melbourne, Australia. His 1975 book *Animal Liberation* has been called "the bible of the animal liberation movement." Singer, the principal founder of that movement, remains active in working to end human exploitation and abuse of animals. The following essay comes from the prologue to his 1985 book *In Defense of Animals*. Tracing the history of contemporary human "speciesism"—human beings' assumption that they are superior to other species—Singer builds a case for valuing the life and welfare of every creature as highly as our own.

Although there were one or two nineteenth-century thinkers who asserted that animals have rights, the serious political movement for animal liberation is very young, a product of the 1970s. Its aims are quite distinct from the efforts of the more traditional organizations, like the Royal Society for the Prevention of Cruelty to Animals, to stop people from treating animals cruelly. Even these traditional concerns, however, are relatively recent when seen in the context of 3,000 years of Western civilization, as a brief glance at the historical background to the contemporary animal liberation movement will show.

Concern for animal suffering can be found in Hindu thought, and the Buddhist idea of compassion is a universal one, extending to animals as well as humans, but our Western traditions are very different. Our intellectual roots lie in ancient Greece and in the Judeo–Christian tradition. Neither is kind to those not of our species.

In the conflict between rival schools of thought in ancient Greece, it was the school of Aristotle that eventually became dominant. Aristotle held the view that nature is a hierarchy in which those with less reasoning ability exist for the sake of those with more reasoning ability. Thus plants, he said, exist for the sake of animals, and animals for the sake of man, to provide him with food and clothing. Indeed, Aristotle took his logic a step further—the barbarian tribes, which he considered obviously less rational than the Greeks, existed in order to serve as slaves to the more rational Greeks. He did not quite have the nerve to add that philosophers, being supremely rational, should be served by everyone else!

Nowadays we have rejected Aristotle's idea that less rational human beings exist in order to serve more rational ones, but to some extent we still retain that attitude towards nonhuman animals. The social reformer Henry Salt tells a story in his autobiography, *Seventy Years among Savages* (an account of a life lived entirely in England), of how, when he was a master at Eton, he first broached the topic of vegetarianism with a colleague, a distinguished science teacher. With some trepidation he awaited the verdict of the scientific mind on his new beliefs. It was: "But don't you think that animals were sent to us for food?" That response is not far from what Aristotle might have said. It is even closer to the other great intellectual tradition of the West—a tradition in which the following words from Genesis stand as a foundation for everything else:

> And God said, Let us make man in our image, after our likeness: and let them have domination over the fish of the sea, and over the fowl of the air, and over the cattle, and over all the earth, and over every creeping thing that creepeth upon the earth.
> So God created man in his own image. . . .
> And God blessed them, and God said unto them, Be fruitful, and multiply, and replenish the earth, and subdue it; and have dominion over the fish of the sea, and over the fowl of the air, and over every living thing that moveth upon the earth.

Here is a myth to make human beings feel their supremacy and   5
their power. Man alone is made in the image of God. Man alone is given dominion over all the animals and told to subdue the earth. One may debate, as environmentally concerned Jews and Christians have done, whether this grant of dominion entitles human beings to rule as petty despots, doing as they please with the unfortunate subjects placed under their jurisdiction, or whether it was not rather a kind of stewardship, in which humans are responsible to their Lord for the proper care and use of what has been placed in their custody. One can point to one or two Christian figures, like John Chrysostom and Francis of Assisi, who have shown compassion and concern for nonhuman Creation. (Though even the stories about Francis are conflicting. There is one episode in which a disciple is said to have cut a trotter off a living pig in order to give it to a sick companion. According to the narrator, Francis rebuked the disciple—but for damaging the property of the pig owner, not for cruelty to the pig!) So far as the history of Western attitudes to animals is concerned, however, the "dominion" versus "stewardship" debate and that over the true nature of the teachings of Francis are both beside the point. It is beyond dispute that mainstream Christianity, for its first 1,800 years, put nonhuman animals outside its sphere of concern. On this issue the key figures in early Christianity were unequivocal. Paul scornfully rejected the thought that God might care about the

welfare of oxen, and the incident of the Gadarene swine, in which Jesus is described as sending devils into a herd of pigs and making them drown themselves in the sea, is explained by Augustine as having been intended to teach us that we have no duties towards animals. This interpretation was accepted by Thomas Aquinas, who stated that the only possible objection to cruelty to animals was that it might lead to cruelty to humans—according to Aquinas, there was nothing wrong *in itself* with making animals suffer. This became the official view of the Roman Catholic Church to such good—or bad—effect that as late as the middle of the nineteenth century Pope Pius IX refused permission for the founding of a Society for the Prevention of Cruelty to Animals in Rome, on the grounds that to grant permission would imply that human beings have duties to the lower creatures.

Even in England, which has a reputation for being dotty about animals, the first efforts to obtain legal protection for members of other species were made only 180 years ago. They were greeted with derision. The [*London*] *Times* was so dismissive of the idea that the suffering of animals ought to be prevented that it attacked proposed legislation that would stop the "sport" of bull-baiting. Said that august newspaper: "Whatever meddles with the private personal disposition of man's time or property is tyranny." Animals, clearly, were just property.

That was in 1800, and that bill was defeated. It took another twenty years to get the first anticruelty law onto the British statute books. That any consideration at all should be given to the interests of animals was a significant step beyond the idea that the boundary of our species is also the boundary of morality. Yet the step was a restricted one because it did not challenge our right to make whatever *use* we chose of other species. Only cruelty—causing pain when there was no reason for doing so but sheer sadism or callous indifference—was prohibited. The farmer who deprives his pigs of room to move does not offend against this concept of cruelty, for he is considered to be doing only what he thinks necessary to produce bacon. Similarly, the scientist who poisons a hundred rats in order to determine the lethal dose of some new flavoring agent for toothpaste is not regarded as cruel, merely as concerned to follow the accepted procedures for testing the safety of new products.

The nineteenth-century anticruelty movement was built on the assumption that the interests of nonhuman animals deserve protection only when serious human interests are not at stake. Animals remained very clearly "lower creatures" whose interests must be sacrificed to our own in the event of conflict.

The significance of the new animal liberation movement is its challenge to this assumption. Taken in itself, say the animal liberationists, membership of the human species is not morally relevant. Other creatures on our planet also have interests. We have always assumed that we are justified in overriding their interests, but this bald assumption is simply species–selfishness. If we assert that to have rights one must be a member of the human race, and that is all there is to it, then what are we to say to the racist who contends that to have rights you have to be a member of the Caucasian race, and that is all there is to it? Conversely, once we agree that race is not, in itself, morally significant, how can species be? As Jeremy Bentham[1] put it some 200 years ago:

> The day *may* come when the rest of the animal creation may acquire those rights which never could have been withholden from them but by the hand of tyranny. The French have already discovered that the blackness of the skin is no reason why a human being should be abandoned without redress to the caprice of a tormentor. It may one day come to be recognized that the number of the legs, the villosity of the skin, or the termination of the *os sacrum*[2] are reasons equally insufficient for abandoning a sensitive being to the same fate.

Someone might say: "It is not because we are members of the hu- 10 man species that we are justified in overriding the interests of other animals; it is because we are rational and they are not." Someone else might argue that it is because we are autonomous beings, or because we can use language, or because we are self-conscious, or because we have a sense of justice. All these contentions and more have been invoked to justify us in sacrificing the interests of other animals to our own.

One way of replying would be to consider whether nonhuman animals really do lack these allegedly important characteristics. The more we learn of some nonhuman animals, particularly chimpanzees but also many other species, the less able we are to defend the claim that we humans are unique because we are the only ones capable of reasoning, or of autonomous action, or of the use of language, or because we possess a sense of justice. I shall not go into this reply here because it would take a long time and it would do nothing for the many species of animals who could not be said to meet whatever test was being proposed.

There is a much shorter rejoinder. Let us return to the passage I have quoted from Bentham, for he anticipated the objection. After dismissing the idea that number of legs, roughness of skin, or fine details of bone formation should "trace the insuperable line" between those who have moral standing and those who do not, Bentham goes on to ask what else might mark this boundary:

[1]**Jeremy Bentham** (1748–1832): English philosopher who founded utilitarianism.—Ed.
[2]*os sacrum:* Bottom of the spine, distinguished in humans by the absence of a tail.—Ed.

> Is it the faculty of reason, or perhaps the faculty of discourse? But a
> full-grown horse or dog is beyond comparison a more rational, as
> well as a more conversable animal, than an infant of a day or a week
> or even a month, old. But suppose they were otherwise, what would
> it avail? The question is not, Can they *reason?* nor Can they *talk?* but,
> *Can they suffer?*

Bentham is clearly right. Whatever the test we propose as a means of
separating human from nonhuman animals, it is plain that if all nonhuman animals are going to fail it, some humans will fail as well. Infants
are neither rational nor autonomous. They do not use language and
they do not possess a sense of justice. Are they therefore to be treated
like nonhuman animals, to be fattened for the table, if we should fancy
the taste of their flesh, or to be used to find out if some new shampoo
will blister human eyeballs?

Ah, but infants, though not rational, autonomous, or able to talk,
have the potential to become adult humans—so the defender of human supremacy will reply to Bentham. The relevance of potential is
another complicated argument that I shall avoid by the stratagem of focusing your attention on another class of humans who would fail the
proposed test: those unfortunate enough to have been born with brain
damage so severe that they will never be able to reason, or talk or do
any of the other things that are often said to distinguish us from nonhuman animals. The fact that we do not use them as means to our ends
indicates that we do not really see decisive moral significance in ratio-
nality, or autonomy, or language, or a sense of justice, or any of the
other criteria said to distinguish us from other animals. Why do we
lock up chimpanzees in appalling primate research centers and use
them in experiments that range from the uncomfortable to the agoniz-
ing and lethal, yet would never think of doing the same to a retarded
human being at a much *lower* mental level? The only possible answer is
that the chimpanzee, no matter how bright, is not human, while the
retarded human, no matter how dull, is.

This is speciesism, pure and simple, and it is as indefensible as the
most blatant racism. There is no ethical basis for elevating membership
of one particular species into a morally crucial characteristic. From an
ethical point of view, we all stand on an equal footing—whether we
stand on two feet, or four, or none at all.

That is the crux of the philosophy of the animal liberation move- 15
ment, but to forestall misunderstanding I had better say something immediately about this notion of equality.

It does *not* mean that animals have all the same rights as you and I
have. Animal liberationists do not minimize the obvious differences between most members of our species and members of other species. The
rights to vote, freedom of speech, freedom of worship—none of these

Doonesbury

BY GARRY TRUDEAU

can apply to other animals. Similarly, what harms humans may cause much less harm, or even no harm at all, to some animals. If I were to confine a herd of cows within the boundaries of the county of, say, Devon, I do not think I would be doing them any harm at all; if, on the other hand, I were to take a group of people and restrict them to the same county, I am sure many would protest that I had harmed them considerably, even if they were allowed to bring their families and friends, and notwithstanding the many undoubted attractions of that particular county. Humans have interests in mountain-climbing and skiing, in seeing the world and in sampling foreign cultures. Cows like lush pastures and shelter from harsh weather. Hence to deny humans the right to travel outside Devon would be to restrict their rights significantly; it would not be a significant restriction of the rights of cows.

Here is another example, more relevant to real problems about our treatment of animals. Suppose we decided to perform lethal scientific experiments on normal adult humans, kidnapped at random from public parks for this purpose. Soon every adult who entered a park would become fearful of being kidnapped. The resultant terror would be a form of suffering additional to whatever pain was involved in the experiments themselves. The same experiments carried out on nonhuman animals would cause less suffering overall, for the nonhuman animals would not have the same anticipatory dread. This does not mean, I hasten to add, that it is all right to experiment on animals as we please, but only that if the experiment is to be done at all, there is *some* reason, compatible with the equal consideration of interests, for preferring to use nonhuman animals rather than normal adult humans.

There is one point that needs to be added to this example. Nothing in it depends on the fact that normal adult humans are members of our species. It is their capacity for knowledge of what may happen to them that is crucial. If they were not normal adults but severely brain-damaged humans—orphans perhaps, or children abandoned by their parents—then they would be in the same position as nonhuman animals at a similar mental level. If we use the argument I have put forward to justify experiments on nonhuman animals, we have to ask ourselves whether we are also prepared to allow similar experiments on human beings with a similar degree of awareness of what is happening to them. If we say that we will perform an experiment on monkeys but not on brain-damaged human orphans, we are giving preference to the humans just because they are members of our own species, which is a violation of the principle of equal consideration of interests.

In the example I have just given the superior mental powers of normal adult humans would make them suffer more. It is important to recognize that in other circumstances the nonhuman animal may suffer more because it cannot understand what is happening. If we capture a wild animal, intending to release it later, it may not be able to distinguish our relatively benign intentions from a threat to its life: general terror may be all it experiences.

The moral significance of taking life is more complex still. There is furious controversy about the circumstances in which it is legitimate to kill human beings, so it is no wonder that it should be difficult to decide whether nonhuman animals have any right to life. Here I would say, once again, that species in itself cannot make a difference. If it is wrong to take the life of a severely brain-damaged abandoned human infant, it must be equally wrong to take the life of a dog or a pig at a comparable mental level. On the other hand, perhaps it is *not* wrong to take the life of a brain-damaged human infant—after all, many people think such infants should be allowed to die, and an infant who is "allowed to die" ends up just as dead as one that is killed. Indeed, one could argue that our readiness to put a hopelessly ill nonhuman animal out of its misery is the one and only respect in which we treat animals better than we treat people.

The influence of the Judeo-Christian insistence on the God-like nature of human beings is nowhere more apparent than in the standard Western doctrine of the sanctity of human life: a doctrine that puts the life of the most hopelessly and irreparably brain-damaged human being —of the kind whose level of awareness is not underestimated by the term "human vegetable"—above the life of a chimpanzee. The sole reason for this strange priority is, of course, the fact that the chimpanzee is not a member of our species, and the human vegetable is biologically human. This doctrine is now starting to be eroded by the acceptance of abortion, which is the killing of a being that is indisputably a member of the human species, and by the questioning of the value of applying all the power of modern medical technology to saving human life in all cases.

I think we will emerge from the present decade with a significantly different attitude towards the sanctity of human life, an attitude which considers the quality of the life at stake rather than the simple matter of whether the life is or is not that of a member of the species *Homo sapiens*. Once this happens, we shall be ready to take a much broader view of the wrongness of killing, one in which the capacities of the being in question will play a central role. Such a view will not discriminate on the basis of species alone but will still draw a distinction between the seriousness of killing beings with the mental capacities of normal human adults and killing beings who do not possess, and never have possessed, these mental capacities. It is not a bias in favor of our own species that leads us to think that there is greater moral significance in taking the life of a normal human than there is in taking the life of, for example, a fish. To give just one reason for this distinction, a normal human has hopes and plans for the future: to take the life of a normal human is therefore to cut off these plans and to prevent them from ever being fulfilled. Fish, I expect, do not have as clear a conception of themselves as beings with a past and a future. Consequently, to kill a fish is not to prevent the fulfillment of any plans, or at least not of any long-range future plans. This does not, I stress, mean that it is all right, or morally trivial, to kill fish. If fish are capable of enjoying their lives, as I believe they are, we do better when we let them continue to live than when we needlessly end their lives, though when we cut short the life of a fish, we are not doing something as bad as when we needlessly end the life of a normal human adult.

The animal liberation movement, therefore, is *not* saying that all lives are of equal worth or that all interests of humans and other animals are to be given equal weight, no matter what those interests may be. It *is* saying that where animals and humans have similar interests—we might take the interest in avoiding physical pain as an example, for it is an interest that humans clearly share with other animals—those interests are to be counted equally, with no automatic discount just because one of the beings is not human. A simple point, no doubt, but nevertheless part of a far-reaching ethical revolution.

This revolution is the culmination of a long line of ethical development. I cannot do better than quote the words of that splendid nineteenth-century historian of ideas, W. E. H. Lecky. In his *History of European Morals* Lecky wrote: "At one time the benevolent affections embrace merely the family, soon the circle expanding includes first a class, then a nation, then a coalition of nations, then all humanity, and finally, its influence is felt in the dealings of man with the animal world." Lecky anticipated what the animal liberationists are now saying. In an earlier stage of our development most human groups held to a tribal ethic. Members of the tribe were protected, but people of other tribes could be robbed or killed as one pleased. Gradually the circle of protection expanded, but as recently as 150 years ago we did not include blacks. So African human beings could be captured, shipped to America, and sold. In Australia, white settlers regarded Aborigines as a pest and hunted them down, much as kangaroos are hunted down today. Just as we have progressed beyond the blatantly racist ethic of the era of slavery and colonialism, so we must now progress beyond the speciesist ethic of the era of factory farming, of the use of animals as mere research tools, of whaling, seal hunting, kangaroo slaughter, and the destruction of wilderness. We must take the final step in expanding the circle of ethics.

Analyzing Issues and Arguments

1. According to Peter Singer, what is the traditional Western attitude toward animals? What are the sources of that attitude?
2. What is the central tenet of the animal liberation movement? What actions are dictated by this tenet?
3. Does Singer argue primarily *for* his own views or *against* opposing views? What are the key points of his argument?

Writing about Issues and Arguments

In paragraph 9 Singer asks, "Once we agree that race is not, in itself, morally significant, how can species be?" Write an argumentative essay responding to this question, either by rebutting Singer's implied answer or by stating and supporting it.

CARL COHEN

The Case Against Animal Rights

Carl Cohen is a professor at the University of Michigan Medical School in Ann Arbor. He received his doctorate in philosophy from UCLA and writes frequently on social and political issues. He has also been a guest lecturer in Peru, at the Hebrew University of Jerusalem, and at the University of Otago in New Zealand. "The Case against Animal Rights" is excerpted from a longer essay that appeared in the *New England Journal of Medicine* on October 2, 1986. In it Cohen defends what Peter Singer calls "speciesism" (p. 64) and rebuts some of the principal arguments for animal rights.

Using animals as research subjects in medical investigations is widely condemned on two grounds: first, because it wrongly violates the *rights* of animals,[1] and second, because it wrongly imposes on sentient creatures much avoidable *suffering*.[2] Neither of these arguments is sound. The first relies on a mistaken understanding of rights; the second relies on a mistaken calculation of consequences. Both deserve definitive dismissal.

Why Animals Have No Rights

A right, properly understood, is a claim, or potential claim, that one party may exercise against another. The target against whom such a claim may be registered can be a single person, a group, a community, or (perhaps) all humankind. The content of rights claims also varies greatly: repayment of loans, nondiscrimination by employers, noninterference by the state, and so on. To comprehend any genuine right fully, therefore, we must know *who* holds the right, *against whom* it is held, and *to what* it is a right.

Alternative sources of rights add complexity. Some rights are grounded in constitution and law (for example, the right of an accused to trial by jury); some rights are moral but give no legal claims (for example, my right to your keeping the promise you gave me); and some rights (for example, against theft or assault) are rooted both in morals and in law.

[1]Regan, T. *The Case for Animal Rights*. Berkeley: University of California Press, 1983.
[2]Singer, P. *Animal Liberation*. New York: Avon Books, 1977.

The differing targets, contents, and sources of rights, and their inevitable conflict, together weave a tangled web. Notwithstanding all such complications, this much is clear about rights in general: they are in every case claims, or potential claims, within a community of moral agents. Rights arise, and can be intelligibly defended, only among beings who actually do, or can, make moral claims against one another. Whatever else rights may be, therefore, they are necessarily human; their possessors are persons, human beings.

The attributes of human beings from which this moral capability arises have been described variously by philosophers, both ancient and modern: the inner consciousness of a free will (Saint Augustine);[3] the grasp, by human reason, of the binding character of moral law (Saint Thomas);[4] the self-conscious participation of human beings in an objective ethical order (Hegel);[5] human membership in an organic moral community (Bradley);[6] the development of the human self through the consciousness of other moral selves (Mead);[7] and the underivative, intuitive cognition of the rightness of an action (Prichard).[8] Most influential has been Immanuel Kant's emphasis on the universal human possession of a uniquely moral will and the autonomy its use entails.[9] Humans confront choices that are purely moral; humans—but certainly not dogs or mice—lay down moral laws, for others and for themselves. Human beings are self-legislative, morally *auto-nomous.*

Animals (that is, nonhuman animals, the ordinary sense of that word) lack this capacity for free moral judgment. They are not beings of a kind capable of exercising or responding to moral claims. Animals therefore have no rights, and they can have none. This is the core of the argument about the alleged rights of animals. The holders of rights must have the capacity to comprehend rules of duty, governing all including themselves. In applying such rules, the holders of rights must recognize possible conflicts between what is in their own interest and what is just. Only in a community of beings capable of self-restricting moral judgments can the concept of a right be correctly invoked.

[3]St. Augustine. *Confessions.* Book Seven. 397 A.D. New York: Pocket Books, 1957: 104–26.
[4]St. Thomas Aquinas. "Summa Theologica." 1273 A.D. *Philosophic Texts.* New York: Oxford University Press, 1960: 353–66.
[5]Hegel, G. W. F. *Philosophy of Right.* 1821. London: Oxford University Press, 1952: 105–10.
[6]Bradley, F. H. "Why Should I Be Moral?" 1876. *Ethical Theories.* Ed. A. I. Melden. New York: Prentice Hall, 1950: 345–59.
[7]Mead, G. H. "The Genesis of the Self and Social Control." 1925. *Selected Writings.* Ed. A. J. Reck. Indianapolis: Bobbs-Merrill, 1964: 264–93.
[8]Prichard, H. A. "Does Moral Philosophy Rest on a Mistake?" 1912. *Readings in Ethical Theory.* Ed. J. Hospers, W. Sellars. New York: Appleton-Century-Crofts, 1952: 149–63.
[9]Kant, I. *Fundamental Principles of the Metaphysic of Morals.* 1785. New York: Liberal Arts Press, 1949.

Humans have such moral capacities. They are in this sense self-legislative, are members of communities governed by moral rules, and do possess rights. Animals do not have such moral capacities. They are not morally self-legislative, cannot possibly be members of a truly moral community, and therefore cannot possess rights. In conducting research on animal subjects, therefore, we do not violate their rights, because they have none to violate.

To animate life, even in its simplest forms, we give a certain natural reverence. But the possession of rights presupposes a moral status not attained by the vast majority of living things. We must not infer, therefore, that a live being has, simply in being alive, a "right" to its life. The assertion that all animals, only because they are alive and have interests, also possess the "right to life"[10] is an abuse of that phrase, and wholly without warrant.

It does not follow from this, however, that we are morally free to do anything we please to animals. Certainly not. In our dealings with animals, as in our dealings with other human beings, we have obligations that do not arise from claims against us based on rights. Rights entail obligations, but many of the things one ought to do are in no way tied to another's entitlement. Rights and obligations are not reciprocals of one another, and it is a serious mistake to suppose that they are.

Illustrations are helpful. Obligations may arise from internal commitments made: physicians have obligations to their patients not grounded merely in their patients' rights. Teachers have such obligations to their students, shepherds to their dogs, and cowboys to their horses. Obligations may arise from differences of status: adults owe special care when playing with young children, and children owe special care when playing with young pets. Obligations may arise from special relationships: the payment of my son's college tuition is something to which he may have no right, although it may be my obligation to bear the burden if I reasonably can; my dog has no right to daily exercise and veterinary care, but I do have the obligation to provide these things for her. Obligations may arise from particular acts or circumstances: one may be obliged to another for a special kindness done, or obliged to put an animal out of its misery in view of its condition—although neither the human benefactor nor the dying animal may have had a claim of right.

Plainly, the grounds of our obligations to humans and to animals are manifold and cannot be formulated simply. Some hold that there is a general obligation to do no gratuitous harm to sentient creatures (the

10

---

[10]Rollin, B. E. *Animal Rights and Human Morality*. New York: Prometheus Books, 1981.

principle of nonmaleficence); some hold that there is a general obligation to do good to sentient creatures when that is reasonably within
one's power (the principle of beneficence). In our dealings with animals, few will deny that we are at least obliged to act humanely—that
is, to treat them with the decency and concern that we owe, as sensitive
human beings, to other sentient creatures. To treat animals humanely,
however, is not to treat them as humans or as the holders of rights.

A common objection, which deserves a response, may be paraphrased as follows:

> If having rights requires being able to make moral claims, to grasp
> and apply moral laws, then many humans—the brain-damaged, the
> comatose, the senile—who plainly lack those capacities must be
> without rights. But that is absurd. This proves [the critic concludes]
> that rights do not depend on the presence of moral capacities.[1,10]

This objection fails; it mistakenly treats an essential feature of humanity as though it were a screen for sorting humans. The capacity for
moral judgment that distinguishes humans from animals is not a test to
be administered to human beings one by one. Persons who are unable,
because of some disability, to perform the full moral functions natural
to human beings are certainly not for that reason ejected from the
moral community. The issue is one of kind. Humans are of such a kind
that they may be the subject of experiments only with their voluntary
consent. The choices they make freely must be respected. Animals are
of such a kind that it is impossible for them, in principle, to give or
withhold voluntary consent or to make a moral choice. What humans
retain when disabled, animals have never had.

A second objection, also often made, may be paraphrased as follows:

> Capacities will not succeed in distinguishing humans from the other
> animals. Animals also reason; animals also communicate with one an-
> other; animals also care passionately for their young; animals also
> exhibit desires and preferences.[11,12] Features of moral relevance—ra-
> tionality, interdependence, and love—are not exhibited uniquely by
> human beings. Therefore [this critic concludes], there can be no solid
> moral distinction between humans and other animals.[10]

This criticism misses the central point. It is not the ability to com-   15
municate or to reason, or dependence on one another, or care for the
young, or the exhibition of preference, or any such behavior that marks

---

[11]Hoff, C. "Immoral and Moral Uses of Animals." *New England Journal of Medicine*. 1980; 302:
115–18.

[12]Jamieson, D. "Killing Persons and Other Beings." *Ethics and Animals*. Ed. H. B. Miller, W. H.
Williams. Clifton, N. J.: Humana Press, 1983: 135–46.

the critical divide. Analogies between human families and those of monkeys, or between human communities and those of wolves, and the like, are entirely beside the point. Patterns of conduct are not at issue. Animals do indeed exhibit remarkable behavior at times. Conditioning, fear, instinct, and intelligence all contribute to species survival. Membership in a community of moral agents nevertheless remains impossible for them. Actors subject to moral judgment must be capable of grasping the generality of an ethical premise in a practical syllogism. Humans act immorally often enough, but only they—never wolves or monkeys—can discern, by applying some moral rule to the facts of a case, that a given act ought or ought not to be performed. The moral restraints imposed by humans on themselves are thus highly abstract and are often in conflict with the self-interest of the agent. Communal behavior among animals, even when most intelligent and most endearing, does not approach autonomous morality in this fundamental sense.

Genuinely moral acts have an internal as well as an external dimension. Thus, in law, an act can be criminal only when the guilty deed, the actus reus, is done with a guilty mind, mens rea. No animal can ever commit a crime; bringing animals to criminal trial is the mark of primitive ignorance. The claims of moral right are similarly inapplicable to them. Does a lion have a right to eat a baby zebra? Does a baby zebra have a right not to be eaten? Such questions, mistakenly invoking the concept of right where it does not belong, do not make good sense. Those who condemn biomedical research because it violates "animal rights" commit the same blunder.

In Defense of "Speciesism"

Abandoning reliance on animal rights, some critics resort instead to animal sentience—their feelings of pain and distress. We ought to desist from the imposition of pain insofar as we can. Since all or nearly all experimentation on animals does impose pain and could be readily forgone, say these critics, it should be stopped. The ends sought may be worthy, but those ends do not justify imposing agonies on humans, and by animals the agonies are felt no less. The laboratory use of animals (these critics conclude) must therefore be ended—or at least very sharply curtailed.

Argument of this variety is essentially utilitarian, often expressly so;[13] it is based on the calculation of the net product, in pains and pleasures, resulting from experiments on animals. Jeremy Bentham, comparing horses and dogs with other sentient creatures, is thus commonly

[13]Singer, P. "Ten Years of Animal Liberation." *New York Review of Books*. 1985; 31: 46–52.

quoted: "The question is not, Can they reason? nor Can they talk? but, Can they suffer?"[14]

Animals certainly can suffer and surely ought not to be made to suffer needlessly. But in inferring, from these uncontroversial premises, that biomedical research causing animal distress is largely (or wholly) wrong, the critic commits two serious errors.

The first error is the assumption, often explicitly defended, that all 20 sentient animals have equal moral standing. Between a dog and a human being, according to this view, there is no moral difference; hence the pains suffered by dogs must be weighed no differently from the pains suffered by humans. To deny such equality, according to this critic, is to give unjust preference to one species over another; it is "speciesism." The most influential statement of this moral equality of species was made by Peter Singer:

> The racist violates the principle of equality by giving greater weight
> to the interests of members of his own race when there is a clash
> between their interests and the interests of those of another race. The
> sexist violates the principle of equality by favoring the interests of his
> own sex. Similarly the speciesist allows the interests of his own
> species to override the greater interests of members of other species.
> The pattern is identical in each case.[2]

This argument is worse than unsound; it is atrocious. It draws an offensive moral conclusion from a deliberately devised verbal parallelism that is utterly specious. Racism has no rational ground whatever. Differing degrees of respect or concern for humans for no other reason than that they are members of different races is an injustice totally without foundation in the nature of the races themselves. Racists, even if acting on the basis of mistaken factual beliefs, do grave moral wrong precisely because there is no morally relevant distinction among the races. The supposition of such differences has led to outright horror. The same is true of the sexes, neither sex being entitled by right to greater respect or concern than the other. No dispute here.

Between species of animate life, however—between (for example) humans on the one hand and cats or rats on the other—the morally relevant differences are enormous, and almost universally appreciated. Humans engage in moral reflection; humans are morally autonomous; humans are members of moral communities, recognizing just claims against their own interest. Human beings do have rights; theirs is a moral status very different from that of cats or rats.

I am a speciesist. Speciesism is not merely plausible; it is essential for right conduct, because those who will not make the morally rele-

---

[14]Bentham, J. *Introduction to the Principles of Morals and Legislation.* London: Athlone Press, 1970.

vant distinctions among species are almost certain, in consequence, to misapprehend their true obligations. The analogy between speciesism and racism is insidious. Every sensitive moral judgment requires that the differing natures of the beings to whom obligations are owed be considered. If all forms of animate life—or vertebrate animal life?—must be treated equally, and if therefore in evaluating a research program the pains of a rodent count equally with the pains of a human, we are forced to conclude (1) that neither humans nor rodents possess rights, or (2) that rodents possess all the rights that humans possess. Both alternatives are absurd. Yet one or the other must be swallowed if the moral equality of all species is to be defended.

Humans owe to other humans a degree of moral regard that cannot be owed to animals. Some humans take on the obligation to support and heal others, both humans and animals, as a principal duty in their lives; the fulfillment of that duty may require the sacrifice of many animals. If biomedical investigators abandon the effective pursuit of their professional objectives because they are convinced that they may not do to animals what the service of humans requires, they will fail, objectively, to do their duty. Refusing to recognize the moral differences among species is a sure path to calamity. (The largest animal rights group in the country is People for the Ethical Treatment of Animals; its codirector, Ingrid Newkirk, calls research using animal subjects "fascism" and "supremacism." "Animal liberationists do not separate out the *human* animal," she says, "so there is no rational basis for saying that a human being has special rights. A rat is a pig is a dog is a boy. They're all mammals.")[15]

Those who claim to base their objection to the use of animals in 25 biomedical research on their reckoning of the net pleasures and pains produced make a second error, equally grave. Even if it were true—as it is surely not—that the pains of all animate beings must be counted equally, a cogent utilitarian calculation requires that we weigh all the consequences of the use, and of the nonuse, of animals in laboratory research. Critics relying (however mistakenly) on animal rights may claim to ignore the beneficial results of such research, rights being trump cards to which interest and advantage must give way. But an argument that is explicitly framed in terms of interest and benefit for all over the long run must attend also to the disadvantageous consequences of not using animals in research, and to all the achievements attained and attainable only through their use. The sum of the benefits of their use is utterly beyond quantification. The elimination of horrible disease, the increase of longevity, the avoidance of great pain, the saving of lives, and the improvement of the quality of lives (for humans and for animals) achieved through research using animals is so incalculably great

[15]McCabe, K. "Who Will Live, Who Will Die?" *Washingtonian*. August 1986: 115.

that the argument of these critics, systematically pursued, establishes not their conclusion but its reverse: to refrain from using animals in biomedical research is, on utilitarian grounds, morally wrong.

When balancing the pleasures and pains resulting from the use of animals in research, we must not fail to place on the scales the terrible pains that would have resulted, would be suffered now, and would long continue had animals not been used. Every disease eliminated, every vaccine developed, every method of pain relief devised, every surgical procedure invented, every prosthetic device implanted—indeed, virtually every modern medical therapy is due, in part or in whole, to experimentation using animals. Nor may we ignore, in the balancing process, the predictable gains in human (and animal) well-being that are probably achievable in the future but that will not be achieved if the decision is made now to desist from such research or to curtail it. . . .

Finally, inconsistency between the profession and the practice of many who oppose research using animals deserves comment. This frankly ad hominem observation aims chiefly to show that a coherent position rejecting the use of animals in medical research imposes costs so high as to be intolerable even to the critics themselves.

One cannot coherently object to the killing of animals in biomedical investigations while continuing to eat them. Anesthetics and thoughtful animal husbandry render the level of actual animal distress in the laboratory generally lower than that in the abattoir. So long as death and discomfort do not substantially differ in the two contexts, the consistent objector must not only refrain from all eating of animals but also protest as vehemently against others eating them as against others experimenting on them. No less vigorously must the critic object to the wearing of animal hides in coats and shoes, to employment in any industrial enterprise that uses animal parts, and to any commercial development that will cause death or distress to animals. . . .

Scrupulous vegetarianism, in matters of food, clothing, shelter, commerce, and recreation, and in all other spheres, is the only fully coherent position the critic may adopt. At great human cost, the lives of fish and crustaceans must also be protected, with equal vigor, if speciesism has been forsworn. A very few consistent critics adopt this position. It is the reductio ad absurdum of the rejection of moral distinctions between animals and human beings. . . .

Analyzing Issues and Arguments

1. What is the thesis of Carl Cohen's essay? Where and how does he state it?

2. What are the logical steps in Cohen's reasoning in paragraph 4? Do you agree with his conclusion? Why or why
not?
3. In his closing paragraph, Cohen uses the term "reductio ad
absurdum." What does it mean? What value judgment does it
indicate on Cohen's part?

Writing about Issues and Arguments

Compare and contrast Cohen's "The Case against Animal Rights" with
Peter Singer's "Ethics and the New Animal Liberation Movement"
(p. 64). What points do both writers address? How do their argumentative techniques differ? Who makes the more convincing case? Write an
essay on the question of animal rights, using these two essays as sources.
If you prefer, you can turn this essay into a research paper by drawing
on additional sources. (See "Suggestions for Further Reading,"
pp. 332–342.)

MAKING CRITICAL CONNECTIONS

1. What do you think animal rights advocate Peter Singer (p. 64) would say about Richard Schroeder's proposed golf course, as Charles C. Mann and Mark L. Plummer describe it in "The Butterfly Problem" (p. 26)? What do you think Thomas Palmer (p. 42) would say about Schroeder's plan? On what points, if any, might Singer and Palmer agree?
2. What comments does Thomas Palmer make about Native Americans' reaction to technology? How would you expect Joseph Bruchac (p. 54) to respond to Palmer's comments?
3. What ideas presented in David Foster's "Beyond Spotted Owls" (p. 62) were suggested some thirty years earlier by Aldo Leopold (p. 4)? Judging from "A Logger's Lament" (p. 20), how would Leila L. Kysar respond to the ecosystem management plan discussed in Foster's article?
4. Which writers represented in this chapter seem most sympathetic to Joseph Bruchac's point of view in "The Circle Is the Way to See"(p. 54)? On what specific evidence in their essays do you base your answer?
5. Look at Aldo Leopold's comparison of the biota with a pyramid in "Toward a Land Ethic" (p. 4), at Paul and Anne Ehrlich's comparison of the earth with an airplane in "The Rivet Poppers" (p. 13), and at Leila L. Kysar's comparison of a forest with a wheat field in "A Logger's Lament"(p. 20). Create an analogy of your own that embodies your view of an ecosystem or some other aspect of humankind's relationship with other species. With Leopold, the Ehrlichs, or Kysar as a model, write an essay using your analogy to present your position.

2

What Should We Do about Our Garbage?

POINTS OF VIEW

In 1991, a zoologist reported to the journal *Nature* that he'd just returned from an uninhabited Pacific atoll 292 miles from the nearest inhabited island and 3,000 miles from the nearest continent. On a 1.5 mile stretch of beach he found, among other things: 14 plastic crates; 71 plastic bottles; 268 unidentified or broken plastic pieces; 113 buoys and 66 pieces of buoys that were mostly plastic; a plastic coat hanger; and three plastic cigarette lighters. "If so much rubbish is washed ashore on small and extremely isolated islands," he concluded, "it makes one wonder just how much more is still floating on the surface of the oceans."

And that was in 1991, when plastic accounted for about 20 percent of municipal solid waste. Plastic production has grown 10 percent a year for the past 30 years, says the EPA, and about half our municipal solid waste will be plastic by the year 2000. How much plastic flotsam will be on that beach then?

> — JoAnn C. Gutin, "Okay, Okay — Here's Another Look at Plastics," *E Magazine* (May/June 1994)

In an environmentally sustainable economy, waste reduction and recycling industries will replace the garbage collection and disposal companies of today.

In such an economy, materials use will be guided by a hierarchy of options. The first priority, of course, is to avoid using any nonessential item. Second is to directly reuse a product—for example, refilling a glass beverage container. The third is to recycle the material to form a new product. Fourth, the material can be burned to extract whatever energy it contains, as long as this can be done safely. The option of last resort is disposal in a landfill.

Most materials used today are discarded after one use—roughly two-thirds of all aluminum, three-fourths of all steel and paper, and an even higher share of plastic. Society will become dramatically less energy-intensive and less polluting only if the throwaway economy is replaced by one that reuses and recycles. Steel produced entirely from scrap requires only one-third as much energy as that produced from iron ore. Newsprint from recycled paper takes 25–60 percent less energy to make than from virgin wood pulp. And recycling glass saves up to a third of the energy embodied in the original product.

Reuse brings even more dramatic gains. For example, replacing a throwaway beverage bottle with one made from recycled glass reduces energy use by roughly a third, but replacing it with a refillable glass bottle can cut energy use by nine-tenths.

—Lester R. Brown, Christopher Flavin, and Sandra Postel,
*Saving the Planet: How to Shape an Environmentally
Sustainable Global Economy* (1991)

What *is* the purpose of pollution control? Is it for its own sake? Of course not. If we answer that it is to make the air and water clean and quiet, then the question arises: what is the purpose of clean air and water? If the answer is, to please the nature gods, then it must be conceded that all pollution must cease immediately because the cost of angering the gods is presumably infinite. But if the answer is that the purpose of clean air and water is to further human enjoyment of life on this planet, then we are faced with the economists' basic question: given the limited alternatives that a niggardly nature allows, how can we best further human enjoyment of life? And the answer is, by making intelligent marginal decisions on the basis of costs and benefits. Pollution control is for lots of things: breathing comfortably, enjoying mountains, swimming in water, for health, beauty, and the general delectation. But so are many other things, like good food and wine, comfortable housing and fast transportation. The question is not which of these desirable things we should have, but rather what combination is most desirable. To determine such a combination, we must know the rate at which individuals are willing to substitute more of one desirable thing for less of another desirable thing.

—Larry E. Ruff, "The Economic Common Sense of Pollution,"
The Public Interest (Spring 1970)

INTRODUCTION

In the last quarter of the twentieth century, shopping has overtaken baseball as the U.S. national pastime. The novelist Alexander Theroux has compared shopping with recreational fishing: a quest we embark on less to meet a need than for the pleasure of casting about and seeing what we can hook. Many a purchase—like many a perch—is tossed away soon after it is reeled in.

What we buy, however, leaves a larger mark on the environment than what we catch. Canned tuna, for instance, arrives in the kitchen wrapped in a metal cylinder and an inked paper label—products of long manufacturing processes that began with mining ore and felling trees. Once the can is opened, what becomes of it? Its usefulness is over. Unless it is redefined as raw material for another round of manufacturing, it becomes garbage: tossed into a plastic-bag-lined bin, hauled away by truck to a landfill or incinerator.

A barge called the *Mobro* made headlines in 1987 as it sailed from place to place vainly seeking somewhere to dump its cargo of municipal solid waste—garbage from the town of Islip, Long Island. Controversy has flourished ever since: Is the United States (and possibly the whole world) on the verge of being buried under its own garbage? Can we reasonably expect to go on manufacturing, consuming, and discarding without running out of dumping space? Should we drastically alter our habits in order to save the planet, or can we depend on our technological ingenuity to solve the problem (if there really is a problem)?

These are the questions debated in this chapter. We begin with an indictment by Donella H. Meadows of one common *bête noire* in "The New World of Plastics—Not New Enough." Are milk jugs and tampon applicators swamping our landfills? What should we do with our broken calculators and clocks, Barbie dolls, and ballpoint pens? Recycle them? Burn them? Avoid buying them in the first place? According to archaeologist William Rathje—founder of the Garbage Project—and coauthor Cullen Murphy, the furor over plastics is overblown. In "What's in a Landfill?" they report that excavations reveal paper to be a much bigger problem, occupying more space and lasting nearly as long. Rathje's and Murphy's conclusions about the longevity of items in landfills are questioned by Chris Clarke, whose "The Thirty-Year-Old Carrot" rebuts the widely publicized assertion that "nothing degrades in a landfill."

A popular alternative to throwing things away is examined by *Consumer Reports* magazine in "Recycling: Is It Worth the Effort?" The editor of *Garbage* magazine, Patricia Poore, criticizes municipal recycling plans in "America's 'Garbage Crisis': A Toxic Myth." Poore's conviction that there is plenty of room for new landfills, especially if supplemented with incinerators, is reinforced by Judd H. Alexander in "The Advantages of Incineration." State-of-the-art combustors, Alexander asserts, are effective and safe—despite the widespread public fears stoked by opponents such as environmental biologist Barry Commoner. Commoner explains why he disagrees in "The Hazards of Incineration," a discussion of toxic ash and other health hazards and a description of one community's successful battle against a proposed incinerator. Finally, Michael Satchell's "Trashing the Reservations?" looks at efforts by some businesses and government agencies to barter for dumping space on Indian reservations—a literal last-ditch attempt to put municipal solid waste and hazardous wastes out of sight, out of mind.

DONELLA H. MEADOWS

The New World of Plastics—
Not New Enough

Donella H. Meadows is a systems analyst, journalist, international coordinator of research management institutions, and farmer. Since 1982 she has taught in the Environmental Studies Program at Dartmouth College. From 1970 to 1972 Meadows was on the MIT team that produced the global computer model World 3 for the Club of Rome. The controversial report she coauthored, *The Limits to Growth* (1972), was banned in the Soviet Union and investigated by President Nixon's staff. Meadows's other influential books include *Beyond the Limits: Confronting Global Collapse, Envisioning a Sustainable Future* (1992) and *The Global Citizen* (1991), a collection of her nationally syndicated newspaper columns. With her husband, Dennis Meadows, she founded and coordinates the International Network of Resource Information Centers, which promotes sustainable, high-productivity resource management. "The New World of Plastics," from *The Global Citizen,* addresses the garbage problem at its source: our society's high output of objects that are both disposable and immortal.

The world of plastics is in a mess these days because it has made a mess. Polyethylene, polystyrene, polyvinyl chloride, and all the other polys are piling up on roadsides, in the ocean, and in landfills. They are likely to last several hundred years there after serving us for a few weeks or hours—if indeed they could be said to serve us at all. The primary role of many plastics is to catch our attention in a store, for which purpose they are garishly shaped and colored with, among other things, toxic heavy metals. Environmentalists say the dumps are filling up not with packaging but with marketing.

Until we noticed the dumps filling up, most of us never thought about the stream of plastics flowing through our lives—18 million tons each year, of which 6.5 million tons is packaging, and over 3 billion dollars' worth is plastic bags in which to throw the other plastics out. Now everyone has panicked. In February 1989 the American Paper Institute counted the following bills pending in state legislatures (not counting those at the federal level)—66 proposed bans on non-biodegradable packaging, 12 packaging taxes, 74 source separation and recycling mandates, and 19 requirements that state governments purchase recycled materials.

It's not fair to blame plastics for our trash problem, says the industry. They make up only 4 to 7 percent of municipal solid waste (by weight—by volume it's more like 20 to 30 percent). But plastics are the focus of most legislation, perhaps because they are the fastest growing constituent of trash, because they are used for so many trivial purposes, and because they are so nearly immortal.

Immortality is one of the qualities that makes plastics useful, of course. They are impervious to bacteria, acid, salt, rust, breakage, almost any agent except heat, and some of them can even stand up to heat. If they didn't junk up our lives so, we would regard them as miracle substances—long, long hydrocarbon chains, crafted to take on any properties we want. Plastics can be transparent or opaque, hard as steel or pliant as silk, squeezable or rigid, moldable into any conceivable shape.

And, environmentalists would say, they are made from depleting oil 5 and gas wrested from the ends of the earth, transported, spilled, refined in energy-consuming, hazardous-waste-generating processes, synthesized, and disposed of carelessly. They are messy from beginning to end. If we were properly charged the full human and environmental costs of our plastics, we would not eliminate them—they are far too useful for that—but we would treat those specialized molecules with the respect they deserve. We would not use them for a few days or hours and throw them out.

The standard environmental formula for dealing with precious but polluting materials is simple. Reduce, reuse, recycle, in that order, and then, as a last resort, dispose with care. Of course, the plastics industry makes money in the inverse order. It is looking for a way to keep us buying millions of tons of plastics each year—and to have them miraculously disappear when we throw them away.

Therefore, industry's favorite answers to the plastics problem are two: incineration and degradation.

As a descendant of petroleum, plastic burns beautifully. Like all hydrocarbons, it combusts into carbon dioxide, a greenhouse gas, plus a host of other pollutants. Some of them derive from additives such as heavy metals (which end up either in air emissions or incinerator ash). Others, like the toxic dioxins and furans, come from high-temperature reactions between hydrocarbons and chlorine. Polyvinyl chloride (PVC) releases so much hydrochloric acid when it burns that it corrodes incinerators. For that reason one incinerator manufacturer recommends keeping PVC out of incinerated trash.

Incineration can recapture a small fraction of the energy put into making plastics. Degradation doesn't even do that.

Degradable plastics come in two forms: biodegradable and pho- 10 todegradable. The biodegradable kind mixes the long plastic molecules, which nothing in nature can digest, with starch, which microorganisms will happily munch away. Depending on the material strength required and the rate of degradation, the starch percentage varies, but it's usually something like 6 percent starch to 94 percent plastic.

On the side of the road a bottle or bag made of biodegradable plastic slowly falls apart into tiny shards of undegradable plastic. The bottle or bag disintegrates, the plastic is still there. Presumably it is inert and harmless, but no one really knows the implications of a world filled with plastic sand.

In a landfill, biodegradation happens slowly, if at all. Nothing degrades well in a landfill. William Rathje, an anthropologist from the University of Arizona, drills core samples from old landfills and finds intact food, paper, and cloth that are twenty years old. He can date the layers exactly because he can read the newspapers. Landfills are not compost heaps. They haven't the proper air circulation, moisture content, mixture of nutrients, or communities of microorganisms to encourage natural breakdown.

Of course, there's no sunlight in a landfill, either. Photodegradable plastics have chemical links built into their molecular chains that fall apart when hit by ultraviolet radiation in sunlight. The breakdown products are shorter chains, not so much plastic sand as plastic powder. If the plastic is polyethylene and the chains are short enough, soil organisms then appear to take over and digest them—the only evidence I've seen of real plastic biodegradation. But several months of photodegradation are necessary to begin the process.

Promoters of photo- and biodegradable plastics admit, when pressed, that neither can extend the lives of landfills one bit. They only help with the problem of litter. They are designer molecules to do away with the ugly evidence of our unwillingness to pick up after ourselves.

Recycling at least slows the waste stream and lets the plastics serve 15 several times before discard. Only about 2 percent of the plastics we use are now recycled (as opposed to 29 percent of aluminum and 21 percent of paper), but that's not because it can't be done. Plastics are the easiest of all materials to recycle. Basically they just need to be shredded, remelted, and re-formed. The industry itself grinds and reuses 5 billion pounds of plastic scrap a year.

Two things are in the way of serious plastics recycling—separation and purification. Consumers can put paper and cans in separate waste containers, but they can't tell the difference between polypropylene and polystyrene. Bottlers have set up a voluntary coding system, which stamps resin types on 8-ounce and larger containers. But that does not help us separate the myriad other forms of plastics, including squeezable bottles with several kinds laminated together. (In a true recycling society such unseparable mixed-material containers would be banned.)

Some separation is easy, though. Some recycling centers now collect high-density polyethylene (HDPE) milk bottles and polyethylene terephthalate (PET) soda bottles. They are not, unfortunately, made back into milk and soda bottles because of the problem of purification. One person in a thousand might have used a bottle to hold roach poison or kerosene before throwing it away, and contaminants could have permeated the plastic — to come out later into the milk or soda.

Therefore, recycled plastics are not used to package edibles. Reclaimed HDPE and PET are made into carpet fibers, cushion stuffing, and scouring pads. Mixed plastics are made into lumberlike poles, posts, stakes, and slats for never-rotting barns, docks, fences, road markers, and pilings. These processes are better than nothing, but they are not real recycling. They will screech to a halt when we have as many immortal cushions and flowerpots as we need. The only recycling processes that can work in the long run are those that return materials to their same use — soda bottles to soda bottles, milk containers to milk containers.

Reuse is preferable to recycling because it takes less energy and causes less pollution to wash out a coffee cup, say, and refill it, than it does to crush it, melt it, and re-form it. Because of the contamination problem, most plastic containers cannot be reused commercially. They can be at home, however, because you know whether you've put roach poison in a cup or not. A real environmentalist would never use a plastic hot cup only once.

But then a real, real environmentalist wouldn't drink from a plastic 20 cup at all. He or she would remember that the world once worked fairly smoothly with washable china cups. Recycling is better than disposal, reuse is better than recycling, but reduction is best of all. It's easier to deal with a flood by turning it off at its source than by inventing better mopping technologies.

Many European countries, which have had to confront the finiteness of their landfills sooner than we have, simply ban PET soda bottles. Furthermore, they require glass bottles to be made in standard-shaped half-liter and liter sizes, so any bottle can be refilled by any beverage company. Europeans cheerfully return glass bottles in handy, reusable (plastic) cases and do not seem to regard it as an infringement of their basic freedoms.

Solutions like these — reduction solutions, solutions that distinguish the plastics we need from the plastics we don't need — will not come from industry. They will come through the political process and through the market, as we finally charge ourselves, one way or another, the real cost of producing and disposing of plastics.

Analyzing Issues and Arguments

1. What recommendations does Donella H. Meadows make regarding the use and disposal of plastics?
2. What two groups does Meadows identify as representing opposing viewpoints on the plastics issue? What features of her essay indicate an effort to present both viewpoints impartially?
3. Whose side do you think Meadows really is on? How can you tell?

Writing about Issues and Arguments

"The standard environmental formula for dealing with precious but polluting materials is simple. Reduce, reuse, recycle, in that order, and then, as a last resort, dispose with care" (para. 6). From the time you wake up in the morning until you leave home, what plastic objects play a role in your life? Write an essay explaining Meadow's formula, illustrating each of the four categories with examples from your own belongings.

IN THE NEWS

Truly Fashionable Recycling: Plastic Bottles Get New Life as Polyester Fiber

Mary Martin

> A longer version of the following article appeared in the *Boston Globe* on March 2, 1994. Mary Martin is a freelance business and technology writer who lives in Cambridge, Massachusetts.

This spring, you may pay a premium to wear the plastic soda bottles you threw into the recycling bin last summer. It's called "eco-wear" and it's coming to a store or catalog near you.

From L. L. Bean in Freeport, Maine, to Patagonia in Ventura, California, retailers are shipping new products that they say combine traditional quality with environmental sensitivity. Consumers will soon begin to see fleece jackets, hiking boots, backpacks, and kids' clothes made from recycled plastic bottles that have been spun into polyester fiber.

If the fabric represents new life for soda bottles, it has also injected new excitement into the U.S. textile industry. At the industry's big outdoor-wear show in Reno last month, vendors say they were swamped with interest in the born-again polyester.

"It's not really a fad; it's a trend," says Richard Van Dernoot, chairman of Starensier Inc. in Newburyport, a manufacturer of the fabric. Consumers usually have the last word on trends, but companies throughout the textile industry have already bought into this one. Millions have been invested in research, equipment, and marketing, involving businesses from recyclers to retailers.

In January, Starensier and partner Martin Color-Fi Inc. of South Carolina 5 introduced what they call the first-ever woven fabric made of 100 percent postconsumer recycled beverage bottles, NatureTex 100. Each yard contains eight, two-liter plastic bottles.

Less than a year ago, Van Dernoot says, he began selling the recycled-polyester fabric and was "immediately inundated with requests." Orders have now exceeded a million yards. Moreover, the company says it is negotiating with a fast-food chain to recycle polyester uniforms—baling and chopping the fabric to reuse the polyester once again.

"We're really at the brink of not having to use more natural resources" to produce polyester, Van Dernoot says.

"There's been tremendous acceptance at the manufacturers' level," says Jeffrey Bowman, merchandising manager for Malden Mills in Lawrence, the largest textile producer in the state. Bowman believes the fabric, made from PET (polyethylene terephthalate) plastic, could constitute up to 80 percent of his company's polyester production within five years. The fabric consists of about 50 percent recycled and 50 percent "virgin" polyester, made by Hoechst Celanese Corporation, one of the nations' largest polyester producers and a major player in the PET-fiber market.

Early versions of the recycled fiber looked and felt bad, says Bowman, but last summer Malden was finally satisfied with the fleece it spun from Hoechst fiber. Marketed as Polartec, Bowman says it is indistinguishable from more traditional polyester and is being made into thermal underwear, outerwear, shirts, and tights. His opinion was reinforced when the company brought in a panel of textile specialists to pick out the partly recycled material and they couldn't do better than a 50–50 guess.

At nearby EastPak, the backpack company in Haverhill, fascination with 10 the fabric sparked a new product line and ad campaign for the spring.

"We haven't shipped piece one to a store yet," says Henry Friedman, vice president. "The jury is still out. But it's a great concept and it makes a lot of sense." EastPak uses Starensier's woven material and continues to offer a lifetime guarantee on its products.

The only drawback so far? Price. Because the process of breaking down bottles and purifying the polyester is more difficult than starting from scratch, it costs more. Textile manufacturers say the fabric cost is 5 percent to 20 percent higher than comparable virgin polyester. EastPak is betting that some customers, at least, will pay an extra $10 for a backpack that is made from 100 percent recycled fibers.

"We generate in this country every hour approximately 2.5 million bottles," says Van Dernoot of Starensier. "By 1995, half our landfills will be closed, and 30 percent of our landfills are taken up by plastic bottles."

According to Jane Henriques of the American Textile Manufacturers Institute, the mainstream introduction of PET fabrics "has the potential to be a landmark, a watershed" event for the U.S. textile industry. "High tech is the only way to stay alive against imports," she observes. In this case, technology has benefited the environment and helped carve a new, green, made-in-the-U.S. market niche.

                                                                                      ■

Analyzing Issues and Arguments

1. Why are textile manufacturers enthusiastic about recycling plastic bottles into polyester fabrics?
2. Do you think Donella H. Meadows would regard this form of recycling as the best solution to the problem of plastic garbage? Why or why not?

WILLIAM RATHJE AND CULLEN MURPHY

What's in a Landfill?

Archaeologist William Rathje is a professor of anthropology at the University of Arizona, Tucson. He founded and directs the university's Garbage Project, which has excavated, sorted, and classified more than a hundred tons of landfill contents over the past two decades in its quest for data on what Americans throw away. Cullen Murphy is managing editor of and a frequent contributor to the *Atlantic Monthly;* he also writes the comic strip *Prince Valiant,* which his father illustrates. "What's in a Landfill?" comes from Rathje and Murphy's book *Rubbish! The Archaeology of Garbage* (1992). In this excerpt the authors debunk several popular misconceptions about landfills and defend such common targets as fast-food packaging and plastics.

The Garbage Project began excavating landfills primarily for two reasons, both of them essentially archaeological in nature. One was to see if the data being gleaned from garbage fresh off the truck could be cross-validated by data from garbage in municipal landfills. The second, which derived from the Garbage Project's origins as an exercise in the study of formation processes, was to look into what happens to garbage after it has been interred. As it happens, the first landfill excavation got under way, in 1987, just as it was becoming clear—from persistent reports about garbage in the press that were at variance with some of the things the Garbage Project had been learning—that an adequate knowledge base about landfills and their contents did not exist. It was during this period that news of a mounting garbage crisis broke into the national consciousness. And it was during this period that two assertions were given wide currency and achieved a status as accepted fact from which they have yet to be dislodged. One is that accelerating rates of garbage generation are responsible for the rapid depletion and present shortage of landfills. The other is that, nationwide, there are few good places left to put new landfills. Whether these propositions are true or false—they happen, for the most part, to be exaggerations—it was certainly the case that however quickly landfills were being filled, the public, the press, and even most specialists had only the vaguest idea (at best) of what they were being filled up *with*. . . .

Although many Garbage Project studies have relied on garbage weight for comparative purposes, volume is the critical variable when it comes to landfill management: Landfills close not because they are too heavy but because they are too full. And yet reliable data on the volume taken up by plastics, paper, organic material, and other kinds of garbage once it has been deposited in a landfill did not exist in 1987. The Garbage Project set out to fill the gap, applying its usual sorting and weighing procedures to excavated garbage, and then adding a final step: a volume measurement. Measuring volume was not a completely straightforward process. Because most garbage tends to puff up with air once it has been extracted from deep inside a landfill, all of the garbage exhumed was subjected to compaction, so that the data on garbage volume would reflect the volume that garbage occupies when it is squashed and under pressure inside a landfill. The compactor used by the Garbage Project is a thirty-gallon cannister with a hydraulic piston that squeezes out air from plastic bags, newspapers, cereal boxes, mowed grass, hot dogs, and everything else at a relatively gentle pressure of 0.9 pounds per square inch. The data on garbage volume that emerged from the Garbage Project's landfill excavations were the first such data in existence.

What do the numbers reveal? Briefly, that the kinds of garbage that loom largest in the popular imagination as the chief villains in the filling up and closing down of landfills—fast-food packaging, expanded polystyrene foam (the material that coffee cups are made from), and disposable diapers, to name three on many people's most-unwanted list —do not deserve the blame they have received. They may be highly visible as litter, but they are not responsible for an inordinate contribution to landfill garbage. The same goes for plastics. But one kind of garbage whose reputation has thus far been largely unbesmirched— plain old paper—merits increased attention.

Over the years, Garbage Project representatives have asked a variety of people who have never seen the inside of a landfill to estimate what percentage of a landfill's contents is made up of fast-food packaging, expanded polystyrene foam, and disposable diapers. In September of 1989, for example, this very question was asked of a group attending the biennial meeting of the National Audubon Society, and the results were generally consistent with those obtained from surveys conducted at universities, at business meetings, and at conferences of state and local government officials: Estimates at the Audubon meeting of the volume of fast-food packaging fell mainly between 20 and 30 percent of a typical landfill's contents; of expanded polystyrene foam, between 25 and 40 percent; and of disposable diapers, between 25 and 45 percent. The overall estimate, then, of the proportion of a landfill's volume that is taken up by fast-food packaging, foam in general, and disposable diapers ranged from a suspiciously high 70 percent to an obviously impossible 115 percent.

Needless to say, fast-food packaging has few friends. It is designed   5 to be bright, those bold reds and yellows being among the most attention-getting colors on a marketer's palette; this, coupled with the propensity of human beings to litter, means that fast-food packaging gets noticed. It is also greasy and smelly, and on some level it seems to symbolize, as do fast-food restaurants themselves, certain attributes of modern America to which modern Americans remain imperfectly reconciled. But is there really all that much fast-food packaging? Is it "straining" the capacity of America's landfills, as a 1988 editorial in the *New York Times* contended?

The physical reality inside a landfill is, in fact, quite different from the picture painted by many commentators. Of the more than fourteen tons of garbage from landfills that the Garbage Project has sorted, fewer than a hundred pounds was found to consist of fast-food packaging of any kind—that is, containers or wrappers for hamburgers, pizzas, chicken, fish, and convenience-store sandwiches, plus all the accessories, such as cups, lids, straws, sauce containers, and so on, plus all the boxes and bags used to deliver food and other raw materials to the fast-food restaurant. In other words, less than one-half of one percent of the weight of the materials excavated from nine municipal landfills over a period of five years (1985–89) consisted of fast-food packaging. As for the amount of space that fast-food packaging takes up in landfills—a more important indicator than weight—the Garbage Project estimate after sorting is that it accounts for no more than one-third of one percent of the total volume of a landfill's contents.

What about expanded polystyrene foam—the substance that most people are referring to when they say Styrofoam (which is a registered trademark of the Dow Chemical Corporation, and is baby blue in color and used chiefly to insulate buildings)? Expanded polystyrene foam is, of course, used for many things. Only about 10 percent of all foam plastics that were manufactured in the period 1980–89 were used for fast-food packaging. Most foam was (and is) blown into egg cartons, meat trays, coffee cups (the fast-food kind, yes, but mainly the plain kind that sit stacked upside down beside the office coffee pot), "peanuts" for packing, and the molded forms that protect electronic appliances in their shipping cases. All the expanded polystyrene foam that is thrown away in America every year, from the lowliest packing peanut to the most sophisticated molded carton, accounts for no more than 1 percent of the volume of garbage landfilled between 1980 and 1989.

Expanded polystyrene foam has been the focus of many vocal campaigns around the country to ban it outright. It is worth remembering that if foam were banned, the relatively small amount of space that it takes up in landfills would not be saved. Eggs, hamburgers, coffee, and stereos must still be put in *something*. The most likely replacement for foam is some form of coated cardboard, which can be difficult to recycle and takes up almost as much room as foam in a landfill. Indeed, in cases where cardboard replaced foam, it could often happen that a larger volume of cardboard would be needed to fulfill the same function fulfilled by a smaller volume of foam. No one burns fingers holding a foam cup filled with coffee, because the foam's insulating qualities are so effective. But people burn their fingers so frequently with plastic- or wax-coated cardboard coffee cups (and all cardboard hot-drink cups are coated) that they often put one such cup inside another for the added protection.

As for disposable diapers, the debate over their potential impact on the environment is . . . vociferous and complex. . . . Suffice it to say for present purposes, though, that the pattern displayed by fast-food packaging and expanded polystyrene foam is apparent with respect to diapers, too. People *think* that disposable diapers are a big part of the garbage problem; they are not a very significant factor at all.

The three garbage categories that, as we saw, the Audubon respon- 10 dents believed accounted for 70 to 115 percent of all garbage actually account, together, for only about 3 percent. The survey responses would probably have been even more skewed if respondents had also been asked to guess the proportion of a typical landfill's contents that is made up of plastic. Plastic is surrounded by a maelstrom of mythology; into the very word Americans seem to have distilled all of their guilt over the environmental degradation they have wrought and the culture of consumption they invented and inhabit. Plastic has become an object of scorn—who can forget the famous scene in *The Graduate* (or quote it properly)?—no doubt in large measure because its development corresponded chronologically with, and then powerfully reinforced, the emergence of the very consumerist ethic that is now despised. (What Mr. McGuire, a neighbor, says to Benjamin Braddock is: "I just want to say one word to you. Just one word. Are you listening? . . . Plastics. There is a great future in plastics. Think about it.") Plastic is the Great Satan of garbage. It is the apotheosis of the cheap, the inauthentic; even the attempts to replace or transform plastic—such as the recent ill-fated experiments with "biodegradable" plastic . . . —seem somehow inauthentic.

There are legitimate causes for concern about plastic, particularly with respect to its manufacture. For the moment the issue is the volume of plastics in landfills. Two statistics have received wide circulation. The first, which appears repeatedly in the press, is that while plastics may make up only 7 percent of all municipal solid waste by weight, they make up some 30 percent of municipal solid waste by volume. This 30 percent figure has a history: It comes from a report published

CATHY copyright 1989, Cathy Guisewite. Reprinted with permission of Universal Press Syndicate. All rights reserved.

by, and available (for $300) from, the International Plastics Consultants Corporation (IPCC), based in Stamford, Connecticut, a group that was set up to promote the recycling of plastic. . . . To estimate the volume of various categories of garbage after such garbage has been crushed and compacted, the researchers obtained from the pertinent trade associations and businesses whatever data they had on the bulk density (that is, the volume per unit weight) of items that have been squashed and baled for transport, usually for shipment to recycling facilities.

There were, of course, a few problems. While the bulk density of some types of paper items, such as newsprint and corrugated cardboard, could be evaluated with a certain precision, because these items get recycled and records are kept, the IPCC had to assume that the bulk density of nonrecycled paper items for which they had no data, such as cereal boxes, paper towels, and tissues, was the same as that of recyclable paper. Similarly, the IPCC had to assume that the bulk density of all nonrecycled plastics, from toothbrushes to tables, was the same as the bulk density for the kinds of recyclable plastic for which it had data—primarily PET (polyethylene terephthalate) plastic soda bottles, the kind that most soft drinks now come in. And, of course, there being no trade associations for yard waste, food waste, and many other kinds of garbage, the International Plastics Consultants Corporation had to settle for reasonable estimates of the bulk density of all these garbage categories. The IPCC ended up by concluding that plastics made up 27 percent of a typical landfill's contents, a figure that in news reports was then rounded up to 30 percent.

The second estimate that one encounters with some regularity for the volume of plastics in landfills is 20 percent. The provenance of this figure is a 1988 Franklin Associates study of landfill constituents by weight and volume. This figure is inflated because Franklin Associates (as its researchers readily admit) excluded the huge category "construction and demolition debris"—which accounts for about 12 percent by volume of a typical landfill's contents—from their estimation of the total landfill pie, thereby reducing the size of the pie and magnifying the relative proportions of the other constituents. The problem with construction and demolition debris, insofar as Franklin is concerned, is the same one faced by the IPCC: no one keeps records on it. There is no trade association for construction and demolition debris in Washington, [D.C.] and, because local communities are not normally responsible for collecting and carting away such debris, as they are other kinds of garbage, very often not even haphazard documentation exists. And besides, the federal government does not technically consider construction and demolition debris to be municipal solid waste (though it ends up in municipal landfills). For these reasons construction and demolition debris was simply left out of the picture. By Franklin's account, not one ounce of construction and demolition debris—not one cinderblock, two-by-four, or rebar rod—has technically entered American landfills during the past thirty years.

The Garbage Project's methodology has not been quite as sophisticated as that of Franklin or the IPPC: Garbage Project personnel simply measured by weight and volume everything exhumed from sample municipal-solid-waste landfills. The results differ from the Franklin and IPCC numbers. In landfill after landfill the volume of all plastics—foam, film, and rigid; toys, utensils, and packages—from the 1980s amounted to between 20 and 24 percent of all garbage, as sorted; when compacted along with everything else, in order to replicate actual conditions inside a landfill, the volume of plastics was reduced to under 16 percent.

Even if its share of total garbage is, at the moment, relatively low, is 15 it not the case that plastics take up a larger proportion of landfill space with every passing year? Unquestionably a larger number of physical objects are made of plastic today than were in 1970 or 1950. But a curious phenomenon becomes apparent when garbage deposits from our own time are compared with those from strata characteristic of, say, the 1970s. While the number of individual plastic objects to be found in a deposit of garbage of a constant size has increased considerably in the course of a decade and a half—more than doubling—the proportion of landfill space taken up by these plastics has not changed; at some landfills, the proportion of space taken up by plastics was actually a little less in the 1980s than it was in the 1970s.

The explanation appears to be a strategy that is known in the plastics industry as "light-weighting"—making objects in such a way that the objects retain all the necessary functional characteristics but require the use of less resin. The concept of light-weighting is not limited to the making of plastics; the makers of glass bottles have been light-weighting their wares for decades, with the result that bottles today are 25 percent lighter than they were in 1984. (That is why bottles in landfills are likely to show up broken in the upper, more-recent, strata, whereas lower strata, holding garbage from many years ago, contain many more whole bottles.) Environmentalists might hail light-weighting as an example of source reduction. Businessmen embrace it for a different reason: sheer profit. Using fewer raw materials for a product that is lighter and therefore cheaper to transport usually translates into a competitive edge, and companies that rely heavily on plastics have been light-weighting ever since plastics were introduced. PET soda bottles had a weight of 67 grams in 1974; the weight today is 48 grams, for a reduction of 30 percent. High-density polyethylene (HDPE) milk jugs in the mid-1960s had a weight of 120 grams; the weight today is about 65 grams, for a reduction of more than 45 percent. Plastic grocery bags had a thickness of 30 microns in 1976; the thickness today is at most 18 microns, for a reduction of 40 percent. Even the plastic in disposable diapers has been light-weighted, although the super-absorbent material that was added at the same time (1986) ensures that even if diapers enter the house lighter they will leave it heavier than ever. When plastic gets lighter, in most cases it also gets thinner and more crushable. The result, of course, is that many more plastic items can be squeezed into a given volume of landfill space today than could have been squeezed into it ten or twenty years ago.

This fact has frequently been met with skepticism. In 1989, Robert Krulwich, of the CBS network's "Saturday Night with Connie Chung" program, conducted a tour of the Garbage Project's operations in Tucson, and he expressed surprise when told about the light-weighting of plastics. He asked for a crushed PET soda bottle from 1989 and tried to blow it up. The light plastic container inflated easily. He was then given a crushed PET soda bottle found in a stratum dating back to 1981—a bottle whose plastic would be considerably thicker and stiffer. Try as he might, Krulwich could not make the flattened container inflate.

One item that has not been light-weighted during the past few decades is your typical daily newspaper—the messenger that repeatedly carries warnings about the garbage crisis. A year's worth of copies of the *New York Times,* for example, weighs about 520 pounds and occupies a volume of about 1.5 cubic yards. A year's worth of the *Times* is the equivalent, by weight, of 12,480 empty aluminum cans or 48,793 Big Mac clamshell containers. It is the equivalent, by volume, of 18,660 crushed aluminum cans or 14,969 crushed Big Mac clamshells.

Newspapers epitomize the part of the garbage problem that gets the least amount of attention: paper. During the 1970s futurists and other writers, perceiving the advent of an electronic society, heralded the new paperless workplace, the new paperless culture. "One of the most startling features of the Computer Revolution," Christopher Evans wrote in *The Micro Revolution* (1979) "is that print and paper technology will appear as primitive as the pre-Caxtonian handcopying of manuscripts seems to us. In sum, the 1980s will see the book as we know it, and as our ancestors created and cherished it, begin a slow but steady slide into oblivion." Predictions like that one were never quite believable even in their heyday, when the consequences of the advent of copying machines were already apparent. It is obvious by now that computers, far from making paper obsolete, have made it possible to generate lengthy hard-copy documents more easily than ever before. A computer with a printer is, in effect, a printing press, and there are now fifty-five million of these printing presses in American homes and offices, where twenty years ago there had been only typewriters. With respect to paper, advancing technology is not a contraceptive but a fertility drug. For one thing, as technology in general has become more and more sophisticated, with more and more components, the engineering specifications needed to describe complex systems have necessarily become more and more voluminous. One environmental consulting group recently publicized the assertion that if all the paper stored on a typical American aircraft carrier were removed, the ship would rise three inches in the water. Garbage Project researchers have been unable to substantiate that claim, but it is definitely the case that, prognostications to the contrary, paper has managed to hold its own among the components of the U.S. solid-waste stream. Edward Tenner, an executive editor at Princeton University Press, recently observed:

"The paperless office, the leafless library, the inkless newspaper, the cashless, checkless society—all have gone the way of the Empire State Building's dirigible mooring, the backyard helipad, the nuclear-powered convertible, the vitamin-pill dinner, and the Paperwork Reduction Act of 1980."

For all the competition since the 1950s from plastic, metal, 20 construction-and-demolition debris, and nonpaperaceous organics, paper's contribution to a landfill's contents has remained relatively even, at well over 40 percent. . . . Newspapers alone may take up some 13 percent or more of the space in the average landfill—nearly as much as all plastics. Paper used in the packaging of consumer goods has grown in volume by about a third since 1960. Nonpackaging paper— computer paper, stationery, paper plates and cups, junk mail—has doubled in volume. The volume of discarded magazines has likewise doubled, to about 1.2 percent—about as much as all the thrown-away fast-food packaging and expanded polystyrene foam combined.

One noteworthy contributor to a landfill's paper content is the telephone book. Dig a trench through a landfill and telephone books can be seen to stud some strata like currants in a cake. They are thrown out regularly, once a year; in the city of Phoenix, that means almost twelve pounds of phone books annually (one yellow pages and one white pages) for every business and household. And their expansion in number seems to know no bounds. First there are the normal "Baby Bell" phone books published by the seven regional phone companies, often two or three of them per household in a city of average size. Then come the many competing brands of yellow pages published by rivals to the Bell system companies: Reuben H. Donnelly and GTE Directories are the biggest, but there are some two hundred other yellow pages publishers. And then there are phone books that target specific businesses, or senior citizens, or juveniles, or members of different ethnic groups. Miniature, paperback book–sized phone books have recently appeared for people who have car phones, to ride beside them on the front seat. In most cases phone books are made of paper of such low quality that recycling is difficult, although some end uses do exist.

The avalanche of paper, like everything else about garbage, needs to be seen in perspective. Paper is not inherently a bad thing. There are many uses for paper that end up *limiting* the generation of garbage. The skillful packaging of food products, to give just one example, cuts down markedly on the wastage of foods. But for all paper's virtues, an inarguable fact remains: If garbage volume is ever to be significantly reduced, paper is the foe that must be faced. The task of getting some control over paper is made all the more necessary by the fact that paper and many other organics . . . tend not so much to degrade in landfills as to mummify. They do not, in other words, take up appreciably less and less space as time goes by.

The following chart, which contrasts the findings of a 1990 Roper Poll with recent Garbage Project data, helps to summarize the difference between mental and material realities with respect to landfills. The percentages in the Roper column indicate the proportion of respondents identifying a particular item as a major cause of garbage problems.

	Roper (%)	Actual Volume in Landfills (%)
Disposable diapers	41	<2
Plastic bottles	29	<1
Large appliances	24	<2
Newspapers	11	~13
All paper	6	>40
Food and yard waste	3	~7
Construction debris	0	~12

Misperceptions such as these are not harmless. They can lead to policies and actions that are counterproductive.

In commemoration of Earth Day, 1990, the New York Public Interest Research Group launched a campaign against the use of certain highly visible and famously odious forms of garbage, such as fast-food containers, aseptic packaging (juice boxes), and disposable diapers, and it urged members of allied environmental groups to spread the word "through newsletters and other publications." One can appreciate the good intentions—as well as the irony of the means of communication employed. . . .

Misconceptions about the interior life of landfills are profound— 25 not surprisingly, since so very few people have actually ventured inside one. There is a popular notion that in its depths the typical municipal landfill is a locus of roiling fermentation, of intense chemical and biological activity. That perception is accompanied by a certain ambivalence. A landfill is seen, on the one hand, as an environment where organic matter is rapidly breaking down—biodegrading—into a sort of rich, moist, brown humus, returning at last to the bosom of Mother Nature. Biodegradation, in this view, is something devoutly to be desired, an environmentally correct outcome of the first order, perhaps even part of God's plan. Romantic thinking about biodegradation is widespread. It lies behind such dubious ventures as the proposed development by the British company London International of a biodegradable latex condom. On the other hand, coexisting with the romance of biodegradation, there is the view of a landfill as an environment from which a toxic broth of chemicals leaches into the surrounding soil, perhaps to pollute groundwater and nearby rivers and lakes. What both views of landfills have in common is the assumption that a great deal of biodegradation is taking place.

Some biodegradation *is* taking place—otherwise landfills would produce none of the large amounts of methane, or of the trace emissions of benzene, hydrogen sulfide, chlorinated hydrocarbons, and other gases, that they do in fact produce. The truth is, however, that the dynamics of a modern landfill are very nearly the opposite of what most people think. Biologically and chemically, a landfill is a much more static structure than is commonly supposed. For some kinds of organics, biodegradation goes on for a little while, and then slows to a virtual standstill. For other kinds, biodegradation never really gets under way at all. Well-designed and managed landfills seem to be far more apt to preserve their contents for posterity than to transform them into humus or mulch. They are not vast composters; rather, they are vast mummifiers. Furthermore, this may be a good thing. For while there are positive things to say about biodegradation, the more of it that occurs in a landfill, the more opportunities there will be for the landfill's contents to come back to haunt us.

When the Garbage Project set up shop, in 1972, its focus was not on the garbage crisis, and . . . it did not begin by excavating landfills. The initial emphasis was on gaining insights into people's behavior, and the garbage examined was fresh off the truck. Although the invasive odor of fresh garbage at least hinted that some degree of putrefaction was probable, the issue of biodegradability was not addressed. Project members simply assumed—like everyone else—that widespread biodegradation was the inevitable lot of the organic material dumped into landfills.

In hindsight, it is clear that clues to the actual state of affairs existed long before the Garbage Project undertook extensive investigations. One clue involved a report by an environmental consulting firm which noted that although more than half of all municipal solid waste consists of materials that are at least in theory biodegradable, for some reason, even twenty or thirty years after being closed, most landfills have settled no more than a few feet at most. Another clue involved data on landfill methane production, which in most cases amounts to no more than 50 percent of what it theoretically should be, and in some cases amounts to as little as 1 percent. A third clue was an account by the archaeologist Rodolfo Lanciani, published in 1890, of his excavation at an ancient Roman garbage dump on the Esquiline Hill, which revealed that much of the garbage from imperial times had yet to fully decompose.

"On the day of the discovery of the above-mentioned stone, June 25, 1884," Lanciani writes, "I was obliged to relieve my gang of workmen from time to time, because the smell from that polluted ground (turned up after a putrefaction of twenty centuries) was absolutely unbearable even for men so hardened to every kind of hardship as my excavators."

The true state of affairs revealed itself when the Garbage Project's research priorities began shifting increasingly to public-policy issues involving garbage—and the research venue began shifting increasingly to landfills. Instead of garbage that was at most a few days old, researchers began dealing with garbage that was ten, twenty, thirty years old—sometimes even older. Various artifacts began to accumulate in the Project's storage bins, particularly in the form of old newspapers with intriguing or resonant headlines: "Apollo Orbits Moon," July 30, 1971 (*Arizona Republic*); "Customs Men Bar Hippies to Cut Mexican Dope Flow," October 18, 1967 (*Phoenix Gazette*); "40 Red MIGs Downed or Hit During Week," April 5, 1952 (*Phoenix Gazette*); "Hint Dropped by Truman Suggests He May Not Be Candidate for President," January 8, 1952 (*Tempe Daily News*). As noted earlier, newspapers are extremely valuable for the purpose of dating garbage deposits, and they were of course entertaining curiosities in their own right. In the tradition of "The Emperor's New Clothes," though, it took a visitor to one landfill excavation—at the Mallard North landfill, in Elgin, Illinois—to point out the obvious. Casting his eyes one day in June of 1988 over the ranks of sorting bins holding stacks and stacks of old newspapers, he said: "I thought newspapers were supposed to biodegrade." . . .

Once broached, the subject of biodegradability became the target 30 of a major research program. The first question to answer was: After a period of ten or fifteen years, how much paper and other organic garbage remains in landfills; that is to say, how much does not become transformed into methane and humus? There is, of course, some variability from landfill to landfill, but when the volume of paper items is combined with those of food waste, yard waste, and wood (mostly lumber used in construction), the overall volume of organic material recovered from the nine U.S. landfills excavated by the Garbage Project is extraordinarily high. For example, organics represented 32.5 percent of the ten- to fifteen-year-old garbage excavated at the Naples [Florida] Airport landfill, 50.6 percent of the garbage of the same age excavated at Mallard North, and 66.5 percent of the garbage of that age at Rio Salado, in Phoenix. Organics in four twenty- to twenty-five-year-old samples from the landfill at Sunnyvale, California, represented some 40 percent of the sampled garbage. Organics in four Rio Salado samples from the 1950s accounted for 49 percent of the samples' total volume. Almost all the organic material remained readily identifiable: Pages from coloring books were still clearly that, onion parings were onion parings, carrot tops were carrot tops. Grass clippings that might have been thrown away the day before yesterday spilled from bulky black lawn and leaf bags, still tied with twisted wire but ripped open by garbage trucks and landfill bulldozers. Whole hot dogs have been found in the course of every excavation the Garbage Project has done, some of them in strata suggesting an age upwards of several decades. . . .

. . . The chemistry of biodegradation inside a landfill is a highly complex and problematic process; among other things, to the extent that biodegradation does occur, the activity is highly variable from place to place throughout the landfill. The puzzle hasn't been completely put together yet, though already pieces have been discovered that just don't seem to fit. . . . The pattern that has been revealed through archaeological excavations of landfills so far accords with what is known of the typical life cycle of a field of methane wells: They vent methane in fairly substantial amounts for fifteen or twenty years after the landfill has stopped accepting garbage, and then methane production drops off rapidly, indicating that the landfill has stabilized. Henceforward, it would seem, the landfill won't be changing very much at all.

Analyzing Issues and Arguments

1. What figures does Donella H. Meadows give in "The New World of Plastics" (page 86) for the volume of plastics in landfills? What figures do William Rathje and Cullen Murphy give here? What appear to be the reasons for the discrepancy?
2. What reasons do Rathje and Murphy give for the proliferation of paper in landfills? What other reasons can you think of?
3. What kinds of evidence do Rathje and Murphy supply for their conclusion that very little biodegradation takes place inside a landfill? Which evidence (if any) do you find most convincing?

Writing about Issues and Arguments

Regarding plastics, on what points do Rathje and Murphy agree with Meadows? On what points do these authors disagree? What aspects and implications of plastics disposal does Meadows consider that Rathje and Murphy do not? On the basis of these two selections, write an essay analyzing the role of plastics in the "garbage crisis" and giving your recommendations.

CHRIS CLARKE

The Thirty-Year-Old Carrot

Chris Clarke is the editor of *Terrain* (formerly the *Ecology Center Newsletter*), a publication of the Ecology Center in Berkeley, California. In the following essay, which appeared in the September 1991 issue of the *Newsletter,* Clarke rebuts some of the conclusions that have been drawn from William Rathje's work with the Garbage Project (see p. 93) and examines their political implications.

"Nothing degrades in a landfill"—or at least that's what the recent cliché would have us believe. Pictures of thirty-year-old carrots and readable newsprint from the Truman years have been reprinted widely of late, and the story of William Rathje's exhumation of the above items from Arizona landfills has been one of the most-repeated anecdotes in the solid waste biz for the past couple of years.

The story is a useful one, as for many years people have assumed that the coffee grounds, banana peels, and old *Sunday Examiners* they put in the trash magically go to a place known as "away," never to confront them again. As recycling and source reduction advocates have been saying for years, it just ain't so. The trash we throw "away" today will plague our descendants for generations unless we reclaim that material for further use.

But, as is the case with most useful stories, the moral depends on the motives of the storyteller. The tale of the mummified carrot has been adopted by the industries who profit by the glut of trash filling our landfills, and reinterpreted to support their goals. What was a cautionary tale warning of the persistence of our past mistakes is now used to convince us that those mistakes are not so bad after all.

The truth of the matter is that things put into a landfill *do* degrade. Anyone who works designing or operating landfills will tell you that degradation of trash is a continuous fact of life. Landfills would be much easier to operate than they are if nothing broke down inside them. Operators are constantly battling the settling, leaching, and methane bubbling that large-scale decomposition causes. Some trash breaks down fairly quickly in a landfill. Though an individual object may hang on for a very long time, degradation of the bulk of material in the landfill proceeds at a fairly constant rate. Like the span of human life, the longevity of human garbage covers a pretty wide range. It's a matter of statistics. (You wouldn't be taken very seriously if you paraded a one-hundred-year-old couple in front of the media, claiming that "nobody dies at age sixty." But that's what the "nothing degrades . . ." people are basically doing.)

Though Rathje's project is illuminating as to just how long some things will hang on to their original form in a landfill, to go from that point to state "nothing really degrades in a landfill" is to make a serious methodological error. When Rathje and his garbologists dug through the Tucson landfill, the stuff that had degraded *wasn't there to be studied*. At least not in a form recognizable to us.

Be that as it may, the trash industry (including both the waste management types and the ones who *make* the trash) has adopted this false conclusion as one of its axioms.

Landfill operators, who have a vested interest in maintaining a low level of public opposition to their industry, have shown remarkable restraint in not adopting the "permanent storage" line to defend their third-quarter earnings. Perhaps this is due to the fact that landfill operators spend huge amounts of time and capital trying desperately to retard the degradation of landfilled material, and trying as well to capture the breakdown products of the stuff as it does degrade. Some landfills even make money selling methane, the primary breakdown product of organic matter in landfills, to utilities as a source of energy. (The fact that banks are willing to take assumed income from methane sales into account when lending money to landfill operators is pretty good evidence that degradation occurs at a constant rate.)

Still, where battle lines are drawn around siting of new landfills, you can bet that citizens concerned about leachate and emissions are being reassured by PR flacks that their fears are unfounded, since "nothing degrades in a landfill."

Styrofoam makers and other plastic manufacturers have been having a field day with the Rathje study. After all, one of the chief environmentalist objections to their product has been the fact that it sticks around for millennia where natural materials would decompose and provide food for microorganisms. Styrofolk claim not only that since "nothing degrades in a landfill," natural materials have no advantage over styro, but also that since styro does not degrade, it provides a stable fill for landfills. Hmmm, lets see . . . paper cups aren't better than styro because neither degrades, and furthermore, styro is better than paper because paper degrades and styro doesn't. I don't get it.

Incidentally, though *bio*degradation is often retarded in landfills due to lack of oxygen, styrofoam will degrade *chemically* if it is landfilled along with any of the number of solvents that attack polystyrene. One of those solvents is humic acid, which is produced when organic matter biodegrades. Styro is just plain not inert in a landfill.

To set the record straight: everything degrades. Current landfill technology may slow the rate of deterioration down for some materials (while accelerating rates for other materials) but whether an object is in a landfill, a compost pile, or deep space, it breaks down eventually. Landfills are the site of constant and fairly rapid biodegradation of many materials. Methane production, organic acid leachate, and fill settling are constant problems which are directly caused by this degradation.

The real moral of the thirty-year-old-carrot story is not that land-fills are efficient preservers of discarded materials, but merely that they are very inefficient compost piles. If you're counting on something breaking down when you discard it, you might as well put it in a real compost pile. Otherwise, the best destination for the stuff you can't avoid or reuse is the recycling center.

Analyzing Issues and Arguments

1 What are Chris Clarke's main areas of agreement and disagreement with William Rathje regarding landfills?
2. According to Clarke, what useful message can be drawn from the idea that "nothing degrades in a landfill"? In his view, what self-serving message can be drawn from the same idea, and who has been drawing it?
3. For what audience did Clarke apparently write this essay? What change does he hope to make in their beliefs? In their actions?

Writing about Issues and Arguments

Should retailers of take-out coffee dispense their product in cups made of coated paper, polystyrene foam, or some other substance? Write an essay defending your answer, using Clarke's "The Thirty-Year-Old Carrot," Rathje and Murphy's "What's in a Landfill?" (p. 93), and Donella H. Meadows's "The New World of Plastics—Not New Enough" (p. 86) as sources.

CONSUMER REPORTS

Recycling: Is It Worth the Effort?

This article appeared in the February 1994 issue of *Consumer Reports*. The magazine is published by Consumers Union, "a nonprofit organization established in 1936 to provide consumers with information and advice on goods, services, health, and personal finance." *Consumers Reports* (which accepts no advertising) regards all its articles as representative of the magazine and does not identify their authors. "Recycling: Is It Worth the Effort?" evaluates the arguments for and against recycling on the individual, local, and national levels and comes up with the answer that yes, recycling is "part of the solution to our waste-disposal problem."

People feel good about recycling. It's a simple, direct, and daily way to feel you're helping the environment. "In the first week in November 1992, more adults took part in recycling than voted," says Jerry Powell, editor of *Resource Recycling* magazine and chair of the National Recycling Coalition. "We're more popular than democracy."

Some 5,400 cities and towns had curbside recycling programs in 1992—five times as many as in 1988. And forty-one states have official recycling goals, ranging from plans to recycle 25 percent of all garbage within a few years to Rhode Island's ambitious target of 70 percent.

Clearly, recycling has taken hold. But are we really "saving the Earth" by dutifully filling our bins? Like most environmental questions, this one doesn't have a simple answer.

Recycling does help to keep garbage out of landfills and incinerators, both of which pose environmental problems. But recycling has its limitations. It will never fully replace other methods of garbage disposal. Moreover, the greatest problems with landfills and incinerators come from the disposal of toxic metals and hazardous wastes—and so far recycling has done little to solve those problems.

Recycling's greatest advantage may not be at the dump, but at the factory. Making new products out of recycled materials almost invariably produces much less air and water pollution, and uses up much less energy, than making the products out of virgin raw material.   5

What Garbage Crisis?

In 1987, the nation watched as a stinking, bedraggled garbage barge called the *Mobro* spent several weeks searching vainly for a place that would take its cargo, municipal solid waste from Islip, Long Island. That well-publicized incident symbolized the growing fear that the United States was running out of places to put its garbage, and helped to fuel interest in recycling.

The nomadic garbage barge wasn't what it seemed; it turns out the *Mobro* episode was caused by a private waste hauler trying to make a quick buck by dumping Islip's trash as cheaply as possible. And the "garbage crisis" the *Mobro* symbolized hasn't materialized in the way that many feared it would. On a national scale, we're still far from running out of places to put our trash.

But if the country doesn't yet have a national garbage crisis, there are some very serious local problems. New York, New Jersey, and some other densely populated states are finding that their trash is becoming more and more difficult to dispose of. In those areas, recycling as much garbage as possible can be more cost-effective than trucking trash farther and farther away to be buried.

On a national level, too, recycling is becoming more cost-effective as garbage disposal becomes more expensive. New regulations from the U.S. Environmental Protection Agency set strict guidelines on how and where landfills can be built. These regulations will raise the price of sending trash to landfills—not only because the new landfills are costly to build, but because many old ones will be shut down. According to one recent estimate, roughly 20 percent of all the country's landfills may have to close under the new regulations.

The regulations were designed to correct what had become a seri- 10
ous problem. Until quite recently, most American cities and towns that didn't burn their trash simply dumped garbage out in the country, or on the poor side of town—frequently in a swamp that seemed unusable for anything else. Such landfills, especially the wet ones, emit methane and other gases and can leach a variety of poisons into adjacent surface water and groundwater.

New landfills minimize those hazards. They are built with strong liners to protect water supplies and are supposed to be covered daily with dirt to seal in their contents. Some of the methane they produce can be captured and sold as fuel. New landfills must also be situated in areas where the chance of leakage into groundwater is low.

The EPA's regulations should make landfills a safer option for disposing of trash than they were in the past. But even well-designed landfills will eventually begin to leak as the decades go by.

Incinerators pose an even greater environmental risk. Old incinerators, many of which are still operating, belch all manner of toxic pollutants. New incinerators are equipped with air-pollution control devices to capture emissions. Nevertheless, the devices are not 100 percent effective, and even modern incinerators release some lead, mercury, and other toxic substances. Moreover, all incinerators produce a highly

Since 1960, the total municipal solid waste generated in the U.S. has more than doubled. The proportion put in landfills rose rapidly until the mid-1980s, but since has leveled off. Recycling and incineration are filling the gap.

Some materials take more energy to produce than others. But for all, the energy required to make a ton of material is substantially less when recycled materials are used—even counting the energy used to collect and process recyclables.

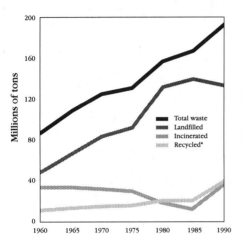

*Includes 4.2 million tons composted in 1990; no composting in previous years.
SOURCE: Franklin Associates for U.S. Environmental Protection Agency

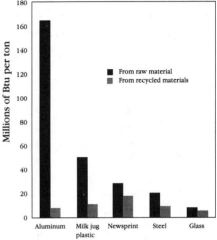

SOURCE: Yale University Program on Solid Waste Policy

toxic ash that must be buried in landfills—and that may eventually leak out of landfills into the environment.

Ultimately, landfills and incinerators pose environmental risks because of some of the things that go into them, such as toxic metals and hazardous wastes. Recycling, at least as it's currently practiced, will remove only a fraction of those hazards from the waste stream. But recycling helps by minimizing the overall amount of trash that needs to be buried or burned and the number of new landfills and incinerators that need to be built. Whether a city faces a "garbage crisis" or not, there are both environmental and practical reasons for communities to try to recycle much of their trash.

Does Recycling Pay?

While American cities and towns have increasingly looked to recycling 15 programs as an option, they have often found that the economics of recycling works against them. Recycling most materials is a costly and

cumbersome undertaking, at least at the beginning, and it's been difficult for many communities to recover the costs quickly.

First, there's the initial investment in extra trucks and sorting
equipment and the cost of paying people to run them. Most communities with curbside collection use separate trucks for picking up recyclables and garbage, increasing their costs in labor and equipment.

To make matters worse, picking up recyclables costs more than
picking up the same quantity of trash. For one thing, most municipalities have only been doing it for a few years and haven't yet settled on
the optimal method. Magazines that cover the recycling industry are
filled with articles discussing the merits of various trucking and sorting
systems.

Also, garbage trucks can squash, or compact, what they collect;
most recycling trucks don't, because compacting makes it difficult to
sort the material later on. As a result, the recycling trucks fill up long
before they've reached their maximum weight load.

Most municipalities collect their recyclable containers "commin-
gled," that is, jumbled together in one bag or bin, often with paper set
out separately. These eventually make their way to a kind of decon-
struction factory called a Materials Recovery Facility, or MRF (pro-
nounced "Murph"), where recyclable materials are sorted—by machine if possible, by hand if not—and sent on to brokers or directly to
the factories that will reuse them. With their heavy machinery and
their dependence on hand-sorting materials such as paper, plastic, and
glass, MRFs are expensive to build and to run.

Together, the costs of pickup and processing easily outstrip the cur- 20
rent value of recycled material. A widely quoted study by Waste Management of North America Inc., the nation's largest private garbage
hauler and landfill operator, found that the company spends an average
of $175 a ton to pick up and sort the recyclables that most communi-
ties include in their curbside programs—glass, aluminum, steel cans,
newspaper, and plastic—but receives only $40 a ton for them. (The
chief culprit appears to be plastic, whose collection and sorting costs
are extraordinarily high compared with its value.)

The cost of recycling, of course, must be compared with the cost
of disposing of trash by other means. In some areas, that comparison
makes recycling look like a bargain. Newark, New Jersey, spends $158
to pick up a ton of garbage and dispose of it at the local incinerator; recycling, by contrast, costs the city $130 to $140 a ton. In the future,
the higher costs of landfills and incinerators built to new environmental
standards may make recycling an equally economical choice for many
more cities.

Another economic factor that would make a huge difference
would be an increase in the value of recyclable materials. Prices for re-

cycled materials have been depressed over the last few years, both because a global recession has led to lower prices for raw materials overall and because the increase in community recycling programs has flooded the market. But as recently as 1988, recycled materials fetched an average of $100 a ton—much more than their current value. At those prices, even cities with plenty of cheap landfill space would find recycling attractive.

The thing that would increase prices most effectively, of course, would be a rise in manufacturers' use of recycled materials. Shifting from raw to recycled materials requires a substantial investment that may take years to recoup. But more and more industries are making the shift, driven by public demand and environmental legislation.

Replacing Raw Materials

"The problem with throwing away a ton of cardboard is not that it's going to hurt somebody if you burn it or bury it," says John Schall, an environmental economist. "The problem is that you have to make the next ton of cardboard by cutting down trees, which has immensely greater environmental impact than disposing of it."

Many analysts have now compared the environmental impact of us- 25
ing virgin raw materials—both in harvesting or mining the materials, and in preparing them for use in factories—versus the environmental costs of collecting, sorting, and remanufacturing recycled materials. In almost every case, using recycled materials has substantial environmental benefits.

An unusually thorough analysis done by the Tellus Institute, a Boston environmental consulting group and think tank, found that a major benefit of using recycled materials is that it saves energy. And energy use is responsible for the major environmental impacts of production: the depletion of nonrenewable resources, the air pollution, the generation of greenhouse gases that may contribute to global warming, and so on. Using recycled materials can make a huge difference in energy use in some cases (see graph p. 111). Recycling also reduces the environmental impact of obtaining raw materials in the first place.

If using recycled materials makes so much sense, why haven't manufacturers been doing it all along? In some cases, they have. The aluminum industry discovered the economies of recycling more than two decades ago, and tissue, cardboard, and boxboard manufacturers have used scrap paper for years. Recycling is built into the steel industry. One of the two major types of steelmaking furnace must have 25 to 30 percent scrap metal to function properly; the other type runs on 100 percent scrap.

Nevertheless, most manufacturing industries are still geared to run on virgin rather than recycled materials, driven by the relative abundance and low cost of virgin resources in the United States. For some materials, such as paper, there are also Government subsidies for virgin materials.

Factories have a huge infrastructure designed to use virgin materials, and retooling to use recycled materials can be very expensive. When the QUNO Corporation, a Canadian newsprint manufacturer, decided to equip its Ontario mill to use more than 50 percent recycled pulp, it spent 50 million in Canadian dollars to build an immense new de-inking plant containing two repulping machines, each the size of a small house, and five de-inking tanks, each the size of a boxcar. Union Carbide Incorporated, one of the nation's major suppliers of plastic, had to build a new $10-million factory in order to recycle bottles made from plastic that it had produced in the first place.

Virgin material often has another clear advantage over recycled: 30 consistent quality. Recycled materials come largely from distracted householders who may or may not follow the dictates of their local recycling program. Contamination isn't a factor for steel or aluminum, but it can compromise the quality—and marketability—of glass, plastic, and paper.

Glass-making factories that accept recycled bottles, for instance, must go to great lengths to exclude contaminants that, because of their different melting points, can ruin entire furnace-loads of glass. These include clear Pyrex baking dishes, windowpanes, and light bulbs, all of which are indistinguishable from container glass after they have been broken and mixed together. By contrast, sand and limestone, the raw materials of glass, are pure.

Manufacturers have needed an incentive to overcome those obstacles and move toward using recycled materials. Much of the incentive has come from public opinion.

"As we looked over our products, plastic packaging showed up at the top of the public-concern list," says Tom Rattray, associate director for environmental quality at the Procter & Gamble Company "People liked the fact that it was flexible and unbreakable, but environmentally they felt it was the worst." Responding to consumer demand, Procter & Gamble jump-started large-scale plastics recycling virtually single-handedly by beginning to use recycled plastics in its detergent bottles.

Recently, a consortium of major American companies, including Time Incorporated, the Prudential Insurance Company, Johnson & Johnson, and McDonald's Corporation, announced they were banding together, with the encouragement and advice of the Environmental Defense Fund, to increase their own use of recycled paper and to encourage other companies and institutions to follow suit. This effort should get the paper industry's attention: The participating organizations buy more than $1 billion worth of paper and paper products every year.

As useful as private-sector initiatives have been, they haven't been 35 enough for some materials. Despite P&G's enormous market clout, for instance, only 15 percent of high-density polyethylene bottles—the kind the company uses for its detergent jugs—were recycled in 1992.

The next wave in recycling may be spurred by legislation. Over the past several years, fourteen states have passed laws specifying a minimum recycled content for newspapers; another fifteen states have similar voluntary agreements with newspaper publishers. Once publishers started shopping in earnest for suppliers of recycled newsprint, the paper industry responded with alacrity. Since 1989, the industry has spent $2 billion to triple the number of mills making recycled newsprint in North America.

Last October, a White House executive order required the federal government to use only paper that is at least 20 percent recycled fiber. Though the government accounts for only 2 percent of the total printing and writing paper market, the order is expected to set a de facto standard for similar public and private initiatives, and thus promote the national effort to recycle paper. That effort has already been largely successful: More than 38 percent of all paper, and 56 percent of all newspaper, was recycled in 1992. This year, for the first time since it has kept track of such figures, the industry projects that we will recycle more paper than we put into landfills.

One ambitious legislative experiment is Germany's so-called Dual System. This system was set up by a law that covers all forms of packaging, from shipping containers to toothpaste boxes. The law requires manufacturers either to meet recycling quotas (at least 60 percent of various materials must be recycled) or to take back all the packaging they put on the market.

The German law has effectively created an industry-supported solid-waste management system side by side with the conventional, government-supported one; hence, the system's name. It has also forced manufacturers to become more innovative in their packaging. For instance, products are now shipped to retailers in reusable plastic containers instead of cardboard boxes.

What Recycling Isn't Doing

Americans are currently recycling well over 30 percent of several major 40 materials, including paper, glass containers, and steel and aluminum cans. Yet in 1992, we diverted only 17 percent of municipal solid waste from burning or burial—a total that included the composting of yard waste, a specialized kind of recycling. . . .

Why don't those numbers match up? The main reason is that the commonly recycled materials make up less of municipal solid waste than you'd expect. Steel and aluminum cans, glass bottles, plastic containers, newspaper, and cardboard account for only about a third of our discards by weight. Even if half that material were recovered, recycling it would reduce the amount to be buried or incinerated by only about 15 percent.

Recycling programs have barely begun to deal with much of the waste that pours daily into landfills and incinerators: food wastes, textiles, shreds of plastic wrap, baby diapers, durable plastics that can't be re-melted, and broken and obsolete products ranging from headless Barbie dolls to rotary dial phones. Some of those products are too dirty or germ-laden to recycle; others are too difficult to disassemble into recyclable components using current technology; and still others are laden with toxic materials. . . .

But other items could, with a little effort and know-how, be diverted from burial or burning. Hazardous wastes, for instance, could be separated out for proper disposal. Food wastes could be composted at home or as part of a municipal program. Textiles and plastic wrap that's not contaminated with food could be recycled, as they are now in a few communities.

Still other categories of materials have been left out of most municipal recycling programs because they aren't even officially considered municipal solid waste. Yet they turn up in landfills in great quantities. William Rathje, a University of Arizona archaeologist, has studied the contents of people's trash cans and dug up old landfills to find out what's in them. In landfill after landfill, he has consistently found that about 12 percent of what's buried is waste from construction—chunks of concrete, splintered wood, old windows, and so on. Some efforts to reuse these materials are now under way, but they're still at an early stage.

Manufacturers can make a difference as well. Some have now be- 45
gun designing their products with recycling in mind. And others have made an effort to remove toxic metals from products that will eventually be discarded; the mercury content of alkaline batteries, for instance, has dropped precipitously in a few years.

The Best Solution: Use Less

Environmentalists often urge the public to "reduce, reuse, recycle." Significantly, recycling is third on the list—less desirable than reusing material or reducing the amount we buy and use in the first place.

A key part of environmental planning is what's being called "source reduction"—the design or purchasing choices that reduce the amount of materials used for a given purpose. It's an area in which packaged-goods manufacturers have been particularly active in recent years. For example, nonreusable glass containers, on average, weighed 44 percent less in 1987 than in 1972.

In 1991 the McDonald's Corporation, working in concert with environmental groups, practiced source reduction when it replaced polystyrene foam "clamshell" hamburger boxes with thin paper-and-polyethylene wraps. Though the hamburger boxes could theoretically be recycled (at great expense and bother) and the paper-and-plastic wraps could not, the switch reduced the volume of waste from burger containers by 90 percent, and the volume of cardboard needed to transport the packaging by 85 percent. To achieve the same result by recycling, the company would have had to retrieve and recycle 9 out of 10 burger boxes—a practical impossibility.

In a similar way, many manufacturers have begun selling their products in a form that minimizes packaging. Concentrates of products from fruit juice to laundry detergent have proliferated on supermarket shelves in recent years. And many cleaning products, such as Wisk detergent and Downy fabric softener, now come in compact packages designed to refill reusable bottles.

Consumers have already started to choose source-reduced packag- 50 ing on environmental principles, and many may soon have an economic incentive as well. Some experts are now recommending that cities charge households different fees according to the amount of trash they generate. In most cities, residents now pay for municipal trash collection through their general property taxes, and pay the same amount whether they habitually fill one small trash can or four big ones. But some cities, such as Seattle, have started to bill households directly, with the price rising sharply for every additional trash can. (These cities generally charge nothing to pick up recyclable materials.) Such a volume-based system can have a big impact: In one rural New York town that tried it, the amount of trash buried in the local landfill decreased by more than half, and the recycling rate more than doubled, within a year.

What You Can Do

Because all forms of trash disposal—including recycling—have environmental impacts, the best thing a consumer can do is to avoid buying new things whenever possible. Think like the thrifty nineteenth-century New Englanders, whose motto was "Use it up, wear it out, make it do." Things can be bought used rather than new, fixed rather than thrown away. The reverse side of scrap paper can be used for

Reprinted with special permission of King Features Syndicate.

grocery lists or children's art projects; plastic take-out containers can be reused to store leftovers.

When you do need to buy, you can practice source reduction by shopping for products, for instance, that have as little packaging as possible. That means buying concentrates and mixing up products at home; buying refills when available; and buying the largest-sized package on the shelf.

The next step after source reduction is to buy products that use recycled materials in their manufacture or packaging. Recycling will work only if manufacturers buy and use recycled materials, and consumer choice helps drive manufacturers' decisions. For that reason, "The only true recycler is someone who uses recycled products," says Jerry Powell, editor of *Resource Recycling.*

It's easier to buy recycled materials for some product categories than for others. Virtually every kind of paper—from 3x5 cards to stationery to fax paper—now comes in a recycled version. You won't find food packaged in recycled plastic; the U.S. Food and Drug Administration doesn't permit it. But an increasing number of nonfood plastic packages have recycled content and say so on the label. Packaging made from glass, steel, or aluminum automatically has a high recycled content.

Finally, it is important to recycle whatever you can in your com- 55 munity—and to do it right. Remember that you are helping to supply the nation's industrial raw materials, and follow your locality's specific recycling instructions to the letter. If your town doesn't want plastic detergent jugs or magazines, don't put them out. If it asks you to remove the lids of containers before recycling, remove them. Otherwise, you may unwittingly contaminate the pool of recycled material your community collects, and risk making it unusable.

Analyzing Issues and Arguments

1. According to *Consumer Reports,* what are the main reasons for a city or town to require residents to recycle paper, plastics, metals, and glass? What are the main arguments against such recycling?
2. What recycled materials are most widely used in manufacturing, and why?
3. What kinds of municipal solid waste are hardest to recycle, and why?

Writing about Issues and Arguments

What do you think should be your own town's or city's policy on residential recycling? Write an essay explaining and supporting your position, using the selections you have read so far in this chapter as sources.

PATRICIA POORE

America's "Garbage Crisis": A Toxic Myth

Patricia Poore is the editor and publisher of *Garbage: The Independent Environmental Quarterly*. A former anthropology major, she became interested in people's attitudes toward recycling and waste disposal when she visited India at the age of seventeen. Poore began her magazine publishing career with *Old House Journal* in New York City. In 1989 she founded *Garbage,* a magazine known for attacking corporate and environmentalist orthodoxies. "America's 'Garbage Crisis': A Toxic Myth" appeared in the March 1994 issue of *Harper's* magazine, adapted from Poore's longer article "Is Garbage an Environmental Problem?", which appeared in theNovember/December 1993 issue of *Garbage*. As her essay's title implies, Poore condemns costly, time-consuming efforts to solve the so-called garbage crisis as "foolish and extremely wasteful."

Let us recall, for a moment, the *Mobro*—the infamous garbage barge that, in 1987, laden with an increasingly ripe pile of waste, wandered from port to port in search of a home. The *Mobro,* which was carrying plain old municipal solid waste—household garbage—occasioned headlines about the nation's looming "garbage crisis": we were throwing away too much, our landfills were running out of space, and soon the seas would be full of *Mobro*s, all looking for a place to dump our trash. And yet here we are, seven years later, and our landfills are not overflowing; our waterways are not crowded with wandering barges. What happened to the garbage crisis?

The environmental movement continues to focus its attention on garbage and recycling, as if household garbage were the single most important issue we face and recycling the only solution. Of course, garbage does have an environmental impact; so does almost everything, from prairie-grass fires to the breath you just took. But, contrary to the rhetoric of some environmentalists, garbage is not a serious environmental hazard. True hazards are ones that threaten human lives and health. There are plenty of these, including toxic waste (which is quite distinct from household garbage), groundwater pollution, and urban smog. Compared with these real crises, the problems of municipal garbage disposal pale. There are times and places when household garbage *can* cause environmental problems—like when toxic runoff leaches into drinking water—but these are increasingly rare. Newer landfills are double-lined, piped, vented, leachate-tested, and eventually capped. These new standards have made current American waste management safer by far than ever before.

Some critics argue that we shouldn't downplay the threat of garbage because of its symbolic value to the environmentalist agenda. Environmental organizations are well aware of the emotional power of garbage: nothing can trigger a bounteous direct-mail response or inspire a powerful grass-roots campaign like the threat of a new landfill or incineration plant. But when symbols like the *Mobro* barge are used to divert attention and money from more pressing environmental and social problems, the symbol itself becomes a threat.

If there is a garbage crisis, it is that we are treating garbage as an environmental threat and not as what it is: a manageable—though admittedly complex—civic issue. Although many old urban landfills are reaching their capacity, the reality is that there is—and always will be —plenty of room in this country for safe landfill. We've chosen to look at garbage not as a management issue, however, but as a moral crisis. The result is that recycling is now seen as an irreproachable virtue, beyond the scrutiny of cost-benefit analysis. But in the real world, the money municipalities spend on recycling is money that can't be spent on schools, libraries, health clinics, and police. In the real world, the sort of gigantic recycling programs that many cities and towns have embarked upon may not be the best use of scarce government funds.

These programs were often sold to local taxpayers as money-saving   5 ventures. In fact, the costs associated with consumer education, separate pickup (often in newly purchased trucks), hand- and machine-sorting, transfer stations, trucking, cleaning, and reprocessing are considerably higher than initial estimates, far higher than receipts from buyers of recyclables, and, in many areas, higher than disposal costs.

Putting aside financial concerns, let's consider other justifications for the recycling-above-all-else movement. Do we need recycling to extend the life of landfills? No. Landfill sites, in fact, are not scarce, and incineration remains a reasonable and safe option. The most ambitious collection programs still leave well over half of municipal waste to be disposed of, so recycling cannot completely replace disposal facilities, even if we needed it to.

Do we need recycling to save resources? No, not in the real world. The reason recycling is unprofitable is that most of the materials being recycled are either renewable (paper from tree farms) or cheap and plentiful (glass from silica). Aluminum *is* profitable to recycle—and private concerns were already recycling it before the legislated mandates.

Recycling is beginning to lose its halo as its costs become apparent and its effect on the volume of waste is found to be smaller than anticipated. Quotas and fines may force people to separate their trash, but they can't create industrial markets for the waste we recycle. Recycling can work, very effectively, on a region-by-region and commodity-by-commodity basis. But recycling as a government-mandated garbage-management option has largely failed.

Although the special attention we pay to garbage, to the exclusion of more serious environmental threats, may be irrational, it does make a certain emotional sense. We as individuals are intimate with our trash, which makes it a more tangible issue than, say, groundwater contamination. Nobody particularly likes garbage; nobody likes taking it out or paying to have it hauled away. We feel we should be able to control it. Furthermore, controlling it—whether by banning plastics or sorting materials neatly at curbside—alleviates consumer guilt. "There," we say, tossing our bundled newspapers on the curb, "I've done my part for the environment."

But for all the psychological benefit that approach may confer, it is 10 distracting us from much more pressing national problems. Trash-handling issues should be debated and decided regionally, and those decisions have to be based, at least in part, on economics. That can't happen when one option—recycling—is elevated by environmentalist rhetoric into a national moral imperative. We have real environmental problems to worry about: We have to protect the water supply. We must improve the quality of the air we breathe. We need a better plan for energy management. And we have to monitor toxic waste more effectively. In that context, it is foolish and extremely wasteful to expend so much effort wringing our hands (and spending our money) on garbage.

Analyzing Issues and Arguments

1. What is the thesis of Patricia Poore's essay? Where and how does she state it?
2. What beliefs and actions does Poore argue for? What beliefs and actions does she argue against?
3. In paragraph 4, Poore writes: "We've chosen to look at garbage not as a management issue . . . but as a moral crisis." What does she mean?

Writing about Issues and Arguments

How serious is the "garbage crisis," and what should we do about it? On the basis of the selections you have read in this chapter so far, write an essay evaluating the problem and recommending steps toward a solution.

Supreme Court's Decision on Waste Disposal Raises Environmental Eyebrows

David Holmstrom

The following article appeared in the *Christian Science Monitor* on June 28, 1994. David Holmstrom is a staff writer for the *Monitor* who covers a variety of social issues.

To the United States Supreme Court, garbage is interstate commerce.

Up until a month ago, Clarkstown, New York, and hundreds of other towns and cities in twenty-seven states thought garbage was a local resource.

In deciding the case known as *C. & A. Carbone Inc. v. Clarkstown,* the high court struck down "flow-control" laws that had assured local municipalities that they could process or transfer their garbage through local plants.

The court ruled that flow-control laws enabled local governments to "hoard a local resource" and had excluded others from access to it in order to engage in the interstate business of trash collection and disposal.

The court said that only the U.S. Congress can regulate interstate com-   5
merce.

This marketplace approach could bring down the cost of waste disposal, some experts say, but the decision has implications beyond access to a town's garbage. It raises questions about disposal of waste in the United States, and the environmental impact.

"Flow control is one mechanism that allows cities and counties to finance solid-waste facilities," says Eddie Coker, executive director of the Huntsville, Alabama, Solid Waste Disposal Authority. "There are many places in the United States where private enterprise is not interested in building facilities."

Many cities and counties, under a state or federal mandate to provide environmentally safe disposal of waste, used industrial bonds to build disposal facilities or incinerators. Many cities' landfills had either been shut down for environmental reasons or filled to capacity.

Huntsville, for instance, has $111 million in outstanding debt for its facility, charging a "tipping fee" of $39 a ton to dump there. The facility processes 275,000 tons of waste a year. "If you guarantee the flow," Mr. Coker says, "and then some of the waste goes to another facility, you are liable for the lost revenue."

Instead of obligating itself with industrial bonds, Clarkstown contracted   10
with a private company to build and operate a waste-transfer facility. The town guaranteed 120,000 tons of trash each year for five years. In turn the company would charge $81 a ton in "tipping fees" to any truck unloading at the facility.

After five years, Clarkstown owns the transfer facility for a fee of $1.

When the town passed an ordinance requiring that all waste generated in

Clarkstown must be delivered to the town facility, a legal issue for the Supreme Court was created.

A local company, C. & A. Carbone, operated a waste facility in Clarkstown, and was caught sending town trash to Indiana. The company challenged the constitutionality of the Clarkstown law.

"Very little has changed at our transfer station because of the decision," says Richard Glickel, Clarkstown deputy attorney. "In fact, we may end up with more business coming in from New Jersey where tipping fees are higher than ours."

The irony is that the Clarkstown facility separates and processes waste 15 material from many sources, then compacts it and sends it out of state on huge trailers to be disposed of in landfills or incinerators. "The Supreme Court has already said you can't treat trash coming into your state in a discriminatory fashion," Glickel says. "You can't double the tipping fees. The Clarkstown case was about restricting the outflow of trash, and the court said no to that too."

For hundreds of towns with bonds to pay off, and for the bond issuers, it's too early to tell what impact the decision will have on tipping fees or trash movement. "If the Clarkstown facility processes more waste from New Jersey," says a New Jersey town council member, "it means garbage from New Jersey is processed in New York and sent to Indiana for disposal. You've got to ask if there is a better way to do it."

"We support the Supreme Court decision," says Neil Seldman, director of waste utilization at the Institute for Local Self-Reliance in Washington, D.C. "The bottom line as we see it is that flow control is a tool for government to support uneconomical facilities, and reward inefficiency."

What the Institute wants is for Congress to tell local and state governments to adopt strategies to ban all out-of-area wastes.   ■

Analyzing Issues and Arguments

1. What are "flow-control" laws? On what grounds did the Supreme Court reject them as unconstitutional?
2. In your opinion, is the Supreme Court's decision flawed from an environmental standpoint? Why or why not?

JUDD H. ALEXANDER

The Advantages of Incineration

Before his retirement, Judd H. Alexander served as an executive vice president of American Can Company and of the James River Corporation and as chairman of Keep America Beautiful, Incorporated. He also was an adjunct professor in the graduate school of Forestry and Environmental Science at the State University of New York, Syracuse. "The Advantages of Incineration" comes from his 1993 book *In Defense of Garbage*. In this excerpt, Alexander argues that incineration is a safe, cost-effective way to dispose of municipal solid waste, despite claims to the contrary by activists like Barry Commoner (see p. 134).

In 1960, 31 percent of our municipal solid waste [MSW] was incinerated. Twenty-eight years later, the share of garbage consigned to combustion had declined to just over 7 percent.[1] When the old municipal incinerators were shut down, they were seldom replaced with new burners meeting current codes. As a result, even though our population and our per capita generation of solid waste was growing slowly, we began sending an extra 17 percent share of our MSW to landfills. Modern municipal-waste-combustion facilities bear about the same relationship to the incinerators of thirty years ago that state-of-the-art landfills do to the old dumps of the same period. Modern combustors are not only more efficient, they are substantially more considerate of public health and welfare than any waste-burning system used in recorded history. How can it be that garbage burning has shown so much improvement while its use has declined so precipitously in a nation struggling to find answers to disposal needs? For the answer, we must turn once again to an examination of popular beliefs.

. . . Waste burning with energy recovery earns the number three position in the EPA hierarchy of disposal choices, ahead of landfilling.[2] In numerous polls, the public expresses its acceptance of this concept with one additional twist, illustrated by a recent survey in Cincinnati. Citizens there expressed support for garbage burning as a national disposal option,

[1] U.S. Environmental Protection Agency, *Characterization of Municipal Solid Waste in the United States: 1990 Update* (Washington, D.C.: U.S. Government Printing Office, 1990).
[2] Elsewhere Alexander notes that in its 1989 booklet "The Solid Waste Dilemma: An Agenda for Action," the EPA advocated an integrated waste management system comprising (in order of preference) reduction, recycling, burning, and landfill.—(Ed.)

with better than 60 percent favoring the idea. Yet, when they were asked a second question about their receptivity to such a facility in their neighborhood or community, they rejected the concept for local use.

The effectiveness of neighborhood resistance has been a key deterrent to the siting of MSW combustors. No one wants a waste incinerator placed in their neighborhood, for very practical reasons. They are concerned about increased truck traffic, odors, and falling property values. But most of all they are concerned about danger! Danger has been the primary weapon of resistance for foes of waste combustion. The information feeding the fear is supplied by environmental newsletters and books such as Dr. Barry Commoner's *Making Peace with the Planet*.[3] The Environmental Defense Fund's *Recycling and Incineration*[4] and *Rush to Burn: Solving America's Garbage Crisis?*[5] are a little more tolerant of the process, but both of these popular studies emphasize the negatives. The key bogeymen in the environmental advice are greenhouse gases, dioxin, heavy metals, and the toxicity of the ash produced by the combustors.

There is little logic to these positions. Hunter Taylor, a well-known consulting engineer in the power industry, examined the gases issue in a paper[6] presented to an international conference on MSW combustion cosponsored by the EPA and Environment Canada in 1991. His analysis found that decomposition in landfills released ten times more greenhouse gas per ton of MSW than burning it in modern WTE [waste-to-energy] facilities.[7] In this study, methane and nitrous oxide, which are respectively twenty-five times and 250 times more effective per molecule at trapping solar heat than carbon dioxide, were converted into equivalent quantities of CO_2 to facilitate comparisons. Further, the greenhouse gases released when garbage is burned in conjunction with energy recovery should receive an offset credit for the reduction in CO_2 the process achieves, because WTE incinerators reduce the need to burn other fuels.

Dioxins and Heavy Metals

The dioxin issue is even more interesting. Dioxins are a family of 5 chemicals which are unwanted by-products of some manufacturing op-

---

[3]Barry Commoner, *Making Peace with the Planet* (New York: Pantheon Books, 1990).

[4]Richard A. Denison and John Ruston, *Recycling and Incineration: Evaluating the Choices*, for the Environmental Defense Fund (Washington, D.C.: Island Press, 1990).

[5]*Newsday, Rush to Burn: Solving America's Garbage Crisis?* (Washington, D.C.: Island Press, 1989).

[6]Hunter F. Taylor, "The Ten Myths of Municipal Waste Combustion and the Fundamentals and Politics of Garbage," paper presented at International Conference on Municipal Waste Combustion sponsored by EPA and Environment Canada, April 1989.

[7]**Waste-to-energy:** Incinerators that generate electricity.—ED.

erations. They occur in nature because they are produced by such processes as volcanoes, forest fires, and burning wood in stoves or fireplaces. Dioxins occur in such small amounts that they were not an issue until the late 1970s when improved methods for measuring minute amounts of matter were developed. Testing procedures on the toxicity of the material involved massive feeding of dioxins to laboratory animals. When tumors developed in some species, particularly rats and guinea pigs, dioxins were declared toxic to humans. Soon, they were called "the most potent carcinogen ever tested," and "one of the most deadly poisons known to man." Dioxin's presence was behind "Agent Orange" suits, the Love Canal evacuation, the closing of the town of Times Beach, Missouri,[8] and the huge expenditures required of industry to lower its unintentional production of dioxins below detection levels—under ten parts per quadrillion. (A part per quadrillion is not a lot. It is equivalent to one second in 31.7 million years.)

The dioxin threat has been an important rallying point for local resistance to garbage-burning plants because trace quantities of dioxin can be created in incinerators. It can be formed in burning when benzene rings contained in wood, paper, leather, and meat combine with the chlorine which is in products such as salt (including road salt), textiles, paper, food scraps, salad dressing, tap water, and PVC [polyvinyl chloride] plastic. PVC, about half chlorine by weight, is in garbage since . . . 8 percent of it is used for packaging. WTE engineers point out that dioxins contained in products burned in incinerators are destroyed at combustion temperatures of over 1,700° F and new dioxins—which do not include the most virulent forms—are not formed at temperatures below 2,400° F. Therefore, modern MSW incinerators are designed to operate within that temperature range.

No less an authority than Commoner, called by his publisher "one of the world's leading environmental scientists," has been in the forefront of resistance to WTE combustors. The dioxin threat has been a key reason for his opposition. In the index to his recent book *Making Peace with the Planet* he cites references to dioxin in five chapters and on thirty-two pages. He states: "The chief dioxin hazard appears to be its extraordinary ability to enhance the incidence of cancer. In animal experiments, it increases the incidence of cancer at dose levels lower than any other synthetic compound."[9]

Now, a strange thing has happened. Authoritative toxicologists and chemists are saying that the toxicity of dioxin has been vastly over-

[8]**Love Canal:** A community in Niagara Falls, New York, evacuated in 1978 as a result of toxic dumping. **Agent Orange:** A dioxin-contaminated defoliant used during the Vietnam War. (See Commoner's discussion, p. 134.) **Times Beach, Missouri:** The presence of dioxin-contaminated soil led to the evacuation of this town in 1982.—ED.

[9]Commoner, *Making Peace*, 30.

stated. Dr. Bruce Ames, the noted biochemist and the chief proponent of animal testing to determine human toxicity to specific chemicals, has changed his position. He now contends that animal tests are fundamentally flawed because the sheer size of the dosages—even when they are nontoxic—can cause rapid cell division, leading to cancer-causing mutations.[10] Drinking a glass of orange juice, Ames has noted, carries more risk than consuming the government mandated "acceptable dose limit" of dioxin.[11] Toxicologists have always insisted that "the dose makes the poison." Dr. Laura Greene of Cambridge Associates points out in her public lectures that fifty or sixty aspirins taken at one time will kill almost anyone, yet few people consider aspirin to be a poison. It should also be noted that the massive doses of dioxins which affected rats and guinea pigs so adversely had no effect on hamsters.

In early 1991, Dr. Vernon Houk, the director for the government's Center for Environmental Health and Injury Control and the official who ordered the Times Beach evacuation, announced that he was no longer concerned about the levels of dioxin in the Missouri town because scientific studies have shown that low doses of dioxin pose minimal health risks.[12] In August 1991, EPA administrator William K. Reilly announced the agency would begin a year-long review of its toxicity standards for the chemical—six-one-thousand-trillionths of a gram per kilogram of body weight.[13] Canada and several European countries already have standards that are 170 to 1,700 times less stringent than those in this United States.

There is another piece of empirical evidence that may influence 10 the decision. Other than a temporary rash, no one has ever become seriously ill from exposure to dioxin. In his chapter on the trash crisis, Commoner points out that when a factory explosion in Seveso, Italy, in 1977 dusted a nearby neighborhood with "only a few pounds of dioxin," it forced the evacuation of the area due to the appreciation for "the extraordinary toxicity of dioxin."[14] He failed to add that even though the people of Seveso were exposed to relatively huge quantities of dioxin, they suffered no long term after-effects; there has been no increase in cancer or unusual incidents of birth defects among the affected civilians. The early reaction by environmental leaders to the good news of the revised estimate of risk from this chemical has been silence or denial. As for the municipal-waste-combustion industry, it

[10]Joan O'C. Hamilton, "Heresy in the Cancer Lab: Biochemist Bruce Ames Insists Some Carcinogens Aren't So Deadly," *Business Week,* October 15, 1990.
[11]Alton Chase, "Eco-Pundits Prey on Our Love for Calamity," *Detroit News,* August 4, 1991.
[12]Reed Irvine, "The Dioxin Un-Scare—Where's the Press?" *Wall Street Journal,* August 6, 1991.
[13]Keith Schneider, "U.S. Officials Say the Dangers of Dioxin Were Exaggerated," *New York Times,* August 15, 1991.
[14]Commoner, *Making Peace,* 110.

sees dioxin as a nonissue. Its newest technology controls the release of dioxins to infinitesimal levels, far below even the current overzealous limits required by the EPA.

A second area of controversy between the environmental community and the power industry concerns the danger of incinerator ash because it contains trace quantities of heavy metals (so does sewage sludge). Environmentalists are concerned that the ash poses a health risk through groundwater contamination; the industry insists it does not. Taylor, the combustion authority, believes there is a logical explanation for this difference in opinion. The environmentalists' concern is based on laboratory tests which show metals, particularly lead and cadmium, can be leached from the ash. Laboratories use an accelerated testing method to make this determination. They apply "aggressive" acidic leaching fluids to incinerator ash samples which do leach out traces of metal. The industry analysis, on the other hand, is based on tests of leachate taken from actual monofills ("ash only" landfills) over a twenty-year period which show no heavy metal content. Taylor points out that ash is slightly alkaline which tends to neutralize the effects of rain which is mildly acidic.[15] There should be a way for the parties to resolve this difference.

Another way to reduce the presence of heavy metals is to not burn them in the first place. The president of one of the largest operators of WTE mass burners[16] has estimated that three-quarters of the lead and cadmium in the ash in his operations come from one source—batteries. They are not difficult to collect separately because they take so little space. Communities with burners should be especially conscious of the need to keep batteries out of incinerators. A smaller source of heavy metals was their use as pigments and stabilizers in some plastic products and in some printing inks. Already, the packaging industries are close to eliminating them from all inks, and they have made significant progress in reducing them in other products. Manufacturers have a real incentive to make such reductions. Heavy metals are bad for the workers who make the product, bad for recycling, and bad for disposal.

Another feature of incinerators is often overlooked in the United States. The Japanese call their burners "cleansing devices" because high-temperature burning destroys pathogens in discards. There is no infectious material in incinerator ash or in gaseous emissions. A final indicator on the risks of garbage combustion is circumstantial, but intriguing. The three industrialized countries that are most dependent on incineration for the disposal of nonrecycled MSW discards are

---

[15]Personal communication, 1991.
[16]**Mass burners:** Incinerators that burn unseparated waste.—ED.

Switzerland (77 percent), Japan (72 percent), and Sweden (55 percent). The citizens of the same three nations, out of ninety-three countries reviewed, have longer life expectancies at birth than do the people of any other nation in the world.[17]

Analyzing Issues and Arguments

1. According to Judd H. Alexander, what are the "popular beliefs" that have restricted the spread of MSW combustors as a way of disposing of garbage?
2. On what grounds does Alexander accuse Barry Commoner of misleading his readers in his account of the evacuation of Seveso, Italy? How convincing do you find his argument?
3. Look back at Edward O. Wilson's comparison of exemptionalists and environmentalists on page 1. In which category would you place Alexander, and why?

Writing about Issues and Arguments

How do the location and nature of a community affect what kind of waste-disposal program will work best there? For instance, would a city with heavy air pollution (such as Los Angeles) be advised to choose a different method of waste disposal from a village on a windy seacoast? Write an essay explaining whether and why you would rather have your community install a state-of-the-art landfill or an MSW combustor to dispose of local garbage.

IN THE NEWS

Fetal Harm, Not Cancer, Is Called the Primary Threat from Dioxin

Keith Schneider

The following news story is excerpted from a longer article that appeared in the *New York Times* on May 11, 1994. Keith Schneider is an environmental reporter for the *Times*. Before writing this article, Schneider had

[17]U.S. Bureau of the Census, *Statistical Abstract of the United States 1990* (Washington D.C.: U.S. Government Printing Office, January 1990).

written a controversial and widely criticized series of stories downplaying the dangers of dioxin. (See note 13, p. 129.)

In a report on dioxin, a group of scientists at the Environmental Protection Agency has concluded that cancer is not the most serious health hazard at common exposure levels. Of greater concern, the report said, are subtle effects on fetal development and the immune system that may be the result of very low levels of exposure.

The scientists said that most adults and children already have levels of dioxin in their bodies at or near the concentrations that cause such fetal and immune system problems in laboratory animals.

This new assessment of the risk of dioxin, one of a class of toxic chlorine-based compounds present everywhere in the environment, comes in a draft summary of a 2,000-page report scheduled to be made public this summer.

The conclusion that current levels of exposure may already pose human health problems is based on new mathematical assumptions that have not been published in scientific journals.

And it has already caused a storm of dissent in federal agencies, principally   5
in the Food and Drug Administration and the Department of Agriculture, which have the primary responsibility for insuring the safety of food. The summary was discussed yesterday by officials from the F.D.A. and the department, as well as from the environmental agency and the Department of Health and Human Services.

Dioxin and its sister toxic compounds, PCB's and furans, are by-products of heating or burning chlorine-based chemicals through incineration or manufacturing. About five hundred pounds of the chemicals are produced every year across the country and enter the environment mostly from smokestacks. Minute quantities fall to the earth and become part of the food chain through animal fat, milk, eggs, and fish, which are the largest sources of human exposure, the summary said.

Officials with the Clinton administration said the draft summary pointed toward several new steps the government could take to reduce dioxin levels in the environment, including new pollution controls on medical, garbage, and hazardous waste incinerators, which the summary identified as important sources of dioxin emissions.

But the officials, all of whom declined to be identified because they were told by their superiors not to talk to reporters, also said the government would continue to recommend that Americans continue to lower the amount of fat they eat, not only to lower the risk of cardiac disease, but also to reduce their intake of dioxins. . . .

Dr. Lynn Goldman, the environmental agency's Assistant Administrator for Prevention, Pesticides, and Toxic Substances, cautioned that the summary is the first attempt to characterize all the data on dioxins that have been amassed over the last three years for the agency's $6 million dioxin reassessment. It is almost certain, she said, that the summary will be revised before the entire multivolume study is made public by the Clinton administration, perhaps as early as next month. . . .

The draft summary made these principal findings: 10

■ Dioxins may cause increases in several types of cancer, but the data were still equivocal and the risks were primarily concentrated in chemical industry workers and victims of accidents exposed to exceptionally high levels.

■ A very sound data base has developed in the last two decades to support the view that dioxins cause reproductive and developmental problems in fish, birds, and mammals, and that such effects are "likely to occur at some levels in humans."

■ There is strong evidence that exposure to dioxins causes suppressed immune systems in animals, leading to greater incidence in disease in animals exposed to low, moderate, and high levels of the compounds. The authors of the summary report said they were worried that because dioxins affect cell growth and confuse biological signals early in fetal development, "the human embryo may be very susceptible to long-term impairment of immune function from in-utero effects."

■ There is evidence in several human epidemiology studies, and in animal studies, that dioxin causes lower testosterone levels in men who are heavily exposed, may slightly increase the risk of diabetes, and may be a factor in causing endometriosis in women exposed to high levels. . . .   ■

Analyzing Issues and Arguments

1. Describe the human health risks dioxin poses, according to this article.
2. How does the information presented in this article affect your assessment of Judd H. Alexander's arguments in favor of incineration? Explain.

BARRY COMMONER

The Hazards of Incineration

Time magazine has called environmental biologist Barry Commoner "the Paul Revere of ecology" and "a professor with a class of millions." Since 1966 Commoner has directed the Center for the Biology of Natural Systems, an environmental and energy research institute now at Queens College of the City University of New York. His writings frequently appear in publications from *The New Yorker* to the *Environmental Law Reporter.* Among Commoner's most influential books are *Science and Survival* (1966), on the effects of radioactive fallout on human health; *The Closing Circle* (1971), on the link between population and other environmental and social problems; and *The Poverty of Power* (1976), on the economics and politics of U.S. energy policy. "The Hazards of Incineration" comes from *Making Peace with the Planet* (1990). Besides enumerating the dangers to human health from burning municipal solid waste, Commoner describes one community group's political fight against an incinerator planned by the New York City Department of Sanitation.

For a long time, especially in rural areas, trash was simply piled up at the town dump. Later, in order to cover the malodorous mess, holes were dug and soil was layered over the trash periodically, creating what was euphemistically called a "sanitary landfill." But a hole is, after all, a nonrenewable resource: it fills up. Even disposing of trash in this simple way becomes more difficult as the hole fills and then becomes a mound, until, as it grows, trucks are unable to climb the progressively steeper slopes and the landfill must be abandoned. Then, since the trash keeps coming, a new, more distant, more expensive landfill must be found. In this way, like any other nonrenewable resource, landfills become progressively more costly simply by being used.

Apart from this basic fault, landfills are serious sources of environmental pollution. Often poorly controlled, they are likely to receive wastes—unwanted pesticides and other chemicals, waste motor oil, used cleaning fluids and solvents—that readily leach out of the landfill into underground water supplies and nearby surface waters. Moreover, the landfill's organic waste putrefies and ferments, producing inflammable methane and other gases, some of them quite noxious, that pollute the surrounding air. Thus, there is an inevitable conflict between the landfill's unhappy and inherently limited lifetime and the incessant, increasing flow of trash that it must accommodate. The problem became acute in the 1980s, especially in heavily populated areas such as the East Coast, and the cost of depositing trash in a landfill, the "tipping fee," began to rise rapidly. The national average tipping fee, which had been relatively constant until 1984, more than doubled in the next four years; fees in the Northeast were then nearly twice the national average.

Understandably, municipal officials began to look for a way out of this progressively more difficult situation. It appeared in the form of an old idea: burning the trash. This was a practice frequently employed in a futile effort to reduce the nasty impact of decaying dumps. In the 1950s and 1960s, a number of U.S. cities built trash-burning incinerators, and apartment houses used them to burn their own residents' trash. But the Clean Air Act Amendments of 1970 established new emission standards that the incinerators could not meet; a few added emission control devices, but most were closed down.

Again, the relentless flow of trash continued to burden the landfills' diminishing capacity. Then late in the 1970s, municipal officials were visited by salesmen for a new type of incinerator, now graced with a disingenuous name: "resource recovery plant." (The resource recovered was steam or electricity, produced from the heat generated by burning the trash.) This development was not so much a response to the trash problem as to a problem in another sector of the economy—electric power production. With the collapse of the U.S. nuclear power industry in the late 1970s and with excess capacity in most electric utilities, a number of large corporations were faced with the prospect of losing heavy investments in their power plant manufacturing facilities. To make up for canceled power plant contracts, some of them, including the "Big Four" of nuclear power (Westinghouse, Babcock & Wilcox, Bechtel, and Combustion Engineering) decided to sell trash-burning incinerators instead. The *Wall Street Journal,* in reporting sharp budget cuts at the Westinghouse nuclear power unit, commented that "the company's entry into several new energy-related businesses, notably the burgeoning waste-to-energy field, should soften somewhat the nuclear business' decline." The urgent need to find orders for nearly idle power plant manufacturing facilities generated high-pressure sales efforts. David L. Sokol, president of Ogden-Martin, an incinerator company not associated with the power plant industry, has described the situation this way:

> Late in the seventies, intrigued by synergistic opportunities, new companies entered the [incinerator] field. Many were equipment vendors trying to increase boiler sales; or engineering/construction services firms, seeking lucrative design contracts; or other vendors. An overabundance of electrical capacity, leading to a decline in new utility power plant projects, precipitated their aggressive entry into refuse-to-energy.

The sales campaign was successful. Touting incinerators as "proven 5 technology" and the only alternative to increasingly costly landfills, between 1983 and 1987 power plant manufacturers and several independent companies sold 173 incinerators, costing an average of about $100 million each. A symptom of the cozy relations that developed between city officials and the incinerator industry was the creation, by the U.S. Conference of Mayors, of a subsidiary, the National Resource Recovery Association, which promotes incinerators. Since landfills accounted for 90 percent of trash disposal in the early 1980s, the industry appeared to be on the verge of a huge boom, reminiscent of the early days of nuclear power.

But the curious link between nuclear power plants and trash-burning incinerators persisted. Just as nuclear power failed because it *created* an environmental hazard—radiation—so incinerators turned out to be gravely hampered by the same sort of self-generated environmental hazard, in this case dioxin. In the late 1970s, several technical reports about the stack emissions of European trash-burning incinerators noted the presence of the best-known (and believed to be the most toxic) of the family of 210 compounds commonly called dioxins— 2,3,7,8-tetrachlorodibenzo-p-dioxin, usually abbreviated as 2,3,7,8-TCDD. Not much attention was paid to this information in the United States until an incinerator in Hempstead, Long Island, was tested in early 1980 to determine why its stack emissions were so malodorous. There was no reason to blame dioxin for this problem, but, because a chemical related to it had been found in the emissions, samples were sent to a laboratory at Wright State University in Dayton, Ohio, that specializes in dioxin tests. They contained significant amounts of dioxin. An intense controversy erupted, first among technicians about the validity of the results, and later in the community about their significance. Finally, concerns about the hazard and about technical problems in operating the plant led to its closing. By then a number of cities, among them New York, had decided to build "resource recovery" plants to divert the endless stream of trash from their rapidly filling —or rather, mounting—landfills. The New York City Department of Sanitation (DOS) decided to build the first of eight planned incinerators—a plant designed to burn 3,000 tons of trash per day—at a site in the Brooklyn Navy Yard that the U.S. Navy had ceded to the city.

The DOS plan was opposed by the people who live in the residential community adjacent to the Navy Yard, Williamsburg. At first, they objected to the heavy truck traffic that the incinerator would generate; the DOS responded by agreeing that the trash would be carried to the incinerator by barge. But then word came from Hempstead about dioxin emissions, creating in the minds of the residents a new concern about the health effects of incinerator emissions. They were poorly prepared to deal with the problem. Dioxin had been detected as a highly toxic impurity in chlorinated herbicides such as 2,4,5-T in the 1960s. But it was unknown as an environmental pollutant until 1973, when it was discovered in fish contaminated, during the war in Vietnam, with the defoliant Agent Orange. In 1977, following a chemical plant explosion in Seveso, Italy, that spread only a few pounds of dioxin over a nearby neighborhood but nevertheless required evacuation of the area, the extraordinary toxicity of dioxin was widely appreciated, if still poorly understood.

When Williamsburg residents raised questions about the dioxin hazard, the DOS was ill prepared to answer. The initial response was a blanket assertion that there would be no adverse health effects of any kind from incinerator operations. Then, in August 1983, when the issue of dioxin emissions had become unavoidable, the commissioner of sanitation responded by asserting (in a *New York Times* op-ed article) that "unsorted garbage can be burned without producing dioxins."

Such assertions raised problems for the residents, who had heard, for example, that the Hempstead incinerator emitted dioxin from its stack. Desiring explanations, they sought expert advice. The previously mentioned Center for the Biology of Natural Systems, which I direct, is a research institute that has, as one of its purposes, helping communities solve environmental and energy problems. Accordingly, we responded by accepting the residents' invitations to informational meetings, at which DOS representatives were heard as well. In response to the DOS claim that incinerators do not produce dioxin, we produced contrary evidence: a series of reports from European incinerators showing that each of them produced dioxin in their emissions. Confronted with this evidence, the DOS retreated to a new position: the incinerator furnace would be hot enough to destroy the dioxin. But this contradicted the fact that tests of various incinerators showed that dioxin was emitted even at such elevated furnace temperatures.

The inconsistencies in these claims only reinforced the residents' 10 protests, and whenever the proposed incinerator was considered—hearings were held before the New York City Board of Estimate, several Community Boards, and a Citizens' Advisory Committee set up by DOS—dioxin dominated the discussion. It became clear that the public acceptance of the proposed incinerator would stand or fall on the expected effect of the dioxin emissions on the people exposed to them.

Such a risk assessment calls for a series of technical evaluations, beginning with the assumed rate at which dioxin will be emitted from the incinerator's stack. Then it is necessary to work out how the emitted material will spread downwind from the stack, in particular the amount to which a person will be exposed at the point where the concentration is highest. With this information in hand, the amount of the environmental dioxin that is likely to enter such a person's body is computed. Finally, by comparing that number with the rate of cancer incidence observed in laboratory animals exposed to measured amounts of dioxin, the risk of cancer to a person exposed to the highest expected concentration over a seventy-year lifetime is estimated. This "maximum lifetime cancer risk" is generally used as a measure of the health hazard from the incinerator's dioxin emissions.

These evaluations call upon an extraordinary range of scientific disciplines: the chemistry of combustion; the physics of air movement and dust settling (part of the emitted dioxin is attached to fine dust particles, "fly ash," produced in the incinerator combustion chamber); the movement of dioxin through the food chain; the physiological mechanisms that can carry airborne dioxin into the body (inhalation, ingestion, and absorption through the skin); the biochemistry of the cancer process (at best a poorly understood area of science); the influence of each of the 210 related substances commonly called "dioxin" on the cancer process, as determined from animal tests; determination, from the measured effects on cancer incidence in laboratory animals, of the expected occurrence of cancer in the exposed population.

The DOS turned over the task of preparing this risk estimate to a firm of engineering consultants contracted to prepare a *Preliminary Draft Environmental Impact Statement*. Their cancer risk assessment concluded that the maximum lifetime cancer risk from dioxin emitted by the Navy Yard incinerator would be 0.13 per million. Since EPA generally regards a risk of one per million acceptable, this result supported the DOS position that there is no significant risk from exposure to the incinerator's dioxin emissions.

The Williamsburg residents had no way of challenging this conclusion, derived as it was from an elaborate technical analysis hardly accessible to the public. At CBNS, however, we could critically review the DOS risk assessment—and it did not stand up under scrutiny. A major fault was the assumption that dioxin would enter the body only through the lungs, although an earlier study had shown that much more would be ingested, for example by children licking their dust-encrusted fingers. The risk assessment also ignored the fact that incinerators emit most of the 210 different compounds that fall under the common rubric of dioxin. Instead, the consultant estimated the risk from only the best-known compound, 2,3,7,8-TCDD.

Correcting for such defects, and accepting the DOS assumption 15 about the amount of dioxin the incinerator would emit, we at CBNS concluded that the maximum lifetime cancer risk would be 29 per million rather than 0.13 per million—well above the one-per-million guideline.

Pressed by the residents—and voters—of Williamsburg, the New York City Board of Estimate held public hearings at which these discrepancies and other objections to the incinerator were aired. The upshot was a Board of Estimate request that the DOS hire a new consultant to do another, "independent" analysis of the dioxin cancer risk. The new consultant adopted most of CBNS's corrections to the original risk assessment and reported that the maximum lifetime cancer risk would be 5.9 per million—a difference from CBNS's value of 29 per million readily encompassed by the uncertainties inherent in such estimates. In any case, the original DOS assessment now appeared to be between 45 and 223 times too low, and clearly in excess of the guideline.

One of the purposes of issuing an environmental impact statement as a "preliminary draft" is to allow for improvements before the final document is produced. In this respect, the procedure worked well, resulting in two separate reviews that corrected the original document's grossly underestimated assessment of the dioxin risk. This correction raised the issue of the incinerator's environmental acceptability, a matter that would presumably be addressed in further versions of the environmental impact statement. The DOS took an innovative, if astonishing, approach to this commendable process of amelioration: the dioxin risk assessment was simply eliminated from the subsequent draft, and eventually from the final environmental impact statement, perhaps on the view that no news is good news.

At this point, the incinerator project moved into the next administrative stage: extending hearings before an administrative law judge of the New York State Department of Environmental Conservation (DEC) in which the application for a construction permit was defended by the city and attacked by the opponents. The DEC noticed the strange omission of a cancer risk assessment in the final environmental impact statement and required the company that proposed to build the incinerator to produce one. Yet another consultant was hired. The new risk assessment concluded that the maximum lifetime cancer risk from the incinerator emissions would be 0.78 per million—once more conveniently within the guideline. This consultant took a very creative approach to the risk assessment. He decided that dioxin would take a novel path into people's bodies. Dioxin-contaminated fly ash would be emitted from the plant stack, then, descending to ground level, it would somehow mix with a ten-centimeter layer of soil. After being enormously diluted by the soil, the dioxin would come in contact with people through soil particles scattered into the environment.

There are a couple of things wrong with this picture. In the first place, dioxin will not readily penetrate the soil; it is so firmly bound to soil particles that, according to several studies, dioxin will hardly penetrate more than a few millimeters of soil when deposited on it as dust. It is also a fact that there is not much soil exposed to descending dust in Brooklyn; houses and paving cover most of the borough. The absurdity of this concept suggests that it was invented in order to justify an enormous reduction in the computed exposure. A well-known feature of environmental impact statements is their considerable length, due to an enormous amount of often unnecessary, irrelevant discussion and computations. In this case, the consultant went to great trouble to determine how much dioxin people would absorb by eating the fish from the lake in Brooklyn's Prospect Park—something very few people are sufficiently rash to do. Correcting for its errors and absurdities, the new risk assessment actually leads to a maximum lifetime cancer risk of twelve per million—a rather good agreement with both the earlier estimates by CBNS and with the DOS's special dioxin report.

The debate over the Navy Yard incinerator's cancer risk assessment 20 —a kind of technological tennis match with the DOS and its consultants on one side and the Williamsburg community (with considerable support from the New York Public Interest Research Group) and CBNS on the other—has helped to improve the method of making such assessments. Before the debate, there was little agreement over the relevance of a number of the crucial factors that influence the dioxin cancer risk, such as the route of exposure. Since then, apart from newly introduced notions, such as the invention of a bucolic, soil-covered Brooklyn, most incinerator cancer risk assessments have at least considered the relevant factors. Most of the results are similar, generally ranging upward from the one-per-million guideline to twenty or more, indicating that according to this single criterion of health risk, the trash-burning incinerator is at best marginal and more likely unacceptable. The credit for this advance must go to the Williamsburg residents who have forced the municipality to test its hired consultants against independent analyses. The controversy has also encouraged new studies on the occurrence of dioxin in the environment. A recent one shows that dioxin is widespread in the air in Ohio, nearly all of it originating from incinerators that burn trash or sewage sludge.

The environmental controversies that have troubled the incinerator industry can be traced back to its power plant ancestry. Power plants are designed to convert as much as possible of their fuel's energy into steam and electricity. Hence their emphasis on high combustion efficiencies —that is, the completeness with which the fuel is burned and the energy released—that can range up to 99.999 percent. The industry engineers assumed that mixed trash could be burned as efficiently as coal or oil and that only 0.001 percent of its combustible material would be left unburned. They assumed that if the furnace temperature is high enough to combust it, any toxic material in the trash would also be 99.999 percent destroyed, eliminating any environmental hazard. This explains the claim that an incinerator operating at a high enough furnace temperature and combustion efficiency would destroy dioxin, and that those incinerators that emitted dioxin were poorly operated. Yet when CBNS examined the data from a series of incinerator tests, we found no statistically significant relation between dioxin emissions and either furnace temperature or combustion efficiency. Thus, the data failed to support the theory—derived from power plants—on which the incinerator engineers relied to control dioxin emissions. The incinerator engineers also failed to reckon with the extraordinary toxicity of dioxin, which renders exposure to soil contaminated with 0.0000001 percent of it (one part per billion) unacceptable according to EPA guidelines.

Rather sobered by the fact that the industry was eagerly building huge incinerators without adequately understanding their operation, at least with respect to toxic emissions such as dioxin, at CBNS we went back to basics. In the chemical engineering literature, we found several reports of experiments indicating that fly ash can catalyze chemical reactions, including the addition of chlorine to unchlorinated dioxins. We also realized that the six-carbon rings (two of them) that make up dioxin and furan molecules occur in trash in the form of lignin, a common constituent of wood and therefore of paper. Lignin is likely to break down in the furnace, releasing these ring compounds, which, bound to fly ash particles, could then react with chlorine to form dioxins and furans. We also found a report of a Dutch investigator who showed that when paper was burned together with the chlorinated plastic polyvinyl chloride, dioxin was produced, whereas very little was produced when paper alone was burned. Finally, realizing that organic compounds such as lignin breakdown products would bind to fly ash only at relatively low temperatures (less than 500°C), we devised a hypothesis that dioxin, rather than being destroyed in the furnace, is actually *synthesized* in the cooler parts of the incinerator—that is, as the hot combustion gases flow from the furnace to the stack. So the crucial test of this theory was to measure the amount of dioxin in the flue gases leaving the furnace and later, when they had cooled down, at the base of the stack.

As it happened, the Canadian environmental agency, Environment Canada, which has a well-developed system of incinerator testing, produced the necessary data. In 1984, in an incinerator on Prince Edward Island, Canada, they found that while the dioxin content of the flue gas leaving the furnace was negligible, significant amounts were present in the gas entering the control device at the base of the stack. Dioxin must have been synthesized in between the furnace and the control device, in the cooler parts of the incinerator. It is now generally accepted, by the incinerator industry as well as government agencies, that dioxin is synthesized in trash-burning incinerators.

This conclusion transformed the problem of controlling the incinerator's environmental impact, at least with respect to dioxin. It meant that the incinerator *created* dioxin as it operated. Some dioxin is present in trash because paper is frequently contaminated with it as a result of chlorine bleach, which is often used to process wood pulp. Dioxin in such paper products is likely to be destroyed in the furnace if it is hot enough. But more is synthesized in the incinerator, and as a result, the trash-burning incinerator is a net producer of dioxin—an unintended dioxin factory. Depending on the efficiency of the control devices installed to precipitate fly ash, some of the newly formed dioxin will emerge from the stack into the air, while the remainder will be found in the fly ash trapped in the control device. In one form or another, the incinerator *creates* an environmental dioxin problem.

The industry has responded to this new understanding of how 25 their incinerators work by introducing new control devices, generally a scrubber that cools and adds lime to the flue gases, followed by a fabric filter, which can usually capture 90 to 95 percent of the dioxin. While such controls correspondingly reduce the amount of dioxin emitted from the stack, they do so not by destroying it, but by transferring it to the fly ash captured by the scrubber and filter. Instead of entering the environment through the air, now most of the dioxin enters the environment when the fly ash is removed from the control device and disposed of.

Incinerator ash depositories vary a great deal. In Saugus, Massachusetts, incinerator ash (fly ash and the "bottom ash" that falls through the furnace grate) has been dumped on top of an old landfill, which itself is situated in a marsh. Residents are exposed to toxic materials as the ash is carried in the wind and its leachable components reach the water. In the town of Glen Cove, Long Island, incinerator ash was for a time piled in a parking lot, poorly protected from the elements. On the other hand, now most states' regulations require that, because of its toxicity, incinerator ash must be deposited in special landfills protected by liners and leachate control systems. But this adds considerably to the cost of operating the incinerator. Like the nuclear power plant before it, the trash-burning incinerator becomes progressively more costly as remedies are needed to control its inherent environmental defects.

A chief reason for the new regulations is the discovery that in addition to dioxin, fly ash is heavily contaminated with toxic metals, especially lead and cadmium. Lead occurs in discarded batteries, and to a lesser extent in electronic equipment. Cadmium also occurs in batteries and in certain plastics. These metals are released and vaporized in the heat of the incinerator furnace and then become trapped along with the fly ash in the control system. On the other hand, mercury, which also occurs in certain batteries, is so easily vaporized that most of it passes through the control system, out the incinerator stack, and into the air.

Thus, in the course of less than ten years a great deal has been learned about the environmental impact of trash-burning incinerators. Once regarded as a "proven technology" that created no environmental hazard, incinerators are now known to emit enough highly toxic compounds to create a risk of cancer and other diseases that is at best borderline, and more often unacceptable according to existing guidelines. The incinerator fly ash is so heavily contaminated with lead and cadmium as to frequently meet the EPA's official definition of "hazardous substance" and therefore subject to very strict disposal rules.

Even if incinerator emissions do meet regulatory requirements, their impact on the environment is likely to exceed levels that have already been rejected in regard to other activities. For example, according to Dr. Peter Montague of the Environmental Research Foundation in Princeton, New Jersey, a proposed "state-of-the-art" incinerator for Falls Township, Pennsylvania, burning 2,250 tons of trash per day would emit five tons of lead annually. This equals the annual emissions from 2,500 automobiles using leaded gasoline. He points out that leaded gasoline is being phased out in part because of its health hazards, and asks, "Does it make sense to now burn garbage and introduce a new lead hazard?" Similarly, the proposed incinerator would emit seventeen tons of mercury per year, an unwarranted environmental hazard when compared with the effort made by paper companies to reduce their emissions below one ton per year. Apart from these pollutants, the annual emissions from this incinerator would also include 580 pounds of cadmium, 580 pounds of nickel, 2,248 tons of nitrogen oxides, 853 tons of sulfur dioxide, 777 tons of hydrogen chloride, 87 tons of sulfuric acid, 18 tons of fluorides, and 98 tons of dust particles small enough to lodge permanently in the lungs. The incinerator's fly ash, which would contain a number of hazardous metals (lead, cadmium, chromium, and nickel), is to be deposited in a special landfill protected by a plastic liner to prevent leaching into groundwater. The metals will remain toxic for millennia; but the liner is guaranteed not to leak for only twenty years. Coincidentally perhaps, the legal responsibility of the incinerator operator, Wheelabrator Environmental Systems, for the ash also expires after twenty years.

Clearly, trash-burning incinerators have serious environmental defects. But they reveal a failing that is even worse: the incinerator industry has been building these devices without fully understanding how they operate, at least with respect to their impact on the environment. 30

In the absence of public opposition, the scientific challenges that led to this new knowledge would never have occurred. But the industry has hardly been grateful for this help. According to the industry and its collaborators, public opposition to incinerators is not an expression of a *social* concern but of a narrow, personal one: fear of the untoward effects on one's own health, one's immediate neighborhood, and the value of one's property. The incinerator industry's public relations experts have created a cute term—NIMBY (not in my backyard)—to convince us that the opposition to incinerators is simply a built-in narrow-minded approach to any unpleasant intrusion into the neighborhood, a generic impulse to keep anything nasty out of one's backyard.

According to H. Lanier Hickman, Jr., the executive vice president of the Governmental Refuse Collection and Disposal Association, an organization that has been engaged in promoting incinerators, NIMBY is a social disease:

> The NIMBY syndrome is a public health problem of the first
> order. It is a recurring mental illness that continues to infect the
> public.

His answer to public opposition to incinerators is a "campaign to wipe out this disease."

To Calvin R. Brunner, a waste industry consultant, the real threat is anarchy:

> More than a century ago de Tocqueville warned us of may be [*sic*]
> too much democracy in America. Because everyone felt equal to
> everyone else, he projected that this would eventually lead to
> anarchy. . . . Is it possible that the NIMBYists will play a large part in
> proving de Tocqueville right in his assertions about democracy being
> an untenable form of government?

According to *Newsweek:*

> Forget Love Canal . . . Arrest the NIMBY patrols.

It turns out, however, that NIMBY is a myth. A detailed study of 35 opposition to incinerators done for the State of California Waste Management Board tells us instead that:

> Public opposition to waste disposal facilities is a recent phenomenon.
> Prior to the rise of the environmental movement in the 1970s, waste
> facilities aroused little public concern, and rarely were facilities closed
> due to local opposition.

People have begun to worry about their backyards not because of a recent epidemic of antisocial selfishness, but—as the California report states—because "government and industry's failure to properly dispose of wastes received widespread publicity, which resulted in increasing public anxiety about the dangers associated with *all* waste facilities." What motivates the public in their opposition to incinerators is their concern not so much with the sanctity of their own backyard as with the quality of the environment that they share with the rest of society; this concern is not merely personal, but social as well.

Analyzing Issues and Arguments

1. Why and how did Barry Commoner become involved in the dispute between residents of Williamsburg and the New York City Department of Sanitation over the proposed Brooklyn Navy Yard incinerator? How objective do you think Commoner's report of that case is? On what evidence do you base your opinion?
2. According to Commoner, what is the worst failing of the incinerator industry? Based on what you have read about incinerators in this chapter, do you agree with his assessment? Why or why not?
3. At what points does Commoner use rhetorical devices such as metaphor and humor? How do these devices affect the impact of his argument?

Writing about Issues and Arguments

How serious a health hazard is dioxin? Compare and contrast Commoner's assessment with Judd H. Alexander's (p. 126). Consider also the "In the News" articles by Keith Schneider and David G. Savage (p. 131). Using these selections as sources, write an essay either supporting or opposing incineration as the method of choice for disposing of municipal solid waste. You may wish to draw on additional sources as well. (See "Suggestions for Further Reading," p. 332.)

IN THE NEWS

High Court's Trash Ruling a Blow to Cities

David G. Savage

> The following article is excerpted from a news story that appeared in the *Los Angeles Times* on May 3, 1994. David G. Savage is a *Times* staff writer who covers the Supreme Court.

In a costly setback for cities that burn their trash, the Supreme Court ruled Monday that ash left by garbage incinerators may be hazardous waste and as such requires disposal in expensive special landfills.

Until Monday, city officials and the Environmental Protection Agency had maintained that federal law exempted municipal incinerators from requirements governing hazardous waste.

But in a strict reading of the law, the high court said the exemption set by Congress applies only to trash that goes into an incinerator, not to the ash that comes out.

The ruling will have its greatest impact in such cities as Chicago and New York, which dispose of much of their garbage through incineration. . . .

In 1992, incinerators burned thirty-four million tons of municipal trash, 5 or about 17 percent of the nation's solid waste. Advocates of the giant trash burners say that they save space in landfills while creating energy—the equivalent of thirty-one million barrels of oil per year. Incinerators reduce trash by 90 percent, leaving the remaining 10 percent as ash for disposal.

The ash is typically dumped in regular landfills. But critics argue that it may be toxic and hazardous because it includes metal from cans, batteries, and other discarded items, and should instead be disposed of in much safer, and more costly, hazardous waste dumps.

Under the court's ruling, operators of incinerators will be required to test their ash. If it is found to be high in metals, such as lead and cadmium, the material will have to be treated as hazardous waste. City officials say it costs an average of $452 per ton to dump hazardous waste, more than ten times the $42-per-ton average cost for dumping in a landfill.

"This creates a real disincentive for the use of incinerators," said David B. Hird, a Washington attorney representing the National League of Cities, which joined in opposing the suit.

But environmentalists hailed the ruling and said that it will encourage conservation and recycling.

Other environmentalists said municipal operators can comply with the 10 law by screening out heavy metal items before they enter the incinerator. . . .   ■

Analyzing Issues and Arguments

1. How do you think Judd H. Alexander and Barry Commoner would respond to the Supreme Court's ruling regarding the disposal of incinerator ash?
2. In your opinion, how might municipalities develop programs to make incinerator ash less hazardous?

Massachusetts Ships Out Its Waste Problems: Destination Often Poor, Rural Towns

Scott Allen

> A longer version of the following news story appeared in the *Boston Globe* on February 16, 1994. Scott Allen is a staff writer for the *Globe* who covers the environment.

A depressed coal-mining town in Utah will get Greater Boston's sewage sludge. A farm community near the infamous Love Canal in New York takes toxic chemicals from Massachusetts factories. Radioactive waste from this state's hospitals and nuclear plants goes to a South Carolina city where more than 20 percent of the people live in poverty.

Massachusetts, a state that consistently tops the national list for tough environmental laws, is sending our worst waste problems to other states. Rather than build hazardous waste landfills and other facilities here, we ship some of our most obnoxious wastes out of state, often to poor, isolated communities.

Phyllis Johnson of East Carbon, Utah, found that out the hard way last fall when the Massachusetts Water Resources Authority signed a deal to ship sewage sludge to her city of 1,600 if it cannot be sold as fertilizer. The MWRA had faced intense opposition to the agency's plan to build a landfill in Walpole.

"I used to think of Massachusetts as a progressive place, but not anymore," said Johnson, whose community agreed to host a landfill to raise cash after the closure of two coal mines. "If it's not safe enough for Massachusetts, why is it safe enough for us?"

Few would contend that Massachusetts intentionally dumps on the poor   5 and weak. But this state's environmental laws have made it virtually impossible to dispose of toxic or radioactive wastes here. As a result, waste goes where the rules are less strict.

Massachusetts pays dearly for the privilege of shipping waste away—the MWRA will pay $1.25 million a year to the Utah landfill just to reserve space for sludge. Massachusetts does take care of its ordinary household garbage: the state approved so many trash incinerators in the last fifteen years that the state now imports trash. But that cannot erase this state's reputation for exporting its worst waste problems.

Today—after thirteen years of trying to avoid it—a Massachusetts panel may finally vote to look for a site in this state to dispose of low-level radioactive waste from labs, nuclear-power plants, and hundreds of other sources. Until now, Massachusetts negotiators have tried in vain to find another state willing to take the waste. Now, the last landfill that was willing, located in

Barnwell, South Carolina, is scheduled to close its doors to Massachusetts on July 1. . . .

Kathryn Visocki, director of the group that manages the Barnwell, South Carolina, landfill, said officials from every state come up with reasons not to build a radioactive waste repository. But, faced with Barnwell's closure, fourteen other states have gone ahead with repository plans, leaving the Bay State far behind.

Communities that host waste disposal facilities are often well paid for the risk, making waste disposal a growth industry in some areas. South Carolina's Legislature agreed to keep the Barnwell landfill open an extra eighteen months to get $90 million in fees. Residents of Barnwell largely support the repository.

Likewise, East Carbon Mayor Paul Clark pushed for the vast 2,400-acre 10 landfill in his town as a way to bring revenues and employment to the declining Utah community. So far, East Carbon Development Corporation officials estimate they have pumped $25 million into the local economy.

Leo Roy, Massachusetts's undersecretary for environmental affairs, said Barnwell and East Carbon are waste management success stories. The communities benefit, the facilities are well-managed, and, at least in East Carbon, he says, the land is better suited for waste disposal than any place in Massachusetts.

"Waste should be managed where it can be managed most safely," Roy said. "East Carbon, Utah, gets very little rainfall. That isn't a bad place to put solid waste."

But that does not stop the nagging feeling in states that import a lot of waste that they are a "dumping ground." Seventy-one percent of South Carolina residents say they would rather see Barnwell close to outsiders than collect more waste fees. And, in East Carbon, Utah, Phyllis Johnson nearly won a City Council race last year on a pledge to stop the landfill.

"The people of Massachusetts had better be aware . . . if they send the stuff here, we truly believe this will be a Superfund site," Johnson said. The Superfund program pays to clean up the nation's most contaminated hazardous-waste sites.

Massachusetts activists who fight disposal facilities here say they are quite 15 aware of how poor and weak communities in other states disproportionately receive this state's waste. But they say they would rather reduce the amount of waste created in the first place than build new disposal facilities here.

"All these storage facilities, incinerators, or landfills: No one wants to live next to these. In Massachusetts, the solution is first to cut down on all of the stuff," said Matt Wilson, an organizer of a new group, Don't Waste Massachusetts. "Talk to people who have been fighting facilities: They feel that Massachusetts is on the right track."

The Massachusetts legislature has passed an aggressive law that helps industry cut back on its use of chemicals, a measure being emulated across the country. Likewise, political pressure from activists has helped reduce the low-level radioactive waste generated in Massachusetts by more than 80 percent since 1985.

Undersecretary Roy said Massachusetts's record of pushing waste reduction and recycling shows that this state is not just dumping on other states. "Other states could be angry at us if we were cavalier and said we don't care —out of sight, out of mind. We're not doing that," he said.   ▪

Analyzing Issues and Arguments

1. Are you convinced by Leo Roy's and Matt Wilson's justifications for their state's exportation of waste? Why or why not?
2. What might the residents of East Carbon, Utah, and Barnwell, South Carolina, learn from the Williamsburg, New York, residents described by Barry Commoner (p. 134)?

"THEY DIDN'T TELL ME WHAT TO DO WITH IT. I THOUGHT THEY TOLD YOU WHAT TO DO WITH IT."

MICHAEL SATCHELL

Trashing the Reservations?

Michael Satchell is a senior writer for *U.S. News & World Report,* where "Trashing the Reservations?" appeared on January 11, 1993. Satchell looks at the dilemma that financially strapped Native Americans face when they are approached by waste disposal companies and government agencies seeking a repository for garbage and hazardous wastes.

For Native Americans, it's a modern twist on an old aphorism: Beware of white men bearing gifts. The nation's Indian tribes, most of them impoverished and ignored, suddenly find themselves being wooed with offers cumulatively amounting to hundreds of millions of dollars. There is, of course, a catch: The Indians are being asked to accept what the rest of America increasingly wants no part of—garbage, toxic waste, landfills, incinerators, and nuclear-waste dumps. To some tribes, the offers represent a financial windfall and an economic development opportunity. To others, they are an ill-disguised bribe and a Faustian bargain.

In the past three years, commercial waste-management companies have approached scores of tribes to locate municipal garbage or hazardous-waste-disposal facilities on their reservations. Most offers have been quickly rejected, some have been seriously considered, a handful are in the works, and two will open this year. The U.S. Department of Energy, desperate to find storage space for the mounting caches of high-level radioactive waste from the nation's 109 commercial nuclear-power plants, is offering tribes multimillion-dollar economic aid packages in return for housing spent fuel rods on their lands.

The specter of garbage dumps and nuclear-waste vaults strikes a nerve among Native Americans, who pride themselves on reverence for the land. In fact, many reservations suffer from some of the nation's worst environmental neglect. In the East, for example, PCBs, fluoride, and other toxic chemicals migrating from adjacent industrial dump sites have badly contaminated New York's Mohawk reservation and have ruined its once viable farming, fishing, and sport-hunting economy. In the West, the Navajos' scenic red-rock vistas have been poisoned by uranium tailings and scarred by strip mining.

Some of the damage is self-imposed. Unlined garbage pits and midnight dumping have turned some reservations into polluted eyesores. Poverty and unemployment have forced tribes to exploit their

natural resources beyond sustainability. Many overgraze their range-
lands, overcut timber, and overuse pesticides. This last practice boosts
crop yields but contaminates streams, kills fish, and sickens wildlife.
Says Roderick Ariwite of the National Tribal Environmental Council,
"We've raped our homelands to maintain our economies."

Against this ruinous ecological backdrop, the issue of waste disposal 5
on the reservations is irradiated with controversy. "Entrepreneurs pushing these poisonous technologies are hoping to take advantage of the
chronic unemployment, pervasive poverty, and sovereign status of Indian tribes," argues Bradley Angel of Greenpeace. But Mervyn Tano of
the Council of Energy Resource Tribes, an economic-development
group, says Native Americans have a responsibility to consider any legitimate means of providing jobs and economic security for themselves.
"Greenpeace and other groups are trying to define what is right and
wrong for the tribes," Tano says. "Who are these people telling Indians
what to do?"

In the waste-trade wrangle, one tribe's trash is another's treasure.
Take Southern California's Kumeyaay Indian Campo band. Their critical need for economic development on a welfare-dependent reservation is tempered by an overriding consideration: pride. "We don't want
casinos and bingo because we don't want to be a playground for non-
Indians," says tribal member Michael Connolly. "And we'd starve before we'd sell beads or pose for pictures."

Preferring trash to tourism, the Campo this spring plan to begin construction of a 400-acre landfill that will take 3,000 tons of San Diego
County garbage each day. And later this year, the adjacent La Posta reservation will begin burying or recycling garbage and toxic wastes, including motor oil, industrial solvents, and cleaning fluids, at a new disposal facility of their own. While neither tribe will discuss the finances of their
new waste-disposal activities, the profits are expected to be substantial.

For the Oglala Sioux on South Dakota's Pine Ridge reservation,
pride is also paramount when it comes to attracting commerce and jobs
to a reservation where annual per capita income averages $2,000 and
unemployment runs at 80 percent. One of the poorest tribes in the nation, the Oglala Sioux seriously considered getting into the trash business but recently decided against it—a decision that cost them at least
$30 million in potential royalties. "Our policy is always to protect our
lands," says Rinard Yellow Boy, the tribe's director of solid waste. "We
do not want to harm Mother Earth."

Where to dispose of an annual 900 million tons of municipal
garbage, industrial toxic waste, and sewage sludge is an increasingly urgent national problem. Since the 1970s, more than two-thirds of the
nation's landfills have been closed, and 2,000 of the remaining 6,500
will be shut down within five years as stricter environmental requirements are imposed or as they reach capacity. Nuclear waste poses even

greater problems. Some 20,000 tons of high-level, deadly poisonous radioactive wastes are temporarily stored underwater in reactor pools or in sealed casks at seventy-three commercial power plants in thirty-four states. By the end of the century, some 42,000 tons of waste will have accumulated—enough to cover a football field to a depth of 18 to 20 feet.

By law, the Department of Energy must take charge of these wastes 10 by 1998. But the planned permanent repository, deep inside Yucca Mountain, Nevada, remains mired in legal and political controversy that will delay its opening at least until the year 2010, and likely far longer.

Desperate to find temporary storage for the waste, the government has targeted Indian reservations. With their quasi-sovereign status and their need for money and jobs, tribal lands are perceived as the most receptive venues. To date, sixteen tribes—and four sparsely populated rural counties in the West—have applied for or have received federal grants to get into the nuclear-waste business.

New Mexico's Mescalero Apaches, the most aggressive, have been awarded $300,000 so far to study suitable sites on their reservation, and they could apply for an additional $2.8 million in research funds. If a $2 billion "monitored retrievable storage" (MRS) facility is built to house the wastes until a permanent repository is opened, the tribe can negotiate for potentially tens of millions of dollars in reciprocal aid for roads, jobs, housing, clinics, and other development—to be paid from a nuclear-power-industry fund.

The MRS facility, which would resemble a small, well-guarded industrial park, would also generate jobs for tribal members and tax revenues for tribal coffers. "It's a remake of an old story," says tribal chairman Wendell Chino. "This time, it's the Indians arriving in the nick of time to rescue the government's nuclear wagon train."

Unfortunately, Uncle Sam's train still isn't rolling fast enough. Fearful that MRS projects will not be in place in time to meet the 1998 deadline, the DOE is now floating the idea of shifting large amounts of hot waste into emergency temporary storage at nuclear-weapons plants in South Carolina and Idaho and at several unnamed military bases. Such a move is certain to create a firestorm of environmental controversy. But for Native Americans willing to embrace what the rest of America spurns, the nuclear-waste crunch could mean a wagon train filled—literally—with glowing economic opportunities.

Analyzing Issues and Arguments

1. What are the positive aspects of storing garbage and hazardous wastes on Indian reservations? What are the negative aspects? What evidence (if any) in "Trashing the Reservations?" suggests whether author Michael Satchell is for or against the idea?

2. What statements by Satchell and others cited in his article suggest that racism is a factor in the quest to dispose of wastes on tribal reservations? How big a factor does racism appear to be?
3. At what points and in what ways does Satchell use historical references? How are these references relevant to the present issue?

Writing about Issues and Arguments

Who should decide what happens to garbage, and how should those decisions be made? Write an essay exploring these questions, using as sources Satchell's article as well as Scott Allen's and John Bellamy Foster's "In the News" pieces (p. 146 and below).

IN THE NEWS

"Let Them Eat Pollution":
The Logic of the Free Market

John Bellamy Foster

> The following article is the first part of a longer piece that appeared in the January 1993 issue of *Monthly Review*. John Bellamy Foster is a professor of sociology at the University of Oregon. His most recent book is *The Vulnerable Planet* (1993).

On December 12, 1991, Lawrence Summers, chief economist of the World Bank, sent a memorandum to some of his colleagues presenting views on the environment that are doubtless widespread among orthodox economists, reflecting as they do the logic of capital accumulation, but which are seldom offered up for public scrutiny, and then almost never by an economist of Summers's rank. This memo was later leaked to the British publication *The Economist,* which published part of it on February 8, 1992, under the title "Let Them Eat Pollution." The published part of the memo is quoted in full below:

> Just between you and me, shouldn't the World Bank be encouraging *more* migration of the dirty industries to the LDCs [Less Developed Countries]? I can think of three reasons:
>   (1) The measurement of the costs of health-impairing pollution depends on the foregone earnings from increased morbidity and mortality. From this point of view a given amount of health-impairing pollution should be done in the country with the lowest cost, which will be the country of the lowest wages. I think the

economic logic behind dumping a load of toxic waste in the lowest-wage country is impeccable and we should face up to that.

(2) The costs of pollution are likely to be nonlinear as the initial increments of pollution will probably have very low cost. I have always thought that underpopulated countries in Africa are vastly *under*polluted; their air quality is probably vastly inefficiently low [sic] compared to Los Angeles or Mexico City. Only the lamentable facts that so much pollution is generated by nontradeable industries (transport, electrical generation) and that the unit transport costs of solid waste are so high prevent world-welfare-enhancing trade in air pollution and waste.

(3) The demand for a clean environment for aesthetic and health reasons is likely to have very high income-elasticity. The concern over an agent that causes a one-in-a-million change in the odds of prostate cancer is obviously going to be much higher in a country where people survive to get prostate cancer than in a country where under-five mortality is 200 per thousand. Also, much of the concern over industrial atmospheric discharge is about visibility-impairing particulates. These discharges may have very little direct health impact. Clearly trade in goods that embody aesthetic pollution concerns could be welfare-enhancing. While production is mobile the consumption of pretty air is a nontradeable.

The problem with the arguments against all of these proposals for more pollution in LDCs (intrinsic rights to certain goods, moral rights, social concerns, lack of adequate markets, etc.) [is that they] could be turned around and used more or less effectively against every Bank proposal for liberalization.

The World Bank later told *The Economist* that in writing his memo Summers had intended to "provoke debate" among his Bank colleagues, while Summers himself said that he had not meant to advocate "the dumping of untreated toxic wastes near the homes of poor people." Few acquainted with orthodox economics, however, can doubt that the central arguments utilized in the memo were serious. In the view of *The Economist* itself (February 15, 1992), Summers's language was objectionable but "his economics was hard to answer."

Although its general meaning could not be clearer, this entire memo deserves to be summarized and restated in a way that will bring out some of the more subtle implications. First, the lives of individuals in the third world, judged by "foregone earnings" from illness and death, are worth less—the same logic says frequently hundreds of times less—than . . . [those] of individuals in the advanced capitalist countries, where wages are often hundreds of times higher. The low wage periphery is therefore the proper place in which to dispose of globally produced toxic wastes if the overall economic value of human life is to be maximized worldwide. Second, third world countries are "vastly *under*polluted" in the sense that their air pollution levels are "inefficiently low" when compared with highly polluted cities like Los Angeles and

Mexico City (where schoolchildren had to be kept home for an entire month in 1989 because of the abysmal air quality). Third, a clean environment can be viewed as a luxury good pursued by rich countries with high life expectancies where higher aesthetic and health standards apply; worldwide costs of production would therefore fall if polluting industries were shifted from the center to the periphery of the world system.

Hence, for all of these reasons the World Bank should encourage the migration of polluting industries and toxic wastes to the third world. Social and humanitarian arguments against such world trade in waste, Summers concludes, can be disregarded since they are the same arguments that are used against all proposals for capitalist development. . . . ∎

Analyzing Issues and Arguments

1. What are the ethical implications of Summers's memo? Do you agree with John Bellamy Foster's analysis?
2. From an ethical standpoint, what is the difference, if any, between Summers's recommendations and the U.S. government's policy of offering Native American tribes the opportunity to host landfills and toxic-waste sites? On what evidence do you base your answer?

MAKING CRITICAL CONNECTIONS

1. Are disposable plastics a serious problem or not? Compare and contrast the different viewpoints expressed on this issue by Donella H. Meadows (p. 86) and William Rathje and Cullen Murphy (p. 93). Whose position do you find most convincing, and why?

2. Lester R. Brown, Christopher Flavin, and Sandra Postel in "Points of View" (p. 83) list a hierarchy of options for materials use: reduce, reuse, recycle, burn, dispose of in a landfill. Think of a common garbage-producing situation, such as moving to a new apartment or having a party. How could you apply this hierarchy to the types of garbage that such a situation would produce?

3. Write an essay comparing and contrasting the pros and cons of the various methods of garbage disposal (including recycling) you have read about in this chapter.

4. Some of the selections in this chapter, such as the *Consumer Reports* article "Recycling: Is It Worth the Effort?" (p. 109) and Judd H. Alexander's "The Advantages of Incineration" (p. 126), mention changes in consumer habits that will be needed for a particular garbage disposal strategy to work effectively (for example, separating different plastics for recycling; removing batteries from household trash for incineration). Choose such a case and write an essay evaluating how realistic the behavioral change is. Then analyze the steps that government, other organizations, or individuals could take to motivate this change.

5. What should we do about our garbage? Do you think there is a "garbage crisis"? If so, what are its characteristics and its causes, and what steps can be taken to solve it? If not, what current policies do you credit for managing garbage effectively, and what changes do you anticipate will be needed in the future to ensure that no such crisis occurs? Write an essay explaining your position, using the selections in this chapter as sources. (You may also want to draw on additional sources.)

3

Global Warming:
Crisis or Hysteria?

POINTS OF VIEW

[The] need for immediate action on the greenhouse effect . . . is the result of two menacing features, demons if you will, of global warming: irreversibility and the lag time between emissions and effects. These characteristics distinguish global warming from other environmental issues, and they have the vicious consequence of increasing the need for an urgent response while at the same time making it politically difficult to implement one.

> — Michael Oppenheimer and Robert H. Boyle,
> *Dead Heat: The Race against the Greenhouse
> Effect* (1990)

The threat of global warming will be used to justify nothing less than changing how we live. Private cars will give way to public transport. Every source of greenhouse gases will be regulated. The reduction of cattle herds may be justified on the grounds that their backsides emit too much methane; besides, they are too high on the food chain anyway. Then we will discover that carbon dioxide is neither the only nor the most important greenhouse gas by volume. Regulating methane, for instance, will involve curtailing rice production and other forms of agriculture. (When the regulators can reach termites I must leave what will be done to the reader's imagination.) Water vapor, by far the largest greenhouse gas, opens up limitless possibilities. In short, agriculture, industry, transportation, practically everything can be regulated with the aim of (or in the guise of) limiting global warming. One of many worries is that if the proponents have their way, by the time we know whether and to what extent global warming has occurred, the United States will have started down the path to deindustrialization, so that the knowledge and organizational capacity to cope with climate change will also have deteriorated.

> —Aaron Wildavsky, Introduction to *The Heated Debate:
> Greenhouse Predictions versus Climate Reality*
> by Robert C. Balling, Jr. (1992)

Research in lieu of action is unconscionable. Those who argue that we should do nothing until we have completed a lot more research are trying to shift the burden of proof even as the crisis deepens. This point is crucial: *a choice to "do nothing" in response to the mounting evidence is actually a choice to continue and even accelerate the reckless environmental destruction that is creating the catastrophe at hand.*

We need to act now on the basis of what we know. Some scientists believe that we are in danger of passing a kind of point of no return, after which we will have missed the last good opportunity to solve the problem before it spirals out of our control. If we choose not to act, will we indeed pass that point?

— Al Gore, *Earth in the Balance* (1992)

Gaia is the theory of an evolving system of two tightly coupled and indivisible parts: the living organisms of the earth and their material environment. In this evolutionary theory, the self-regulation of climate and chemical composition are emergent properties of the system. In general terms Gaia predicts evolution to proceed gradually during long periods of homeostasis, punctuated by sudden, simultaneous changes in both organisms and environment, changes that move the system to a new and different homeostatic state. . . .

. . . Whether or not Gaia is an accurate description of the earth, it forces a different view from that of conventional wisdom, a view that could be crucial to understanding the consequences of pollution and other environmental disturbances. From a Northern Hemispheric human view, we see glaciations as a disaster, but Gaia theory sees the glaciations as a preferred state, one in which life is more vigorous. . . . When seen this way, the current interglacial [warming] appears as a planetary fever, a pathology. The swings of temperature between glacials and interglacials could be the oscillations of a control system near the limits of its capacity to regulate. Seen this way, pollution by greenhouse gases and the widespread destruction of natural habitat are further insults to a weakened system. If we force the system too far from the preferred cool state, a sudden transition could occur, leading to a new homeostasis, possibly at a much higher global temperature.

The American geochemist Wallace Broecker has warned that geophysical processes alone could lead to surprises in the greenhouse effect. Gaia as an active control system can speed and intensify such surprises. The expected warming by the greenhouse effect may at first be masked by a system response, for example, such as an increased cloudiness. We might then become complacent, or argue that the greenhouse effect has been overstated, only to be surprised by a catastrophic climate change when the system is overwhelmed.

—James Lovelock, "Rethinking Life on Earth"
Earthwatch, (September/October 1992)

Twenty years from now, we will more fully appreciate the effects of modest warming and CO_2 enhancement. We will see longer growing seasons, summer temperatures that do not change much (except that sum-

mers will tend to be longer), warmer nights, not much change in day temperatures, and a greener planet. . . . On warm nights we will look out on green fields and wonder how we could have been so foolish.
Historians in the twenty-first century will note that, even by the mid-1980s, the best available data indicated that the then Popular Vision of climate catastrophe was a failure.

—Patrick J. Michaels, *Sound and Fury:The Science and Politics of Global Warming* (1992)

INTRODUCTION

As the United States expanded in the late-nineteenth century, while the Industrial Revolution added factory smoke and other detritus to the landscape, some prescient souls began to worry about civilization's impact on its surroundings. Early environmentalists focused on two main goals. *Preservation* involved keeping undeveloped land in (or near) its natural state. "In Wildness is the preservation of the world," Henry David Thoreau told audiences in the 1860s. With human society encroaching on more and more territory, another critical concern was *conservation:* managing people's use of land to protect existing ecosystems. (See Aldo Leopold's "Toward a Land Ethic," p. 4).

When the United States dropped the first nuclear bombs on the Japanese cities of Hiroshima and Nagasaki in 1945, the scope of environmental concerns changed. Radiation entered the American consciousness. So did the array of pesticides and other poisons humankind was releasing into the air, water, and soil. Rachel Carson (p. 1) was a pioneer in this second phase of environmental activism.

Now our sense of stewardship extends beyond our parks and forests, beyond our national boundaries, to encompass the whole earth. We have realized that human activity may actually affect the sustainability of the planet. In this chapter we consider one of the most critical issues currently facing humanity: the possibility that our technology, by changing the mix of gases in the atmosphere, has triggered a process that will alter the earth's climate. The basis of this threat is the greenhouse effect, a natural phenomenon in which atmospheric gases regulate how heat from the sun warms the earth. Over the past century, human inventions such as the internal combustion engine have greatly increased the amount of carbon dioxide and certain other gases being released into the atmosphere. As this shift in composition affects the atmosphere's greenhouse functioning, the result may be global warming: a rise in the earth's temperature.

The Australian physician and activist Helen Caldicott explains the greenhouse effect and discusses the mechanics, probability, and possible impact of global warming in "The Greenhouse Effect." Caldicott argues forcefully for immediate and drastic changes in the way we live, to prevent the potential catastrophe of a warmer earth. In contrast, Dixy Lee Ray—former governor of Washington and chair of the Atomic Energy Commission in the early 1970s—sees no plausible evidence that global warming is under way, much less that human technology is responsible for it. On the contrary, she asserts in "Greenhouse Earth" that technology is our best hope for solving the problem if it should become serious. A more detailed look at scientists' viewpoints and methodology comes from climatologist Stephen H. Schneider in "The Global Warming Debate Heats Up," along with criticism of the media's role in distorting the issue.

British scientist James Lovelock has hypothesized that all life on earth works as a unit to keep the planet's temperature and chemistry suitable for existing plants and animals. Can Gaia—this collective action of earth's living creatures—prevent global warming? Two writers better known for science fiction, Isaac Asimov and Frederick Pohl, consider this possibility and some other proposed remedies in "Gaia and Global Warming." More dramatic potential weapons against global warming—front-line technologies from the field of geoengineering— are described in "Changing the World," from *The Economist* magazine. Finally, writer Bill McKibben examines the implication of such high-tech fixes for life on earth as we know it in "The End of Nature."

HELEN CALDICOTT

The Greenhouse Effect

Australian physician and antinuclear activist Helen Caldicott cofounded the international group Physicians for Social Responsibility, and founded Women's Action for Nuclear Disarmament and International Physicians to Save the Environment. Among her books are *Nuclear Madness: What You Can Do* (1978) and *Missile Envy: The Arms Race and Nuclear War* (1984). She has won numerous international awards and appeared frequently on television and radio as well as in documentary films. In the late 1970s and 1980s Caldicott lived in New England while she taught at Harvard University Medical School and worked with the antinuclear movement. "The Greenhouse Effect" comes from her 1992 book *If You Love This Planet: A Plan to Heal the Earth.* In it she analyzes the global warming problem, vividly depicts its potential impact, and recommends a broad program of changes to avert it.

The earth is heating up, and the chief culprit is a gas called carbon dioxide. Since the late nineteenth century, the content of carbon dioxide (CO_2) in the air has increased by 25 percent. Although this gas makes up less than 1 percent of the earth's atmosphere, it promises to have devastating effects on the global climate over the next twenty-five to fifty years.[1] Carbon dioxide is produced when fossil fuels—coal, oil, and natural gas—burn, when trees burn, and when organic matter decays. We also exhale carbon dioxide as a waste product from our lungs, as do all other animals. Plants, on the other hand, absorb carbon dioxide through their leaves and transpire oxygen into the air.

Carbon dioxide, along with other rare man-made gases, tends to hover in the lower atmosphere, or troposphere, covering the earth like a blanket. This layer of artificial gases behaves rather like glass in a glasshouse. It allows visible white light from the sun to enter and heat up the interior, but the resultant heat or infrared radiation cannot pass back through the glass or blanket of terrestrial gases. Thus the glasshouse and the earth heat up.

In one year, 1988, humankind added 5.66 billion tons of carbon to the atmosphere by the burning of fossil fuels, and another 1 to 2 billion tons by deforestation and the burning of trees. Each ton of carbon produces 3.7 tons of carbon dioxide.[2]

[1]United Nations Environment Program (UNEP), *The Greenhouse Gases* (Nairobi, 1987).
[2]Lester R. Brown et al., *State of the World, 1990: A Worldwatch Institute Report on Progress toward a Sustainable Society* (New York: W. W. Norton, 1990), 18.

But carbon dioxide accounts for only half of the greenhouse effect. Other gases, the so-called trace gases, which are present in minute concentrations, are much more efficient heat trappers.[3] Chlorofluorocarbons (CFCs) are ten to twenty thousand times more efficient than carbon dioxide. Methane is also very efficient (twenty times more effective than carbon dioxide) and is released at the rate of 100 liters per day from the intestine of a single cow. For example, Australia's cows make an annual contribution to global heating equivalent to the burning of thirteen million tons of black coal (about half the coal used in Australia per year). The scientists Ralph Laby and Ruth Ellis, from the Australian Commonwealth Institute and Research Organization, have developed a slow-release capsule that diminishes by 20 percent the production of methane by bacteria in the rumen of cows. (Methane is also a wonderful gas for heating and lighting houses; for example, Laby and Ellis estimated that two cows produce enough methane to heat and light an average house!)[4] Further sources of methane are garbage dumps, rice paddies, and termites. Nitrous oxide is another greenhouse gas, a component of car and power plant exhausts, of chemical nitrogenous fertilizers, and of bacterial action in heated, denuded soil. Nitrous oxide has increased by 19 percent over preindustrial levels and methane by 100 percent.[5] A report from the World Wide Fund for Nature published in August 1991 stated that carbon dioxide emissions from aircraft flying at altitudes of ten to twelve kilometers account for 1.3 percent of the global warming. However, the nitrous oxide that aircraft also emit is an extremely efficient heat trapper at that height and may increase global warming by 5 to 40 percent.[6]

Within fifty years, the "effective carbon dioxide concentration" (CO_2 and trace gases) will probably be twice that of preindustrial levels, raising global temperatures 1.5° to 5.5°C (2.7° to 10°F).[7] Because many scientific variables—heat trapping by clouds, change in radiation over melting ice caps, and so on—are not well understood, this rise in temperature could be as high as 10°C (18°F). Other scientists say the earth could cool several degrees. But all agree that we are in trouble.[8]

Such a rapid change in climatic conditions has never occurred in human history. If global heating were at the lower predicted level, it

[3]Stephen Schneider, "The Changing Climate," *Scientific American*, Sept. 1989, 70–79.

[4]Mike Seccombe, "An Ill Wind That Only Does Cows Good," *Sydney Morning Herald*, July 18, 1989.

[5]Brown et al., *State of the World, 1990*, 17.

[6]"Another Culprit of the Greenhouse Effect: Jet Aircraft," *Sydney Morning Herald*, Aug. 27, 1991.

[7]UNEP, *Greenhouse Gases*; Schneider, "Changing Climate"; Michael Lemonick, "Feeling the Heat," *Time*, Jan. 2, 1989.

[8]Phillip Shabecoff, "Cloudy Days in Study of Warming World Climate," *International Herald Tribune*, Jan. 19, 1989.

would match the 5°C warming associated with the end of the last ice age, eighteen thousand years ago. But this change would take place ten to a hundred times faster.[9] And at present temperatures, a 5°C increase would cause global temperatures to be higher than at any other time during the last two million years.[10]

What will happen to the earth? Let us look at a worst-case scenario. Changes of climate could have devastating consequences in the tropical forests and food-growing areas of the world, causing extinction of many plant and animal species over a few years, in evolutionary terms. Dust bowls could develop in the wheat belt of the United States, creating a situation like that described in *The Grapes of Wrath*, and the productive corn and wheat belt might migrate north into Canada and into the Soviet Union.[11]

Already the futures markets are speculating that productive banana and pineapple plantations will develop in the middle of arid Australia. Cyclones, tidal waves, and floods will almost certainly affect temperate areas of the world, which were previously immune to such catastrophes.[12]

Sea levels will probably rise as the warming oceans expand, and great areas of land will be flooded, particularly during storms. Rivers, lakes, and estuaries will have their courses and boundaries changed forever. This will disturb the hatching habitats of millions of fish.[13]

Because about one-third of the human population lives within 10 sixty kilometers of the sea, millions, or even billions, of people will either be killed by floods or storms or be forced to migrate to higher levels, thereby severely dislocating other urban and rural populations. These refugees will create chaos as they move into established rural areas, towns, and cities. Food production will already have been disrupted by the change in climate, and a redistribution of the scarce remaining resources will probably not happen.[14]

As sea levels rise, beautiful cities, including Venice and Leningrad, will be submerged, and even Westminster Abbey and the houses of Parliament, in London, will be threatened. Many beautiful, exotic Pacific islands will be underwater. Sea levels could rise seven feet (2.2 meters) by the year 2100, according to the U.S. Environmental Protection Agency.[15]

[9]Schneider, "Changing Climate."
[10]Walter H. Corson, ed., *The Global Ecology Handbook: What You Can Do about the Environmental Crisis.* (Boston: Beacon Press, 1990), 232.
[11]Lemonick, "Feeling the Heat."
[12]Ibid.
[13]Ibid.
[14]Corson, ed., *Global Ecology Handbook,* 233.
[15]Ibid., 232.

It is possible that the polar ice caps will melt; alternatively, the Antarctic snow cover might increase in volume as warm air induces a buildup of snow-forming clouds over the South Pole.[16] (Warm air promotes the evaporation of water from the earth's surface, thereby thickening the cloud cover.)

The aquatic food chain will be threatened because the base of the pyramid of the ocean food chain—algae and plankton—will be seriously affected. These ubiquitous single-celled plants are food for primitive life forms and are themselves consumed by more evolved species of fish. Some forms of algae and plankton will be threatened by rising sea temperatures, and many are extremely sensitive to UV light. . . . Therefore, as the temperature rises and as the ozone diminishes,[17] this essential element of the food chain will be jeopardized.

Moreover, plankton and algae, together with trees and plants, are nature's biological traps for elemental carbon from atmospheric carbon dioxide, 41 percent being trapped in sea plants and 59 percent in land plants. Higher concentrations of atmospheric carbon dioxide will promote the growth of algae. But if algae are threatened by global warming and ozone depletion, this hypothetical fertilizer effect will become irrelevant. By increasing the atmospheric concentration of carbon dioxide from man-made sources, we are thus also threatening the survival of trees, plants, algae, and plankton.

Forests, too, are terribly vulnerable to climatic change and ozone 15 destruction. Because temperature changes will be relatively sudden, specific tree species will not have thousands of years to migrate to latitudes better suited to their survival, as they did at the end of the last ice age. When the ice cap slowly retreated northward, the spruce and fir forests moved from the area of the United States into Canada at the rate of one kilometer per year. Although some plants that adapt rapidly will thrive under changed circumstances, most forests will die, and along with them many animal and bird species.[18]

Interestingly, although sudden global warming will kill large numbers of trees, increased carbon dioxide concentrations will actually stimulate the growth of those that remain, because the gas is a plant food during photosynthesis and thus acts as a fertilizer.[19] Therefore, as forests become extinct in the unusually hot climate, some food crops and surviving trees will grow bigger and taller. Unfortunately, many

---

[16]UNEP, *Greenhouse Gases.*

[17]**ozone:** A gas in the stratosphere that screens out most dangerous ultraviolet (UV) radiation. Many atmospheric scientists believe that the earth's protective ozone layer is being depleted primarily as a result of chlorofluorocarbon (CFC) emissions.—ED.

[18]Schneider, "Changing Climate."

[19]UNEP, *Greenhouse Gases.*

"I CAN REMEMBER WHEN EVERYONE WAS SKEPTICAL ABOUT THE GREENHOUSE EFFECT."

weeds are even more responsive to high carbon dioxide levels than crop plants are, and they will almost certainly create adverse competition.[20]

Another factor to consider in this rather dire biological scenario is that faster-growing crops utilize more soil nutrients. Hence more artificial fertilizer will be needed, and, since electricity is required for its production, more carbon dioxide will be added to the air. But nitrogen-containing fertilizers themselves release the greenhouse gas nitrous oxide into the air.[21] In addition, as soil heats, vegetable matter decays faster, releasing more carbon dioxide. These are just a few of the interdependent and variable effects of global warming that are so difficult to calculate.

When forests are destroyed by greenhouse and ozone deforestation, or by chainsaw and bulldozer deforestation, massive quantities of rich topsoil will be lost forever as floods and erosion wash it out to sea. Downstream waterways will overflow their banks as rain pours off the denuded high ground, and when the floods subside, the once deep rivers will be silted up from the eroded topsoil. Large dams designed

[20]Corson, ed., *Global Ecology Handbook,* 233.
[21]UNEP, *Greenhouse Gases;* Schneider, "Changing Climate."

for predictable rainfalls could collapse and drown downstream populations, and associated hydroelectric facilities would then be destroyed.

Decreased rainfall in other parts of the world will reduce stream
runoff. For example, a rise of several degrees Celsius could deplete water levels in the Colorado River, causing severe distress for all communities that depend upon the river for irrigation, gardening, drinking
water, and so forth. The water quality will also suffer, because decreased volumes will not adequately dilute toxic wastes, urban runoff,
and sewage from towns and industry.[22] Until April 1991, when rain
began to fall again in some quantity, California experienced a severe
five-year drought, whose impact was rapidly becoming critical. After
this April rainfall, the California drought continued unabated. That
may be an omen of worse to come.

Cities will be like heat traps. For instance, Washington, D.C., at   20
present suffers one day per year over 38°C and thirty-five days over
32°C (100°F and 90°F). By the year 2050, these days could number
twelve and eighty-five, respectively.[23] In that case, many very young
and many old and infirm persons would die from heat stress, and there
would be a general temptation to turn on air conditioners, which . . .
use CFCs and electricity, whose generation produces more carbon
dioxide. People will thus be in a catch-22 situation—damned if they
do and damned if they don't. . . .

How did the problem of atmospheric degradation become so
alarming, and what are the solutions?

When CFC was first concocted, in 1928, nobody understood the
complexities of atmospheric chemistry, and during subsequent decades
scientists really believed that chlorofluorocarbons were ideal for refrig-
eration, air conditioners, plastic expanders, spray cans, and cleaners for
silicon chips.[24] Industry became so heavily invested in its production
that it now finds it very difficult to cut back, even though the environmental consequences of not doing so will be severe. . . .

In the early years of the Industrial Revolution, no person could
have predicted the atmospheric havoc that the internal-combustion engine and coal-fired plants would wreak. Even during the 1930s and
1940s, when General Motors, Standard Oil, Phillips Petroleum, Fire-
stone Tire and Rubber, and Mack Manufacturing (the big-truck
maker) bought up and destroyed the excellent mass transit systems of
Los Angeles, San Francisco, and most other large U.S. cities in order to

[22]Schneider, "Changing Climate."
[23]UNEP, *Greenhouse Gases.*
[24]UNEP, *Action on Ozone.*

induce total societal dependence on the automobile, global warming was a vague future threat.[25] These companies were subsequently indicted and convicted of violating the Sherman Antitrust Act.

But now that we understand the coming disaster, we are in a position to act. In order to act, we must be willing to face several unpleasant facts.

Fact Number One.   The United States, constituting only 5 percent of the earth's population, is responsible for 25 percent of the world's output of carbon dioxide.[26] It uses 35 percent of the world's transport energy, and an average-size tank of gasoline produces between 300 and 400 pounds of carbon dioxide when burned.[27] Together, the United States and the Soviet Union consume 44 percent of the world's commercial energy.[28]

In China, by contrast, there are 300 million bicycles, and only one person in 74,000 owns a car. Each year three times more bicycles than cars are produced. Domestic bicycle sales in 1987 came to 37 million —more than all the cars bought worldwide.[29] Motor vehicles globally produce one-quarter of the world's carbon dioxide, and in the United States transportation (cars, buses, trains, and trams [streetcars]) produces 30 percent of all the carbon dioxide. Transport consumes about one-third of all the energy consumed globally. The United States also produces 70 percent of the carbon monoxide gas (which leads to deoxygenation of the human blood), 45 percent of the nitrous oxides (which cause acid rain), and 34 percent of the hydrocarbon chemicals (many of which are carcinogenic).[30]

In 1985, there were 500 million motor vehicles in the world, 400 million of them cars. Europeans and North Americans owned one-third of these.[31]

Fact Number Two.   In order to reduce carbon dioxide production, cars must be made extremely fuel efficient, and some computer models and prototype automobiles can indeed achieve 60 to 120 miles per gallon (mpg) by means of lightweight materials and better design.[32] But these techniques are not being employed. In 1987, U.S. car manufacturers

[25]Jonathan Kwitny, "The Great Transportation Conspiracy," *Harper's,* Feb. 1981, 14–21.

[26]"What the U.S. Should Do," *Time,* Jan. 2, 1989, 65.

[27]Jeremy Leggett, ed., *Global Warming: The Greenpeace Report* (New York: Oxford University Press, 1990).

[28]Corson, ed., *Global Ecology Handbook,* 192

[29]Brown et al., *State of the World, 1990,* 120.

[30]Corson, ed., *Global Ecology Handbook,* 192; Leggett, ed., *Global Warming,* 261, 262.

[31]Leggett, ed., *Global Warming,* 269.

[32]Ibid., 289.

dropped most of their research on fuel-efficient cars, and in 1986 the fuel-efficient standard, or minimum mpg, in the States was only 26 mpg.[33] In 1991, it was still only 27.5 mpg, and the Bush administration has resisted any move to increase fuel efficiency in cars.[34] In fact, the president's new energy plan of 1991 barely deals with these issues, and does not deal at all with mass transportation. It is more efficient to transport hundreds of bodies in one train than hundreds of single bodies in hundreds of cars. Furthermore, the construction of sleek state-of-the-art trains would constructively reemploy the one in eight people in California who currently are employed producing weapons of mass destruction.[35] Far more people will work in this wonderful new civilian industry than in the obsolete weapons industry, because the military sector is capital intensive, whereas the civilian sector is labor intensive. The corporation that first accepts this challenge could become the world's leading producer of global mass transit systems and could earn huge profits while saving the planet.

Cars can be fueled with solar energy. In 1990, an international solar car race across Australia was held. The cars achieved the acceptable speed of approximately 60 mph. They were slow to accelerate, but who needs cars that go from 0 to 90 mph in a matter of seconds? Cars can also be fueled with natural gas, which generates less carbon dioxide than gasoline does, and with alcohol. By investing heavily in this form of energy, Brazil has been helped to become somewhat energy independent. In 1988, alcohol provided 62 percent of Brazil's automotive fuel. Although alcohol is relatively expensive, it gives off 63 percent less carbon emission than gasoline. This excellent form of energy production is renewable, and marginal land can be used to grow crops that can be converted into alcohol. The United States already produces twenty million barrels of alcohol by the fermentation of corn. As oil prices climb, alcohol will obviously become a viable fuel alternative.[36]

Cars can also be fueled with hydrogen; the technology is available. One can drink the exhaust of a car powered by hydrogen, because when hydrogen burns it produces pure water. Unfortunately, major U.S. auto companies seem resistant to being inventive and creative. They stick to old, outdated designs and have even resorted to copying the latest Japanese designs—a rather sorry setback for an industry that once led the world in automobile technology. It could overtake the

---

[33]Corson, ed., *Global Ecology Handbook*, 205.
[34]Ibid.
[35]Helen Caldicott, *Missile Envy* (New York: Morrow, 1984), 208.
[36]Brown et al., *State of the World, 1990*, 26.

Japanese industry by manufacturing solar-, hydrogen-, and alcohol-powered cars, while helping to save the planet.

Fact Number Three.   Bicycles use human energy and save global energy. They are clean, efficient, and healthful for human bodies. Roads must give way to bicycle tracks. In China, special bicycle avenues with five or six lanes are separated from motorized traffic and pedestrians.[37] This sort of planning is required by a large percentage of the population of the United States and of the Western world. The arrangement is simple, easy, cheap, and clean. Distant, large-scale supermarkets and shopping malls accessible only by car will become obsolete as people demand small, convenient shops within walking distance of their homes. We can reestablish small community shopping centers, where people meet each other and socialize and where the emphasis is on the community rather than on consumerism. What a healthy, exciting prospect!

Fact Number Four.   Buildings can be made extremely energy efficient. Improved designs for stoves, refrigerators, and electric hot-water heaters can increase energy efficiency by between 5 and 87 percent. The sealing of air leaks in houses can cut annual fuel bills by 30 percent, and double-paned insulated windows greatly reduce energy loss. Superinsulated houses can be heated for one-tenth of the average cost of heating a conventional home. In the United States, 20 percent of the electricity generated is used for lighting, but new fluorescent globes are 75 percent more efficient than conventional globes. Theoretically, then, the country could reduce its electricity usage for lighting to 5 percent of the total.[38] This, together with other conservation measures, would cause the closing down and mothballing of all nuclear reactors in the States, because 20 percent of all the electricity used there is generated by nuclear power.[39]

I lived in the beautiful city of Boston for fourteen years and grew to love the old New England houses. But now that I am more aware of the fate of the earth, I realize that these are totally inappropriate dwellings. They are big, rambling, leaky, and inefficient. The vast quantities of oil required to heat these large volumes of enclosed air through a long Boston winter adds to carbon dioxide greenhouse warming. When these handsome houses were built, in the last century, no one imagined that the earth would someday be in jeopardy. Fuel supplies seemed endless, and the air was relatively clean.

[37]Ibid., 128.
[38]Corson, ed., *Global Ecology Handbook*, 203–4.
[39]Ibid.

Houses of that kind can be made somewhat fuel efficient by the insulation of walls, ceilings, and windows and by the sealing of all leaks. To encourage such reform, the federal government must legislate adequate tax incentives, for in the long run these will provide insurance for our children's future.

Actually, solar buildings are now in an advanced stage of design and 35 development. The need is for legislation that requires all new buildings, residential and office, to be solar designed—with large heat-trapping windows oriented toward the south and with floors made of tiles and cement, which trap the sun's heat during the day, and appropriate window insulation, which retains the heat at night. Solar hot-water panels and solar electricity generation are relatively cheap and state-of-the-art. Firms that manufactured such equipment would make large profits. Householders would benefit because they would become independent of the utilities; they could even sell back electricity to the local utility at off-peak hours. Indeed, some Americans are already vendors of electricity.

Solar technology would then become highly efficient and cheap, and a huge market would open up in the Third World. The industrialized countries could assist billions of people to bypass the fossil-fuel era, so they could generate electricity from solar and wind power and use solar cookers and solar hot-water generators. This is a signal solution to the problem of ongoing global warming. The First World must help the Third World bypass the fossil-fuel era if the earth is to survive.

Attention should also be given to the strange high-rise buildings covered in tinted glass that seem to be in vogue in many U.S. cities. These are not solar buildings. The windows cannot be opened to allow ventilation during the summer, and they must be cooled with air conditioners, which use ozone-destroying CFCs and carbon dioxide–producing electricity. In the winter, heat leaks from the windows like water through a sieve. And these buildings are generally lit up like Christmas trees at night, for no apparent purpose, by energy-inefficient lighting. Dallas, Houston, and Los Angeles boast numerous of these monstrosities, many of which now sit empty and idle, built by speculators who cashed in on the savings and loan scandal. (I used to wonder as I traveled through the United States in the 1980s why the Sun Belt was thriving. Now we know! This prosperity was a by-product of the deregulation of the savings and loan industry by the Reagan administration.)

We all must become acutely conscious of the way we live. Every time we turn on a switch to light a room, power a hair dryer, or toast a piece of bread, we are adding to global warming. We should never have more than one light bulb burning at night in our house unless there are two people in the house in different rooms—then two bulbs. Lights must not be left on overnight in houses or gardens for show, and all lights must be extinguished in office buildings at night.

Clothes dryers are ubiquitous and unnecessary. In Australia, we dry our clothes outside in the sun, hung by pegs from a line. Americans can do the same in the summer, and in the colder climes, like Boston's, clothes can be hung on lines in the cellars in the winter. In some American cities there are laws prohibiting people from hanging clothes on lines outside, on grounds that it is not aesthetically pleasing. This method of drying offers, in fact, an easy and efficient step toward the reduction of atmospheric carbon dioxide and radioactive waste. Clothes dryers use over 10 percent of the electricity generated in the States,[40] a large fraction of that generated by nuclear power. And bear in mind that electrically operated doors, escalators, and elevators all contribute to global warming. . . .

Renewable energy sources (wind, solar, geothermal, and so on) [40] could theoretically provide a total energy output equal to the current global energy consumption. Today these sources already provide approximately 21 percent of the energy consumed worldwide and are freely available to be developed further.[41]

Solar power will soon yield electricity as cheap as coal-fired electricity. In fact, scientists at the U.S. Solar Energy Research Institute estimate that photovoltaic solar systems could supply over half the U.S. electricity within forty to fifty years. This technology will decrease in price as it is mass produced, modified, refined, and made more efficient. Solar water and household heating is already widespread in Australia, Greece, and the Middle East.[42]

Wind power offers an obvious and benign technique that is being used to generate electricity in many countries, including Greece, China, Australia, Israel, Belgium, Italy, Germany, Britain, the United States, and Denmark. Since 1974, fifty thousand wind machines have been built, mainly in California and Denmark. Wind "farms" cover areas of the desert between Los Angeles and Palm Springs, and by the year 2030 wind power could provide 10 percent of the world's energy.[43]

Geothermal power, which taps into the intrinsic heat and lava trapped below the earth's crust, is already being used to good advantage in New Zealand, Iceland, and Hawaii, and there is much potential for its use in

---

[40]Ibid.
[41]Leggett, ed., *Global Warming*, 231.
[42]Ibid., 25.
[43]Ibid., 24, 25.

the United States, Soviet Union, and Central America. Output is increasing by 15 percent per year.[44]

Tidal power utilizes the twice daily changes in sea levels to generate electricity. It is suitable only for certain coastlines, but it certainly offers great possibilities in places where the tides vary twenty to a hundred feet per day. Wave power is another dynamic area awaiting development.

Hydropower has been expanding by 4 percent annually worldwide, 45 and the potential for further expansion is vast.[45] Hydroelectric and geothermal power provides over 21 percent of the world's electricity.[46] Electricity generated at dams and waterfalls crosses borders and can be used in other countries; for instance, New England uses Canadian hydroelectricity. Hydroelectric dams that flood large areas of natural forests are ecologically dangerous, and careful planning is essential before and during their construction.

Cogeneration is a wonderful method for harnessing heat usually wasted in factories. One technique, used extensively in the Soviet Union and in Scandinavia, is to heat water and pipe it to warm whole towns and cities. Another is to use waste steam to drive electricity-generating turbines, to run refrigerators, and to power industrial machinery. An ordinary power plant is 32 percent efficient, but a cogenerator consuming the same amount of fuel is 80 percent efficient.[47]

Conservation can save large quantities of energy. Society must invest in highly efficient light bulbs, refrigerators, stoves, cars, and street lighting. Energy-efficient equipment uses one-third to one-half less energy than does conventional technology. Much of it has already been invented, but monopolistic corporations tend to encourage distribution of inefficient equipment, thus leading to increased electricity consumption. For example, General Electric manufactures not only nuclear reactors but also hair dryers, toasters, stoves, and refrigerators. Is it not therefore in GE's best interests to encourage people to use more electricity with less efficient appliances and to use electric brooms, electric hedge clippers, and electric lawn mowers instead of ones operated by muscle power?

But energy-efficient investments are much cheaper financially and ecologically than the building and operating of coal or nuclear plants. Patents for wonderful energy-saving inventions abound, but most inventors lack the money to develop their product. And corporations seem uninterested in pursuing or financing such inventions.

Not least, utilities hide enormous government subsidies that they

---

[44]World Commission on Environment and Development (WCED), *Our Common Future* (New York: Oxford University Press, 1987), 193.
[45]Ibid., 192.
[46]Corson, ed., *Global Ecology Handbook,* 93.
[47]Ibid., 205; WCED, *Our Common Future,* 200.

receive for fossil fuels and nuclear power. This deception makes renewable energy appear to be more expensive. Because utilities enjoy an almost total monopoly in energy advertising and technologies of energy production, it is very hard to understand and dissect their propaganda. Solar-heating systems and photovoltaic cells endow people with energy self-reliance, but clearly such self-sufficiency is not and will not be seen to be in the best interests of the utilities.

Trees and other plants (biomass) are sources of energy mainly in the 50 developing world. In India, people even burn pats of cow dung for cooking. But inhabitants of these countries often decimate their forests for short-term survival. I have seen Indian women spend a whole day walking to a patch of trees, gather the wood, and walk home for another day in order to cook food for their families. The burning of wood adds to atmospheric carbon dioxide.

Deforestation is leading to desertification in many countries—to creeping deserts and utter destruction of the land. Brazil is even using parts of the Amazon forest to fuel iron ore smelters.[48] So wood is not necessarily a good fuel and needs to be replaced by solar, wind, and other kinds of power. Still, garbage and agricultural wastes can be used to produce methane, an excellent gas for cooking and heating. Biomass supplies 12 percent of the energy worldwide and up to 50 percent in some poor countries.[49]

Industrial efficiency has been shown to have enormous potential. It must be developed on a massive scale, for industry uses 40 to 60 percent of the available energy in the developed countries and 10 to 40 percent in the developing countries.[50]

If all fossil fuels were taxed to avoid climate change, the ecosphere could be brought into a relatively stable equilibrium. In the United States, this tax would raise the price of electricity by 28 percent and that of a gallon of gasoline by seventeen cents, but it would produce $60 billion in revenue, and this money could then be earmarked for alternative-energy facilities and conservation. In India, the tax would raise $17.5 billion.[51] The international community within the United Nations must endorse this tax proposal. According to the Worldwatch Institute report of 1990, in order to stabilize atmospheric greenhouse gas concentrations by 2050, net carbon emissions will need to be reduced by two billion tons per year. So, given a probable global population of eight billion by then, all people will require levels of net carbon emissions similar to India's today, which is only one-eighth of the cur-

[48]Sting and Jean-Pierre Dutilleux, *Jungle Stories: The Fight for the Amazon* (London: Barrie & Jenkins, 1989), 4.
[49]Brown et al., *State of the World, 1990*, 25.
[50]WCED, *Our Common Future*, 199.
[51]Lester R. Brown et al., *State of the World, 1990*, 36.

rent levels in Western Europe. Furthermore, 20 percent of the global carbon tax could be diverted to Third World reforestation, benign energy production, and renewable energy sources.[52]

A 12 percent reduction in global greenhouse gas emissions by 2000 seems an appropriate interim goal if we are to achieve a stabilization of carbon dioxide concentrations by 2050. This means that the United States and the Soviet Union would have to reduce carbon dioxide production by 35 percent over the next ten years. To be fair, though, Kenya and India could actually increase carbon dioxide emissions, because they produce so little at present. If we fail to make these important decisions and if the industrial countries maintain present-day emission levels, the Third World, by emulating the First World, could increase the quantity of carbon dioxide by some 20 to 30 percent by the year 2000 and by 50 to 70 percent by 2010, as its fuel use and population base expand.[53]

I don't think we have any choice in these matters, and the sooner   55
we knuckle down to the task, the sooner we can reassure our children that they will inherit a viable future.

Analyzing Issues and Arguments

1. What value-laden words in Helen Caldicott's opening paragraph show her attitude toward the changes she describes? What neutral words might Caldicott have substituted if she preferred not to reveal her position so early?
2. According to Caldicott, who is likely to be most affected by global warming, and why? Who is likely to be least affected, and why?
3. Do the dramatic predictions in this selection represent a best-case scenario, a worst-case scenario, or a reasonable probability? Where does Caldicott answer this question? How does the language she uses in her predictions clarify or obscure her estimate of their actual likelihood?

Writing about Issues and Arguments

1. Which of Caldicott's recommendations for decreasing the world's output of greenhouse gases do you think are most and least realistic? Write an essay reviewing her proposals, with the goal of developing a workable plan for minimizing global warming.

[52]Ibid., 37.
[53]Ibid., 35, 36.

Developing Nations Top List of Carbon Dioxide Producers

Randy Smith

> The following story ran in newspapers throughout the country on April 18, 1994. Randy Smith is a staff writer for the Washington, D.C., bureau of the Associated Press. He covers the Department of Transportation and the Census Bureau.

Developing nations have become the leading producers of carbon dioxide, surpassing the more industrialized countries, the Energy Department reported yesterday.

As of 1992, the developing nations produced 52 percent of the world's energy-related carbon dioxide emissions, up from 43 percent in 1970, the report said.

Increased use of fossil fuels for transportation and electricity were cited as the primary factors in the growth as the poorer nations move toward modern economies.

At the same time, the twenty-four major developed nations increased their energy-related carbon emissions much more slowly, using more water power and nuclear generation in place of polluting fuels such as coal and oil, the report said.

In the developed nations, overall energy use increased 40 percent between 1970 and 1992, while carbon emissions were up 28 percent.   5

Carbon dioxide increases in the atmosphere have produced concern among many scientists and environmentalists in recent years about the potential greenhouse effect.

Because carbon dioxide absorbs some radiation and reflects other types, they worry that larger amounts of it in the air could trap heat from the sun, causing the earth to overheat.

Overall, world emissions of energy-related carbon dioxide grew from four billion metric tons in 1970 to six billion in 1992. A metric ton is 2,205 pounds.   ▪

Analyzing Issues and Arguments

1. Why, according to the article, are carbon dioxide emissions up in developing nations and down in industrialized ones?
2. What steps do you think Caldicott would recommend for developing countries that are trying to lower their carbon dioxide emissions?

DIXY LEE RAY WITH LOU GUZZO

Greenhouse Earth

Dixy Lee Ray, a marine biologist who championed the nuclear industry, was governor of Washington State from 1977 to 1981. She chaired the Atomic Energy Commission (AEC) under President Richard Nixon from 1973 to 1975; served briefly as assistant secretary of state for Oceans, International Environmental and Scientific Affairs under President Gerald Ford; and was a longtime member of the zoology faculty at the University of Washington. Ray died in 1994, the same year she and Lou Guzzo published *Environmental Overkill.* Guzzo, a former managing editor at the *Seattle Post-Intelligencer,* is a reporter, TV commentator, teacher, and editor who also has written a biography of Ray. Guzzo was a member of the International Atomic Energy Commission from 1973 to 1974, then public affairs director of Ray's bureau at the State Department, and later policy counselor to Governor Ray. "Greenhouse Earth" comes from the first book Ray wrote with Guzzo— *Trashing the Planet: How Science Can Help Us Deal with Acid Rain, Depletion of the Ozone, and Nuclear Waste (Among Other Things)* (1990). In this excerpt Ray explains why drastic action to avert global warming is inappropriate and probably pointless.

The year 1988 ended on a high note of environmental hysteria about global warming, fueled by an unusually hot, dry summer (in the United States). Testifying at a Senate hearing, NASA's James Hansen claimed that the high temperatures presaged the onset of the long debated "greenhouse effect" caused by increased carbon dioxide (CO_2) in the atmosphere.[1]

Forgotten was the harsh winter of 1982, or of 1978, when, for example, barges carrying coal and heating oil froze in river ice and more than two hundred people lost their lives in the cold weather.

Only days after *Time* magazine featured a doomed, overheated earth as its "man of the year" for 1988, Alaska experienced the worst cold in its history. The freezing weather set in on January 12, 1989. Twenty different locations in our most northerly state recorded their lowest-ever temperatures, mainly in the range of −50 to −65 degrees Fahrenheit. At Tanana, near Fairbanks, −75 degrees Fahrenheit was reached. (The all-time low recorded anywhere in Alaska was −80 de-

---

[1] James E. Hansen, 1988, *The Greenhouse Effect: Impacts on Current Global Temperatures and Regional Heat Waves,* testimony given before the Senate Committee on Energy and Natural Resources, typewritten report.

grees in January 1971 at a Prospect Creek pipeline station.) The cold persisted; it did not moderate and begin to move south until the first week of February. Old-timers agreed that no such cold had ever been experienced before, and they expressed amazement that the temperature remained a chilly −16 degrees Fahrenheit along the coast even with an 81-knot wind blowing. This was unheard of, since usually it is coldest when the wind is quiet. In early February, the cold seeped down from Alaska along both sides of the Rocky Mountains, bringing near-record lows both to the Pacific Northwest and throughout the Midwest south to Texas and eventually to the mid-Atlantic and New England states. Proponents of the "greenhouse-is-here-global-warming-has-begun" theory were very quiet during these weeks.

To be fair, even if the projected greenhouse warming should occur, no one would expect it to happen all at once or without intervening cold spells. So let's examine the situation more closely.

Of course, the earth, with its enveloping blanket of atmosphere,   5 constitutes a "greenhouse." This fact has never been at issue. Indeed, were it not for the greenhouse function of air, the earth's surface might be like the moon, bitterly cold (−270 degrees Fahrenheit) at night and unbearably hot (+212 degrees Fahrenheit) during the day. Although the amount of solar energy reaching the moon is essentially the same as that reaching earth, the earth's atmosphere acts like a filter. Of the incoming solar radiation, about 20 percent is absorbed in the atmosphere, about 50 percent reaches and warms the earth's surface, and the rest is reflected back into space. As the earth's surface is warmed up, infrared radiation is emitted. It is the presence of CO_2 (and water vapor, methane, hydrocarbon, and a few other gases) in the atmosphere that absorbs the long wavelength infrared radiation, thereby producing the warming "greenhouse effect." This accounts for a net warming of the earth's atmosphere system of about 55 degrees Fahrenheit. Without this natural greenhouse, it would be difficult to sustain life on this planet.

All the important "greenhouse gases" are produced in nature, as well as by humans. For example, CO_2 comes naturally from the respiration of all living organisms and from decaying vegetation. It is also injected into the atmosphere by volcanoes and forest and grass fires. Carbon dioxide from man-made sources comes primarily from burning fossil fuels for home and building heat, for transportation, and for industrial processes. The amount of CO_2 released into the atmosphere is huge and it is commonly believed that it is divided about evenly between natural and man-made sources.

Hydrocarbons come from growing plants, especially coniferous trees, such as fir and pine, and from various industries. In the transportation arena, hydrocarbons result from incomplete oxidation of gasoline. Both hydrocarbons and methane also enter the atmosphere through the metabolism of cows and other ruminants. It is estimated that American cows produce about 50 million tons of these gases per year—and there is no control technology for such emissions. Methane seeps into the air from swamps, coal mines, and rice paddies; it is often "flared" from oil wells. The largest source of greenhouse gas may well be termites, whose digestive activities are responsible for about 50 billion tons of CO_2 and methane annually. This is ten times more than the present world production of CO_2 from burning fossil fuel. Methane may be oxidized in the atmosphere, leading to an estimated one billion tons of carbon monoxide per year. All in all, the atmosphere is a grand mixture of gases, in a constant state of turbulence, and yet maintained in an overall state of dynamic balance.

But now this balance appears to be disturbed as CO_2 and the other major greenhouse gases are on the rise, increasing their concentration in the air at a rate of about 1 percent per year. CO_2 is responsible for about half of the increase. Analysis of air bubbles trapped in glacial ice and of carbon isotopes in tree rings and ocean sediment cores indicate that CO_2 levels hovered around 260 to 280 parts per million from the end of the last ice age ten thousand years ago) till the mid-nineteenth century, except for an anomalous rise 300 years ago. And these measurements also show that CO_2 concentrations have varied widely (by 20 percent) as the earth has passed through glacial and interglacial periods. While today's 25 percent increase in CO_2 can be accounted for by the burning of fossil fuels, what caused the much greater increases in the prehistoric past?

The present increase has brought the CO_2 level to 340 parts per million, up about 70 parts per million. If we add the greater amounts of methane, hydrocarbons, and so forth, there is now a total of about 407 parts per million of greenhouse gases. This is large enough so that from the greenhouse effect alone we should have experienced a global warming of about two to four degrees Fahrenheit. But this has not happened.

The observed and recorded temperature pattern since 1880 does not fit with the CO_2 greenhouse warming calculations. During the 1880s, there was a period of cooling, followed by a warming trend. The temperature rose by one degree Fahrenheit during 1900 to 1940, then fell from 1940 to 1965, and then began to rise again, increasing by about 0.3 degrees Fahrenheit since 1975. When all these fluctuations are analyzed, it appears unlikely that there has been any overall warming in the last fifty years. And if the temperature measurements taken in the northern hemisphere are corrected for the urban effect—the so-called "heat island" that exists over cities due mainly to the altered albedo[2] from removing vegetation—then it is probable that not only

10

[2]**albedo**   The ratio of light reflected by a planet to that received by it.—ED.

has there been no warming; there may have been a slight cooling. It all depends on whose computer model you choose to believe.

Clearly, there is still something that is not understood about global conditions and about the weather links between the oceans and the atmosphere. Have the experts fully taken into account the role of the sea as a sink or reservoir for CO_2, including the well-known fact that much more CO_2 dissolves in cold water than in warm? Interest in the greenhouse gases and projections of global warming has stimulated greater interest in the role that the oceans play in influencing moderately or even drastically changing global climate. The oceans hold more CO_2 than does the atmosphere, sixty times more. Complex circulation patterns that involve waters of different temperature, together with the activities of marine organisms that deposit carbonate in their skeletons, carry carbon dioxide to the depths of the ocean.

Recall that all the public furor about global warming was triggered in June 1988, when NASA scientist James Hansen testified in the U.S. Senate that the greenhouse effect is changing the climate now! He said he was 99 percent sure of it, and that "1988 would be the warmest year on record, unless there is some remarkable, improbable cooling in the remainder of the year."[3] Well, there was. Almost while Dr. Hansen was testifying, the eastern tropical Pacific Ocean underwent a remarkable, improbable cooling—a sudden drop in temperature of seven degrees. No one knows why. But the phenomenon is not unknown; it is called La Niña to distinguish it from the more commonly occurring El Niño, or warm current, and it has happened nineteen times in the last 102 years.

Dr. Hansen did not consider the possibility of La Niña, because his computer program does not take sea temperatures into account. Yet the oceans cover 73 percent of the earth's surface.

When people, including scientists, talk "global," it is hard to believe that they can ignore 73 percent of the globe, but obviously they sometimes do. It is all the more astonishing to ignore ocean-atmosphere interactions, especially in the Pacific, when it is well established that El Niño has profound and widespread effects on weather patterns and temperatures; does it not follow that La Niña may also? Indeed, some atmospheric scientists credit the severely cold winter of 1988–89 to the earlier temperature drop in the tropical Pacific.

Once again, since the greenhouse gases are increasing, what's keep- 15 ing the earth from warming up? There are a number of possible explanations. Perhaps there is some countervailing phenomenon that hasn't been taken into account; perhaps the oceans exert greater lag than expected and the warming is just postponed; perhaps the sea and its carbonate-depositing inhabitants are a much greater sink than some

[3]"Hansen vs. the World on the Greenhouse Effect," *Science,* Vol. 244, pp. 1041–43, 2 June 1989.

scientists believe; perhaps the increase in CO_2 stimulates more plant growth and removal of more CO_2 than calculated; perhaps there is some other greenhouse gas, like water vapor, that is more important than CO_2; perhaps varying cloud cover provides a greater feedback and self-correcting mechanism than has been taken into account; perhaps. . . . The fact is, there is simply not enough good data on most of these processes to know for sure what is happening in these enormous, turbulent, interlinked, dynamic systems like atmosphere and oceanic circulation. The only thing that can be stated with certainty is that they do affect the weather. So also do forces outside the planet, and in a moment we'll look at the sun in this regard.

First, we must acknowledge that some zealots in the greenhouse issue make much of deforestation, especially in the tropical rainforests, but this topic is marked more by emotion bordering on hysteria than on solid scientific data. Good measurements on CO_2 uptake and oxygen production in tropical rainforests are lacking. Such information could be critical, because we know that in temperate climates mature trees and climax forests add little in the way of photosynthetic activity and consequent CO_2 removal from the atmosphere. Mature trees, like all living things, metabolize more slowly as they grow old. A forest of young, vigorously growing trees will remove five to seven tons more CO_2 per acre per year than old growth.[4] There are plenty of good reasons to preserve old-growth forests, but redressing the CO_2 balance is not one of them. If we are really interested (as we should be) in reducing atmospheric CO_2, we should be vigorously pursuing reforestation and the planting of trees and shrubs, including in urban areas, where local impacts on the atmosphere are greatest.

Reforestation *has* been going on through enlightened forestry practices on private lands by timber companies and as a result of changes in agriculture and land use. In the United States, the average annual wood growth is now more than three times what it was in 1920, and the growing stock has increased 18 percent from 1952 to 1977. Forests in America continue to increase in size, even while supplying a substantial fraction of the world's timber needs.[5]

Finally, it should be kept in mind that when a tree is cut for timber, it will no longer remove CO_2 from the atmosphere, but it won't release its stored carbon either—until or unless it is burned or totally decayed. In the whole deforestation question, it would be interesting to try to determine what effect the deforestation of Europe had on temperature

---

[4]John Rediske, 1970, "Young Forests and Global Oxygen Supply," *Weyerhauser World*, Vol. 2, No. 4, April 1970.

[5]Roger Sedjo and Marion Clausen (Resources for the Future), 1989, "Prices, Trade, and Forest Management," *Econ Update*, Reason Foundation, Vol. 3, No. 8, April 1989.

and climate in the nineteenth century, and, similarly, what the effect was of the earlier deforestation of the Mediterranean area and the Middle East.

If we study history, we find that there is no good or widely accepted explanation for why the earth's temperature and climate were as they were at any particular time in the past, including the recurring ice ages and the intervening warm periods. What caused the "little ice age" of the late seventeenth century and why was it preceded by 800 years of relative warmth? Is all this really due to human activity? What about natural phenomena? Recent studies of major deep-sea currents in the Atlantic Ocean suggest a causative relation to the onset of ice ages.[6] Occasional unusual actions by nature can release great quantities of CO_2 and other greenhouse gases [in]to the atmosphere.

I received my lesson in humility, my respect for the size and vast 20 power of natural forces on May 18, 1980. For those who might not instantly recognize that date, it was a Sunday, a beautiful spring morning when at 8:31 Mount St. Helens erupted with the force of more than 500 atomic bombs. Gases and particulate matter were propelled 80,000 feet, approximately 15 miles, into the stratosphere and deposited above the ozone layer. The eruption continued for nearly twelve hours and more than four billion tons of earth were displaced.[7]

Because Mount St. Helens is relatively accessible, there were many studies conducted and good data are available on the emissions—at least those that occurred after May 18. For the remaining seven months of 1980, Mount St. Helens released 910,000 metric tons of CO_2, 220,000 metric tons of sulfur dioxide, and unknown amounts of aerosols into the atmosphere. Many other gases, including methane, water vapor, carbon monoxide, and a variety of sulfur compounds were also released, and emissions still continue to seep from the crater and from fumaroles and crevices.

Gigantic as it was, Mount St. Helens was not a large volcanic eruption. It was dwarfed by Mount St. Augustine and Mount Redoubt in Alaska in 1976 and 1989 and El Chicon in Mexico in 1982. El Chicon was an exceptionally sulfurous eruption. The violence of its explosion sent more than 100 million tons of sulfur gases high into the stratosphere. Droplets of sulfuric acid formed; these continue to rain down onto the earth's surface. The earth, at present, appears to be in a period of active volcanism, with volcanic eruptions occurring at a rate of about one hundred per year. Most of these are in remote locations, where accurate measurement of the gaseous emissions is not possible, but they

[6]Wallace S. Broecker and George H. Denton, 1990, "What Drives Glacial Cycles," *Scientific American*, Vol. 262, No. 1, p. 48ff.

[7]*The 1980 Eruptions of Mount St. Helens*, Washington Geological Survey Professional Paper 1250, Peter W. Lipman and Donald R. Mullineaux, editors, 1981.

must be considerable. Some estimates from large volcanic eruptions in the past suggest that all of the air polluting materials produced by man since the beginning of the industrial revolution do not begin to equal the quantities of toxic materials, aerosols, and particulates spewed into the air from just three volcanoes: Krakatoa in Indonesia in 1883, Mount Katmai in Alaska in 1912, and Hekla in Iceland in 1947.[8] Despite these prodigious emissions, Krakatoa, for example, produced some chilly winters, spectacular sunsets, and a global temperature drop of 0.3 degrees Centigrade, but no climate change. From written records, we also know that the famous "year without a summer" that followed the eruption of Mount Tambora in 1816 meant that the summer temperature in Hartford, Connecticut, did not exceed 82 degrees Fahrenheit. No doom.

We can conclude from these volcanic events that the atmosphere is enormous and its capacity to absorb and dilute pollutants is also very great. This is no excuse, of course, to pollute the air deliberately, which would be an act of folly. But it does give us some perspective on events.

So far, we have considered only those phenomena that occur on earth that might influence global temperature, weather, and eventually the climate. "Weather" means the relatively short-term fluctuations in temperature, precipitation, winds, cloudiness, and so forth, that shift and change over periods of hours, days, or weeks. Weather patterns may be cyclic, more or less repeating themselves every few years. The "climate," on the other hand, is generally accepted to be the mean of weather changes over a period of about thirty years. Weather may change rapidly, but the climate may remain essentially the same over thousands of years, as it probably has for the last eight thousand years.

Now, what about the effects on weather of extraterrestrial phe-[25] nomena? After all, it is the sun that determines the climate on earth—but the role of the sun, with its ever-shifting solar radiation, is generally ignored as being inconsequential in affecting shorter-term weather patterns. But is this really so?

Consider: the earth shifts in its position relative to the sun. Its orbit is eccentric, varying over a period of 97,000 years. The inclination of the earth's axis shifts with respect to the ecliptic over a cycle of 41,000 years, and the precession of the equinox[es] varies over a period of 21,000 years.[9] How do these shifts affect the amount of solar radiation reaching the earth? Some astronomers believe that at least for the last

---

[8]Margaret Maxey, 1985, *Technology and a Better Environment,* National Council for Environmental Balance, Inc., P.O. Box 7732, Louisville, KY 40207.

[9]**ecliptic:** The sun's apparent annual path through the heavens. **precession of the equinoxes:** The change from year to year (precession) in the two dates when night and day are the same length (equinoxes).—ED.

500,000 to one million years, these phenomena are related to the initiation and dissipation of glacial and interglacial intervals.

Although it may seem to us that the sun is stable and stationary, it is in fact whirling through the Milky Way galaxy, taking its family of planets with it. Activity on the sun itself goes through periods of relative quiet and then erupts into flares and protuberances, sunspots, and gigantic upheavals that "rain" solar material out into space.[10] One recent solar storm was measured at 43,000 miles across. This produced the largest solar flare ever recorded. Some of the increased solar radiation from such storms reaches the earth and disrupts radio communication and television transmission and increases the aurora borealis.[11] Solar activity in the form of storms seen as sunspots has a span of roughly eleven years. It seems that the sunspots whirl clockwise for about eleven years, then reverse and go counterclockwise for another eleven years. This interval is an average and may vary from seven to seventeen years. The controlling mechanism for this reversal is unknown.

Then there is another variable. The sun "flickers"; that is, it dims and brightens slightly over a period of about seventy years. When it dims, the sunspots attain lower maxima. When the sun brightens, the sunspots have higher maxima than "normal." Although this dimming and brightening has been suspected for some time, the first actual measurement of such a "flicker" was made on April 4, 1980, when a satellite measuring solar radiation outside the earth's atmosphere recorded a 0.2 percent drop in radiation. Changes in solar radiation are now routinely measured.

Coupled with the activity of the sun, there is the moon's gravitational force, to which the earth's waters respond daily and in twenty-eight-day cycles of tides. Also, there are twenty-year and sixty-year tidal cycles, as well as longer ones. Moreover, the solid land also responds to the moon's gravitational force, but because we move with the ground, we do not feel it. Recently, a 556-year variation in the moon's orbit around the earth was analyzed; some meteorologists believe that the occasional confluence of all these sun-and-moon cycles may trigger dramatic changes in ocean currents and temperatures. And it is now widely acknowledged that the oceans are a major influence on the climate. There is also a 500-to-600-year cycle in volcanic activity, which appears to be near a peak at the present time.

Let's consider again. Does all this variability in solar activity really 30 have anything to do with weather or climate? No one knows for certain. But studies are continuing, and Dr. John Eddy of the National Center for Atmospheric Research has found an interesting correlation

[10]Doreen Fitzgerald, 1990, *Sun Meets Earth,* Vol. 8, Nos. 1 and 2.
[11]John Douglas et al., 1989, "A Storm from the Sun," *EPRI Journal,* July/August 1989.

between decades of low sunspot activity and cold periods, such as the "little ice age" of the seventeenth century, when there was a virtual absence of sunspot activity between 1645 and 1715, and decades of high sunspot activity with warm temperatures on earth.[12]

Since the sunspot cycle is not perfectly regular and varies considerably, how do scientists determine the extent of sunspot activity that occurred decades or centuries ago? This is a neat piece of scientific detective work that merits a brief explanation. It involves another extraterrestrial phenomenon—cosmic radiation.

Cosmic rays consist of high-energy particles that enter the earth's atmosphere from outer space. These energetic particles split the nuclei of atmospheric gases, giving rise to some of the background radiation to which all living organisms are exposed. Among the fission products are Potassium-40 and Carbon-14, which get into the food chain and are eaten (by animals) or absorbed (by plants), and that is one of the reasons that the bodies of all living organisms are radioactive. Of these two fission products, it is Carbon-14 that is the most interesting for tracing events in the past.

C-14, whose half-life is a relatively short 5,570 years, is being produced continuously in the atmosphere (through interaction with cosmic rays) and is continuously taken up by *living* organisms, but not by dead ones. Therefore, by measuring the amount of C-14 in dead or fossil material, one can infer the date of death. This is called carbon-dating. C-14 is a very good but not perfect clock of history, because the assumption is that the formation of C-14 is not only continuous but also that it occurs at a steady rate. But what Dr. Eddy has determined is that the rate of formation varies with the amount of cosmic radiation, which, in turn, varies with the amount of sunspot activity, because high solar activity also creates more solar wind that can compress the earth's magnetic field. This stronger field is more effective in shielding cosmic rays from the earth's atmosphere, which means that less C-14 is formed during periods of high sunspot activity. Less C-14 equates with warmer periods on earth.

Taking advantage of these phenomena, Dr. Eddy measured the C-14 radioactivity in tree rings in trees that are up to five thousand years old. Keep in mind that the years (rings) of low C-14 equate with years of high solar activity and warm temperatures. Dr. Eddy recorded twelve prolonged periods with either unusually cold or unusually mild winters over the last five thousand years. These correlations between solar activity and weather on earth seem good; his measurements identified the terrible winter of 1683–84, also recorded in the novel *Lorna*

[12]John Eddy, 1982, "C-14 Radioactivity in Tree Rings," *Access to Energy*, Vol. 9, No. 7, March 1982, Box 2298, Boulder, CO 80306.

Doone, when trees in Somerset, England, froze and many exploded from the buildup of internal ice.

If Dr. Eddy's work and theory hold up, the mid–twentieth century 35 was an unusually warm period, and the earth may be set soon to enter a slow return to cooler temperatures. Besides, in geologically recent times, ice ages recur about every eleven thousand to twelve thousand years, and it is now eleven thousand years since the last one. How do all these complications interact with the greenhouse effect? Again, no one really knows. All we can say with confidence is that it is probably more complicated than many environmentalists seem to believe.[13]

When we consider all of the complex geophysical phenomena that might affect the weather and climate on earth, from changes in ocean temperatures and currents, volcanic eruptions, solar storms, and cyclic movements of heavenly bodies, it is clear that none of these is under human control or could be influenced by human activity. Is the "greenhouse effect" and its theoretical enhancement by increases in atmospheric CO_2 from human sources more powerful or capable of overshadowing all other planetary influences? Until the supporters of the man-produced-CO_2-caused-global-warming-theory can explain warm and cold episodes in the past, we should remain skeptical.[14] What caused the 80 parts per million increase in CO_2 during a hundred-year period three hundred years ago and the high peak— many times anything measured since—of 130,000 years ago?

The alteration of the chemical content of the air by *human* production of greenhouse gases, however, is something that man *can* control. And because no one knows what the ultimate consequences of heightened CO_2 might be, it is reasonable and responsible to reduce human contribution wherever possible.

Fortunately, there are ways to accomplish this. For starters, we can phase out the use of fossil fuel for making electricity and turn to the established and proven technology that has no adverse impact on the atmosphere—nuclear power. The energy of the atom now produces 20 percent of the electricity in the United States—more than the total of all electricity used in 1950. The number of nuclear power plants can be increased.[15]

[13]William Nierenberg, Robert Jastrow, and Frederick Seitz, 1989, *Scientific Perspectives on the Greenhouse Problems,* George C. Marshall Institute, 11 DuPont Circle, No. 506, Washington, D.C. 20036.

[14]Richard S. Lindzen, 1990, "Some Coolness Concerning Global Warming," *Journal of the American Meteorology Society,* Vol. 71, No. 3, March 1988.

[15]Support for nuclear power comes not only from the U.S. Council on Energy Awareness— 1988 Midyear Report: *Taking Another Look at Nuclear,* 23 June 1988—but also from Robert M. White, president of the National Academy of Engineering, in testimony before the Senate Committee on Commerce, Science, and Transportation, 13 July 1988, and a news release from Senator Tim Wirth, 18 July 1988.

Second, we can shift to an essentially all-electric economy, utilizing electricity for direct heating of buildings and homes and extending the use of electric processes in industry. With enough electricity available, it can also be used to desalinate sea water and purify the fresh water sources that have become polluted. It can also be used to split water and obtain hydrogen, which has great potential as a clean fuel for transportation. Its "burning" produces only water vapor.

And we can turn, once again, to electric buses and trains, and 40 eventually to electric automobiles.

None of these shifts away from fossil fuels will be easy or fast, but if we have an abundance of electricity from nuclear power plants, it can be done. That would leave fossil fuels for the important synthetics and plastics industries, and for the manufacture of medicinals, pesticides, and fertilizers.

There are also two important caveats; though steps to reduce CO_2 production may be possible for an advanced, highly technical, industrialized society with plenty of electricity, the infrastructure to make use of it, and money to spend, the story is different in the nonindustrialized world. In China, for example, 936 million metric tons of coal were burned in 1987. Who is going to tell China to stop or to change? What alternative do the Chinese have? No matter what we in the Western world do, the amount of CO_2 arising from human use of fossil fuel will not be significantly reduced.[16]

The second caveat is to remember that draconian measures intended to make rapid and large decreases in CO_2 formation won't do much good if they are so costly that they seriously impede the economy and degrade our standard of living without achieving the desired result. Certainly the level of atmospheric CO_2 is increasing, but nothing in all our knowledge of weather and climate guarantees that global warming will inevitably occur. It may, or it may not; the uncertainties are legion. The computer models are too simplistic and include too many estimates and guesses and too little about the role of the hydrosphere, both water vapor and the oceans.[17]

Notwithstanding all this, deliberate, reasoned steps can and should be taken to lower CO_2 emissions; responsible stewardship of the planet demands no less.

Finally, let's suppose that a worst case scenario does develop and 45 that global warming does occur. If the warming caused polar ice to melt, only that on land, as in the Antarctic continent (or the glaciers of

---

[16]Hugh W. Ellsaessar, 1989, "A Review of the Scientific American Article: Managing Planet Earth," *20th Century Energy and Environment,* November/December 1989.

[17]Warren T. Brookes, "The Global Warming Panic," *Forbes,* 25 December 1989.

Reprinted with permission from *The Colorado Springs Gazette Telegraph*.

Greenland), would materially affect global sea level. When ice floats, as in the Arctic Ocean, it already displaces approximately the same amount of water that would result if it were to melt. (There would be some slight thermal expansion.) Whether Arctic ice stays solid or melts would no more cause the sea level to rise than ice cubes melting would cause a full glass of ice water to overflow.

Analysis of sea level data since 1900 indicates that the oceans may be rising at a rate of 10 to 25 centimeters per century (about 0.1 inch per year). The data are very sketchy and uncertain. The sea rise, if it is real, is not uniform and other phenomena, such as land subsidence or upthrust, the building and erosion of beaches by weather, and the variation of inshore currents, could all affect the few measurements that are available.

Some scientists postulate that the west Antarctic ice sheet, which is anchored on bedrock below sea level, could melt and add enough water to raise the world sea level by 6 or 7 meters. This would be disastrous for most coastlines, but if it should happen, it would probably take several hundred years, and there is currently neither observational evidence nor scientific measurements to indicate that it is under way. In

fact, new measurements show that the glaciers in Antarctica are growing, not melting.[18]

Air temperatures in Antarctica average −40 degrees Centigrade. A
five-degree rise in air temperature to −35 degrees Centrigrade is certainly not enough to melt ice. But somewhat warmer sea water (above
one degree Centigrade) might get under the ice sheet and start it slip-
ping into the sea; then it would float and displace an enormous volume
of water, causing the sea level to rise. But this is also a very unlikely
"what if?" with no evidence to support it. . . .

The historian Hans Morgenthau wrote in 1946:

> Two moods determine the attitude of our civilization to the
> social world: confidence in the power of reason, as represented by
> modern science, to solve the social problems of the age, and despair
> at the ever renewed failure of scientific reason to solve them.
>
> The intellectual and moral history of mankind is the story of
> inner insecurity, of the anticipation of impending doom, of
> metaphysical anxieties.

John Maddox, editor of the prestigious British journal *Nature,* has 50
said that "these days there also seems to be an underlying cataclysmic
sense among people. Scientists don't seem to be immune to this."

Well, they ought to be. And we ought to remember that using our
technology will go a long way toward averting those cataclysmic events
and the "doom-is-almost-here" philosophy that seems to have so much
appeal. Scientists owe it to society to show the way to a better life and
an improved environment—through quality technology.

Analyzing Issues and Arguments

1. In "Greenhouse Earth," what central thesis is Dixy Lee Ray trying
   to persuade her readers to accept? What belief is she trying to
   persuade readers to reject? What evidence does she offer to support
   her position?
2. Specifically, what action does Ray advocate taking—or resisting?
   Which of her arguments (if any) do you find most convincing?
   Why?
3. What ideas and recommendations appear in both "Greenhouse

[18]Charles R. Bentley, 1990, "Recent Data from Measurements of Antarctic Glaciers," *Insight,* 15
January 1990.

Earth" and Helen Caldicott's "The Greenhouse Effect" (p. 161)? On what ideas and recommendations do Ray and Caldicott disagree?

Writing about Issues and Arguments

1. Reread Edward O. Wilson's comparison of exemptionalists and environmentalists (p. 1). How do you think Wilson would classify Ray, and why? How do you think he would classify Helen Caldicott, and why? Write an essay using Wilson's concept to compare and contrast the ideas presented in "Greenhouse Earth" and "The Greenhouse Effect."

IN THE NEWS

A Review of *Trashing the Planet*

Daniel B. Botkin

Daniel B. Botkin's review of *Trashing the Planet* ran in the *New York Times Book Review* on September 30, 1990. Botkin is professor of biology and environmental studies at the University of California, Santa Barbara. His most recent books are *Discordant Harmonies: A New Ecology for the Twenty-First Century* (1990) and *Forest Dynamics: An Ecological Model* (1993).

At first glance, *Trashing the Planet* seems to be an exposé of environmental problems, but it is really a call for nuclear power and technology. Dixy Lee Ray, the former governor of Washington, and Lou Guzzo, a Seattle journalist, suggest that the outcry over environmental problems is vastly overblown, that we have little to fear from acid rain, upper atmosphere ozone declines, or pesticides. They dwell on the great advantages of technology and seem bewildered that we have lost faith in its progress. Searching for a culprit, the authors seize on environmentalists, failing to understand that today our society genuinely questions the nineteenth-century idea of progress and is concerned by negative effects of the machine age. Their call for strict, narrow disciplinary approaches ignores the truth that nature knows no such boundaries and that solutions to environmental problems require experts willing to think beyond their own disciplines. The style of *Trashing the Planet* jumps from yellow journalistic attacks on environmentalist enemies to woodenly written textbook discussions of environmental mechanisms. At their best, the authors call for an objective analysis of environmental issues, a perception of environmental problems in terms of acceptable and unacceptable risks, and an honest appraisal of whether there are threshold effects for pollutants. But these positive qualities are lost in emotionalism, rhetoric, and unfair selection of facts. In short, *Trashing the Planet* falls victim to the very tendencies it condemns.   ∎

Revenge of the Wackos

Will Nixon

> Will Nixon's review of Dixy Lee Ray's *Environmental Overkill* was part of a review of three environmental "backlash" books, including Rush Limbaugh's *The Way Things Ought to Be* and Ronald Bailey's *Eco-Scam: The False Prophets of Ecological Apocalypse* (see p. 231). Entitled "Revenge of the Wackos," the review ran in the November/December 1993 issue of *E: The Environmental Magazine,* where Nixon is associate editor.

Let me confess, before anyone complains about the smell of bias rising from this review, that I am indeed one of Rush Limbaugh's "long-haired maggot-infested FM-type environmentalist wackos." I've been known to birdwatch before breakfast, eat camping food at home, and wear a hemp baseball hat to protest chemical cotton. We're a peaceful bunch, my maggots and I, so we were shocked to open Limbaugh's monumental best-seller, *The Way Things Ought to Be,* to read that we want "to roll us back, maybe not to the Stone Age, but at least to the horse-and-buggy era." I'd quote further, but my mastodon is now eating his book.

Green-bashing has become a popular conservative sport. . . .

Dixy Lee Ray is the queen bee of green-bashing. Limbaugh blesses her new book, *Environmental Overkill,* with a cover blurb: "A way must be found to get this book into the hands of as many Americans as possible." My maggots and I would suggest theft, except that Ray's enthusiasm for radiation might set off the store alarms. ("For those who do not like radioactivity, the earth is no place to live," she writes in an earlier book, *Trashing the Planet.*) Ray had a colorful career before she took up green-bashing, serving as a chairman of the Atomic Energy Commission and as a governor of Washington State. Progressives mostly remember her dogs, which she named after *Seattle Times* reporters and made her staffers walk, but Limbaugh treats her as an oracle of science. She sprays the page with numbers and quotes from Ph.Ds, dedicates *Environmental Overkill* to "factual information about basic science," and writes with overbearing confidence. "Whatever happened to common sense?" she asks repeatedly.

What really drives Ray, though, is her Pavlovian need to disprove almost everything that environmentalists say. Dixy World is the photo negative of Mother Gaia. Acid rain is "manna from heaven," she writes, loaded with nitrogen and sulfur, "nutrients, essential for plant growth." Wetlands are villains, breeding grounds for mosquitoes that carry malaria, encephalitis, yellow fever, and River Blindness. So it goes, as she flip-flops every issue of our day. The Northern Spotted Owl lives in forty-year-old trees; the toxic wastes buried at Love Canal didn't even cause one common cold; and a thinner ozone layer may be good for people, especially the elderly, since increased ultraviolet radiation could strengthen their bones.

My maggots and I enjoyed our visit to Dixy World, until a reality probe   5
landed from *Science* magazine. For all of her protestations to the contrary, Ray quotes outsider scientists rather than those in the mainstream. *Science* dug into her theory that volcanoes blow much bigger holes in the ozone layer than do human chemicals, an idea which delights Limbaugh, and found that much of her information comes from a source funded by supporters of Lyndon LaRouche, a jailbird who keeps running for president with plans to colonize Mars. She goofed, too, in writing that Mount St. Augustine, which blew up in Alaska in 1976, spewed 570 times as much chlorine into the atmosphere as CFCs did that year. The U.S. Geological Survey speculated that a volcanic eruption 700,000 years ago released that much gas, based on its measurements of the much smaller Mount St. Augustine blast, which belched only a fourth as much chlorine as civilization did in 1976. . . .   ▪

Analyzing Issues and Arguments

1. On what grounds do both Daniel B. Botkin and Will Nixon object to the style and substance of Dixy Lee Ray's writings?
2. What do you think Nixon's own writing style reveals about his assumptions regarding his audience? What similarities and differences can you identify between his rhetorical approach and Botkin's?

STEPHEN H. SCHNEIDER

The Global Warming Debate Heats Up

Stephen H. Schneider is a leading international climatologist and environmental policy analyst. A professor of biological sciences at Stanford University, he is also affiliated with the Climate and Global Dynamics Division of the National Center for Atmospheric Research in Boulder, Colorado. Schneider has published more than one hundred papers and numerous books on the climate and its complex relationships with the earth and human beings. For the past twenty years he has been particularly interested in the public policy implications of still uncertain climatic forecasts. James Lovelock (see p. 158) called *The Coevolution of Climate and Life* (1984), which Schneider coauthored with Randi Londer, "inspiring and most important." The following excerpt comes from the 1990 epilogue to Schneider's 1989 book *Global Warming: Are We Entering the Greenhouse Century?* In it he explains the consensus among scientists about global warming—and the media sensationalism that he feels has obscured the facts.

Critics maintain four principal objections to the likelihood of global warming. First, the scientific basis for projecting future climate change is so uncertain that no responsible scientists would dare propose immediate policy responses. Second, those who suggest that a hundred years or more of unprecedented climate change (what I have called the Greenhouse Century) is being built into the future are just "environmental activists" whose ideological agenda aims to destroy the free market system. On the other hand, those who argue that there are unlikely to be any significant effects are, by contrast, thoughtful senior scientists protecting the public's interests. Third, decade-to-decade temperature changes over the past one hundred years aren't consistent with climate model predictions of the effects of increasing greenhouse gases; thus the model projections are probably exaggerated. And fourth, it's too expensive to do anything about global warming anyway. The only thing to do now is wait and see what happens—after all, the changes probably won't be great and may be beneficial even if they occur. So say the most strident critics.

The debate became so intense that in 1990 the U.S. National Academy of Sciences invited the principal scientific opponents of activism on global warming to debate the scientific "establishment" that has consistently reaffirmed its confidence in its own 1.5°C to 4.5°C

warming estimates for the middle of the next century. President Bush's Chief of Staff, John Sununu, cited these oppositionist critics to justify a go-slow approach to joining international efforts to regulate emissions of atmospheric pollutants that have the potential to cause unprecedented climate change in the twenty-first century. As long as the United States refuses to limit its emissions, Great Britain, France, Canada, Japan, and other nations are also unlikely to act. Thus, the U.S. refusal to agree to specific curbs on some of its emissions is having a major impact on the shape of the Greenhouse Century.

The debate has strayed far from reason and civility on occasion. *Forbes* magazine, for example, placed an ad on the back page of the *New York Times* (February 7, 1990), praising itself for courageous journalism in debunking global warming as "Hype Not Heat" and belittling the issue with the headline "No Guts, No Story." "Global warming effects," *Forbes* said, "would be at worst minimal." Editorial cartoons in support of warming controls advocates escalated the media circus. One showed Sununu as a devil whispering in the president's right ear, "To hell with the future, let's go for short-term profit." Bush is flicking an angel, William Reilly, the Environmental Protection

Agency administrator, off his left ear as Reilly reminds him of his campaign promise to be the "Environmental President." When debate degenerates to such inanity, it's no wonder the public and most politicians are confused about what the real problem is, let alone what to do about it. . . .

Typical projections of global warming possibilities (see the graph below) into the twenty-first century have been drawn by a group of scientists convened by the International Council of Scientific Unions. They show warming from a moderate half degree Celsius (.9°F) up to a catastrophic 5°C (9°F) or greater before the end of the next century. I do not hesitate to call the latter figure catastrophic because it is the magnitude of warming that occurred between about fifteen thousand and five thousand years ago: from the end of the last ice age to our present interglacial epoch. It took nature some five thousand to ten thousand years to accomplish that warming, which was accompanied by an approximately 100-meter (330-foot) rise in sea level, long distance migration of forest species, radically altered habitats, extinction and evolution of species, and other major environmental changes.

Critics of immediate policy responses to global warming are quick   5

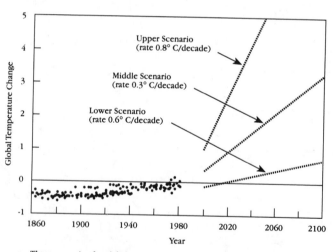

Three scenarios for global temperature change to the year 2100 derived from combining uncertainties in future trace greenhouse gas projections with uncertainties of modeling the climactic response to those projections. Sustained global temperature changes beyond 2° (3.6° F) would be unprecedented during the era of human civilization. The middle to upper range represents climactic change at a pace ten to one hundred times faster than typical long-term natural average rates of change. [Source: J. Jäger, April 1988. Developing Policies for Responding to Climactic Change, A Summary of the Discussions and Recommendations of the Workshops Held in Villach 28 September to 2 October 1987.

to point out the uncertainties that could reduce the average projections of climate models (such as the middle line on the graph). Indeed, most climate modelers include similar caveats in their papers. . . .

The public policy dilemma is how to respond in the absence of conclusive evidence of the effects of global warming. It is my opinion that the scientific community will not be able to provide definitive information over the next decade or so about the precise timing and magnitude of century-long climate changes, especially if research efforts remain at current levels. Policy makers must decide how much information is "enough" to act on and what measures to take to deal with the plausible range of environmental changes. Unfortunately, the probability of such changes cannot be precisely estimated by analytical methods. Rather, we must rely on the intuition of experts, which is why obfuscating media debate impedes policy development.

Fortunately, making intuitive scientific judgments is the purpose of such deliberative bodies as the National Research Council of the U.S. National Academy of Sciences (NAS) and the International Council of Scientific Unions. NAS, for example, regularly convenes a range of experts to estimate the probabilities of various scenarios of change. The deliberations of these panels are removed from the cacophony of media debates that typically highlight only the extreme opposite positions. Half a dozen such assessments[1] over the past ten years have all reaffirmed the plausibility of unprecedented climate change building into the next fifty to a hundred years. In 1990 a United Nations–sponsored group of several hundred international scientists, the Intergovernmental Panel on Climate Change (IPCC), also reaffirmed that plausibility.[2] . . .

One . . . critic, Richard Lindzen, a meteorologist at the Massachusetts Institute of Technology, is himself a member of the National Academy. . . . [In 1989 he suggested] that his intuitive understanding of how the atmosphere worked led him to believe that its "response to doubling of carbon dioxide may readily be one-eighth to one-fourth — or even less—of what is suggested" by the National Research Council consensus of 1.5°C to 4.5°C warming if CO_2 doubled. Lindzen based this "one-eighth to one-fourth" statement upon his intuitive scientific

---

[1]National Research Council, *Carbon Dioxide and Climate: A Scientific Assessment* (Washington, D.C.: National Academy Press, 1979): 11 pp; National Research Council, *Changing Climate: Report of the Carbon Dioxide Assessment Committee* (Washington D.C.: National Academy Press, 1983): 496 pp; National Academy of Sciences, *Current Issues in Atmospheric Change* (Washington D.C.: National Academy Press, 1987): 39 pp., are examples of National Academy reports in which the well-traveled 1.5°C–4.5°C warming range is cited. A current study by the National Research Council's Committee on Science, Engineering, and Public Policy is likely to reaffirm that range, in full awareness of the current debate.

[2]Intergovernmental Panel on Climate Change (IPCC), *Scientific Assessment of Climate Change*, 2nd Draft, March 1990 (Geneva: World Meteorological Organization).

judgment and offered no calculations in the peer-reviewed literature to back it up. Nevertheless, opinion page articles proliferated following Lindzen's statements, and my telephone was busy with reporters and others seeking my response to his assertions that global warming was a vastly overblown environmental scare.

Finally, the December 25, 1989, issue of *Forbes* magazine featured an article whose scientific objectivity was emblazoned colorfully on the cover: "Global Warming Panic: A Classical Case of Overreaction."[3] Excerpts appeared in newspaper opinion pages for weeks following. The piece was by Warren Brookes, an economic journalist who combines sharply worded anti–global warming scientific and policy opinions with *ad hominem* attacks. It's not surprising that such stuff is written, but it is surprising to me that it appears on the opinion pages of respectable newspapers without any attempt to put this nonscientist's scientific arguments in the perspective of the broad consensus. What newspapers tend to do for "balance" is print the contrary views of comparably extreme advocates of radical environmental policies or *laissez-faire* economics. The result is increased confusion and further loss of objectivity and perspective. . . .

. . . Because of public doubt aroused by the *Forbes* story and other 10 commentaries, the National Academy of Sciences and National Academy of Engineering organized debates to inform their most recently convened panel of the critics' views. Lindzen and others were present at the first debate, along with the "establishment scientists": James Hansen, director of NASA's Goddard Institute for Space Studies; V. Ramanathan, a climate expert from the University of Chicago; and Jerry Mahlman, director of the National Oceanic and Atmospheric Administration's Geophysical Fluid Dynamics Laboratory in Princeton. Also attending was my NCAR colleague, Kevin Trenberth, frequently cited as a critic of global temperature trend data.

Trenberth started the discussion, showing how difficult it is to estimate the world's average surface temperature. He noted that ocean temperatures inferred from ships' records in the pre–1900s period were problematic, since they were obtained from thermometers placed in buckets dropped over the side of the boat. Some buckets were made of leather, some of wood; some measurements were taken on the windward side, some to the leeward side of the ship, all of which would affect the readings. He also showed that the fraction of the oceans covered by ship tracks before 1900 was 10 percent to 20 percent at best. One of the Academy panel members asked him if he felt there was any utility at all in the ocean temperature data before 1900 for the purpose of global trend analysis. "Not much," he said. In fact, he commented,

[3]W. T. Brookes, "The Global Warming Panic," *Forbes* (25 December 1989): 96–102.

the corrections due to faulty measurement techniques are typically larger than the inferred climatic trends, which is why no one pays serious attention to them.

Nevertheless, Brookes, Lindzen, and other critics have prominently cited M.I.T. meteorologist Reginald Newell's study suggesting that ocean temperatures were as warm in the 1850s as in the 1950s; thus they argue that no global warming has taken place over the past 150 years. But as noted by Trenberth, pre-1890 thermometer data are not usually regarded as credible in scientific assessments of global trends; coverage is not global and the measurements themselves are unreliable. These reservations did not stand out in the critics' citation of Newell's analysis.

I asked all the assembled scientists at this Academy debate my favorite polling question: "What is your estimate of the probability that the next century will see a global warming of 2°C (3.6°F) or more?" All the atmospheric scientists present, including Lindzen, agreed that there would be warming. He, however, felt the most likely extent of warming was between 0.5°C to 1°C rather than 2°C to 4°C as in typical Academy assessments—and the IPCC estimate. Atmospheric scientists Hansen, Mahlman, Trenberth, and Ramanathan all agreed that 2°C was certainly a reasonable number for the twenty-first century. They assigned the occurrence of a 2°C warming a probability between 60 percent and 90 to 95 percent. Lindzen was the only exception; his probability for 2°C warming was 25 percent—the lowest estimate I've yet heard from any knowledgeable atmospheric scientist. Indeed, several people in the audience—aware of his assertions that global warming is likely to be "one-eighth to one-fourth" of what the Academy presently estimates—expressed surprise to hear that his estimate of the probability of unprecedented warming in the next century differs from mine by less than a factor of 2.5 (25 percent for him versus 60 percent for me). One science writer observing the Academy debate for a major newspaper said to me later, "This 'great debate' is a phony; you guys really disagree scientifically much less fundamentally than most people think." I was glad he discovered it. . . .

Scientists share responsibility with the media for often failing to communicate complex issues clearly to the public. What the general public, as well as politicians and bureaucrats, do not recognize is that most scientists spend their time arguing about what they don't know. Scientists generally consider discussions of accepted ideas boring and a waste of time. This is because the scientific method operates by constant questioning, particularly of issues not yet well substantiated. . . .

We scientists simply have to spend more time differentiating ac- 15 cepted information from what is reliably believed to be true and, most important, from what is highly speculative. The public version of the global warming debate rarely separates those components clearly, thereby leaving the false impression that the scientific community over-all is in intellectual disarray, when, in fact, the IPCC and the National Research Council's consensus of 1.5° to 4.5°C warming in the next century still reflects the best estimate of a wide range of knowledgeable scientists. . . .

. . . Another criticism of global warming projections has been the imperfect match between the warming of the earth and the smooth in-crease in greenhouse gases over the past hundred years. . . . It has been alleged that since most warming in the twentieth century took place up to the 1940s, followed by a cooling at the time the global greenhouse gases were increasing at their fastest, the decade-by-decade temperature trends in the twentieth century cannot therefore be attributed to greenhouse gas build-up.

At first reading that sounds like a valid criticism; but there are sev-eral flaws in the argument. First, nature always fluctuates. Several tenths of a degree Celsius warmings and coolings over decades are part of the natural record and, indeed, are normal. Scientists call these fluctuations "climatic noise." These are not predictable as far as anyone can tell, since they appear to be caused largely by the internal redistribution of energy among the principal reservoirs: the atmosphere, oceans, ice, and land surfaces. Therefore, natural fluctuations could partially explain the sharp warming up to the 1940s, the Northern Hemisphere's cooling to 1975, and possibly even the spectacularly rapid rewarming of the 1980s —the warmest decade in the hundred-year instrumental record. Sec-ondly, we do not know precisely what other potential climatic forcings (that is, processes that could force the climate to change) have been do-ing over the past hundred years. These include energy output from the sun, atmospheric particles from the volcanic eruptions, or particles generated by human activities—or as University of Wisconsin clima-tologist Reid Bryson likes to put it, the "human volcano."

This "forcings" problem is akin to a criminal investigation in which the whereabouts of only one suspect is known and the activities of the other possible suspects were not carefully observed. In this case, the "crime" is the hundred-year 0.5°C (0.9°F) warming trend and the leading "suspect" is the known greenhouse gas increase. Unfortunately, since we do not have quantitatively accurate ways of knowing precisely what the other potential forcings may have been (that is, the un-watched "other suspects"), we can't rule out some possible role for them. . . .

Fortunately, we are now measuring the sun, volcanos, and pollution-generated particles, and can thus account better for their effects. In other words, we finally are checking up on the "other suspects." Thus, as greenhouse gases continue to build up in the future, if greenhouse warming does not take place at roughly the predicted rate during the

1990s and into the twenty-first century, then indeed it will be possible to argue on the basis of some direct evidence that the effect predicted by today's models is off base. Personally, I'll be surprised if there is a major error that overrides the 1.5°C to 4.5°C warming projections.

Let me next address the final, and perhaps the most important, criticism made against action to slow global warming; that immediate policy steps to cut CO_2 emissions are too expensive. The *Forbes* newspaper ad suggests, for example, that if we cut CO_2 emissions the United States will be bankrupt and the Third World impoverished. Indeed, . . . there is substantial Third World opposition to the prospect that they may be deprived of their own industrial revolutions, and of the economic growth experienced in the Victorian period by the then-developing countries using cheap and dirty coal. Since developing Third World countries such as India and China have abundant coal supplies, they would like to use them as low-cost means to industrialization. In 1990, however, these countries have between them some two billion people, whereas in the nineteenth century the entire world didn't have two billion people. The global impact of the developing countries' use of coal to produce even a quarter of our current industrial standard of living would be greater than was ours. Needless to say, such arguments are not met sympathetically in China or India.

It is sensible, I believe, to argue that developing countries need not repeat the Western experience of industrialization with smog-choked cities, acid rain, and inefficient power production, given that modern technology has many better solutions. Unfortunately, developing countries typically respond that high-tech, efficient machinery is more expensive than the traditional options available to them. This dilemma makes obvious the need for a bargain. Countries with technology and capital must provide resources to developing countries, which in return must keep population growth under control and work toward industrial development with the lowest polluting, most efficient technologies, even if they cost more initially.

There have been international efforts afoot to draft an agreement requiring the developed nations to decrease their carbon dioxide emissions by, say, 20 percent by the year 2000, and to cut the projected emissions growth rates in developing countries. This has been strongly opposed by the United States, echoed by Japan, the United Kingdom, the U.S.S.R., and some other countries. The Japanese are unhappy since they're already twice as energy efficient as the United States. They claim it would cost them much more to cut carbon dioxide by 20 percent than the United States, since our very inefficiency gives us more opportunity to cut cheaply. . . .

. . . Supposing each developed country had to reduce its CO_2 impact on the world by something equivalent to 20 percent of its present production. Let's say, continuing the Japanese example, that their quota is to cut 100 million tons of CO_2 annually. Why not structure an international agreement so that the Japanese need to be responsible either for reducing 100 million tons of CO_2 from their own industries, or else paying to cut 150 million tons in another country (or some combination of both)? The obvious candidate is China, since Japanese investment in China for efficient energy production would both reduce acid rain over Japan as well as global CO_2 buildup. It is likely to be much cheaper per unit of CO_2 saved for the Japanese to improve Chinese energy efficiency, since China is starting out so inefficient, than for Japan to improve its own efficiency. At the same time the Chinese would receive extra development assistance, the Japanese would get less acid rain and could buy out of their emissions reduction quota without having to cut emissions at home. Moreover, the Japanese would be creating friendship and markets for their products in the future, whereas the Chinese would be getting more efficient machines with lower long-term operating costs, thereby improving their economy and competitive posture into the twenty-first century. In other words, everybody wins. But first, we need a world emissions agreement that provides incentives for such bargaining and trading to take place. That agreement is what the United States, the United Kingdom, the U.S.S.R., and Japan were balking at in 1989.

Other similar ideas include issuing "tradeable (or leaseable) permits," giving everyone in the world the right to emit a certain amount of CO_2 or some other greenhouse gas.[4] These permits could be traded for cash, food, energy-efficient products, etc. As of the signing of the global agreement, all nations would have equal per capita CO_2 emissions rights. That implies a certain amount of total national emissions. In the future a country could sell or trade these rights or exercise them for development, or increase their population and thereby limit their future emissions per capita. In other words, a fixed per capita emissions right that goes into effect at the signing date would dramatically reduce Third World suspicions that they were being singled out to bear the immediate burden of emission controls.

Critics of emissions reductions cite the supposed annual costs of 25 global warming reduction at tens of billions of dollars—too much to be worth the benefits of climate change abatement. But they often neglect the additional non-greenhouse-effect benefits of emissions reductions: reduced acid rain; reduced air pollution; reduced balance of payments deficits; and lower long-term operating costs of efficient equipment, which reduces the energy costs of manufactured products and enhances competitiveness. Critics who simply cite the potential capital costs of

[4]M. Grubb, "The Greenhouse Effect: Negotiating Targets," Energy and Environmental Program (London: Royal Institute of International Affairs, 1989): 56 pp.

CO_2 reduction write newspaper stories about how many billions or trillions it will cost and scare people away from action. But they often present a very unbalanced view of the distribution of benefits that come with greenhouse gas abatement. Unfortunately, it is very difficult to communicate these benefits in bumper sticker length headlines or in sound bites on the evening news, which is often all the time this complicated story gets. . . .

In summary, then, the greenhouse effect, the heat trapping properties of the atmosphere and its gases and particles, is well understood and well validated as a scientific principle. Indeed, it is as good a theory as there is in the atmospheric sciences. . . .

It is well known that the 25 percent increase in CO_2 documented since the industrial revolution, the 100 percent increase in methane since the industrial revolution, and the introduction of man-made chemicals such as chlorofluorocarbons (also responsible for stratospheric ozone depletion) since the 1950s should have trapped about two extra watts of radiant energy over every square meter of earth. That much is accepted by most climatological specialists. Less well accepted, however, is how to translate those two watts of heat into "x" degrees of surface temperature change, since this involves assumptions about how that heat will be distributed among surface temperature rises, evaporation increases, cloudiness changes, ice changes, and so forth. The factor of two to three uncertainty in global temperature rise projections cited in the National Research Council's reports reflects a legitimate estimate of uncertainty held by most in the scientific community. . . . Finally, . . . predicting detailed regional distribution of climatic anomalies—that is, where and when it will be wetter and drier, whether floods will occur in the spring in California or forest fires in Siberia in August—is highly speculative, although plausible scenarios can be given.

While [computer] climatic models are far from fully verified for future simulations, the present seasonal and ancient climatic simulations, along with satellite observations of atmospheric heat trapping, are strong evidence that state-of-the-art climatic models already have considerable predictive skills. An awareness of what models are and what they can and can't do is probably the best we can ask of the public and its representatives. Then the tough policy problem is how to apply society's values about risk taking in choosing to face the future, given the possible outcomes that climatic models foretell.

The global warming debate takes in both science and politics. But it is essential for the public to understand that disagreements over what to do about the prospect of global warming (a political value issue) are far greater than over the approximate probability that unprecedented climate change is being built into a Greenhouse Century (a scientific debate). . . . The more we debate and the longer we delay slowing down the greenhouse gas emissions, the greater the magnitude of climatic change that we and the rest of life on earth will have to cope with. We are still marching relentlessly into the Greenhouse Century.

Analyzing Issues and Arguments

1. What is Stephen H. Schneider's position on global warming? What information does he evidently expect will do the most to convince readers that his position is valid?
2. Whom does Schneider blame for confusion about global warming? What recommendations does he make to alleviate that confusion?
3. In paragraph 1, Schneider lists the four main objections made by those who reject calls for urgent action against global warming. In what passages does Dixy Lee Ray (p. 176) express these four objections? What additional objections (if any) does Ray present?

Writing about Issues and Arguments

Look at the "critic's . . . four principal objections" that Schneider lists in paragraph 1. Write a short essay in which you use information in "The Global Warming Debate Heats Up" to rebut each of these objections (without going into detail about scientific specifics).

IN THE NEWS

Labs Rely on Computer Models to Predict Changes in Climate

Frank Edward Allen

> The following article ran in the *Wall Street Journal* on June 3, 1992. Frank Edward Allen held many positions at the *Journal*, including environment editor and news editor. In 1994 he was named dean of the journalism school at the University of Montana, Missoula.

If atmospheric carbon dioxide were to double in the next half century or so, how much warmer would the world get?

History offers a lot of clues, but hardly any clear-cut guidance. Nor is it possible to recreate the globe's climate physically in a laboratory. So, in their search for answers, scientists who study the environment's future must rely on mathematical models fed to supercomputers.

Some of the most sophisticated models have been developed at the National Oceanic and Atmospheric Administration's Geophysical Fluid Dynamics Laboratory at Princeton University, the National Aeronautics and Space Administration's Goddard Institute for Space Studies in New York, the National Center for Atmospheric Research in Boulder, Colorado, and the Hadley Center in England.

Modelers use complex equations and mathematical expressions to simulate the interaction of many factors—energy from the sun, composition of the atmosphere, ocean currents, land masses, even basic laws of physics such as the ideal gas laws and the conservation of mass, momentum, and energy. Using the simulations, the huge computers crank out calculations of temperature, pressure, wind speed, humidity, soil moisture, and other variables. They do that by chopping the globe into grid sections and entering data collected at specific geographic locations.

The models used by the most advanced laboratories are called global circu- 5 lation models, or GCMs, which simulate the world's current climate and project the future. In GCMs, the atmosphere is represented as a three-dimensional grid with average horizontal spacing of several hundred kilometers and average vertical spacing of several kilometers. The computers calculate climate only at the intersections of the grid lines. At peak production times, the labs can make nearly a billion computations a second. But despite efforts to simplify, the calculating of just one year in the future can take many hours.

In the late 1980s, a number of labs performed GCMs that reached a similar conclusion: A doubling of carbon dioxide (or an equivalent increase in other gases) would probably warm the earth's surface by an average of about 3 to 5.5 degrees Centigrade. Such an increase, scientists say, would roughly match the warming since the peak of the last ice age, which was some eighteen thousand years ago. But under current conditions, the warming could take effect ten to a hundred times faster.

Given the potential dangers, scientists face increasing pressure to churn out new projections. But they're held back by the shortfall of computing power and by shortcomings that limit the reliability of the models' forecasts.

Precipitation, for example, can occur in small areas—a few square kilometers or less. The same is true for atmospheric turbulence and cloud formation. None of these factors can be simulated directly, so modelers have to express them through "parameters" that can be plugged into the model's crude scale. In this way, small-scale phenomena get lumped together.

Similarly, models of cloud cover have limited reliability. As clouds reflect sunlight back to outer space, they help cool the climate. But they also absorb infrared radiation that bounces up from the earth, which contributes to warming. Which of these effects dominates can depend on the clouds' brightness, size, and height. Satellite measurements show that clouds currently have a net cooling effect: The earth as a whole would be much warmer with cloudless skies. But most computer models don't take all of the variables about clouds into account.

The oceans also exert powerful effects on the climate. They slow any in- 10 crease in global temperature while they themselves are warming. The magnitude of this effect depends on ocean circulation. But the circulation itself may change as the ocean warms.

Jerry Mahlman, director of the NOAA lab at Princeton, acknowledges a further weakness of the current models: their limited ability to project how effects of clouds and oceans will change as the volume of greenhouse gases changes. "We don't know if our best guesses right now are on the high side or the low side of the real number," he says.

Greater precision is coming. Most leading labs now use an eight-processor system called the YM-P, made by Cray Research Inc. Cray recently introduced its C-90 system, which uses sixteen processors and much faster computer chips, increasing overall power about threefold. In a decade or less, labs expect far more powerful, "massively parallel" systems to be available. At peak speeds, they are described as being able to perform as many as a trillion operations a second. This next generation of equipment would be about a thousand times faster than the Cray YM-Ps, at about ten times the cost.

The precision of the analysis and the forecasting also would improve if the earth's surface could be carved up into much smaller areas. That can't be done currently, because averaging temperatures over smaller distances costs the forecasters heavily in computing time. By one lab's estimate, computations take about eight times as long if forecasts are averaged over 250-mile areas instead of 500-mile zones. Accordingly, a single 100-year forecast might take about four months when the areas are 500 miles across. Reduced to 250 miles, it would take almost three years.

But modelers may soon face increased pressure to deliver much sharper geographic predictions. "Nobody lives in the global average," says Dr. Mahlman. "People want to know what's going to happen in the state where they live. These models still paint with a very broad brush." ∎

Analyzing Issues and Arguments

1. What are the shortcomings of current global circulation models (GCMs), according to this article?
2. Do you think the U.S. government should invest more heavily in GCM technology? Why or why not?

IN THE NEWS

Warming of Deep Sea Is Surprising

William K. Stevens

The following article appeared in the *New York Times* on May 10, 1994. William K. Stevens is a science news reporter for the *Times*.

The waters of the Atlantic Ocean deep below the course of Christopher Columbus's 1492 voyage have warmed by nearly six-tenths of a degree Fahrenheit in the last thirty-five years, oceanographers have discovered, a finding that has important implications for the study of global climate change.

The oceans are a critical part of the climate system because they absorb, store, move, and eventually release heat, the system's main driving force. Mathematical models of the system predict that sea-surface temperatures should rise by 3 to 7 degrees if, as many scientists expect, atmospheric concentrations of carbon dioxide double in the next hundred years. The gas, which traps heat in the atmosphere, is produced by the burning of fossil fuels like coal, oil, and natural gas.

The magnitude of the ocean warming detected by the new observations is "broadly consistent" with model predictions of ocean warming for a doubling of carbon dioxide, the oceanographers say in an article in the current issue of the British journal *Nature*. But the researchers found that the greatest warming has taken place not at the surface, as the models predict, but rather at depths of half a mile to 1.6 miles. The average depth of the Atlantic is 2.2 miles.

This warming in the deep ocean is "surprisingly large; it surprised us anyway," said Dr. Harry Bryden, one of the researchers. Dr. Bryden is a physical oceanographer at the James Rennell Center for Ocean Circulation, a government-supported British research institution at Southampton.

Equally surprising, Dr. Bryden said, the warming was remarkably uniform   5 across the entire Atlantic basin along the latitude of 24 degrees north, the latitude of the Bahamas and roughly that of Columbus's first voyage. The scientific expedition took place in 1992 as an "oceanographic tribute" to Columbus and his crew, Dr. Bryden said.

He said it is too early to tell whether the ocean warming is being caused by the carbon dioxide or is a product of natural variability within the interlinked ocean-atmosphere system.

The observations suggest that some of the models of the earth's climate should be corrected, he said. Although the models are the principal tools for predicting climatic change, they are imperfect and evolving.

Based on the results of the models' simulation of the climate, he said, "I would have expected the warming to be largest at the surface," but instead, "we see a certain pattern of temperature change that doesn't particularly agree with most of the current models."

It may be, Dr. Bryden said, that the upper layers of the ocean really are warmest, as most models predict. But it is impossible to tell, he said, because the pattern of surface warming was obscured by the effect of widely varying seasonal temperatures in the atmosphere, which modify the temperature of the sea's topmost layers. The upper few hundred meters of the ocean displayed both warming and cooling that could be attributed to the fact that some of the readings being compared between 1957 and 1992 were taken in different seasons.

If this is true, the picture painted by the new observations "may not be   10 very inconsistent" with what the latest and most sophisticated climate models show, said Ron Stouffer, a climate modeler at the National Oceanic and

Atmospheric Administration's Geophysical Fluid Dynamics Laboratory at Princeton University. These latest models, he said, predict a warming pattern roughly similar to that observed by Dr. Bryden and his colleagues, except for the surface.

In any event, the broader impact of a warming ocean is unclear. Scientists know that when the temperature of the deep ocean changes, it can lead to radically different patterns in the circulation of worldwide oceanic currents, and with them, changes in patterns of surface climate as well.

Is this warming in the Atlantic causing changes in ocean circulation? "We don't know," Mr. Stouffer said.

And Dr. Bryden said that may be the most important implication of the new findings: "We have to know more about how the ocean is changing."   ∎

Analyzing Issues and Arguments

1. How do the oceans influence the world's climate, according to this article?
2. Does the research presented here verify or challenge the reliability of global circulation models (GCMs)? Explain your response.

ISAAC ASIMOV AND FREDERIK POHL

Gaia and Global Warming

Isaac Asimov wrote nearly five hundred books before his death in 1992 at age seventy-two. He is best known for his science fiction novels, from *Pebble in the Sky* (1950) to the acclaimed Foundation series, the last volume of which was published after he died. His other subjects include astronomy, biology, chemistry, physics, the Bible, Shakespeare, Gilbert and Sullivan, humor, and ancient and modern history. Born in the Soviet Union, Asimov moved with his family to Brooklyn, New York, at age three. He graduated from high school at fifteen and sold his first science fiction story at eighteen. After receiving his Ph.D. in chemistry from Columbia University, Asimov became a professor of biochemistry at Boston University's School of Medicine and wrote a textbook on the subject. Frederik Pohl is also an internationally known science fiction writer from Brooklyn. He was the editor of *Galaxy* magazine in the 1960s and science fiction editor at Bantam Books in the 1970s and has lectured at more than two hundred colleges around the world. Pohl's dozens of novels, including *Gateway* (1977), *JEM* (1979), and *The Years of the City* (1984), have won many awards. "Gaia and Global Warming" comes from Asimov and Pohl's 1991 book *Our Angry Earth: A Ticking Time Bomb*. They explain the concept of Gaia (see p. 158), examine its implications for global warming, and explore some proposed remedies for that potential disaster.

We would all like to think that there was something—some benign and superior kind of *Something*—that would step in and save us from the things that are going wrong with our world.

Most people have always had a comforting belief of that sort. In most of human history their nominee for that "something" was usually their god—whatever god they chanced to worship in that time and place—which is why, in parched summers, farmers have long prayed for rain. They still do, but as scientific knowledge grew and began to explain more and more events as the working out of natural law, rather than divine caprice, many people began to wish for a less supernatural (and perhaps a more predictable) protector.

For that reason there was quite a stir in the scientific community when, about twenty years ago, an English scientist named James Lovelock came up with something that came close to filling that bill. Lovelock gave his hypothetical new concept a name. He called it "Gaia," after the ancient goddess of the earth.

When Lovelock published his "Gaia hypothesis" it shook up many scientists, especially the most rational-minded ones, who purely hated so mystical-sounding a concept. It was an embarrassment to them, and the most disturbing part of it was that Lovelock was one of their own number. He did have a reputation as a bit of a maverick, but his scientific credentials were solid. Among other accomplishments, Lovelock was known as the scientist who had designed the instruments for some of the life-seeking experiments that the American spacecraft *Viking* carried out on the surface of Mars.

Yet, in the eyes of his peers, the things that Lovelock was saying   5
verged on the superstitious. Worse, he had the temerity to present his arguments in the form of the orthodox "scientific method." He had drawn the evidence for his proposal from observation and from the scientific literature, as a scientist is supposed to do. That evidence, he said, appeared to show that the entire biosphere of the planet earth—which is to say, every last living thing that inhabits our planet, from the bacteria to the whales, the elephants, the redwood trees, and you and me—could usefully be described as one single, planet-wide organism, each part of it almost as related and interdependent as the cells of our body. Lovelock felt that this collective super-being deserved a name of its own. Lacking inspiration, he turned to his neighbor William Golding (author of *Lord of the Flies*) for help, and Golding came up with the perfect answer. So they called it "Gaia."

Lovelock came to his conclusions in the course of his scientific work while he was trying to figure out what signs of life the instruments he was designing should look for on the planet Mars. It occurred to him that if he had been a Martian instead of an Englishman, it would have been easy to solve that problem the other way around. All a Martian would need was a modest telescope, with a fairly good spectroscope attached, to get the answer. The very composition of earth's air proclaimed the undeniable existence of life. earth's atmosphere contains a great deal of free oxygen, which is a very active chemical. The fact that it was free in such volume in the earth's atmosphere meant that something had to be constantly replenishing it. If that were not true, the atmospheric oxygen would long since have reacted with such other elements as the iron in the earth's surface and thus have disappeared—in just the same way that our own earthly spectroscopes have shown that whatever oxygen there ever was has long since been used up on all of our planetary neighbors, Mars included.

Therefore a Martian astronomer would have understood at once that that constantly oxygen-replenishing "something" could be only one thing. It had to be life.

It is life—living plants—which continually produces that oxygen in our air; it is that same oxygen which life—ourselves and almost every other living member of the animal kingdom—relies on to survive.

Lovelock's insight from that was that life—all terrestrial life combined—was interactive and had the capacity to maintain its environment in such a way that its own continued existence was possible. If some environmental change should threaten life, life would then act to counter the change, in much the same way that a thermostat acts to keep your home comfortable when the weather changes, by turning on the furnace or the air conditioner.

The technical term for this kind of behavior is "homeostatic." According to Lovelock, "Gaia"—the sum total of all life on earth—is a homeostatic system. (To be more technically precise, the proper term is "homeorhetic" rather than "homeostatic" in this case, but the distinction would matter only to specialists.) This self-preserving system not only adapts itself to changes, it even makes changes of its own, altering the environment around it in whatever ways are necessary to its well-being. 10

With that speculation to spur him on, Lovelock began looking for other evidences of homeostatic behavior. He found them in surprising places.

Coral islands, for instance. Coral is made up of living animals. They can only grow in shallow water. Yet many coral islands are slowly sinking, and somehow the coral continues to grow upward just as much as it needs to remain at the proper depth for survival; that's a rudimentary kind of homeostasis.

Then there's the temperature of the earth. The global average temperature has stayed within fairly narrow limits for a billion years or more, although it is known that in that time the radiation from the sun (which is what basically determines that temperature) has been steadily increasing. Therefore the earth should have warmed appreciably. It didn't. How could that happen without some kind of homeostasis?

Even more interesting to Lovelock was the paradoxical question of how much salt there is in the sea. The present salt concentration in the world's oceans is just about right for marine plants and animals to live in. Any significant increase would be disastrous. Fish (and other sea life) have a tough job as it is in preventing that salt from accumulating in their tissues and poisoning them; if there were much more salt in the sea than there is, the job would be impossible and they would die.

Yet, by all normal scientific logic, the seas should be a lot saltier than they are. It is known that the rivers of the earth are continually dissolving salts out of the soil they run through and carrying more and more of those salts into the seas. The water itself which the rivers add each year doesn't 15 stay in the ocean. That pure water is taken out by evaporation by the heat of the Sun to make clouds and ultimately to fall again as rain; while the salts those waters contained have nowhere to go and must stay behind.

We know from everyday experience what happens in that case. If we leave a bucket of salt water exposed in the summer, it will get more and more salty as the water evaporates. Astonishingly, that does not happen in the oceans. Their salt content is known to have remained at just about the same level for all of geological time.

So it is apparent that *something* is acting to remove excess salt from the ocean.

There is one known process that might account for it. Now and then, bays and shallow arms of the ocean are cut off. The Sun evaporates their water and they dry out to form salt beds—which ultimately are covered over by dust, clay, and finally impenetrable rock, so that when the sea ultimately returns to reclaim that area that layer of fossil salt is sealed in and is not redissolved. (When, later on, people dig them up for their own needs we call them salt mines.) In that way, millennium after millennium, the oceans get rid of the excess and keep their salt content level.

It could be simply a coincidence that that balance is maintained so exactly, no matter what else is going on . . . but it could also be another manifestation of Gaia.

But perhaps Gaia shows herself most clearly in the way she has kept 20 earth's temperature constant. As we've mentioned, in the early days of earth the sun's radiation was about a fifth less than it is now. With so little warming sunlight the oceans should have frozen over, but that didn't happen.

Why not?

The reason is that then the earth's atmosphere contained more carbon dioxide than it does now. And there, Lovelock says, Gaia is at work. For plants came along to reduce the proportion of carbon dioxide in the air. As the sun warmed up, the carbon dioxide, with its heat-retaining qualities, diminished—in exact step, over the millennia. Gaia worked through the plants (Lovelock suggests) to keep the world at the optimum temperature for life. . . .

But we must not take too much personal reassurance from Lovelock's theory. The Gaia hypothesis does suggest that life is likely to continue, and even that many species will exist. However, there is nothing in the theory to say that the world will be safe for our grandchildren, because there is nothing in it which predicts that the assortment of species of living things which will survive the present assaults will necessarily include that particular species called *Homo sapiens sapiens*, which is ourselves.

James Lovelock said it himself one day, talking over a cup of coffee with the author of *The Hole in the Sky*, John Gribbin. As Lovelock put it, "People sometimes have the attitude that 'Gaia will look after us.' But that's wrong. If the concept means anything at all, Gaia will look after *herself*. And the best way for her to do that might well be to get rid of us."

Can natural checks and balances save us from the effects of the 25 man-made greenhouse global warming?

No, they can't. They are certainly doing their best, in the face of greater challenges, due to our uncontrolled mining and burning of fossil fuels, than they ever had to face before, but their best is not good enough.

. . . There are many natural processes which operate to remove carbon dioxide from the air (they are technically called "sinks"), such as coal formation and the deep-freeze of dead plant material in the tundras. There are a great many of these natural sinks; but most of them are much too weak to resist the large-scale changes in the atmosphere.

Only two sinks, really, are big enough to make a dent in the problem. The first of them is the world aggregate of living plants, which suck carbon dioxide out of the air to turn it into vegetation. The other is the world's bodies of water, mostly the oceans, which dissolve large quantities of the carbon dioxide out of the atmosphere in much the same way that a cup of coffee dissolves a spoonful of sugar.

The world's living plants are our most valuable sink. When a plant takes in a molecule of carbon dioxide from the air, it uses sunlight to break that molecule down into its component elements, carbon and oxygen; the process is called photosynthesis. The plant uses the carbon that results to build into its own structure; that's how it grows. The plant has no use for oxygen, however, so it exhales the oxygen back to the air—that is how, billions of years ago when plants began to appear, the earth came to have an oxygen atmosphere for us to breathe in the first place.

Plant photosynthesis is a very satisfactory process for human needs 30 —indeed, you could call it indispensable, not just for us but for almost all life on Earth. But we are killing the plants that do the job. We cut down our trees in vast numbers for such trivial reasons as to splinter them into disposable chopsticks for export to the Orient, as well as to use them for paper and lumber or simply to get them out of the way so we can build houses and plant farms.

The habit of destroying woodlands did not begin with our generation. Scientists tell us that the pristine world—the world that existed before the human race became numerous enough, and aggressive enough, to have much of an effect on it—contained almost twice as many forested acres as now remain; it was human beings who destroyed the missing half. But those ancient people who burned or cut down all those trees did not have our chain saws and bulldozers, so they were nowhere nearly as good at it as we are.

It isn't only trees that we are removing from the cycle. We take our toll of everything that is green. We destroy more of that indispensable plant life every time we drain a swamp, or bulkhead a shoreland, or construct a highway, or start a new suburban housing development, or lay a concrete parking lot for a shopping mall. And we do all this on so vast a scale that the vegetative sink is no longer large enough to handle the task of keeping the carbon-dioxide level in check.

As to the sink in the oceans: Water is very good at dissolving carbon dioxide—that's what makes our fizzy drinks like beer and ginger ale possible. Over the ages, the seas have dissolved enormous quantities of the gas, so that now there is far more carbon dioxide dissolved in the global ocean than is free in the atmosphere.

But there is a limit to how rapidly the oceans can take up excess carbon dioxide, and that limit depends on the temperature. If the seas should warm enough, more carbon dioxide will bubble out of solution than there is being dissolved—in just the same way that when you leave ginger ale out overnight it goes flat faster than the same beverage kept in the refrigerator.

In that case, the race that we call the carbon-dioxide exchange be- 35 tween the atmosphere and the oceans will go the wrong way. It will make the situation worse instead of better.

(Nor is the situation any better for the other greenhouse gases. The sinks for methane are similar to those for carbon dioxide, and equally threatened. For the synthetic gases like the chlorofluorocarbons [CFCs] there are no natural sinks at all. None ever arose, since those gases did not exist until we began to manufacture them.)

So Gaia alone can't do the job for us any more. It was primarily through these two carbon-dioxide sinks that she managed to keep the global climate so stable over so many millions of years, but now we've crippled her.

Which brings us to the second question: Is there anything we can do to restore Gaia to health—say, by inventing some technological fix?

That is the question with the "Yes, but" answer. There are a lot of things we might be able to *try* in the attempt to remove surplus greenhouse gases from the air, but no obvious good ones. Some would work too slowly to do us much good, some might not work at all, some might actually make the situation worse.

For instance, we can start planting new trees on the barren lands 40 where the forests have been cut down.

That's the most obvious (and lowest-tech) of all the current proposals. It would probably help considerably, in the long run, but it is an enormous job. To replace the cut-over regions would mean planting the greatest forest in the world, covering an area about the size of Australia.

Reforestation on that scale may well be worth undertaking for many other reasons—for instance, in order to control soil erosion—but it can't solve our present problem. The atmospheric benefits of replanting logged-out areas come too slowly to help us now. It takes anywhere from forty years to several centuries for a newly planted sapling to grow big enough to match the carbon-holding capacity of a mature tree. We don't have that much time to spare.

There have been more technologically "sophisticated" proposals by the dozen. Some are grotesquely unrealistic, though they come from respected institutions: for instance, a Brookhaven National Laboratory project to catch all the carbon dioxide that comes from the world's smokestacks and pump it through vast pipes to the bottom of the sea, where it can dissolve and remain out of the air, at least for a while. (Think of the cost of such a program! Think of the extra carbon dioxide that would be produced by the power plants that ran the pumps that forced all that gas against the pressure of the deep sea.) Two Japanese scientists have a similar idea; they also want to catch all the stack emissions, but then their idea is to pump them through great tanks holding a soup of algae, letting the algae do what plants always do. (Expense again; plus the fact that suitable algae strains would have to be genetically engineered; plus the problem of how you then dispose of the slurry of dead algae that results.) Some are simply inadequate to the task, like the Environmental Protection Agency's March, 1989, suggestions of cutting down on cement production and finding alternative methods of producing rice, meat, and milk. (Again worth doing for other reasons, but not for dealing with the surplus carbon dioxide; the EPA plan would affect only the other greenhouse gas, methane, and only a small fraction of that.) Some might help to ameliorate the carbon-dioxide problem—like the EPA's other suggestion, of replacing fossil-fuel power plants with nuclear reactors—but create serious problems of another kind. (Such problems as the expense of constructing the nuclear plants; the long time delay involved in building such plants, which typically run to a decade or more; the dangers of nuclear plants —such as Chernobyl-style accidents[1]—and the equally worrisome but

---

[1]**Chernobyl-style accidents:** On April 26, 1986, the worst commercial nuclear accident in history occurred at a nuclear power plant in Chernobyl. Chernobyl is located 80 miles north of Kiev, Ukraine, in the former Soviet Union.—ED.

generally overlooked unsolved problems that afflict all such plants, such as the total lack of disposal facilities for their radioactive wastes.)

There are more speculative proposals, too. They represent wishes more than solid, realizable plans, but they are worth a look.

For instance: If natural trees grow too slowly, how about letting the 45 molecular biologists build us some new kind of tree or shrub—one as good at surviving and growing as any weed—that will come to maturity very rapidly, and, what's more, will do it almost anywhere in the world without special care or irrigation, so that we could perhaps spray seeds out of airplanes over the bare Asian hills, or even over the empty Sahara? That's not quite impossible. Conceivably such new tree species could some day be bred. But we don't have them now, and no one presently knows how to start creating them; so that is a wish rather than a plan.

All right, then: How about dispensing with vegetation entirely and going right to inorganic chemistry?

We know that a lot of carbon dioxide does get taken out of the air by chemical means and turned into rocks like limestone. That doesn't happen fast enough naturally to be useful to our present needs, but perhaps science can find a way to speed it up. Can't we just spray some magic fairy dust into the air (let's not call it that; let's call the stuff by the more sober-sounding chemical name of "catalyst")—a high-tech catalyst, then, which would make the process happen quickly, creating great masses of carbon-containing rock which we could then bulldoze underground—or simply leave lying harmlessly around, or even use for building materials?

No. We can't. We don't know how; but even if we did we probably wouldn't dare. Like the sorcerer's apprentice, we would be tempting fate if we started things we might not be able to stop.

If we did have the capacity to speed up some such natural process we would risk it going beyond our control. Then it might keep on removing carbon dioxide past the point we intended it for—perhaps until it got down to that 200 parts per million level that means another Ice Age—or even beyond that, perhaps to the point where there is no atmospheric carbon dioxide at all. That would make our planet almost as cold as Mars. Then we would all die.

So we can't put back the lost trees in time, and we can't expect the 50 inventors to give us a gadget that will make the process stop.

There's only one thing left. We're going to have to do it the hard way . . . if we are to have any hope of doing it at all. That is, we're going to have to cut down on the amount of fossil fuel we burn.

That doesn't mean we have to forswear the use of fossil fuel entirely. That wouldn't be sensible—there are applications to which fossil fuels are vastly better suited than any imaginable alternative—but fortunately it isn't necessary. What we have to do is *reduce* our burning of coal, oil, and natural gas to the point of our Steady-state Allowable Perturbation, or SAP.[2] So let's try to estimate just how much man-made interference we can inflict upon the environment in this area without making things worse.

That means we have to put numbers into the equation. Fortunately, in the race between our production of greenhouse gases and their removal from the atmosphere, we do know some of the necessary numbers. We know, for instance, that the human race now turns out some 50 billion tons of carbon dioxide a year from the burning of fossil fuels. And we know that that's too much.

It's doubtful that there is any way at all to stop the process of global warming entirely, whatever we do. The process has picked up too much momentum, and stopping or reversing it may be simply beyond our capacities. But perhaps we can do the next best thing by slowing it down. If we can do that adequately, then we can at least allow the world time to adjust to the coming climate changes.

We have a number for that. A pair of scientists, one from the 55 Lawrence Berkeley Laboratories in California, the other a climatologist from West Germany, have prepared an estimate of what a tolerable rate of global warming should be. Their conclusion: no more than an increase of a twentieth of a degree every ten years. Any rate of global warming higher than that would result in unacceptable damage to forests and crops.

Even that is very rapid, as natural global change goes. (The warming after the last Ice Age took place at an average of about a *thirtieth* of a degree every ten years.) And it is certainly far less than our present practices would produce. According to a United Nations panel which studied the question in April, 1990, we're likely to experience an increase of about a whole degree every ten years between now and the year 2030. That's twenty times the proposed maximum level.

If we translate that one-twentieth of a degree level into what is produced by carbon dioxide production, holding our temperature rise to safe limits means that we have to make quite drastic cuts in our burning of fossil fuels. Our present discharge of 50 billion tons a year of carbon dioxide would have to come down to about 6 billion tons a year—about as much as we now produce every forty-four days.

So, as a first approximation, anyway, that can be our SAP for carbon-dioxide production. It's formidable. It means that for every

---

[2]**Steady-state Allowable Perturbation (SAP):** The level at which no further environmental damage occurs.—ED.

gallon of oil we now burn, we have to restrict ourselves to a little less than a pint. (And that doesn't even take into account what has to be done about the other greenhouse gases—particularly methane and the CFCs.)

It isn't quite as bad as it sounds, though. We don't have to reduce our *energy* consumption to the same degree. . . . We can start taking advantage of nonpolluting energy sources to make up much of the slack; and we can save a good deal of the rest by using our energy more efficiently.

Still, reducing the rate of warming will certainly be a difficult task, 60 and it is likely to be an expensive one as well.

Just how much this will cost us, in public and private funds, is almost as hard to predict as the fine-screen detail of what the climate changes will mean in your own neighborhood. Some studies are fairly scary. One such modeling of the probable cost of doing what is necessary to achieve this sort of steady state puts the price of change, for the United States alone, at anywhere from $800 billion to more than $3 trillion—and several times that when the changes for the rest of the world are taken into account.

But, in the event, it isn't going to be that bad. Those high cost-estimates show only the loss side of the ledger; there are gains as well.

The money we will save from, for example, more efficient use of energy will go a long way toward meeting those costs. Some estimates even suggest that a conversion to a steady-state energy economy will actually mean a *profit* for the world, in terms of cheaper bills forever after.

. . . It is possible to stave off at least the worst effects of the greenhouse disaster. The ways of doing it are known. It is only the dislocations and difficulties involved in making the transition to a steady-state world that are hard to face.

Analyzing Issues and Arguments

1. What beliefs and actions do Isaac Asimov and Frederik Pohl advocate? Look at James Lovelock's comments on the relationship between Gaia and global warming (p. 158). How do his observations support or conflict with Asimov and Pohl's recommendations?

2. In what respects does the Gaia hypothesis, as explained by Asimov and Pohl, identify the same problems and possible solutions to global warming as other approaches discussed in this chapter? In what respects does adding Gaia to the equation change the problems and solutions?

3. How does Asimov and Pohl's use of stylistic informalities, such as the first-person plural ("we") and contractions ("There's," "It's"), affect the impact of "Gaia and Global Warming"? What other informalities can you identify?

Writing about Issues and Arguments

Asimov and Pohl agree with Dixy Lee Ray ("Greenhouse Earth") on the role of the oceans in dissolving carbon dioxide, but not on the likely results. Whose argument is more convincing, and why? How do the findings reported by William K. Stevens (p. 204) affect your response? Write an essay on this issue, using these three selections as your sources.

THE ECONOMIST

Changing the World

> "Changing the World" is a report on the 1994 annual meeting of the
> American Association for the Advancement of Science (AAAS) in San
> Francisco. It appeared in the February 26, 1994, issue of *The Economist*, a
> worldwide magazine, published in London, featuring economic news for
> nonspecialists. *The Economist* does not credit individual authors for the ar-
> ticles it prints, but regards them as representing the magazine. This article
> looks at some ways scientists are proposing to use advanced technology
> (as Dixy Lee Ray recommends) to create geoengineering remedies for
> global warming in the event that it becomes a serious problem.

Traipsing from room to room at the AAAS conference, you might be
forgiven for thinking that no scientist ever gave up an opportunity to
talk. Yet the organizers of one symposium found that several possible
speakers declined their invitations. The audience, on the other hand,
was eager to attend—the symposium had to be moved to a bigger hall,
and even then it was crammed. The nonspeakers' demurrals and listen-
ers' enthusiasm are linked; the second is the reason for the first.

The session concerned was devoted to geoengineering: deliberately
modifying the climate so as to counteract inadvertent (and undesirable)
changes that have already been made. The target of this engineering is
the global warming that climatologists expect to result from ever-in-
creasing levels of carbon dioxide in the earth's atmosphere. The canonical response to this greenhouse effect is to cut the amount of CO_2 produced by burning fewer fossil fuels. But there are alternatives—which
some scientists do not want to discuss. They worry that the prospect of
mending the climate might reduce efforts to avoid harming it.

Would-be geoengineers have a number of tools at their disposal,
from the more-or-less unexceptionable to the out-of-this-world. CO_2
could be pumped direct from power stations into the ocean depths—
which is where the gas eventually ends up anyway, by way of the atmosphere. It could be sucked out of the atmosphere by growing new
forests, or by fostering photosynthesizing plankton in the sea. Or its effects could be counteracted. Mirrors in space or dust high in the atmosphere could block out some sunlight. Greenhouse gases would still
trap heat—but less heat would get into the greenhouse in the first
place.

Some of these schemes are simply too costly. Pumping CO_2 out of power-station flues and dumping it in the deep oceans looks expensive. It could double the price of power and reduce generator efficiency by 30 percent. Other ideas, though, might be cheaper. One such is to fertilize the oceans with iron. It was suggested by the late John Martin, who had noticed that parts of the world's oceans contained lots of basic nutrients—except iron—but little life.

If the lack of iron has kept life from these waters, adding some   5 could have a huge effect. Plankton would multiply to eat up the nutrients; in doing so they would suck up CO_2. When they died and fell to the ocean floor, it would be removed from climatic concerns. The plankton need only a little iron—one iron atom for 10,000 carbon atoms—so not much metal would be required. A few oil tankers full of iron filings could fertilize all the seas around Antarctica, if the iron could be spread evenly.

The idea has recently been tested, and Richard Barber of Duke University presented the results to the AAAS meeting. Spreading iron around a patch of the equatorial Pacific, the researchers found that it did indeed increase the productivity of small planktonic plants. However, little planktonic animals that live slightly lower in the water soon cottoned on, and what might have been geoengineering became lunch. Not much extra carbon ended up in Davy Jones's locker. But a lot of iron did; it clustered into lumps and sank, out of reach of the plankton after only three days. Dr. Barber and his colleagues find this all scientifically fascinating; but they think planetary engineers will find it discouraging.

Engineering efforts that do not depend on the vagaries of living things look simpler and more predictable. A thin layer of dust could be put into the stratosphere relatively easily and cheaply by battleship guns pointing straight up. There is evidence that this can successfully shield the earth from the sun. The eruption of Mount Pinatubo[1] in 1991 threw 20 million metric tons [22 million U.S. tons] or so of muck into the stratosphere. That pall around the world, which is only now settling, appears to have cooled the surface roughly as computer models would have predicted.

A 1992 report by America's National Research Council suggested that the guns put a Pinatubo's worth of fine dust into the atmosphere every few years, to maintain a shield that would reflect away about 1 percent of the incoming sunlight, reducing its intensity by a few watts per square meter. Such a shield would need constant replenishment, but that is probably just as well, since it makes it easy to remove if necessary. And far from visibly dimming the sky, it might have some aesthetic value, enriching sunsets around the world. For those who do not

---

[1]**Mount Pinatubo**: A volcano located in the northern Phillipines.—ED.

like guns, something similar might be achieved with additives to the exhausts of airliners.

There could be side effects; everything in this field is layered in quite proper caveats. Although there is no biology to complicate things in the stratosphere, the chemistry and physics offer enough complexity to confuse the budding engineer. Ralph Cicerone of the University of California, Irvine, demonstrated as much in his discussion of a different sort of geoengineering. He and his colleagues were looking at ways to patch the hole in the ozone layer over Antarctica, which has been eaten out by chlorine released from chlorofluorocarbons used as refrigerants and aerosol propellants. Dumping propane into the Antarctic stratosphere at the end of winter looked promising; computer models showed that chlorine would get used up in reactions with propane, leaving the ozone layer alone.

Before even breathing a suggestion that a fleet of aircraft should 10 spray stove-fuel over the South Pole, though, Dr. Cicerone and his colleagues checked their findings in a more detailed model, which took account of more chemical reactions. It showed that chlorine had various ways to escape the clutches of propane and put itself back into circulation. The stratosphere is complicated; anyone who wants to put millions of tons of dust into it should bear that in mind.

In principle, it is possible to avoid any side effects. Just put the engineering at a safe distance from the earth. A large mirror poised between the earth and the sun could also reduce the amount of sunlight reaching the planet. Aluminum foil could do the trick, and it might not have to be lifted through the earth's powerful gravity. Strip mines on the moon or nearby asteroids might furnish the raw material, to be smelted *in situ*. The price tag—perhaps a few trillion dollars—is high; but so would be the cost of phasing out fossil fuels.

However, even though a sunscreen made in space does nothing to the earth's environment except deny it a few watts per square meter of light, it would still not be a perfect answer to the few watts per square meter of warming that are expected. Stephen Schneider of Stanford University pointed out that the energy reflected would match the energy trapped by greenhouse gases only on average. Regionally, things would not be so well balanced.

Reflecting sunlight into space from the stratosphere would have fairly even effects around the world; the stratosphere is pretty smooth. But the effects of greenhouse warming are not so evenly spread. The atmosphere varies more lower down, thanks to the surface below it and the weather within it. Land warms up more quickly than the sea, and seas where the water is stratified in unmixed layers warm faster than those where the water circulates a lot. Places with clear skies are more subject to greenhouse warming than cloudy places. So a uniform cooling by a stratospheric shield would not be a return to a preindustrial Eden. It would lower temperatures on average, but it might not limit changes in regional climate anything like as much. It might leave some places cooler than today, and upset regional weather patterns in unpredictable ways.

Dr. Schneider is not ruling out geoengineering. He is pointing out its flaws and uncertainties. Those keen to publicize the threat of global warming find it natural to do so, for fear that geoengineering gives people an excuse to do nothing, or encourages them to rely on an unproven technology with unforeseen side effects. These fears are probably well founded, but they should not prevent discussion of the possibilities. One person's quick fix is another person's timely action. Few argue that technologies that allow people to maintain their standard of living while using less energy are undesirable because they are quick fixes, but some do. It is almost as if humanity deserves to suffer for despoiling its planet, and that to escape by being clever would be morally wrong even if entirely practical.

Reflection from the stratosphere is not the opposite of trapping 15 heat in the lower atmosphere; but discussions of geoengineering provide a mirror image of the traditional global warming debate. That may be why it unsettles some people enough to keep them from joining in. Skeptics about global warming—often of a rightwing and technocratic frame of mind—are often geoengineering enthusiasts. People who live in terror of waves of extinction and disaster seem unwilling even to contemplate doing something positive to avert them.

Two wrongs, they argue, cannot make a right. But that is to believe that changing the environment is wrong in itself, rather than wrong only if it brings about harm. This is not an absurd view; nor is it one that everyone on the planet should be expected to share. Geoengineering, unlike measures to reduce global warming, needs no worldwide consensus. Stopping CO_2 emissions must be a multilateral process, but geoengineering can be unilateral. It might be immoral or unwise for a single superpower to darken the skies; but it is possible.

At its heart, however, the geoengineering debate shares the defining characteristic of all other debates about the climate: it is dominated by uncertainties. All the AAAS speakers pointed out that the effects of any geoengineering project are unpredictable, and that the models are full of uncertainties—uncertainties that are often given less weight in the greenhouse predictions of the same models. The uncertainties do not argue against the principle of geoengineering; they argue in favor of further research. If CO_2 emissions are not curtailed, knowing the benefits and disadvantages of alternative responses to global warming will be crucial, even if they are far from perfect. Preventive medicine is in many ways preferable to radical surgery or chemotherapy. If it fails, though, an educated approach to the alternatives comes in handy.

Analyzing Issues and Arguments

1. According to this article, why are some people reluctant to talk about geoengineering solutions to global warming? What evidence, if any, does the author supply to explain why some potential speakers refused to participate in the AAAS's symposium?
2. What is the author's attitude toward geoengineering? Where is it stated, and where is it implied?
3. Why do you think the author mentions the possibility that geoengineering could be a unilateral rather than a multilateral process (para. 16)?

Writing about Issues and Arguments

"One person's quick fix is another person's timely action" (para. 14). What does "quick fix" mean in this context? How and by whom is the term defined? How is it subsequently applied? Write an essay analyzing the progression of reasoning in this paragraph and the author's use of the expression "quick fix" as part of that progression.

BILL McKIBBEN

The End of Nature

Bill McKibben began writing for *The New Yorker* in 1982, soon after graduating from Harvard University. Besides the hundreds of articles he has published as a staff writer, editor, and contributor to that magazine, his observations on environmental and related issues have appeared in *The New York
Review of Books*, the *New York Times*, *Rolling Stone* (where he was a contributing editor), and other publications. McKibben's books include *The
Age of Missing Information* (1993) and *The Comforting Whirlwind* (1994). He
lives in the Adirondack Mountains in New York State and has written
widely on the challenges facing that huge undeveloped region so close to
major cities. In the following excerpt from his best-known book, *The End of
Nature* (1989), McKibben warns of ecological disaster if the industrialized
world does not change its habits to mitigate the greenhouse effect.

The invention of nuclear weapons may actually have marked the beginning of the end of nature: we possessed, finally, the capacity to over-
master nature, to leave an indelible imprint everywhere all at once.
"The nuclear peril is usually seen in isolation from the threats to other
forms of life and their ecosystems, but in fact it should be seen at the
very center of the ecological crisis, as the cloud-covered Everest of
which the more immediate, visible kinds of harm to the environment
are the mere foothills," wrote Jonathan Schell in *The Fate of the Earth*.
And he was correct, for at the time he was writing (less than a decade
ago!) it was hard to conceive of any threats of the same magnitude.
Global warming was one obscure theory among many. Nuclear
weapons were unique (and they remain so, if only for the speed with
which they work). But the nuclear dilemma is at least open to human
reason—we can decide not to drop the weapons, and indeed to reduce
and perhaps eliminate them. And the horrible power of these weapons,
which has been amply demonstrated in Japan and on Bikini and under
Nevada and many times in our imaginations, has led us fitfully in that
hopeful direction.

By contrast, the various processes that lead to the end of nature
have been essentially beyond human thought. Only a few people knew
that carbon dioxide would warm up the world, for instance, and they
were for a long time unsuccessful in their efforts to alert the rest of us.
Now it is too late—not too late, as I shall come to explain, to ameliorate some of the changes and so perhaps to avoid the most gruesome of

their consequences. But the scientists agree that we have already pumped enough gas into the air so that a significant rise in temperature and a subsequent shift in weather are inevitable.

Just how inevitable we can see from the remedies that some scientists have proposed to save us—not the remedies, like cutting fossil fuel use and saving the rainforests, that will keep things from being any worse than they need to be, but the solutions that might bring things back to "normal." The most natural method anyone has suggested involves growing enormous numbers of trees to take the carbon dioxide out of the air. Take, for argument's sake, a new coal-fired electric generating station that produces a thousand megawatts and operates at 38 percent thermal efficiency and 70 percent availability. To counteract just the carbon dioxide generated by that plant, the surrounding area to a radius of 24.7 kilometers would need to be covered with American sycamore trees (a fast-growing species) planted at four-foot intervals and "harvested" every four years. It might be possible to achieve that sort of growth rate—a government forestries expert told the Senate that with genetic screening, spacing, thinning, pruning, weed control, fire and pest control, fertilization, and irrigation, net annual growth could be "very much higher than at present." Even if it worked, though, would this tree plantation be nature? A walk through an endless glade of evenly spaced sycamores, with the weed-control chopper hovering overhead, and the irrigation pipes gurgling quietly below, represents a fundamental break with my idea of the wild world.

Other proposals get even odder. One "futuristic idea" described in the *New York Times* springs from the brain of Dr. Thomas Stix at Princeton: he proposes the possibility of using a laser to "scrub" chlorofluorocarbons from the earth's atmosphere before they have a chance to reach the ozone layer. Dr. Stix calculates that an array of infrared lasers spaced around the world could "blast apart" a million tons of chlorofluorocarbons a year—a procedure he refers to as "atmospheric processing." Down at the University of Alabama, Leon Y. Sadler, a chemical engineer, has suggested employing dozens of airplanes to carry ozone into the stratosphere (others have suggested firing a continuous barrage of "bullets" of frozen ozone, which would melt in the stratosphere). To deal with the warming problem, Columbia geochemist Wallace Broecker has considered a "fleet of several hundred jumbo jets" to ferry 35 million tons of sulfur dioxide into the stratosphere annually to reflect sunlight away from the earth. Other scientists recommend launching "giant orbiting satellites made of thin films" that could cast shadows on the earth, counteracting the greenhouse effect with a sort of venetian-blind effect. Certain practical problems may hamper these various solutions; Dr. Broecker, for instance, admits that injecting large quantities of sulfur dioxide into the atmosphere would

SYLVIA   **by Nicole Hollander**

Copyright © 1988 by Nicole Hollander.

increase acid rain "and give the blue sky a whitish cast." Still, they just might work. And perhaps, as Dr. Broecker contends, "a rational society needs some sort of insurance policy on how to maintain a habitable planet." But even if they do work—even if the planet remains habitable —it will not be the same. The whitish afternoon sky blessed by the geometric edge of the satellite cloud will fade into a dusk crisscrossed by lasers. There is no way to reassemble nature—certainly not by following the suggestion of one researcher that, in order to increase the earth's reflectivity and thus cool its temperature, we should cover most of the oceans with a floating layer of white Styrofoam chips.

There are some people, perhaps many, to whom this rupture will 5 mean little. A couple of years ago a group of executives went rafting down a river in British Columbia; after an accident killed five of them, one of the survivors told reporters that the party had regarded the river as "a sort of ersatz roller-coaster." Nature has become a hobby with us. One person enjoys the outdoors, another likes cooking, a third favors breaking into military computers over his phone line. The nature hobby boomed during the 1970s; now it is perhaps in slight decline (the number of people requesting permits to hike and camp in the rugged backcountry of the national parks has dropped by half since 1983, even as the number of drive-through visitors has continued to increase). We have become in rapid order a people whose conscious need for nature is superficial. The seasons don't matter to most of us anymore except as spectacles. In my county and in many places around this part of the nation, the fairs that once marked the harvest now take place in late August, while tourist dollars are still in heavy circulation. Why celebrate the harvest when you harvest every week with a shopping cart? I am a child of the suburbs, and even though I live on the edge of the wild I have only a tenuous understanding of the natural world. I can drive past hundreds of miles of fields without ever being able to figure out what's growing in them, unless it's corn. And even farmers have a lessened feel for the world around them. The essayist Wendell Berry quotes from an advertisement for a new tractor: "Outside—dust, noise, heat, storm, fumes. Inside—all is quiet, comfortable, safe. . . . Driver dials 'inside weather' to his liking. . . . He pushbuttons radio or stereo-tape entertainment."

Even this is several steps above the philosophy expressed by a mausoleum director in a full-page newspaper ad that seems to run once a week in my newspaper: "Above-Ground. The Clean Burial. Not Underground with Earth's Disturbing Elements." Four of his "clean, dry, civilized" vaults are already sold out, and a fifth is under construction. While we are still alive, we do sometimes watch a nature program, an account of squid or wildebeest, usually sponsored by Mutual of Omaha. Mostly, however, we watch *L.A. Law*.

Still, the passing of nature as we have known it, like the passing of any large idea, will have its recognizable effects, both immediately and over time. In 1893, when Frederick Jackson Turner announced to the American Historical Association that the frontier was closed, no one was aware that the frontier had been the defining force in American life. But in its absence it was understood. One reason we pay so little close attention to the separate natural world around us is that it has always been there and we presumed it always would. As it disappears, its primal importance will be clearer—in the same way that some people think they have put their parents out of their lives and learn differently only when the day comes to bury them.

Analyzing Issues and Arguments

1. What is Bill McKibben's opinion of geoengineering solutions to global warming, and on what grounds does he base that opinion?
2. "Just how inevitable [global warming is] we can see from the remedies that some scientists have proposed to save us" (para. 3). Do the proposed remedies indeed demonstrate that global warming is inevitable? If so, how? If not, what do they demonstrate?
3. What does McKibben evidently mean by *nature*? How does his definition of *nature* differ from Isaac Asimov and Frederik Pohl's definition of *Gaia* (p. 207)?

Writing about Issues and Arguments

Review the proposed geoengineering remedies for global warming described by McKibben in "The End of Nature," in *The Economist* article "Changing the World," and by Asimov and Pohl in "Gaia and Global

Warming." Which ones sound most promising, and why? Imagine that your job is to evaluate geoengineering projects submitted to a federal agency established to fight global warming. Write a report recommending which projects should (and should not) be funded. You may wish to expand the scope of your report by consulting sources not included in this chapter. (See "Suggestions for Further Reading," p. 338.)

MAKING CRITICAL CONNECTIONS

1. Describe in your own words how the greenhouse effect works, and how and why it may lead to global warming. (You may refer to selections in this chapter, but do not quote or closely paraphrase them.)

2. Look back at Edward O. Wilson's comparison between exemptionalists and environmentalists (p. 1). Which authors represented in this chapter would you place in each category, and why?

3. What is the role of Third World countries, such as India and China, in global warming? How do developing nations pose different problems for the environment from countries at a more advanced stage of development, such as the United States and most European nations? What strategies can be taken, and by whom, to ease the environmental impact of economic and industrial development in the Third World? Write an essay answering these questions, using as sources Helen Caldicott's "The Greenhouse Effect," (p. 161), Dixy Lee Ray's "Greenhouse Earth," (p. 176), Stephen H. Schneider's "The Global Warming Debate Heats Up," (p. 192), and Randy Smith's "Developing Nations Top List of Carbon Dioxide Producers" (p. 175).

4. "The threat of global warming will be used to justify nothing less than changing how we live," declares Aaron Wildavsky (p. 157). Based on your reading in this chapter, do you agree with his prediction? If not, why not? If so, do you also agree with Wildavsky that it would be a disaster for the threat to be used in this way? Why or why not? Write an essay stating and defending your answers to these questions, using as sources at least three selections in this chapter.

5. How should we respond to the threat of global warming? Should people and corporations be required to make the kinds of changes recommended by Caldicott? If so, how can such requirements be implemented? If not, should funds be allocated (by whom?) for geoengineering solutions? Should we delay any action until more information (what kind? how much?) is available? Write an essay stating and defending your views. Use all the selections in this chapter (including the "Points of View" and "In the News" pieces) as sources. You may wish to turn this essay into a research paper by drawing on outside sources as well. (See "Suggestions for Further Reading," p. 338.)

4

How Can We Solve
Our Environmental Predicament?

POINTS OF VIEW

The ecological crisis is essentially beyond "our" control, as citizens or householders or consumers or even voters. It is not something that can be halted by recycling or double-pane insulation. It is the inevitable by-product of our modern industrial civilization, dominated by capitalist production and consumption and serviced and protected by various institutions of government, federal to local. It cannot possibly be altered or reversed by simple individual actions, even by the actions of the millions who will take part in Earth Day — and even if they all went home and fixed their refrigerators and from then on walked to work. Nothing less than a drastic overhaul of this civilization and an abandonment of its ingrained gods—progress, growth, exploitation, technology, materialism, humanism, and power—will do anything substantial to halt our path to environmental destruction, and it's hard to see how the lifestyle solutions offered by Earth Day will have an effect on that.

—Kirkpatrick Sale, "The Trouble with Earth Day,"
Nation (April 30, 1990)

However destructive may be the policies of the government and the methods and products of the corporations, the root of the problem is always to be found in private life. We must learn to see that every problem that concerns us as conservationists always leads straight to the question of how we live. The world is being destroyed—no doubt about it—by the greed of the rich and powerful. It is also being destroyed by popular demand. There are not enough rich and powerful people to consume the whole world; for that, the rich and powerful need the help of countless ordinary people.

The problems we are worried about are caused, not just by other people, but by ourselves. And this realization should lead directly to two more. The first is that solving these problems is not work merely for so-called environmental organizations and agencies, but also for individuals, families, and local communities. . . .

The second realization, that we ourselves, in our daily economic life, are causing the problems we are trying to solve, ought to show us the inadequacy of the language we are using to talk about our connection to the world. The idea that we live in something called "the environment," for instance, is utterly preposterous. This word came into use because of the pretentiousness of learned experts who were embarrassed by the religious associations of "creation" and who thought "world" too mundane. But "environment" means that which surrounds or encircles us; it means a world separate from ourselves, outside us.

The real state of things, of course, is far more complex and intimate and interesting than that. The world that environs us, that is around us, is also within us. We are made of it; we eat, drink, and breathe it; it is bone of our bone and flesh of our flesh. It is also a Creation, a holy mystery, made for and to some extent by creatures, some but by no means all of whom are humans. This world, this Creation, belongs in a limited sense to us, for we may rightfully require certain things of it—the things necessary to keep us fully alive as the kind of creature we are; but we also belong to it, and it makes certain rightful claims upon us: that we care properly for it, that we leave it undiminished, not just to our children, but to all the creatures who will live in it after us. None of this intimacy and responsibility is conveyed by the word "environment."

—Wendell Berry, "Conservation Is Good Work,"
Amicus Journal (Winter 1992)

Although eco-radicals argue that it is only by personally reconnecting with nature that we can save nature, I would argue that the most ecological course for human society is, in fact, to divorce ourselves, and our economy, from the natural world. Our greatest contributions to the environment will come when we're farthest removed from it—in the laboratory, in the voting booth, and in the marketplace. To advocate this notion, which has been labeled "decoupling," is to acknowledge a profound division between humankind and the rest of nature—the very division that many Greens allege is at the root of the ecological crisis. Yet the technological progress that occurs when we disengage from the natural world has already averted ecological devastation many times. Europe, for example, avoided complete deforestation only because early modern smelters substituted coal for charcoal. This process should continue as composites replace steel and as coal begins to yield to solar power—with nature breathing easier everywhere as a result. One must wonder whether self-proclaimed deep ecologists, affirming their communion with nature through shamanistic rituals, will be in a position to supply the world with solar technologies. I suspect, rather, that such a contribution will come, if at all, from high-tech corporations—from firms operating in a social, economic, and technical milieu largely removed from the intricate webs of the natural world.

—Martin W. Lewis, "The Green Threat to Nature"
Harper's (November 1992), adapted from *Green Delusions: An Environmentalist Critique of Radical Environmentalism* (1992)

As C. S. Lewis put it, "Man's power over Nature means the power of some men over other men with Nature as the instrument."

Nature vs. economy, environment vs. development are false dualisms. They are inextricably related, parts of the same whole, set in opposition to one another only by a competitive social order that provides less than subsistence for the many, enormous power and wealth for a few, and a carrot and stick to keep the middle class in the game.

—Mary Zepernick, "Keeping Business in Its Place"
Cape Cod Times (February 11, 1994)

Biologists and economists agree that cooperation cannot be taken for granted. People and animals will cooperate only if they as individuals are given reasons to do so. For economists that means economic incentives; for biologists it means the pursuit of short-term goals that were once the means to reproduction. Both think that people are generally not willing to pay for the long-term good of society or the planet. To save the environment, therefore, we will have to find a way to reward individuals for good behavior and punish them for bad. Exhorting them to self-sacrifice for the sake of "humanity" or "the earth" will not be enough. . . .

Wherever environmentalism has succeeded, it has done so by changing individual incentives, not by exhortation, moral reprimand, or appeals to our better natures. If somebody wants to dump a toxic chemical or smuggle an endangered species, it is the thought of prison or a fine that deters him. If a state wants to avoid enforcing the federal Clean Air Act of 1990, it is the thought of eventually being "bumped up" to a more stringent nonattainment category of the act that haunts state officials. Given that this is the case, environmental policy should be a matter of seeking the most enforceable, least bureaucratic, cheapest, most effective incentives.

—Matt Ridley and Bobbi S. Low,
"Can Selfishness Save the Environment?"
Atlantic Monthly (September 1993)

Let's take a brief look now at what happened while the world was supposedly approaching the limits to growth.

The world's total output of goods and services increased 500 percent since 1950. Not everybody got richer, but the vast majority of people did. Those countries that experienced disappointing economic growth did not do so because they ran up against any environmental limits, but because of wars or devastatingly bad economic policies. . . .

And the future? The World Bank believes, "the opportunity for rapid development is greater today than at any time in history." One of the chief reasons is that policymakers are coming to understand the importance of drastically reducing government interference in the economy and of establishing stable property rights and free markets as the way to create wealth. In addition, new technologies are vastly improving both industrial and agricultural productivity around the world.

The World Bank expects developing countries' economies to expand at an average rate of 4.9 percent per year in the 1990s, while industrial countries will grow at a 3 percent annual rate.

There are no permanent resource shortages—future food supplies are ample, world population will level off before overcrowding becomes a problem, and pollution can be controlled at modest cost. So it appears that the only limit to growth is the human imagination—if we sink back and accept the antigrowth eco-theology we may well condemn our posterity to desperate poverty in a resource-depleted world. Yet this is precisely the world that some radical environmentalists would like us to accept.

—Ronald Bailey, *Eco-Scam:*
The False Prophets of Ecological Apocalypse (1993)

INTRODUCTION

What vaster, more complex challenge has ever faced humanity than preserving our habitat? Most of us accept the need to take care of our own surroundings. We might skip making the bed or vacuuming the rug from time to time, but eventually some combination of training and common sense moves us to reassert order. The larger the territory, the more work involved. Every backyard gardener knows that keeping crabgrass out of the carrot patch and caterpillars off the roses requires constant vigilance. How much more vigilance is needed to care for a forest? An ecosystem? A planet?

Beyond care and attention, we need knowledge. Otherwise we risk killing the carrots along with the crabgrass. Yet—as the selections in this book demonstrate—no definitive instruction manual exists for protecting our environment. Instead we distill information from dozens of fields of study focusing on hundreds of problems, generating thousands of hypothetical solutions. Some of these diagnoses and prescriptions overlap; some conflict. Not all investigators even agree that environmental protection should be a priority—much less how it should be done, or whether our species is in a position to do it.

In this chapter we look at an assortment of answers to the question: How can we solve our environmental predicament? In "Earth First!" Dave Foreman, a founder of the radical group by that name, explains why he renounced moderation in favor of extremism to preserve and restore wilderness. Foreman is a vocal advocate of deep ecology, the view that human beings have no right to place our interests ahead of those of any other species or of the earth as a whole. In "The Problem with Earth First!" Murray Bookchin counters Foreman with a defense of social ecology. Bookchin contends that our very kinship with other species forces human beings to acknowledge our unique place in evolution and in power and that we must seek social solutions to ecological problems. According to Regina Austin and Michael Schill the whole mainstream environmental movement has skewed priorities. In "Activists of Color," they describe the relatively new environmental justice movement, which asserts that human beings—especially those forced to live in polluted surroundings—are more important than animals or wilderness.

Former Environmental Protection Agency administrator William K. Reilly hails a new environmental consciousness on the part of corporate leaders, who recognize that being "green" is good for business. His essay "The Green Thumb of Capitalism" depicts economic growth as essential to effective environmental action. Diane Jukofsky considers specific applications of economics to ecology in "Can Marketing Save the Rainforest?" A growing number of manufacturers, she notes, are helping to preserve valuable tropical rainforests by developing uses for oils and other substances that can be harvested there. Sandra Postel presents a still wider view of the relationship between environmental problems and economics in "Carrying Capacity: Earth's Bottom Line." Armed with grim statistics from around the world, Postel argues that the earth's human population is rapidly exhausting the resources our planet can produce to support us.

Julian L. Simon takes the opposite position in "Should We Conserve?," asserting that scarcity of resources is a fiction—what we use up today, advancing technology will replace tomorrow. Frances Cairncross rebuts some of Simon's ideas and refines others in "Government and the Economics of the Environment." She believes we must accept both the need to conserve the earth's resources and the need for government to play a key role in environmental protection.

DAVE FOREMAN

Earth First!

Dave Foreman worked for the Wilderness Society (founded by Aldo Leopold; see p. 4) from 1973 to 1980. He served as Southwest representative in New Mexico and as issues coordinator in Washington, D.C. In the following excerpt from *Confessions of an Eco-Warrior* (1991), Foreman tells why he left the moderate Wilderness Society and cofounded the radical environmental group Earth First! Foreman edited the *Earth First! Journal* from 1982 to 1988. He currently operates a mail-order bookstore, Dave Foreman's Conservation Bookshelf, and continues to represent the "deep ecology" view within the radical wing of the environmental movement. Among his other writings is *Ecodefense: A Field Guide to Monkeywrenching* (1989).

A major crack in my moderate ideas appeared early in 1979, when I returned from Washington to the small ranching community of Glenwood, New Mexico. I had lived there earlier for six years, and although I was a known conservationist, I was fairly well accepted. Shortly after my return, the *New York Times* published an article on RARE II,[1] with the Gila National Forest around Glenwood as chief exhibit. To my amazement, the article quoted a rancher who I considered to be a friend as threatening *my* life because of local fears about the consequences of Wilderness designations. A couple of days later I was accosted on the street by four men, one of whom ran the town café where I had eaten many a chicken-fried steak. They threatened my life because of RARE II.

I was not afraid, but I was irritated—and surprised. I had been a leading moderate among New Mexico conservationists. I had successfully persuaded New Mexico conservation groups to propose fewer RARE II areas on the Gila National Forest as Wilderness. What had backfired? I thought again about the different approaches to RARE II: the moderate, subdued one advanced by the major conservation groups; the howling, impassioned, extreme stand set forth by off-road-vehicle zealots, many ranchers, local boosters, loggers, and miners. They looked like fools. We looked like statesmen. They won.

---

[1]**RARE II:** Roadless Area Review and Evaluation II, a twenty-month Forest Service effort to determine which national forest lands should be protected in their natural condition (that is, as officially designated wilderness areas).—ED.

The last straw fell on the Fourth of July, 1980, in Moab, Utah. There the local [Grand County] commission sent a flag-flying bulldozer into an area the Bureau of Land Management [BLM] had identified as a possible study area for Wilderness designation. The bulldozer incursion was an opening salvo for the so-called Sagebrush Rebellion, a move by chambers of commerce, ranchers, and right-wing fanatics in the West to claim federal public land for the states and eventual transfer to private hands. The Rebellion was clearly an extremist effort, lacking the support of even many conservative members of Congress in the West, yet BLM was afraid to stop the county commission.

What have we really accomplished? I thought. *Are we any better off as far as saving the earth now than we were ten years ago?* I ticked off the real problems: world population growth, destruction of tropical forests, expanding slaughter of African wildlife, oil pollution of the oceans, acid rain, carbon dioxide buildup in the atmosphere, spreading deserts on every continent, destruction of native peoples and the imposition of a single culture (European) on the entire world, plans to carve up Antarctica, planned deep seabed mining, nuclear proliferation, recombinant DNA research, toxic wastes. . . . It was staggering. And I feared we had done nothing to reverse the tide. Indeed, it had accelerated.

And then: Ronald Reagan. James "Rape 'n' Ruin" Watt became   5 Secretary of the Interior. The Forest Service was Louisiana-Pacific's. Interior was Exxon's. The Environmental Protection Agency was Dow's. Quickly, the Reagan administration and the Republican Senate spoke of gutting the already gutless Alaska Lands bill. The Clean Air Act, up for renewal, faced a government more interested in corporate black ink than human black lungs. The lands of the Bureau of Land Management appeared to the Interior Department obscenely naked without the garb of oil wells. Concurrently, the Agriculture Department directed the Forest Service to rid the National Forests of decadent and diseased old-growth trees. The cowboys had the grazing lands, and God help the hiker, Coyote, or blade of grass that got in their way.

Maybe, some of us began to feel, even before Reagan's election, it was time for a new joker in the deck: a militant, uncompromising group unafraid to say what needed to be said or to back it up with stronger actions than the established organizations were willing to take. This idea had been kicking around for a couple of years. Finally, in 1980, several disgruntled conservationists—including Susan Morgan, formerly educational director for the Wilderness Society; Howie Wolke, former Wyoming representative for Friends of the Earth; Bart Koehler, former Wyoming representative for the Wilderness Society; Ron Kezar, a longtime Sierra Club activist; and I—decided that the time for talk was past. We formed a new national group, which we called Earth First! We set out to be radical in style, positions, philosophy, and organization in order to be effective and to avoid the pitfalls of co-option and moderation that we had already experienced.

What, we asked ourselves as we sat around a campfire in the Wyoming mountains, were the reasons and purposes for environmental radicalism?

- To state honestly the views held by many conservationists.

- To demonstrate that the Sierra Club and its allies were raging moderates, believers in the system, and to refute the Reagan/Watt contention that they were "environmental extremists."

- To balance such antienvironmental radicals as the Grand County 10 commission and provide a broader spectrum of viewpoints.

- To return vigor, joy, and enthusiasm to the tired, unimaginative environmental movement.

- To keep the established groups honest. By stating a pure, no-compromise, pro-earth position, we felt that Earth First! could help keep the other groups from straying too far from their original philosophical base.

- To give an outlet to many hard-line conservationists who were no longer active because of disenchantment with compromise politics and the co-option of environmental organizations.

- To provide a productive fringe, since ideas, creativity, and energy tend to spring up on the edge and later spread into the center.

- To inspire others to carry out activities straight from the pages of *The* 15 *Monkey Wrench Gang* (a novel of environmental sabotage by Edward Abbey), even though Earth First!, we agreed, would itself be ostensibly law-abiding.

- To help develop a new worldview, a biocentric paradigm, an earth philosophy. To fight, with uncompromising passion, for earth.

The name Earth First! was chosen because it succinctly summed up the one thing on which we could all agree: that in *any* decision, consideration for the health of the earth must come first.

In a true earth-radical group, concern for wilderness preservation must be the keystone. The idea of wilderness, after all, is the most radical in human thought—more radical than Paine, than Marx, than Mao.[2] Wilderness says: Human beings are not paramount, earth is not

---

[2]**Paine . . . Marx . . . Mao:** Thomas Paine (1737–1809) Anglo-American political theorist, writer, and revolutionary. Karl Marx (1818–83) German social philosopher; the chief theorist of modern socialism and communism. Mao Zedong (1893–1976) Founder and leader of the People's Republic of China, 1949–1976.—ED.

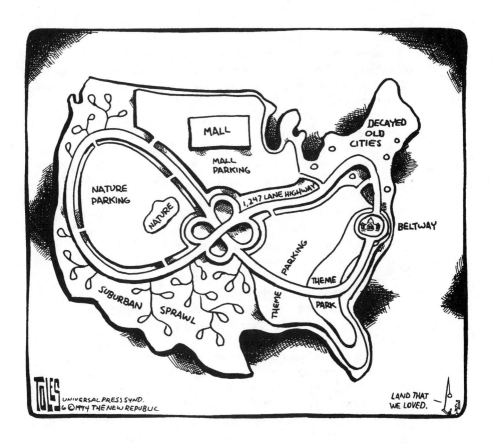

for *Homo sapiens* alone, human life is but one life form on the planet and has no right to take exclusive possession. Yes, wilderness for its own sake, without any need to justify it for human benefit. Wilderness for wilderness. For bears and whales and titmice and rattlesnakes and stink bugs. And . . . wilderness for human beings. Because it is the laboratory of human evolution, and because it is home.

It is not enough to protect our few remaining bits of wilderness. The only hope for earth (including humanity) is to withdraw huge areas as inviolate natural sanctuaries from the depredations of modern industry and technology. Keep Cleveland, Los Angeles. Contain them. Try to make them habitable. But identify big areas that can be restored to a semblance of natural conditions, reintroduce the Grizzly Bear and wolf and prairie grasses, and declare them off limits to modern civilization.

In the United States, pick an area for each of our major ecosystems 20 and recreate the American wilderness—not in little pieces of a thousand acres, but in chunks of a million or ten million. Move out the people and cars. Reclaim the roads and plowed land. It is not enough any longer to say no more dams on our wild rivers. We must begin tearing down some dams already built—beginning with Glen Canyon on the Colorado River in Arizona, Tellico in Tennessee, Hetch Hetchy and New Melones in California—and freeing shackled rivers.

This emphasis on wilderness does not require ignoring other environmental issues or abandoning social issues. In the United States, blacks and Chicanos of the inner cities are the ones most affected by air and water pollution, the ones most trapped by the unnatural confines of urbanity. So we decided that not only should eco-militants be concerned with these human environmental problems, we should also make common ground with other progressive elements of society whenever possible.

Obviously, for a group more committed to Gila monsters and mountain lions than to people, there will not be a total alliance with other social movements. But there are issues in which Earth radicals can cooperate with feminist, Native American, antinuke, peace, civil-rights, and civil-liberties groups. The inherent conservatism of the conservation community has made it wary of snuggling too close to these leftist organizations. We hoped to pave the way for better cooperation from the entire conservation movement.

We believed that new tactics were needed—something more than commenting on dreary environmental-impact statements and writing letters to members of Congress. Politics in the streets. Civil disobedience. Media stunts. Holding the villains up to ridicule. Using music to charge the cause.

Action is the key. Action is more important than philosophical hairsplitting or endless refining of dogma (for which radicals are so well known). Let our actions set the finer points of our philosophy. And let us recognize that diversity is not only the spice of life, but also the strength. All that would be required to join Earth First!, we decided, was a belief in earth first. Apart from that, Earth First! would be big enough to contain street poets and cowboy bar bouncers, agnostics and pagans, vegetarians and raw-steak eaters, pacifists and those who think that turning the other cheek is a good way to get a sore face.

Radicals frequently verge on a righteous seriousness. But we felt 25 that if we couldn't laugh at ourselves we would be merely another bunch of dangerous fanatics who should be locked up—like oil company executives. Not only does humor preserve individual and group sanity; it retards hubris, a major cause of environmental rape, and it is also an effective weapon. Fire, passion, courage, and emotionalism are also needed. We have been too reasonable, too calm, too understanding. It's time to get angry, to cry, to let rage flow at what the human cancer is doing to earth, to be uncompromising. For Earth First! there is no truce or cease-fire. No surrender. No partitioning of the territory.

Ever since the earth goddesses of ancient Greece were supplanted by the macho Olympians, repression of women and earth has gone hand in hand with imperial organization. Earth First! decided to be nonorganizational: no officers, no bylaws or constitution, no incorporation, no tax status, just a collection of women and men committed to the earth. At the turn of the century, William Graham Sumner wrote a famous essay titled "The Conquest of the United States by Spain." His thesis was that Spain had ultimately won the Spanish-American War because the United States took on the imperialism and totalitarianism of Spain. We felt that if we took on the organization of the industrial state, we would soon accept their anthropocentric paradigm, much as Audubon and the Sierra Club already had.

And when we are inspired, we *act.*

Massive, powerful, like some creation of Darth Vader, Glen Canyon Dam squats in the canyon of the Colorado River on the Arizona-Utah border and backs the cold, dead waters of "Lake" Powell some 180 miles upstream, drowning the most awesome and magical canyon on earth. More than any other single entity, Glen Canyon Dam is the symbol of the destruction of wilderness, of the technological ravishment of the West. The finest fantasy of eco-warriors in the West is the destruction of the dam and the liberation of the Colorado. So it was only proper that on March 21, 1981—at the spring equinox, the traditional time of rebirth—Earth First! held its first national gathering at Glen Canyon Dam.

On that morning, seventy-five members of Earth First! lined the walkway of the Colorado River Bridge, seven hundred feet above the once-free river, and watched five compatriots busy at work with an awkward black bundle on the massive dam just upstream. Those on the bridge carried placards reading "Damn Watt, Not Rivers," "Free the Colorado," and "Let It Flow." The five of us on the dam attached ropes to a grille, shouted out "Earth First!" and let three hundred feet of black plastic unfurl down the side of the dam, creating the impression of a growing crack. Those on the bridge returned the cheer.

Then Edward Abbey, author of *The Monkey Wrench Gang,* told the 30 protestors of the "green and living wilderness" that was Glen Canyon only nineteen years ago:

> And they took it away from us. The politicians of Arizona, Utah,
> New Mexico, and Colorado, in cahoots with the land developers,

city developers, industrial developers of the Southwest, stole this treasure from us in order to pursue and promote their crackpot ideology of growth, profit, and power—growth for the sake of power, power for the sake of growth.

Speaking toward the future, Abbey offered this advice: "Oppose. Oppose the destruction of our homeland by these alien forces from Houston, Tokyo, Manhattan, Washington, D.C., and the Pentagon. And if opposition is not enough, then subvert."

Hardly had he finished speaking when Park Service police and Coconino County sheriff's deputies arrived on the scene. While they questioned Howie Wolke and me, and tried to disperse the illegal assembly, outlaw country singer Johnny Sagebrush led the demonstrators in song for another twenty minutes.

The Glen Canyon Dam caper brought Earth First! an unexpected amount of media attention. Membership quickly spiraled to more than a thousand, with members from Maine to Hawaii. Even the government became interested. According to reports from friendly park rangers, the FBI dusted the entire Glen Canyon Dam crack for fingerprints!

When a few of us kicked off Earth First!, we sensed a growing environmental radicalism in the country, but we did not expect the response we received. Maybe Earth First! is in the right place at the right time.

The cynical may smirk. "But what can you really accomplish? 35 How can you fight Exxon, Coors, the World Bank, Japan, and the other great corporate giants of the earth? How, indeed, can you fight the dominant dogmas of Western civilization?"

Perhaps it *is* a hopeless quest. But one who loves Earth can do no less. Maybe a species will be saved or a forest will go uncut or a dam will be torn down. Maybe not. A monkeywrench thrown into the gears of the machine may not stop it. But it might delay it, make it cost more. And it feels good to put it there.

Analyzing Issues and Arguments

1. What does Dave Foreman see as the proper role(s) for the human residents of this planet?
2. From the description in this selection, what appear to have been the goals of Earth First!'s first national gathering at the Glen Canyon Dam? What did that gathering accomplish?
3. Where in this selection does Foreman use logic and reason to convince readers of his points? Where does he use the emo-

tionalism that Earth First! advocates? How would the impact of his argument change if Foreman's approach were entirely reasonable? Entirely emotional?

Writing about Issues and Arguments

Look at the goals Foreman describes in paragraphs 19 and 20. What would they accomplish if achieved? What would it take to achieve them? Write an essay evaluating the desirability and feasibility of these goals. You may wish to draw on other sources in arriving at your evaluation. (See "Suggestions for Further Reading," p. 333.)

IN THE NEWS

A New Conservation Ethic

Bruce Babbitt

> The following op-ed piece ran in the *Los Angeles Times* on June 1, 1994. It was adapted from a speech that Secretary of the Interior Bruce Babbitt delivered at Independence National Park in Philadelphia on May 23, 1994, to mark the beginning of National Parks Week. Babbitt, a former governor of Arizona, was also head of the League of Conservation Voters.

In its 1916 decree creating the National Park Service, Congress explicitly outlined two goals: preserve the designated sites "unimpaired for the enjoyment of future generations," and provide for the public enjoyment of those resources. The conflict between preservation and access has forced a creative tension on the Park Service since its first days. Achieving balance grows more difficult each year.

As challenging as the mission is, the two goals are not contradictory, particularly when one focuses on the nature of the genuine park visitor experience.

The national parks are not about entertainment; Disney, Warner Brothers, and others are masters at that task, and park rangers need not compete with them. Rather, rangers facilitate the American people's encounter with their heritage. The challenge is in bringing the visitor to a more intense appreciation of the natural world.

This framework sets new and clear parameters on methods for accommodating more visitors.

Despite annual increases in visitation, for example, the Park Service will 5
not be in the road-building business. Roads disrupt, divide, and fragment

natural systems that are the very reason for parks; our challenge is in finding new means of visitor transport.

We will not be in the hotel-building business, but will instead work with owners of lands bordering parks so that many overnight needs can be met in gateway communities. These communities can also serve as "staging" areas, where visitors can learn of a park's facilities, collect materials, and shop—all without adding to the milling crowds inside.

Likewise, the service must consider different methods for protecting its resource base, because it is no longer enough to focus on the nature of developments within the park. We must begin to focus on parks not as distinct entities, but as the centers of ecosystems.

At Yellowstone, massive herds of elk and buffalo (and soon, perhaps, gray wolves) do not acknowledge the straight lines on a map; those animals inherited an entire ecosystem, and park staff must work closely with resource managers from other state and federal agencies to protect their migration range.

Everglades National Park is part of a natural system being killed by the invasion of exotic plants (caused by nutrient-rich agricultural runoff) and the diversion of water for residential and commercial uses. That park's fate lies not in the hands of its rangers, but in a massive, multi-agency effort to restore the system.

Sequoia National Park has air-quality problems worse than many large 10 cities, but the problems' source lies in faraway industrial centers along the California coast and in the Central Valley. Clearly, it is no longer sufficient to label land a park and assume it is protected.

Protecting the resource base also means continuing the search for new sites, because America's history and perspectives are always changing. Fifty years ago, there was no Martin Luther King Jr. Historical Site to be preserved, because that chapter in our history had not yet been written.

A century ago, we crossed the Midwest in search of scenic splendor, oblivious to the extraordinary biodiversity being plowed up and taken for granted. The new effort to create a park in the Kansas tall-grass prairie finally acknowledges the importance of that resource.

Generations in search of alpine scenery simply walked on by some of America's most unique ecosystems. One of those regions would be protected by the California Desert Protection Act, ushered through the Senate by Senator Dianne Feinstein, D-Calif. Unsurpassed in its scenic, biological, cultural, and recreational significance, the desert has been ignored too long.

Finally, protection of the resource requires a sounder financial base. A first step would be congressional action to restore discretion to the Interior secretary to set reasonable park entrance fees. Currently, only three of the 367 Park Service sites charge $10 per vehicle, only fifteen charge as much as $5 per car, and Yellowstone's entrance fee is less today than it was in 1915. In addition, Congress can provide collection incentives to park managers by returning to the park half the money collected above the current base.

Though beset by fundamental problems, the National Park Service can 15 fill a unique and immediate role. We are within decades of an environmental collapse. Our urgent task is to communicate to the American people what it means to live more lightly and respectfully on the land.

The national parks must serve as the gateway to the conservation ethic, because if that gateway can't be crossed in our national parks, it can't be crossed anywhere.   ▪

Analyzing Issues and Arguments

1. According to Bruce Babbitt, how should the National Park Service reconcile its two seemingly contradictory goals? What specific recommendations does he make?
2. How are the National Park Service's goals different from those Dave Foreman described in paragraphs 19 and 20 (page 237)? How do you think Foreman would react to Babbitt's recommendations?

MURRAY BOOKCHIN

The Problem with Earth First!

Murray Bookchin is the founder of the social ecology movement, which argues that environmental problems are the direct consequence of humanity's attempt to dominate nature, and that "the very concept of dominating nature stems from the domination of human by human." The son of Russian revolutionary émigrés to New York City, Bookchin joined but then left the Communist youth movement in the 1930s, served in the U.S. army during World War II, and afterward became active in union organizing. During the 1950s and 1960s he began publishing articles and books on such subjects as chemicals in food, the problems of cities, and alternative technologies. Bookchin's books include *Our Synthetic Environment* (1962), *The Limits of the City* (1974), *Toward an Ecological Society* (1981), *The Ecology of Freedom* (1982), and *Remaking Society: Pathways to a Green Future* (1990). In 1989 Bookchin and Dave Foreman (p. 234) debated their contrasting positions in an attempt to heal a schism that was developing within the radical wing of the environmental movement. Their debate led to the book *Defending the Earth: A Dialogue between Murray Bookchin and Dave Foreman* (1991), from which this selection is excerpted.

The ultimate moral appeal of Earth First! is that it urges us to safeguard the natural world from our ecologically destructive societies, that is, in some sense, from ourselves. But, I have to ask, who is this "us" from which the living world has to be protected? This, too, is an important question. Is it "humanity"? Is it the human "species" per se? Is it people, as such? Or is it our particular society, our particular civilization, with its hierarchical social relations which pit men against women, privileged whites against people of color, elites against masses, employers against workers, the First World against the Third World, and, ultimately, a cancerlike, "grow or die" industrial capitalist economic system against the natural world and other life-forms? Is this not the social root of the popular belief that nature is a mere object of social domination, valuable only as a "resource"?

All too often we are told by liberal environmentalists, and not a few deep ecologists, that it is "we" as a species or, at least, "we" as an amalgam of "anthropocentric" individuals that are responsible for the breakdown of the web of life. I remember an "environmental" presentation staged by the Museum of Natural History in New York during the 1970s in which the public was exposed to a long series of exhibits, each depicting examples of pollution and ecological disruption. The exhibit which closed the presentation carried a startling sign, "The Most Dangerous Animal on Earth." It consisted simply of a huge mirror which reflected back the person who stood in front of it. I remember a black child standing in front of that mirror while a white schoolteacher tried to explain the message which this arrogant exhibit tried to convey. Mind you, there was no exhibit of corporate boards of directors planning to deforest a mountainside or of government officials acting in collusion with them.

One of the problems with this asocial, "species-centered" way of thinking, of course, is that it blames the victim. Let's face it, when you say a black kid in Harlem is as much to blame for the ecological crisis as the president of Exxon, you are letting one off the hook and slandering the other. Such talk by environmentalists makes grassroots coalition-building next to impossible. Oppressed people know that humanity is hierarchically organized around complicated divisions that are ignored only at their peril. Black people know this well when they confront whites. The poor know this well when they confront the wealthy. The Third World knows it well when it confronts the First World. Women know it well when they confront patriarchal males. The radical ecology movement needs to know it too.

All this loose talk of "we" masks the reality of social power and social institutions. It masks the fact that the social forces that are tearing down the planet are the same social forces which threaten to degrade women, people of color, workers, and ordinary citizens. It masks the fact that there is a historical connection between the way people deal with each other as social beings and the way they treat the rest of nature. It masks the fact that our ecological problems are fundamentally social problems requiring fundamental social change. That is what I mean by *social* ecology. It makes a big difference in how societies relate to the natural world whether people live in cooperative, nonhierarchical, and decentralized communities or in hierarchical, class-ridden, and authoritarian mass societies. Similarly, the ecological impact of human reason, science, and technology depends enormously on the type of society in which these forces are shaped and employed.

Perhaps the biggest question that all wings of the radical ecology 5 movement must satisfactorily answer is just what do we mean by "nature." If we are committed to defending nature, it is important to clearly understand what we mean by this. Is nature, the real world, essentially the remnants of the earth's prehuman and pristine biosphere that has now been vastly reduced and poisoned by the "alien" presence of the human species? Is nature what we see when we look out on an unpeopled vista from a mountain? Is it a cosmic arrangement of beings frozen in a moment of eternity to be abjectly revered, adored, and untouched by human intervention? Or is nature much broader in meaning? Is nature an evolutionary process which is cumulative and which *includes* human beings?

The ecology movement will get nowhere unless it understands that the human species is no less a product of natural evolution than bluegreen algae, whales, and bears. To conceptually separate human beings and society from nature by viewing humanity as an inherently unnatural force in the world leads, philosophically, either to an antinature "anthropocentrism" or a misanthropic aversion to the human species. . . .

We are part of nature, a product of a long evolutionary journey. To some degree, we carry the ancient oceans in our blood. To a very large degree we go through a kind of biological evolution as fetuses. It is not alien to natural evolution that a species called human beings has emerged over billions of years which is capable of thinking in sophisticated ways. Our brains and nervous systems did not suddenly spring into existence without long antecedents in natural history. That which we most prize as integral to our humanity—our extraordinary capacity to think on complex conceptual levels—can be traced back to the nerve network of primitive invertebrates, the ganglia of a mollusk, the spinal cord of a fish, the brain of an amphibian, and the cerebral cortex of a primate.

We need to understand that the human species has evolved as a remarkably creative and social life-form that is organized to create a place for itself in the natural world, not only to adapt to the rest of nature. The human species, its different societies, and its enormous powers to alter the environment were not invented by a group of ideologues called "humanists" who decided that nature was "made" to serve humanity and its needs. Humanity's distinct powers have emerged out of eons of evolutionary development and out of centuries of cultural development. These remarkable powers present us, however, with an enormous moral responsibility. We can contribute to the diversity, fecundity, and richness of the natural world—what I call "first nature"—more consciously, perhaps, than any other animal. Or, our societies—"second nature"—can exploit the whole web of life and tear down the planet in a rapacious, cancerous manner.

The future that awaits the world of life ultimately depends upon what kind of society or "second nature" we create. This probably affects, more than any other single factor, how we interact with and intervene in biological or "first nature." And make no mistake about it, the future of "first nature," the primary concern of conservationists, is dependent on the results of this interaction. The central problem we face today is that the social evolution of "second nature" has taken a wrong turn. Society is poisoned. It has been poisoned for thousands of years, from before the Bronze Age. It has been warped by rule by elders, by patriarchy, by warriors, by hierarchies of all sorts which have led now to the current situation of a world threatened by competitive, nuclear-armed, nation-states and a phenomenally destructive corporate capitalist system in the West and an equally ecologically destructive, though now crumbling, bureaucratic state capitalist system in the East.

We need to create an ecologically oriented society out of the pres- 10 ent antiecological one. If we can change the direction of our civilization's social evolution, human beings can assist in the creation of a truly "free nature," where all of our human traits—intellectual, communicative, and social—are placed at the service of natural evolution to consciously increase biotic diversity, diminish suffering, foster the further evolution of new and ecologically valuable lifeforms, and reduce the impact of disastrous accidents or the harsh effects of harmful change. Our species, gifted by the creativity of natural evolution itself, could play the role of nature rendered self-conscious.

Analyzing Issues and Arguments

1. On what points does Murray Bookchin disagree with Dave Foreman ("Earth First!", p. 234)? What questions does Bookchin call on Foreman to answer?
2. On what points does Bookchin agree with Foreman? What concepts, phrases, and key words appear in both "Earth First!" and "The Problem with Earth First!"?
3. What actions or changes of behavior does Bookchin advocate?

Writing about Issues and Arguments

"Society is poisoned," writes Bookchin in paragraph 9. "It has been warped by rule by elders, by patriarchy, by warriors, by hierarchies of all sorts." What does he mean? Write a description of a particular society you live in—your neighborhood, your school, your town, your country, or whatever—in which you identify these different kinds of rule, and then show how each one affects the people living under it. Be sure to make it clear whether you agree or disagree with Bookchin's statement. Alternatively, write a description of an imaginary society with none of the hierarchies Bookchin mentions.

REGINA AUSTIN AND MICHAEL SCHILL

Activists of Color

Regina Austin is a professor at the University of Pennsylvania Law School; she has also been a visiting professor at Harvard and Stanford University law schools. Previously, she practiced law with the firm of Schnader, Harrison, Segal, and Lewis. Austin has written on a wide range of topics addressing African American culture, the underground and informal economies, African American feminist legal scholarship, and harassment of low-status employees. Michael Schill is an assistant professor at the University of Pennsylvania Law School, where he teaches in the areas of property law, real estate transactions, and urban affairs. Before joining the faculty there in 1987, he specialized in real estate law with the New York law firm of Fried, Frank, Harris, and Jacobson. "Activists of Color" looks at involvement in environmental issues among African Americans and other minorities as well as those groups' skepticism about the mainstream environmental movement. The selection is excerpted from Austin and Schill's chapter "Black, Brown, Red, and Poisoned" in *Unequal Protection: Environmental Justice and Communities of Color* (1994), edited by Robert D. Bullard.

People of color throughout the United States are receiving more than their fair share of the poisonous fruits of industrial production. They live cheek by jowl with waste dumps, incinerators, landfills, smelters, factories, chemical plants, and oil refineries whose operations make them sick and kill them young. They are poisoned by the air they breathe, the water they drink, the fish they catch, the vegetables they grow, and, in the case of children, the very ground they play on. Even the residents of some of the most remote rural hamlets of the South and Southwest suffer from the ill effects of toxins.[1] . . .

The Path of Least Resistance

The disproportionate location of sources of toxic pollution in communities of color is the result of various development patterns. In some cases, the residential communities where people of color now live were

---

[1]Activist Pat Bryant uses the term "poisoning" in lieu of "pollution" to convey the idea that harm is being caused deliberately with the knowledge and aid of government officials. See Pat Bryant, "Toxics and Racial Justice," *Social Policy* 20 (Summer 1989): 48–52; Pat Bryant, "A Lily-White Achilles Heel," *Environmental Action* 21 (January–February 1990): 28–29.

originally the homes of whites who worked in the facilities that generate toxic emissions. The housing and the industry sprang up roughly simultaneously.[2] Whites vacated the housing (but not necessarily the jobs) for better shelter as their socioeconomic status improved, and poorer black and brown folks who enjoy much less residential mobility took their place. In other cases, housing for African Americans and Latino Americans was built in the vicinity of existing industrial operations because the land was cheap and the people were poor. For example, Richmond, California, was developed downwind from a Chevron oil refinery when African Americans migrated to the area to work in shipyards during World War II.[3]

In yet a third pattern, sources of toxic pollution were placed in existing minority communities. The explanations for such sitings are numerous; some reflect the impact of racial and ethnic discrimination. The impact, of course, may be attenuated and less than obvious. The most neutral basis for a siting choice is probably the natural characteristics of the land, such as mineral content of the soil.[4] Low population density would appear to be a similar criterion. It has been argued, however, that in the South, a sparse concentration of inhabitants is correlated with poverty, which is in turn correlated with race. "It follows that criteria for siting hazardous waste facilities which include density of population will have the effect of targeting rural black communities that have high rates of poverty."[5]

Likewise, the compatibility of pollution with preexisting uses might conceivably make some sites more suitable than others for polluting operations. Pollution tends to attract other sources of pollutants, particularly those associated with toxic disposal. For example, Chemical Waste Management, Incorporated (Chem Waste) has proposed the construction of a toxic waste incinerator outside of Kettleman City, California, a community composed largely of Latino farm workers.[6] Chem Waste also has proposed to build a hazardous waste incinerator

---

[2]See Community Environmental Health Center at Hunter College, *Hazardous Neighbors? Living Next Door to Industry in Greenpoint-Williamsburg* (New York: Hunter College, Community Environmental Health Center, 1989). This study details the nature of the toxic risks posed by industrial concerns in a community composed primarily of Hasidic Jews and Puerto Ricans.

[3]Citizens for a Better Environment, *Richmond at Risk: Community Development and Toxic Hazards from Industrial Polluters* (San Francisco: Citizens for a Better Environment, 1989), pp. 21–22.

[4]Conner Bailey and Charles Faupel, "Environmentalism and Civil Rights in Sumter County, Alabama," pp. 159, 170–171 in *Proceedings of the Michigan Conference on Race and the Incidence of Environmental Hazards,* ed. Bunyan Bryant and Paul Mohai (Ann Arbor: University of Michigan, School of Natural Resources, 1990).

[5]Ibid., p. 171.

[6]Miles Corwin, "Unusual Allies Fight Waste Incinerator," *Los Angeles Times,* February 24, 1991, p. A3.

in Emelle, a predominantly African American community located in the heart of Alabama's "black belt." The company already has hazardous waste landfills in Emelle and Kettleman City.

According to the company's spokeswoman, Chem Waste placed the 5 landfill in Kettleman City "because of the area's geological features. Because the landfill handles toxic waste, . . . it is an ideal spot for the incinerator"; the tons of toxic ash that the incinerator will generate can be "contained and disposed of at the installation's landfill."[7] Residents of Kettleman City face a "triple whammy" of threats from pesticides in the fields, the nearby hazardous waste landfill, and a proposed hazardous waste incinerator. This case is not unique.

After reviewing the literature on hazardous waste incineration, one commentator has concluded that "[m]inority communities represent a 'least cost' option for waste incineration . . . because much of the waste to be incinerated is already in these communities."[8] Despite its apparent neutrality, then, siting based on compatibility may be related to racial and ethnic discrimination, particularly if such discrimination influenced the siting of preexisting sources of pollution.

Polluters know that communities of low-income and working-class people with no more than a high school education are not as effective at marshaling opposition as communities of middle- or upper-income people. People of color in the United States have traditionally had less clout with which to check legislative and executive abuse or to challenge regulatory laxity. Private corporations, moreover, can have a powerful effect on the behavior of public officials. Poor minority people wind up the losers to them both.[9]

People of color are more likely than whites to be economically impoverished, and economic vulnerability makes impoverished communities of color prime targets for "risky" technologies. Historically, these communities are more likely than others to tolerate pollution-generating commercial development in the hope that economic benefits will inure to the community in the form of jobs, increased taxes, and civic improvements.[10] Once the benefits start to flow, the community may be reluctant to forgo them even when they are accompanied by poisonous spills or emissions. This was said to be the case in Emelle, in

---

[7]Ibid., p. A36.

[8]Harvey White, "Hazardous Waste Incineration and Minority Communities: The Case of Alsen, Louisiana," in Bryant and Mohai, *Race and the Incidence of Environmental Hazards*, pp. 142, 148–149.

[9]See Conger Beasley, "Of Pollution and Poverty: Keeping Watch in 'Cancer Alley,' " *Buzzworm* 2 (July–August 1990): 38, 41–42 (describing the Louisiana politics that produced the string of petrochemical plants lining what is known as Cancer Alley).

[10]Robert D. Bullard, "Environmental Blackmail in Minority Communities," in Bryant and Mohai, *Race and the Incidence of Environmental Hazards*, pp. 60, 64–65.

Sumter County, Alabama, site of the nation's largest hazardous waste landfill.[11]

Sumter County's population is roughly 70 percent African American, and 30 percent of its inhabitants fall below the poverty line. Although the landfill was apparently leaking, it was difficult to rally support against the plant among African American politicians because its operations contributed an estimated $15.9 million to the local economy in the form of wages, local purchases of goods and services, and per-ton landfill user fees.[12]

Of course, benefits do not always materialize after the polluter be- 10 gins operations. . . . In other cases, there is no net profit to distribute among the people. New jobs created by the poisonous enterprises are "filled by highly skilled labor from outside the community," while the increased tax revenues go not to "social services or other community development projects, but . . . toward expanding the infrastructure to better serve the industry."[13]

Once a polluter has begun operations, the victims' options are limited. Mobilizing a community against an existing polluter is more difficult than organizing opposition to a proposed toxic waste–producing activity. Resignation sets in, and the resources for attacking ongoing pollution are not as numerous, and the tactics not as potent, as those available during the proposal stage. Furthermore, though some individuals are able to escape toxic poisoning by moving out of the area, the flight of others will be blocked by limited incomes, housing discrimination, and restrictive land use regulations.[14]

Threat to Barrios, Ghettos, and Reservations

Pollution is no longer accepted as an unalterable consequence of living in the "bottom" (the least pleasant, poorest area minorities can occupy) by those on the bottom of the status hierarchy. Like anybody else, people of color are distressed by accidental toxic spills, explosions, and inexplicable patterns of miscarriages and cancers, and they are beginning to fight back, from Maine to Alaska.[15]

To be sure, people of color face some fairly high barriers to effec-

[11]See Robert D. Bullard, *Dumping in Dixie: Race, Class, and Environmental Quality* (Boulder, CO: Westview Press, 1990), pp. 69–73; Bailey and Faupel, "Environmentalism and Civil Rights in Sumter County," pp. 169–170, 172–173.

[12]Bailey and Faupel, "Environmentalism and Civil Rights in Sumter County," p. 163.

[13]Dana Alston, *Taking Back Our Lives: A Report to the Panos Institute on Environment, Community Development, and Race in the United States* (Washington, D.C.: The Panos Institute, 1990), p. 11.

[14]Robert D. Bullard and Beverly H. Wright, "Blacks and the Environment," *Humboldt Journal of Social Relations* 14 (Summer 1987):165, 180.

[15]Robert D. Bullard, *People of Color Environmental Groups Directory 1992* (Riverside, CA: University of California, 1992), pp. i–v.

tive mobilization against toxic threats, such as limited time and money; lack of access to technical, medical, and legal expertise; relatively weak influence in political and media circles; and ideological conflicts that pit jobs against the environment.[16] Limited fluency in English and fear of immigration authorities will keep some of those affected, especially Latinos, quiescent. Yet despite the odds, poor minority people are responding to their poisoning with a grass-roots movement of their own.

Activist groups of color are waging grass-roots environmental campaigns all over the country. Although they are only informally connected, these campaigns reflect certain shared characteristics and goals. The activity of activists of color is indicative of a grass-roots movement that occupies a distinctive position relative to both the mainstream movement and the white grass-roots environmental movement. The environmental justice movement is antielitist and antiracist. It capitalizes on the social and cultural differences of people of color as it cautiously builds alliances with whites and persons of the middle class. It is both fiercely environmental *and* conscious of the need for economic development in economically disenfranchised communities. Most distinctive of all, this movement has been extremely outspoken in challenging the integrity and bona fides of mainstream establishment environmental organizations.

People of color have not been mobilized to join grass-roots envi-   15
ronmental campaigns because of their general concern for the environment. Characterizing a problem as being "environmental" may carry weight in some circles, but it has much less impact among poor minority people. It is not that people of color are uninterested in the environment—a suggestion the grass-roots activists find insulting. In fact, they are more likely to be concerned about pollution than are people who are wealthier and white.[17] Rather, in the view of many people of color, environmentalism is associated with the preservation of wildlife and wilderness, which simply is not more important than the survival of people and the communities in which they live; thus, the mainstream movement has its priorities skewed.

The mainstream movement, so the critique goes, embodies white, bourgeois values, values that are foreign to African Americans, Latino Americans, Asian Americans, and Native Americans. Environmental sociologist Dorceta Taylor has characterized the motivations of those who make donations to mainstream organizations as follows:

---

[16]See generally Dorceta Taylor, "Blacks and the Environment: Toward an Explanation of the Concern and Action Gap between Blacks and Whites," *Environment and Behavior* 22 (March 1989): 175.

[17]Susan Cutter, "Community Concern for Pollution: Social and Environmental Influences," *Environment and Behavior* 13 (1981): 105–124.

> [In part, the] motivation to contribute is derived from traditional Romantic and Transcendental ideals—the idea of helping to conserve or preserve land and nature for one's own present and future use, or for future generations. Such use involves the ability to get away from it all; to transcend earthly worries, to escape, to commune with nature. The possibility of having a transcendental experience is strongly linked to the desire to save the places where such experiences are likely to occur.[18]

Even the more engaged environmentalists, those whose involvement includes participation in demonstrations and boycotts, are thought to be imbued with romantic and transcendental notions that favor nature over society and the individual's experience of the natural realm over the collective experience.

There are a number of reasons why people of color might not share such feelings. Their prospects for transcendental communion with nature are restricted. Parks and recreational areas have been closed to them because of discrimination, inaccessibility, cost, their lack of specialized skills or equipment, and residence requirements for admission.[19] They must find their recreation close to home. Harm to the environment caused by industrial development is not really their responsibility because they have relatively little economic power or control over the exploitation of natural resources. Since rich white people messed it up, rich white people ought to clean it up. In any event, emphasis on the environment in the abstract diverts attention and resources from the pressing, concrete problems that people of color, especially those with little or no income, confront every day.

Nonetheless, communities of color have addressed environmental problems that directly threaten them on their own terms. The narrowness of the mainstream movement, which appears to be more interested in endangered nonhuman species and pristine, undeveloped land than at-risk humans, makes poor minority people *think* that their concerns are not "environmental." Cognizant of this misconception and eschewing terminology that artificially compartmentalizes people's troubles, minority grass-roots environmental activists take a multidimensional approach to pollution problems. Thus, the sickening, poisonous odors emitted by landfills and sewage plants are considered matters of public health or government accountability, while workplace contamination is a labor issue, and lead-based paint in public housing projects is a landlord-tenant problem.[20]

[18]Dorceta Taylor, "Can the Environmental Movement Attract and Maintain the Support of Minorities?" in Bryant and Mohai, *Race and the Incidence of Environmental Hazards*, p. 35.

[19]Taylor, "Blacks and the Environment," pp. 187–190.

[20]Arnoldo Garcia, "Environmental Inequities," *Crossroads* (June 1990), p. 16 (interview with activist Richard Moore).

The very names of some of the organizations and the goals they espouse belie the primacy of environmental concerns. The Southwest Organizing Project of Albuquerque (SWOP) has been very successful in mobilizing people around issues of water pollution and workplace contamination. For example, SWOP fought for the rollback of charges levied against a group of home owners who were forced to hook up with a municipal water system because nitroglycerine had contaminated private wells. SWOP then campaigned to make the federal government assume responsibility for the pollution, which was attributed to operations at a nearby military installation. Yet in a briefing paper titled "Major National Environmental Organizations and the Problem of the 'Environmental Movement,' " SWOP describes itself as follows:

> SWOP does not consider itself an "environmental" organization but rather a community-based organization which addresses toxics issues as part of a broader agenda of action to realize social, racial, and economic justice. We do not single out the environment as necessarily having a special place above all other issues; rather, we recognize that issues of toxic contamination fit within an agenda which can (and in our practical day-to-day work, does) include employment, education, housing, health care, and other issues of social, racial, and economic justice.[21] . . .

In the estimation of the grass-roots folks, . . . race and ethnicity 20 surpass class as explanations for the undue toxic burden heaped on people of color. Activists see these environmental inequities as unfair and unjust—practices that many feel should be illegal. Of course, it is hard to prove that racial discrimination is responsible for siting choices and government inaction in the environmental area, particularly in a court of law. One need only point to the examples of *Bean v. Southwestern Waste Management* (Houston, Texas), *Bordeaux Action Committee v. Metropolitan Nashville* (Nashville, Tennessee), and *R.I.S.E. v. Kay* (King and Queen County, Virginia) to see the limited utility of current antidiscrimination doctrine in redressing the plight of poisoned communities of color.

Environmental activists of color draw a good deal of their inspiration from the modern civil rights movement of the 1960s. That movement was advanced by hard-won Supreme Court decisions. These organizers hope that a civil rights victory in the environmental area will validate their charges of environmental racism, help to flesh out the

[21]Southwest Organizing Project, "Major National Environmental Organizations and the Problem of the 'Environmental Movement,' " (February 1990) (unpublished briefing paper).

concept of environmental equity, serve as a catalyst for further activism, and, just possibly, force polluters to reconsider siting in poor minority communities.

Capitalizing on the Resources of Common Culture

For people of color, social and cultural differences such as language are not handicaps but the communal resources that facilitate mobilization around issues like toxic poisoning. As members of the same race, ethnicity, gender, and even age cadre, would-be participants share cultural traditions, modes, and mores that encourage cooperation and unity. People of color may be more responsive to organizing efforts than whites because they already have experience with collective action through community groups and institutions such as churches, parent-teacher associations, and town watches or informal social networks.[22] Shared criticisms of racism, a distrust of corporate power, and little expectation that government will be responsive to their complaints are common sentiments in communities of color and support the call to action around environmental concerns.

Grass-roots environmentalism is also fostered by notions that might be considered feminist or womanist. Acting on a realization that toxic poisoning is a threat to home and family, poor minority women have moved into the public realm to confront corporate and government officials whose modes of analysis reflect patriarchy, white supremacy, and class and scientific elitism. There are numerous examples of women of color whose strengths and talents have made them leaders of grass-roots environmental efforts.[23]

The organization Mothers of East Los Angeles (MELA) illustrates the link between group culture and mobilization in the people of color grass-roots environmental movement.[24] Persistent efforts by MELA defeated proposals for constructing a state prison and a toxic-waste incinerator in the group's mostly Latino American neighborhood in East Los Angeles.

---

[22]Bullard, *Dumping in Dixie,* pp. 95–98.

[23]See Jim McNeil, "Hazel Johnson: Talkin' Toxics," *In These Times* (May 23–June 5, 1990), p. 4 (interview with the founder of Chicago's Southeast Side's People for Community Recovery); Claude Engle, "Profiles: Environmental Action in Minority Communities," *Environmental Action* (January–February 1990), p. 22 (profiling Jessie Deerln Water, founder of Native Americans for a Clean Environment; Cora Tucker, founder of Citizens for a Better America; and Francesca Cavazos, director of the Maricopa County Organizing Project); Cynthia Hamilton, "Women, Home, and Community: The Struggle in an Urban Environment," *Race, Poverty, and the Environment Newsletter* (April 1990), p. 3.

[24]See Mary Pardo, "Mexican American Women Grassroots Community Activists: 'Mothers of East Los Angeles,' " *Frontiers: A Journal of Women Studies* 11 (1990): 1; Dick Russell, "Environmental Racism," *Amicus Journal* 11 (Spring 1989): 22–23, 29–31.

Similarly, the Lumbee Indians of Robeson County, North Car- 25
olina, who attach spiritual significance to a river that would have been
polluted by a hazardous waste facility proposed by the GSX Corporation, waged a campaign against the facility on the ground of cultural
genocide. Throughout the campaign, "Native American dance, music,
and regalia were used at every major public hearing. Local Lumbee
churches provided convenient meeting locations for GSX planning ses-
sions. Leaflet distribution at these churches reached significant minority
populations in every pocket of the county's nearly 1,000 square miles."[25]

Concerned Citizens of Choctaw defeated a plan to locate a hazardous waste facility on their lands in Philadelphia, Mississippi. The
Good Road Coalition, a grass-roots Native American group based on
the Rosebud Reservation in South Dakota, defeated plans by a Con-
necticut-based company to build a 6,000-acre garbage landfill on the
Rosebud. Local residents initiated a recall election, defeating several
tribal council leaders and the landfill proposal. The project, dubbed
"dances with garbage," typifies the lengths that the Lakota people and
other Native Americans will go to preserve their land—which is an essential part of their religion and culture.

Consider, finally, the Toxic Avengers of El Puente, a group of environmental organizers based in the Williamsburg section of Brooklyn,
New York.[26] The name is taken from the title of a horror movie. The
group attacks not only environmental racism but also adultism and
adult superiority and privilege. The members, whose ages range from
nine to twenty-eight, combine their activism with programs to educate
themselves and others about the science of toxic hazards.

The importance of culture in the environmental justice movement
seems not to have produced the kind of distrust and misgivings that might
impede interaction with white working-class and middle-class groups
engaged in grass-roots environmental activism. There are numerous examples of ethnic-based associations working in coalitions with one another, with majority group associations, and with organizations from the
mainstream.[27] There are also localities in which the antagonism and sus-
picion that are the legacy of white racism have kept whites and African
Americans from uniting against a common toxic enemy. The link between the minority groups and the majority groups seems grounded in

[25]Richard Regan and M. Legerton, "Economic Slavery or Hazardous Wastes? Robeson County's
Economic Menu," in *Communities in Economic Crisis: Appalachia and the South,* John Gaventa and
Alex Willingham, eds. (Philadelphia: Temple University Press, 1990), pp. 146, 153–154.

[26]Marguerite Holloway, "The Toxic Avengers Take Brooklyn," *City Limits* (December 1989),
p. 8.

[27]M. Oliviero, *Minorities and the Environment: An Inquiry for Foundations* (report to the Nathan
Cummings Foundation) (New York: Nathan Cummings Foundation, 1991), pp. 17–18, 21–24.

material exchange, not ideological fellowship. The white groups attacking toxins at the grass-roots level have been useful sources of financial assistance and information about tactics and goals. . . .

People of color have provided the crucial leadership for the growing environmental justice movement in the United States. This movement, in all aspects of its operations, is antielitist, antiracist, class conscious, populist, and participatory. It attacks environmental problems as being intertwined with other pressing economic, social, and political ills. It capitalizes on the social and cultural strengths of people of color and demands in turn that their lifestyles, traditions, and values be respected by polluters and mainstream environmental organizations alike.

The environmental justice movement is still in its embryonic 30 stages. Its ideology has yet to be fully developed, let alone tested. Moreover, it is too easy for outsiders to criticize the trade-offs and compromises poor people and people of color bearing toxic burdens have made. It is important to understand the movement on its own terms if one hopes to make policy proposals that will be of use to those struggling to save themselves. Grass-roots people have proven that they are capable of *leading, speaking,* and *doing* for themselves.

Analyzing Issues and Arguments

1. What reasons do Regina Austin and Michael Schill give in paragraphs 2–8 for the disproportionate siting of landfills, incinerators, and other sources of pollution in communities of color?

2. What demographic groups do Austin and Schill identify within the environmental justice movement? What groups do they identify within the rest of the environmental movement? What views do they express about environmentalism outside communities of color? What role(s) do they identify for whites in the environmental justice movement?

3. Judging from the style, content, and approach of "Activists of Color," how would you describe Austin and Schill's intended audience? How do you think the selection's impact would change if the authors used a less formal tone?

Writing about Issues and Arguments

Write an essay comparing and contrasting Dave Foreman's attitude toward wilderness (p. 234, paras. 18ff) with that of Austin and Schill (paras. 15ff). Whose position do you find more persuasive, and why?

How do you think Austin and Schill might respond to Foreman's statement that the "idea of wilderness . . . is the most radical in human thought" (para. 18)?

IN THE NEWS

No Pattern of Bias Found in Locating Toxic Waste Plants

Robert Braile

> The following news story ran in the *Boston Globe* on May 10, 1994. Robert Braile reports on environmental issues for the *Globe*. An expanded version of this article, entitled "Is Racism a Factor in Siting Undesirable Facilities?," appeared in the Summer 1994 issue of *Garbage* magazine.

Challenging several previous studies, researchers at the University of Massachusetts at Amherst said yesterday that they have found no evidence that minority communities have been targeted as sites for commercial hazardous waste facilities.

Environmental injustices exist, but when it comes to finding sites for incinerators, treatment plants, and other facilities, "there is no national pattern of environmental racism," said Douglas Anderton, professor of sociology and director of the Social and Demographic Research Institute.

Anderton's team examined census tract data from 1970, 1980, and 1990 in regions with 555 waste facilities. All 335 metropolitan areas are included, along with many remote areas.

They concluded that facilities are concentrated in industrial areas but are no more likely to be in areas with large black and Hispanic populations than elsewhere. The study found no evidence for "white flight," the exodus of wealthier whites from areas where facilities are sited, leaving behind a higher percentage of minorities. Areas with and without facilities have experienced growth in minority populations, the study found.

However, several leaders in the environmental justice movement said the 5
research is flawed because the analysis is based on census tracts, areas about 0.74 square miles in size with about four thousand people each. Those units are too large for meaningful analysis and ignore smaller communities with large minority populations where waste facilities are concentrated, the critics said.

"That itself is a sin of omission," said Robert Bullard, a professor of sociology at the University of California at Riverside. "If you are going to do a national study, you should use a methodology that is inclusive."

Anderton said he considers census tracts the smallest, most statistically reliable unit for such analysis.

Critics also said that the study covered only 36,423 of 61,258 tracts, omitting more rural, largely white areas and skewing the results. "If you exclude many of the white communities, you won't find bias," said Benjamin Goldman of the Boston-based Jobs and Environment Campaign.

In addition, the critics said the focus on incinerators and similar facilities ignores the broad range of injustices that minorities face—from Maine's Penobscot tribe, whose river has been contaminated by upstream paper mills, to the children of North Dorchester whose tenements are laced with lead.

"I've seen the evidence with my own eyes," said EPA Regional Adminis- 10 trator John P. DeVillars, who announced a plan to make environmental justice a priority.

The research was funded by a $200,000 grant, most of which was provided by WMX Technologies, one of the country's largest waste facility operators. Anderton denied that the sponsorship influenced the findings and said that if anything, the company's stockholders "want to downplay the findings, because they want to maintain their good relationship" with the movement.

Several earlier studies have concluded that minority and poor communities have borne the brunt of America's waste disposal needs. Based on such findings, an alliance of environmentalists and social justice advocates has forged a movement to address the issue. It gained steam in February when President Clinton directed federal agencies to ensure that their activities do not disproportionately burden minorities and the poor.

Among the earlier studies was a 1983 report by the General Accounting Office that concluded that most of the people living near four hazardous waste landfills in the Southeast were black. A study the same year by Bullard found that twenty-one of Houston's twenty-five incinerators and landfills were in predominantly black neighborhoods. A 1987 report by the United Church of Christ Commission for Racial Justice found that communities across the country within ZIP code range of at least one hazardous waste landfill had twice as many minorities as those without landfills. And a 1992 report by the National Law Journal concluded that minority communities do not fare as well as white communities when it comes to hazardous waste cleanups.

"We certainly do not rule out any specific case of environmental racism, and we do only address siting—only one area of concern for the environmental justice movement," Anderton said. But even so, he said, "we just don't see a pattern of environmental racism." ■

Analyzing Issues and Arguments

1. On what grounds does Douglas Anderton's research team dispute the conclusion drawn by previous studies that incinerators, hazardous waste landfills, and other pollution sources are disproportionately sited in minority communities? On what grounds have critics attacked his study?

2. Where in this article is environmental racism" treated as a matter of deliberate discrimination? Where is it treated as a matter of statistical inequity, without regard for anyone's motives? What specific words and phrases reflect each approach?

WILLIAM K. REILLY

The Green Thumb of Capitalism

A lawyer with degrees from Yale, Harvard, and Columbia universities, William K. Reilly was president of the World Wildlife Fund (WWF) and a longtime environmentalist when the Bush administration named him administrator of the Environmental Protection Agency (EPA) in 1989. At the EPA Reilly quickly made his mark, toughening enforcement of the agency's rules on pollution and toxic waste, preventing the damming of a Colorado river, and shepherding a new version of the Clean Air Act through Congress. Despite George Bush's pledge to be "the environmental president," however, Bush reneged on his promise to elevate the EPA to cabinet status, and others in his administration undercut many of Reilly's efforts. In "The Green Thumb of Capitalism," which appeared in the Fall 1990 issue of *Policy Review,* Reilly argues that a prosperous, growing economy is actually good for the environment. By the time he wrote this article, some critics felt that by defending certain policies and actions the Bush administration—as he does here—Reilly was compromising of his professed goal of protecting the environment. After Bill Clinton became president in 1993, Reilly left the EPA; he is now a senior fellow at the WWF.

Murmurs of agreement rippled through the business world last year when the new chairman of Du Pont, Edgar S. Woolard, declared himself to be the company's "chief environmental officer." "Our continued existence as a leading manufacturer," he said, "requires that we excel in environmental performance."

Ed Woolard has plenty of company these days. The sight of CEOs wrapped in green, embracing concepts such as "pollution prevention" and "waste minimization," is becoming almost commonplace. Businessmen increasingly are acknowledging the value, to their profit margins and to the economy as a whole, of environmentally sound business practices—reducing emissions, preventing waste, conserving energy and resources. Government is trying to help by creating market incentives to curb pollution, by encouraging energy efficiency and waste reduction, and by developing flexible, cost-effective regulatory programs. The recognition by business leaders and government that a healthy environment and a healthy economy go together—that in fact, they reinforce each other—reflects a growing awareness throughout society of this profound reality of modern life.

Less has been said or written, however, about the other side of the coin—the environmental benefits of a prosperous, growing economy. Many environmentalists remain ambivalent—and some openly suspicious—about many forms of economic growth and development. Entire industries are viewed as unnecessary or downright illegitimate by a shifting subset of activist, although not mainstream, environmentalist opinion: offshore oil development, animal husbandry, plastics, nuclear energy, surface mining, agribusiness. These skeptics equate growth with pollution, the cavalier depletion of natural resources, the destruction of natural systems, and—more abstractly—the estrangement of humanity from its roots in nature. Studs Terkel's trenchant comment about corporate polluters—"They infect our environment and then make a good buck on the sale of disinfectants"—remains a common attitude among certain activists. At the grass-roots level, conflicts over industrial

"WE CREATE IT, WE CLEAN IT UP — BUSINESS COULDN'T BE BETTER."

pollution, waste disposal, and new development tend to erupt with particular intensity and passion. One activist recently put it to me directly: In relation to waste incinerators, he said, "People think we're NIMBYs (Not-In-My-Backyard). But we're not. We're NOPEs (Not-On-Planet-Earth)."

The skepticism of some environmentalists toward growth is grounded in painful experience. Historically, economic expansion has led to the exploitation of natural resources with little or no concern for their renewal. At some levels of population and economic activity the damage from such practices was not readily apparent. But growing populations, demands for higher living standards, and widespread access to the necessities of modern life in economically advanced societies— and even in developing countries that provide raw materials to richer consumers—have created steadily increasing pressures on the environment. These include air and water pollution, urban congestion, the careless disposal of hazardous wastes, the destruction of wildlife, and the degradation of valuable ecosystems. Up to half of the wetlands in the lower forty-eight states that were here when the first European settlers arrived are gone; and the United States continues to lose 300,000 to 500,000 acres of this ecologically—and economically—productive resource to development every year. Furthermore, the byproducts of rapid industrialization have become so pervasive that they are altering the chemical composition of the planet's atmosphere, depleting stratospheric ozone, and adding to atmospheric carbon dioxide.

Economic development based on unsustainable resource use cannot   5 continue indefinitely without endangering the carrying capacity of the planet. Old growth patterns must change—and quickly—if we are to ensure the long-term integrity of the natural systems that sustain life on earth.

Great Expectations

To achieve *sustainable* growth—growth consistent with the needs and constraints of nature—we need to secure the link between environmental and economic policies at all levels of government and in all sectors of the economy. Harmonizing economic expansion with environmental protection requires a recognition that there are environmental benefits to growth, just as there are economic benefits flowing from healthy natural systems. Most environmentalists realize this, and a growing number are working creatively toward new policies that serve the long-term interests of both the environment and the economy.

How does economic growth benefit the environment?

First, growth raises expectations and creates demands for environmental improvement. As income levels and standards of living rise and people satisfy their basic needs for food, shelter, and clothing, they can afford to pay attention to the quality of their lives and the condition of their habitat. Once the present seems relatively secure, people can focus on the future.

Within our own country, demands for better environmental protection (for example, tighter controls on land development and the creation of new parks) tend to come from property owners, often affluent ones. Homeowners want to guarantee the quality of their surroundings. On the other hand, environmental issues have never ranked high on the agenda of the economically disadvantaged. Even though the urban poor typically experience environmental degradation most directly, the debate proceeds for the most part without their active participation.

The correlation between rising income and environmental concern 10 holds as true among nations as it does among social groups. The industrialized countries with strong economies and high average standards of living tend to spend more time and resources on environmental issues, and thus to be better off environmentally. Between 1973 and 1984, when Japan emerged as a global economic power, it also took significant steps to clean up its historic legacy of pollution; and the energy and raw materials used per unit of Japanese production decreased by an impressive 40 percent. In contrast, the developing nations, mired in poverty and struggling to stay one step ahead of mass starvation, have had little time and even less money to devote to environmental protection. Some of the world's worst and most intractable pollution problems are in the developing world and Eastern Europe.

Recent United Nations data analyzed by the World Resources Institute (WRI) show that the rivers with the highest levels of bacterial contamination, including urban sewage, are in Colombia, India, and Mexico. The WRI also reports consistently higher levels of sulfur dioxide and particulate air pollution in cities in Eastern Europe and the Third World than in most (although not all) of the cities in the developed world. And it is in Third World countries like Brazil, Indonesia, and Colombia that tropical rainforests are being lost at such alarming rates; while in Africa, India, and China, deserts are growing amid ever-worsening water shortages.

Growth Lowers Birth Rates

Economic growth can mitigate these resource and environmental pressures in the developing nations in two closely related ways: by reducing poverty, and by helping to stabilize population growth. Many global environmental problems result less from the activities of those supposed villains, the profit-hungry multinational corporations, than from the incremental, cumulative destruction of nature from the actions of many individuals—often the poor trying desperately to eke out a living. These actions range from the rural poor in Latin America clearing land for title, for cattle, or for subsistence farming; to gold miners, electroplaters, and small factories releasing toxic substances into the air and water; to farmers ruining fields and groundwater with excessive applications of pesticides.

In the developing nations especially, the population explosion of the past few decades (developing countries have more than doubled in population just since 1960) has greatly intensified the accumulating pressures on the environment. Even though the *rate* of increase is starting to fall in most of the Third World, population growth in countries such as Mexico, the Philippines, Kenya, Egypt, Indonesia, and Brazil has contributed and will continue to contribute to global degradation, to loss of natural resources, to poverty, and to hunger. Continued rapid population growth will cancel out environmental gains, and offset environmental investments.

One widely acceptable strategy that can make an important contribution to lowering fertility rates is education. The World Bank has drawn attention to the close correlation between education of children —specifically, bringing basic literacy to young girls—and reduction in the birth rate. Economic growth also offers hope for some relief. As countries grow economically, their fertility rates tend to decline; in most developed nations the birthrate has dropped below replacement levels, although it is creeping back up in some countries. Stable populations coupled with economic growth mean rising per capita standards of living. Education and economic development are the surest paths to stabilizing population growth.

A Walk on the Supply Side

The benefits of economic growth just described—higher expectations for environmental quality in the industrialized countries, and reduced resource demands and environmental pressures related to poverty and swelling populations in the developing nations—show up on the demand side of the prosperity/progress equation. But economic expansion contributes on the supply side as well—by generating the financial resources that make environmental improvements possible. 15

In the United States, for example, economic prosperity has contributed to substantial progress in environmental quality. The gains this country has made in reducing air and water pollution since 1970 are measurable, they are significant, and they are indisputable. In most major categories of air pollution, emissions on a national basis have either leveled off or declined since 1970. And the improvements are even more impressive when compared with where we would be without the controls established in the early 1970s.

Air emissions of particulates went down by 63 percent between 1970 and 1988; the EPA estimates that without controls particulate emissions would be 70 percent higher than current levels. Sulfur dioxide emissions are down 27 percent; without controls, they would be 42 percent higher than they are now. Nitrogen oxide, which is up about 7 percent from 1970 levels, would have increased by 28 percent without controls. Volatile organic chemicals are down 26 percent; without controls, they would be 42 percent higher than today's levels. Carbon monoxide is down 40 percent; without controls, it would be 57 percent higher than current levels. And without controls on lead, particularly the phase-in of unleaded gasoline, lead emissions to the air would be fully 97 percent higher than they are today. Instead, atmospheric lead is down 96 percent from 1970 levels.

Similar, although more localized, gains can be cited with respect to water pollution. In the Great Lakes, thanks to municipal sewage treatment programs, fecal coliform is down, nutrients are down, algae are down, biological oxygen demand is down. Twenty years ago pollution in Lake Erie decimated commercial fishing; now Lake Erie is the largest commercial fishery in the Great Lakes. The Potomac River in Washington, D.C., was so polluted that people who came into contact with it were advised to get an inoculation for tetanus. Now on a warm day the Potomac belongs to the windsurfers.

It cost the American taxpayers, consumers, and businessmen a great deal of money to realize these gains. The direct cost of compliance with federal environmental regulations is now estimated at more than $90 billion a year—about 1.7 percent of gross national product (GNP), the highest level among Western industrial nations for which data are available. Yet the United States achieved its remarkable environmental progress during a period when GNP increased by more than 70 percent.

We can learn two important lessons from the U.S. experience of the past two decades. First, our environmental commitments were compatible with economic advancement; the United States is now growing in a qualitatively better, healthier way because we made those commitments. And second, it was not just good luck that substantial environmental progress occurred during a period of economic prosperity. Our healthy economy paid for our environmental gains; economic expansion created the capital to finance superior environmental performance.

Eco-Catastrophe in Eastern Europe

The contrast between the U.S. experience and that of the Soviet Union and Eastern Europe over the past two decades is both stark and illuminating. While the United States prospered and made a start on cleaning up, Poland, Hungary, Romania, East Germany, Czechoslovakia, and the Soviet Union were undergoing an environmental catastrophe that will take many years and hundreds of billions of dollars to correct. In Eastern Europe, whole cities are blackened by thick dust. Chemicals make up a substantial percentage of river flows. Nearly two-thirds of the length of the Vistula, Poland's largest river, is unfit even for industrial use. The Oder River, which forms most of Poland's border with East Germany, is useless over 80 percent of its length. Parts of Poland, East Germany, and Romania are literally uninhabitable; zones of ecological disaster cover more than a quarter of Poland's land area. Millions of Soviets live in cities with dangerously polluted air. Military gas masks were issued in 1988 to thousands of Ukrainians to protect them from toxic emissions from a meat-processing plant.

The Soviet Union and its former satellites are plagued by premature deaths, high infant mortality rates, chronic lung disorders, and other disabling illnesses, and worker absenteeism. The economic drain from these environmental burdens, in terms of disability benefits, health care, and lost productivity is enormous—15 percent or more of GNP, according to one Eastern European minister with whom I spoke.

The lifting of the Iron Curtain has revealed to the world that authoritarian, centrally planned societies pose much greater threats to the environment than capitalist democracies. Many environmental principles were undefendable in the absence of private property: Both the factory and the nearby farmland contaminated by its pollution were the property of the state. And the state, without elections, was not subject to popular restraints or reform. Equally important, decisions to forgo environmental controls altogether, in order to foster all-out, no-holds-barred economic development, now can be seen to have done nothing for the economy. The same policies that ravaged the environment also wrecked the economy. There is a good reason that no economic benefits have been identified from all the pollution control costs these nations avoided: Healthy natural systems are a *sine qua non*[1] for all human activity, including economic activity.

What has happened in the United States and Eastern Europe is convincing evidence that in the modern industrial world prosperity is essential for environmental progress. Sustainable economic growth can and must be the engine of environmental improvement; it must pay for the technologies of protection and cleanup.

[1]**sine qua non** [Latin]: "without which not." Something indispensable. —ED.

Cleaner Technologies

The development of cleaner, more environmentally benign technolo- 25
gies clearly makes up a central element in the transition to sustainable
patterns of growth. Technology, like growth, can be a mixed blessing.
Technological progress has given many of the earth's people longer,
healthier lives, greater mobility, and higher living standards than most
would have thought possible just a century ago. Technology has alerted
us to environmental concerns such as stratospheric ozone depletion and
the buildup of "greenhouse" gases in the atmosphere.

But the adverse consequences to the environment from new technology, while neither intended nor anticipated, have also been significant. Twentieth-century industrial and transportation technologies,
heavily dependent on fossil fuels for their energy and on nonrenewable
mineral and other resources for raw materials, have contributed substantially to today's environmental disruptions. So, too, has the widespread use of certain substances—asbestos, chlorofluorocarbons
(CFCs), PCBs, a number of synthetic organic chemicals—which have
proved to be hazardous to human health or the environment, or both.

But if technological development has caused many of the environmental ills of the past and present, it also has a vital role to play in their
cure. This "paradox of technology," as Massachusetts Institute of Technology President Paul Gray calls it, is increasingly accepted by environmentalists and technocrats alike. In fact, some environmentalists and
legislators are more inclined to invest faith in technology even than are
the captains of industry. Gus Speth, a cofounder of the Natural Resources Defense Council and now president of World Resources Institute, has called for a "new Industrial Revolution" in which "green"
technologies are adopted that "facilitate economic growth while
sharply reducing the pressures on the natural environment."

I share this enthusiasm for the promise of technology, especially after observing firsthand the truly encouraging results of bioremediation
in cleaning up Alaska's Prince William Sound after the Exxon *Valdez*
oil spill.[2] When I first saw the full scale of that disaster, my initial
thought was: Where are the exotic new technologies, the products of
genetic engineering, that can help us clean this up? It was immediately
clear that conventional oil spill response technology was overwhelmed.

Not long after the spill, EPA's research and development staff
brought together thirty or so scientists to develop a program of bioremediation. This program does not involve any genetically engineered
organisms—just applications of nutrients to feed and accelerate the
creation of naturally occurring, oil–eating microbes.

---

[2]On March 24, 1989, the oil tanker *Exxon Valdez* ran aground and spilled about 200,000 barrels
of crude oil. More than 400 miles of Alaskan coastline were polluted.—ED.

Having been to Alaska several times to check on the progress of the 30 cleanup, I've seen what bioremediation can do to minimize the effects of a massive crude oil spill—especially below the surface of the shoreline. Those areas of shoreline that were treated only by washing or scrubbing still have unacceptably high levels of subsurface oil contamination—much higher than the areas treated with nutrients. The success of bioremediation is, in fact, virtually the only good news to result from that tragic oil spill.

Biotechnology also has great potential for many other environmental applications: Last February, I urged biotechnology companies to give a high priority to locating and developing microorganisms that can safely and inexpensively neutralize harmful chemicals at hazardous waste sites, as well as other pollutants in the air and water.

Other technologies, such as space satellites and sensors, increasingly sophisticated environmental monitoring and modeling capabilities, will give us the information base we need to respond appropriately to global atmospheric changes. The recent international agreement to phase out ozone-depleting CFCs before the end of this century was greatly facilitated by scientific studies of the Antarctic ozone hole and the rapid development of safe substitutes for CFCs. And continued advancements in medical technology and in our understanding of the role of environmental factors in human health will continue to enhance human life expectancy and freedom from disease.

Commuting by Computer

President Bush recently called attention to the environmental and social benefits of a technological advance known as "telecommuting": working from home or a neighborhood center close to home, sending messages and papers back and forth via fax or computer. By giving Americans an attractive alternative to driving, telecommuting helps reduce harmful auto emissions, from smog precursors to carbon dioxide. It also saves energy, relieves traffic congestion, and according to some studies, can even increase productivity by 20 percent or more.

As a fan of face-to-face communication, who believes also that creativity is often stimulated by the chance encounter, I must confess to a bit of skepticism about some of the virtues attributed to telecommuting. But environmentally and economically, it has incontestable appeal. And as congestion grows in many American cities, the appeal of telecommuting will also increase. Recognizing this, the federal government and several states have tried telecommuting in pilot projects; the EPA is among the federal agencies testing the concept at selected locations.

Many other environmentally beneficial technologies are changing 35 for the better the way humans interact with the environment. Miniaturization, fiber optics, and new materials are easing the demand for natural resources. As older plants and equipment wear out, they are replaced by more efficient, less polluting capital stock. The evolution of energy will continue with clean coal technologies and with the commercialization of economically competitive, nonpolluting, renewable energy technologies such as photovoltaic solar cells. New self-enclosed industrial processes will prevent toxic substances such as lead and cadmium, which are almost impossible to dispose of safely, from entering the ambient environment. The wise manufacturer is already asking new questions about products—not just how will the product be used, but how will it be disposed, and with what effects?

A Resource Saved Is a Resource Earned

Corporations such as Dow, 3M, Monsanto, Du Pont, Hewlett-Packard, Pratt & Whitney, Union Carbide, and others have curtailed emissions and saved resources through a wide variety of successful pollution-prevention techniques. Dow's Louisiana division, for example, recently designed and installed a vent recovery system to recapture hydrocarbon vapors that were being released as liquid hydrocarbons were loaded into barges. The new system recovers 98 percent of the vaporized hydrocarbons, abating hydrocarbon emissions to the atmosphere by more than 100,000 pounds a year.

As environmentalists have been pointing out for years, a pollutant is simply a resource out of place. By taking advantage of opportunities for pollution prevention, companies not only can protect the environment, they can save resources and thus enhance productivity and U.S. competitiveness in an increasingly demanding international market.

Accordingly, the EPA has made the encouragement of pollution prevention one of its leading priorities. At the same time, the administration is pursuing an innovative regulatory approach that builds on traditional command-and-control programs with economic incentives to harness the dynamics of the marketplace on behalf of the environment. By engaging the market in environmental protection, we can send the kind of signals to the economy that will encourage cleaner industrial processes and the wise stewardship of natural resources. The Department of Energy is involved as well; DOE is placing heavy emphasis on increasing energy efficiency and the commercialization of renewable energy technologies.

These governmental efforts are badly needed because the development of environmentally and economically beneficial new technology has been slowed by the high cost of capital in the United States—a direct consequence of the immense federal budget deficit. The deficit drives up interest rates, slows the pace of economic expansion, and discourages modernization and other environmentally friendly investments. While there are many reasons to bring the federal deficit under control, the need to free capital for environmental investments is certainly an important one.

Deficit spending is, unfortunately, not the only government policy 40 inhibiting environmental improvement. A wide range of regulatory requirements and subsidies, in the United States and in many other countries, lead to market distortions that encourage inefficiencies while promoting the unsustainable use of timber, water, cropland, and other resources. The Foundation for Research on Economics and the Environment (FREE), a free-market think tank based in Seattle, Washington, and Bozeman, Montana, has done pioneering work in the field of "New Resource Economics"; FREE argues that hundreds of millions of dollars could be saved and much environmental damage avoided every year by discontinuing subsidized clear-cutting in national forests and by curtailing heavily subsidized water development projects. For similar reasons, the Reagan administration opposed development on coastal barrier islands, which required heavy subsidies for bridges, flood insurance, and seawalls, and also exposed taxpayers to the costs of disaster relief when the inevitable hurricanes devastated the fragile handiwork of human beings.

Accounting for Pollution

One important step toward achieving greater harmony between economic and environmental policies would be for the government to consider seriously some long-overdue changes in the way the nation's economic health and prosperity are evaluated. As environmentalists and economists at think tanks like Resources for the Future have been pointing out for years, traditional economic accounting systems such as GNP and NNP (net national product) are poor measures of overall national well-being. They ignore or undervalue many nonmarket factors that add immeasurably to our quality of life: clean air and water, unspoiled natural landscapes, wilderness, wildlife in its natural setting. President Bush's Clean Air Act proposals for curtailing sulfur dioxide emissions, which are precursors of acid rain, will significantly improve visibility in the northeastern United States. People literally will be able to see farther. But we have not yet found a way to put a price tag on a scenic vista.

At the same time, GNP and NNP fail to discount from national income accounts the environmental costs of production and disposal, or the depletion of valuable natural capital such as lost cropland and degraded wetlands. The Exxon *Valdez* oil spill, a terrible environmental disaster, shows up as a *gain* in GNP because of all the goods and services expended in the clean-up. Without a realistic measure of national welfare, it is difficult to pursue policies that promote healthy, sustainable growth—growth that draws on the interest on stocks of renewable natural capital—in place of policies that contribute to the depletion of the capital itself.

The effort to develop a more comprehensive measure of national welfare should be just one part of an overall national strategy to achieve environmentally sound, sustainable economic growth. Such a strategy should be based on two fundamental premises:

First, economic growth confers many benefits, environmental and otherwise. Growth provides jobs, economic stability, and the opportunity for environmental and social progress. Only through economic growth can the people of the world, and especially the poor and hungry, realize their legitimate aspirations for security and economic betterment. And second, not all growth is "good" growth. What the world needs is healthy, sustainable, "green" growth: growth informed by the insights of ecology and wise natural resource management. . . .

A "Good Growth" Strategy

Good growth means greater emphasis on conservation, greater effi-   45
ciency in resource use, and greater use of renewables and recycling. Good growth unifies environmental, social, and economic concerns, and stresses the responsibility of all individuals to sustain a healthy relationship with nature.

Good growth enhances productivity and international competitiveness and makes possible a rising standard of living for everyone, without damaging the environment. It encourages broader, more integrated, longer-term policy-making. It anticipates environmental problems rather than reacting to the crisis of the moment.

Good growth recognizes that increased production and consumption are not ends in themselves, but means to an end—the end being healthier, more secure, more humane, and more fulfilling lives for all humanity. Good growth is about more than simply refraining from inflicting harm on natural systems. It has an ethical, even spiritual dimension. Having more, using more, does not in the final scheme of things equate to being more.

Good growth can illuminate the path to a sustainable society—a society in which we fulfill our ethical obligations to be good stewards of the planet and responsible trustees of our legacy to future generations.

Analyzing Issues and Arguments

1. What does William K. Reilly mean by "economic growth"?
2. In paragraph 3 Reilly writes: "Studs Terkel's trenchant comment about corporate polluters—'They infect our environment and then make a good buck on the sale of disinfectants'—remains a common attitude among certain activists." Does Terkel's comment apply to the cycle of corporate pollution and cleanup Reilly describes in paragraphs 28 ff? Why or why not?
3. What U.S. government policies does Reilly praise? What policies does he criticize? How does he rate other governments' environmental policies compared with those of the United States?

Writing about Issues and Arguments

In paragraph 7 Reilly asks: "How does economic growth benefit the environment?" Look closely at the answers he offers in paragraphs 8 and 9. Do you think Regina Austin and Michael Schill (p. 248) would agree? Using "Activists of Color" as a source, write an essay responding to Reilly's statements. If you prefer, you can turn this essay into a research paper by drawing on additional sources. (See "Suggestions for Further Reading," p. 333.)

DIANE JUKOFSKY

Can Marketing Save the Rainforest?

Diane Jukofsky is codirector of the Rainforest Alliance's Conservation Media Center, headquartered at the Latin America office of the Alliance in San Jose, Costa Rica. She was the vice president of programs for the Scientists' Institute for Public Information before joining the Alliance, an organization committed to conserving the world's endangered tropical forests. Jukofsky has served as press secretary for U.S. Representative Sam Gejdenson of Connecticut and as editor of the monthly membership magazine for public television station KTCA in Minneapolis–St. Paul. She also has worked as a lobbyist for the Minnesota Conservation Federation and as a public information officer for the National Wildlife Federation. She currently serves on the board of directors of the Rainforest Alliance and World Teach Costa Rica. Jukofsky writes frequently about tropical ecology. In "Can Marketing Save the Rainforest?," which appeared in the July/August 1993 issue of *E Magazine,* she describes efforts by U.S. groups to make preserving rainforests profitable for the people who live there.

Kathryn Alexander saw the green light when she read an article about Cultural Survival, the indigenous-rights group based in Boston. "I was truly inspired," she remembers. Alexander is president of Tropical Botanicals, a California company that produces such sexy-sounding products as "Passionflower Massage Oil" and "Babaçu Nut Body Lotion."

What inspired Alexander to start Tropical Botanicals and its line of rainforest bath products was Cultural Survival's program of buying directly from harvesters in tropical countries, then selling these fruits, nuts, and oils to manufacturers. Like other companies that buy from Cultural Survival, Tropical Botanicals pays a 5 percent premium above market cost, in [its] case for oil from the babaçu palm tree that it whips into a fragrant, creamy lotion. Cultural Survival then turns profits back to the South Americans who gathered the palm fruit.

Use It or Lose It

Alexander is not alone in the rainforest products market. Dozens of beauty products and munchies promise consumers that their purchase is "actually helping to preserve the precious rainforests," as it says in the Tropical Botanicals ad, just to the right of the handsome jaguar.

The concept, roughly, is "use it or lose it," a far cry from when many environmentalists thought that the best way to save wild habitat was to declare it off-limits to the destructive habits of humans. Now, ecologists hope to convince those who live in and near rainforests that the trees and plants in their backyards can provide a continuing source of income.

In 1989, Charles Peters, of the New York Botanical Garden's Insti-   5 tute of Economic Botany, completed a study that finally provided rainforest conservationists with the data they needed to prove that a rainforest is worth more intact than logged or burned for cash crops or cattle pasture, the usual fate of the 50 million acres of tropical forest lost worldwide each year.

Peters and two colleagues found that the fruits and rubber that could be gathered from one hectare (2.5 acres) of Peruvian rainforest could net a harvester $422 a year, *every* year, which adds up to a far more secure future than the $1,000 that hectare would yield, just once, if it were cut for timber.

Now, in Guatemala, Peru, the Philippines, Ecuador, Zambia, Indonesia—in nearly every country where there are still large stands of rainforest remaining—experts are combing the forests to see what might be harvested and sold.

The number of products with origins in the rainforest already on the market seems remarkable—until you consider that half of all the species on earth are found in tropical forests. Oranges, lemons, bananas, pineapples, chocolate, coffee, avocadoes, resins used in paints and varnishes, latex, bamboo, rattan, many dusky-hued hardwoods used to make furniture, and more than forty prescription drugs have their origins in wild tropical plants.

To Market, to Market

People who live in and near tropical forests regularly use hundreds of plant species Westerners have never tasted, smelled, or seen. The two hundred families who live along the Río Capim in Brazil's Amazonia, for example, are "utterly dependent" on plants, says Woods Hole Research Center ethnobotanist Patricia Shanley. "Their daily routines demand an intimate knowledge of the surrounding forest." Not long ago, they asked Shanley and her colleagues for help in determining which plants in their forests might be marketable. Shanley surveyed the nearby forests and found four hundred different plant species. She found trees like bacuri, ushi, and piquia, whose fruits are in demand at local markets, and andiroba and copaiba trees, which yield effective medicinal oils. While these products may have value internationally, Shanley is concerning herself right now with what their worth might be in local and regional markets. "The closest market is three hours away by boat," she explains, "and selling a plant is a whole new concept to people here."

It's a concept that the Río Capim villagers and hundreds of others 10 who live near the forest's edge are learning: There are people willing to pay for the bounty in their backyards. Buyers may be downriver, or on another continent.

The members of the Xapuri Agroextractive Cooperative are rubber tappers in the state of Acre in Brazil. To supplement the income they earn from the latex tapped from rubber trees in the Amazon, they now gather the fruit of Brazil nut trees from the forest floor. Inside each softball-sized fruit are up to twenty nuts, which are brought to a nearby processing plant. There the nuts are dried, shelled, and sorted for shipment to foreign markets.

In 1989, Cultural Survival bought a shipment of Brazil nuts from the rubber tappers and sold them at 5 percent above the market price to a new company called Community Products, which used them in a nut brittle it dubbed "Rainforest Crunch." Cultural Survival returned 100 percent of the profit from the sale to the Xapuri cooperative. Suddenly, a movement was born. According to recently departed director Jason Clay, who founded the organization's rainforest products market-

ing program, Cultural Survival now sells fifteen commodities from ten to fourteen different countries to sixty-six companies. The program has thus far generated about $3 million. All profits are returned to the product harvesters. (Clay is now codirector of the Washington, D.C.–based group Rights and Resources.)

New England Natural Bakers is one of the companies that buys from Cultural Survival. President John Broucek started the company in 1989, "after I read an article about Jason Clay and Community Products."

Broucek first introduced "Save the Forest" granola cereals, then fruit and nut snacks. "We source 95 percent of our products from Cultural Survival," says Broucek. "Any of our ingredients that come from rainforest areas, we buy from them," even though he could be saving a good deal if he bought his Brazil nuts from another source.

Indeed, there's a glut of Brazil nuts on the open market now. "The 15 current market price is about 85 cents a pound," says Clay, "and we're paying about $1.25. . . . Many of the 'green' companies just started. . . . It hurts them to pay so much more than the market price."

Broucek agrees. "We have wrestled with price." But last September Cultural Survival introduced them to a man from the Xapuri cooperative in Brazil. He gave them the whole social and cultural background of that cooperative, and why it is that they charge what they charge. "Hearing about it in the context of the history and plight of the rubber tappers and nut gatherers . . . moved us beyond a decision based strictly on money," says Broucek. "When you take in the political and social ramifications, it takes some of the sting out of the price."

Rainforest Raised?

Rachel Perry Body Care Products has sold rainforest products since the 1970s. In fact, the company has even trademarked the word "rainforest." Three years ago, as Cultural Survival and Rainforest Crunch were making news, Rachel Perry introduced Rainforest Botanical Therapy Body Care products. "We thought that by creating this product line it would help call attention to the rainforest situation," says marketing manager Melinda Rubin.

Rachel Perry buys Brazil nut oil, babaçu, copaiba, agave, banana nut, coconut, and orchids from Cultural Survival and other sources. "We ask that our sources provide us with substantiation that these ingredients were sustainably harvested," explains Rubin.

Like other Cultural Survival customers, Rachel Perry and New England Natural Bakers try to be careful about the claims they make. "We say our goal is to use as many sustainably harvested products as possible. We don't say every product is sustainable," says Rubin.

Product sustainability—or harvesting without damaging the abil- 20 ity of the plant that produced it to produce again—is one of the controversial aspects of rainforest marketing. Clay maintains that the only way to develop sustainable sources is to buy first from the open market—that is, from commercial sources—even though it means that, initially, he really doesn't know how the products were harvested, or by whom or under what conditions. "We use that as a way to get companies interested and convinced that we can supply them with the quantities they want," he says. "All of our initial fifteen commodities were commercially sourced. Now only four are part commercial, part local."

One product Cultural Survival still buys from commercial sources is annatto, a seed that produces a tawny oil that is used in Tropical Botanical's Annatto Natural Bronzing Oil. "We can't guarantee that what comes from commercial sources is sustainably harvested," Clay admits. "We *can* guarantee that the money generated from that sale goes back to set up" a sustainably harvested system.

Even products that are bought from local sources are not necessarily gathered from the rainforest. Cashews, for example, a common ingredient in many rainforest cereals and snacks, come from trees grown in plantations. They are farmed like any crop, planted in rows on land where rainforests once flourished.

"A lot of the products being sold as rainforest products are actually farmed," says Michael Balick, who directs the Institute of Economic Botany. "Some of the products in the stores are from plants that are not sustainably extractable, yet they are being sold as contributions to the movement."

Clay makes no apologies. "We buy cupuaçu from a cooperative near Belem in Brazil," he says. The cooperative's members, says Clay, are recent colonists who moved in and cleared rainforest. Cultural Survival funds helped set up a small processing plant that will buy the fruit from farmers in the area. "If we can't figure out a way for the colonists to make a decent living, they're going to keep cutting down the rainforest and sell it as pasture," Clay warns.

Knudsen & Sons, Incorporated, which buys cupuaçu from Cultural 25 Survival and sells it as one of the company's Tropical Rainforest Juices, describes the fruit as tasting something like a honeydew melon. It grows wild, but many farmers like those in Belem are planting cupuaçu to take advantage of the fruit's new international market. "There are so many people planting cupuaçu," says Woods Hole botanist Shanley, "that it could be a time bomb. The fruit could flood the markets, and that could be the worst thing in the world, because finally these farmers are taking a risk and planting something new."

Michael Saxenian of the environmental group Conservation International (CI), which also works in the production and marketing of rainforest products, shares Shanley's concerns. "We believe that simply taking nontimber products out of the market and selling them is not enough to guarantee that our conservation objectives will be met," he explains. "We work with scientists to study the ecological sustainability of any product that we offer so, while it's always difficult to determine what is a sustainable product, we think we have as sound a scientific basis as possible in making sure that we're not exceeding those limits." CI first identifies what it calls a "hot-spot" ecological system, a natural area rich in biodiversity that faces development threats. Working with the people nearby, CI designs programs that involve community development, conservation science, long-term management and policy work.

CI's first forest product extracted under this multifaceted program was tagua nut, the hard seed of a rainforest palm tree. Tagua nut, sometimes called "vegetable ivory" for its creamy white color and easily carved texture, is sold as buttons, jewelry, and carvings. CI linked up with a community development group outside the Cotacachi-Cayapas Ecological Reserve in Ecuador to establish a locally run business that purchases tagua and resells it to factories on the coast, which in turn shape the tagua into disks for buttons.

"First," says Saxenian, "we did an ecological analysis of the area to determine whether tagua nuts could be sustainably harvested. We also provided capital and some of the infrastructure the community enterprise needed, like scales for weighing the tagua nut, and boats for transporting them."

CI then found three U.S. button manufacturers who would buy the semiprocessed tagua disks, as well as companies who would buy the finished buttons. In the first year of CI's "Tagua Initiative," seven million buttons worth $500,000 were sold. CI is developing similar programs with a variety of products in ecological hot spots in Colombia, Guatemala, Peru, and the Philippines.

Where Cultural Survival says they differ from "the tagua people" is 30 in how profits are spent. "Some of the organizations doing [rainforest product] marketing don't guarantee that all the money goes back to the harvesters," says Clay. "They use some of it for overhead and cost related to consumer education and outreach. Education is important, but we don't think it's appropriate when programs are paid for by the labor of someone who lives in the rainforest."

Michael Balick questions if all the rainforest-product groups have the necessary ecological data to ensure they are not damaging plant populations. For example, how many Brazil nuts can be removed from the forest floor before the ability of the area's slow-growing Brazil nut trees to produce is irreversibly damaged?

"I'm not quite sure the world needs another organization running around the Third World telling people what to plant, so they can cash in on this month's rainforest crunch," he says. "I think what the world needs is more people figuring out how to develop sustainable harvesting systems for rainforest species. This is our goal. We do long-term studies in the mud, in the villages, working with people to see what they utilize and how they utilize it," he explains. "We try to figure out whether their use is sustainable or not and at what level."

Are You Indigenous?

The information that accompanies many rainforest products frequently explains that rainforests are home to hundreds of surviving indigenous tribes who face cultural and physical extinction due to the loss of their homelands. The overt suggestion is that purchase of rainforest products will help save ancient cultures and their territories.

But in fact, only a small percentage of the harvesters of exported rainforest products are indigenous people who live in the rainforest, as did their ancestors before them. The Río Capim villagers are *coboclos,* colonists of mixed European, indigenous, and African descent, who have lived in the region for decades—and not exactly in harmony with the forest. The ancestors of the Xapuri rubber tappers in Brazil were landless farmers who long ago invaded and cleared the forest. CI's tagua collectors in Ecuador are Afro-Ecuadorian, descendants of an ex-slave community. Many harvesters, like the Brazilian farmers who sell cupuaçu to Cultural Survival, are more recent arrivals to the rainforest frontier, where they have hacked out a clearing in the woods to graze cattle and plant subsistence crops—not unlike the European adventurers who first set foot on the shores of the wild New World five hundred years ago.

Jason Clay acknowledges the term "indigenous" is vague, but wonders, "If you've lived in a place for one hundred years, are you indigenous?" He adds, "Cultural Survival works with threatened cultures, sometimes called ethnic groups, sometimes called indigenous, sometimes called nations. We decided that it was OK to work with rubber tappers, although there was a strong sentiment among some in our organization that we shouldn't because rubber tappers are not tribal people, even though their way of life is threatened and they have lived where they are for a long time.

"I think we should work with everybody, because even colonists need to figure out how to do what they're doing better, so they don't just keep cutting forests. And the best way to protect the land rights of indigenous people is to make sure that colonists don't keep moving in on them."

Two companies that purchase products directly from indigenous communities are Natural Nectar of California, and the Body Shop, which is based in England and has dozens of stores in the United States.

Natural Nectar, according to environmental program director Kate Priest, purchases sapayul oil, which is pressed from the seed of the sapote trees that grow in lowland rainforests, from a supplier in Guatemala, who in turn buys the sapote seeds from Maya Indians. Sapayul oil is a main ingredient in the company's Emerald Forest Botanical Shampoo and Conditioner.

Two years ago Natural Nectar wanted to create a "model product that takes resources from the environment in a responsible way," says Priest, "a product that consumers love and that's successful in the market, to prove that you could make enough of a profit that you could channel back some of the profits to the environment you are drawing the resources from." Sapayul oil appealed to the company, says Priest, because "people can relate to the Mayans with their beautiful, thick, healthy, long hair."

The sapote seeds are gathered by a Mayan cooperative, and Priest 40 emphasizes that the impact of Natural Nectar's "arrival into their culture and economy" is being carefully monitored. "We know that if you go in and demand too much of a good thing, you pressure the community too much. They have no experience in a market economy . . . so we spend a lot of time helping people adjust to this."

The Body Shop, which manufactures an extensive and profitable line of beauty products made from natural ingredients, began purchasing Brazil nut oil in 1991 from three small Kayapo Indian communities in northeastern Brazil. Earnings from the sale of the key ingredient in the Body Shop's Brazil Nut Oil Conditioner are administered by elders of the tribe, says Body Shop media relations manager Martyn Evans. "We helped them set their business up, but they control the funds. Profits are used to benefit the community. The goal of the Body Shop's Trade Not Aid program," Evans explains, "is to empower people economically so they can acquire the resources they need to determine their own futures.

"Because of the invading miners and loggers, tribal people's exposure to Western culture is irreversible," he points out. "So do you just build a fence around them or do you help them? With Trade Not Aid, we are saying, 'We want Brazil nut oil to make money, because that's our business. You can supply us with this product, giving you the ability to earn your own money and run your own lives.' The Kayapo are equal partners in a business relationship."

But Susan Meeker-Lowry, director of the Montpelier, Vermont–based nonprofit group Catalyst, and author of *Economics As If the Earth Mattered*, wonders what the long-term effect of rainforest marketing will be on the Kayapo, the Maya villagers, and on CI's tagua-nut gatherers in Ecuador. "I would like to see a plan that helps ensure that the indigenous communities will eventually be running these cooperatives themselves," she says. "We need to ask whether this harvesting process helps them attain tribal land ownership, which is what they really need."

Michael Balick also wonders about the social impacts of rainforest product marketing. "Are they implementing mechanisms for long-term production and insuring the rights of the harvesters? These are complex issues. You can't speak about them in sound bites."

Saving the Rainforest

Satisfied that the ingredients were harvested in a responsible way, and 45 that the profits will benefit, if not an indigenous tribe, at least deserving farmers or rubber tappers and their families, consumers may still wonder, "Just how many acres of rainforest is my purchase going to save?"

"It's difficult to say," acknowledges CI's Michael Saxenian. "We do have anecdotal evidence that suggests we are having a real impact. A 12,000 hectare [30,000 acre] banana plantation was proposed for the site where we are working. The Tagua Initiative was an important topic in the debate in the community . . . and the plans for the plantation were scrapped."

Notes Jason Clay: "I can't say with any kind of conviction that we've saved a hectare of rainforest [but] we have generated a lot of income for as many as twenty thousand people."

Many rainforest product companies donate a portion of their profits to nonprofit groups that support rainforest conservation, chalking up yet another helpful gesture in their favor. Consumers may want to read labels to find out how much is donated, as well as the names of the groups that receive funds. If you're unfamiliar with a group's goals, request more information.

And then, make that purchase. Although, as John Broucek of New England Natural Bakers notes, "The efforts of all these companies put together are not going to have a dramatic effect," the majority of rainforest product companies and organizations are led by people with sincerely good intentions, who are trying to merge heart and business in a positive way. It's a step toward maintaining the forests for the future.

Analyzing Issues and Arguments

1. Who benefits and in what ways when U.S. companies develop markets in this country for tropical rainforest products?

2. Why are buyers of rainforest products concerned about sustainability? How important do you think it is, and why?

3. In her closing paragraph, Diane Jukofsky quotes John Broucek: "The efforts of all these companies put together are not going to have a dramatic effect." In your opinion, is he correct? Why or why not?

Writing about Issues and Arguments

What are the different goals of U.S. groups working with inhabitants of tropical rainforests? Which of these goals sometimes come into conflict? Which goals do you think are most important, and why? Write an essay in which you compare and contrast these groups and then argue in favor of a particular agenda.

IN THE NEWS

Eco-Yearnings

Mary Tannen

> A longer version of the following essay appeared in the *New York Times Magazine* on March 20, 1994. Mary Tannen is a novelist whose most recent books are *After Roy* (1989) and *Easy Keeper* (1992).

I'm scanning the fashion magazines, waiting for Michiko to cut my hair, and I gradually become aware of an eco-phobic theme threading through the beauty ads. A shampoo promises to "discourage environmental damage." A lotion calls itself "environmental skin care." One message begins ominously, "Until the world is a safer place for your hair."

It occurs to me that in order to succeed, the people who make and market cosmetics must be poets for our time. After all, what is more intimate than ointments we rub onto our skin, gels we squeeze into our bath? If we're going to let a lotion into our bathroom, it must speak to our deepest longings and fears. Its advertising, packaging, its very consistency, must follow the path of the Zeitgeist.

Lulled by the sound of the hair dryers, I fall into a reverie, remembering how my mother used to send us out to play in the sun and fresh air—an innocent time when the sun was considered good for us, before chlorofluorocarbons depleted the ozone layer, allowing dangerous UV rays to penetrate the atmosphere, turning sunshine from a blessing into a curse.

And sun is only the most obvious peril, I think, as I step out of the hair salon and into a weird blue haze drifting up from Third Avenue in

Manhattan. What's in that cloud? Asbestos? Sulfuric acid? I know it's eating the obelisk in Central Park. What's it doing to my skin and hair?

On a slow browse through the great cosmetics bazaar of my favorite department store, I sample seductively packaged nostrums that offer protection not only from sun but also from invisible pathogens lurking in the corrupted atmosphere.

At the Prescriptives counter, there's Line Preventor 3 Environmental Skincare, which has a sunscreen as well as vitamins C and E, and BHT—free-radical scavengers that combine with unstable oxygen molecules and render them harmless. It also contains something called "carnosine," which protects against cigarette smoke. You can use it before going into a bar, like donning an anticontamination suit before entering a radioactive zone.

Estée Lauder offers Advanced Night Repair Protective Recovery Complex. The heavy, amber, beveled-glass bottle with dropper brings back comforting medicinal memories. The sleek gold cap reminds me of the preciousness of the substance within. Just four or five drops on face and throat, and I'll sleep easier at night knowing I've done all I can to recover from the assaults of the day.

Alert now to the eco-theme, I see that purveyors of cosmetics are addressing not only our fears of a toxic environment but also our hunger for substances we used to take for granted, such as pure water and air.

"It's mostly water" used to be a derogatory expression. Who would have guessed that a whole line of beauty and bath products—called H₂O Plus— would emerge, boasting water as the main ingredient? With names like Ebb Tide, Sea Spray, and Natural Spring, the bath and shower gels sold at the brightly lighted H₂O Plus store on Madison Avenue promise to restore ordinary tap stuff to its primal state. For a parched face there's Hydraspa Moisture Mist, a slightly viscous clear liquid that delivers water as well as vitamins E and B, aloe, cucumber, chamomile, sea kelp, and the sensation of walking through heavy fog on a deserted Nantucket beach.

And how about air? We used to take it for granted. Oxygen was some colorless gas that floated around. We knew we needed it to live, but it was always there. Now we worry about all sorts of noxious gases coming between us and our oxygen.

Lancaster, sensing our concern, has come up with a lotion to revive suffocating faces: Skin Therapy Vital Oxygen Supply. It is packaged in a cobalt blue bottle (polyurethane but reminiscent of what Proust might have had at his bedside) and, according to its promotional material, will deliver "pure molecular oxygen" to the cells, increasing the skin's oxygen content by 100 percent after fourteen days.

I've ridden in enough elevators with overdoused women to think of perfume as the very antithesis of fresh air. But some of the new fragrances—New West Skinscent for Her, Escape, Sunflowers, and L'Eau d'Issey among them —are formulated to smell, paradoxically, like the absence of smell, like the pure, clean scent of sun-dried wash on the line or a mountain campsite after a storm.

It's not just water and air. With meadows giving way to shopping malls, we feel a hunger deep as DNA for herbs and grasses, roots and barks. The high priests of the cosmetics world, sensing this need, have responded with a blooming profusion of creams and lotions, unguents and potions, based on plants.

"Natural" cosmetics isn't a new idea, I remind myself as I turn into the Body Shop on upper Broadway and spread some Blue Corn Moisture Cream on my hands. The Body Shop, like the *Whole Earth Catalogue,* is a child of the 70s. It still has a 70's look, with its bright mirrors and Pop Art colors, and a 70s crusading spirit (no to animal testing and petrochemicals; yes to products from the rainforest, plant-based cosmetics, recycled packaging, and returning bottles for refills).

As we approach the millennium, there's been a resurgence of interest in 15 eco-aware cosmetics but with a subtle shift in emphasis. Formerly we were concerned about what cosmetics and its packaging were doing to the environment. Now we worry more about what the environment is doing to us.   ▪

Analyzing Issues and Arguments

1. How do the large cosmetics companies mentioned in Mary Tannen's article engage with environmental issues differently than the smaller companies mentioned in Diane Jukofsky's "Can Marketing Save the Rainforest?"
2. Whom does Tannen appear to mean by "we" and "us" (see, for example, paras. 2, 8, 10, and 15)? How does her use of the first-person plural affect the impact of her article?

SANDRA POSTEL

Carrying Capacity: Earth's Bottom Line

Sandra Postel is vice president for research at the Worldwatch Institute, an independent nonprofit organization in Washington, D.C., that analyzes and reports on global environmental trends. She has written and coauthored numerous books and papers on environmental issues, as well as serving since 1989 as associate project director for the institute's annual *State of the World* reports. Before joining Worldwatch, Postel was a consultant specializing in water conservation and groundwater issues for a private firm in California. "Carrying Capacity: Earth's Bottom Line" is excerpted from Postel's chapter by that name in *State of the World 1994.* Here she summarizes the havoc wrought around the world by careless or desperate human exploitation of natural resources and recommends measures for preserving the earth's ability to support us.

It takes no stretch of the imagination to see that the human species is now an agent of change of geologic proportions. We literally move mountains to mine the earth's minerals, redirect rivers to build cities in the desert, torch forests to make way for crops and cattle, and alter the chemistry of the atmosphere in disposing of our wastes. At humanity's hand, the earth is undergoing a profound transformation—one with consequences we cannot fully grasp.

It may be the ultimate irony that in our efforts to make the earth yield more for ourselves, we are diminishing its ability to sustain life of all kinds, humans included. Signs of environmental constraints are now pervasive. Cropland is scarcely expanding any more, and a good portion of existing agricultural land is losing fertility. Grasslands have been overgrazed and fisheries overharvested, limiting the amount of additional food from these sources. Water bodies have suffered extensive depletion and pollution, severely restricting future food production and urban expansion. And natural forests—which help stabilize the climate, moderate water supplies, and harbor a majority of the planet's terrestrial biodiversity—continue to recede.

These trends are not new. Human societies have been altering the earth since they began. But the pace and scale of degradation that started about mid-century—and continues today—is historically new. The central conundrum of sustainable development is now all too apparent: population and economies grow exponentially, but the natural resources that support them do not.

Biologists often apply the concept of "carrying capacity" to questions of population pressures on an environment. Carrying capacity is the largest number of any given species that a habitat can support indefinitely. When that maximum sustainable population level is surpassed, the resource base begins to decline—and sometime thereafter, so does the population.

A simple but telling example of a breach of carrying capacity in-   5 volved the introduction of twenty-nine reindeer to St. Matthew Island in the Bering Sea in 1944. Under favorable conditions, the herd expanded to six thousand by the summer of 1963. The following winter, however, the population crashed, leaving fewer than fifty reindeer. According to a 1968 study by biologist David R. Klein of the University of Alaska, the large herd had overgrazed the island's lichens, its main source of winter forage, and the animals faced extreme competition for limited supplies during a particularly severe winter. Klein concluded that "food supply, through its interaction with climatic factors, was the dominant population regulating mechanism for reindeer on St. Matthew Island."[1]

Of course, human interactions with the environment are far more complicated than those of reindeer on an island. The earth's capacity to support humans is determined not just by our most basic food requirements but also by our levels of consumption of a whole range of resources, by the amount of waste we generate, by the technologies we choose for our varied activities, and by our success at mobilizing to deal with major threats. In recent years, the global problems of ozone depletion and greenhouse warming have underscored the danger of overstepping the earth's ability to absorb our waste products. Less well recognized, however, are the consequences of exceeding the sustainable supply of essential resources—and how far along that course we may already be.

As a result of our population size, consumption patterns, and technology choices, we have surpassed the planet's carrying capacity. This is plainly evident by the extent to which we are damaging and depleting natural capital. The earth's environmental assets are now insufficient to sustain both our present patterns of economic activity and the life-support systems we depend on. If current trends in resource use continue and if world population grows as projected, by 2010 per capita availability of rangeland will drop by 22 percent and the fish catch by 10 percent. Together, these provide much of the world's animal protein. The per capita area of irrigated land, which now yields about a third of the global food harvest, will drop by 12 percent. And cropland area and forestland per person will shrink by 21 and 30 percent, respectively.[2]

[1]David R. Klein, "The Introduction, Increase, and Crash of Reindeer on St. Matthew Island," *Journal of Wildlife Management,* April 1968.

[2]The resource projections for 2010 are not predictions but extrapolations based largely on recent trends—primarily those observed from 1980 to 1990—and current knowledge of the resource base.

The days of the frontier economy—in which abundant resources were available to propel economic growth and living standards—are over. We have entered an era in which global prosperity increasingly depends on using resources more efficiently, distributing them more equitably, and reducing consumption levels overall. Unless we accelerate this transition, powerful social tensions are likely to arise from increased competition for the scarce resources that remain. The human population will not crash wholesale as the St. Matthew Island reindeer did, but there will likely be a surge in hunger, crossborder migration, and conflict—trends already painfully evident in parts of the world.[3]

Wiser and more discriminating use of technology offers the possibility of tremendous gains in resource efficiency and productivity, helping us get more out of each hectare [2.47 acres] of land, ton of wood, or cubic meter of water. In this way, technology can help stretch the earth's capacity to support humans sustainably. Trade also has an important, though more limited role. Besides helping spread beneficial technologies, it enables one country to import ecological capital from another. Trade can thus help surmount local or regional scarcities of land, water, wood, or other resources.

In these ways, technology and trade can buy time to tackle the larger challenges of stabilizing population, reducing excessive consumption, and redistributing wealth. Unfortunately, past gains in these two areas have deluded us into thinking that any constraint can be overcome, and that we can therefore avoid the more fundamental tasks. And rather than directing technology and trade toward sustainable development, we have more often used them in ways that hasten resource depletion and degradation.

The roots of environmental damage run deep. Unless they are unearthed soon, we risk exceeding the planet's carrying capacity to such a degree that a future of economic and social decline will be impossible to avoid.

Driving Forces

Since mid-century, three trends have contributed most directly to the excessive pressures now being placed on the earth's natural systems— the doubling of world population, the quintupling of global economic output, and the widening gap in the distribution of income. The environmental impact of our population, now numbering 5.5 billion, has been vastly multiplied by economic and social systems that strongly

[3]Thomas F. Homer-Dixon et al., "Environmental Change and Violent Conflict," *Scientific American,* February 1993; Norman Myers, *Ultimate Security: The Environmental Basis of Political Security* (New York: W.W. Norton & Company, 1993).

favor growth and ever-rising consumption over equity and poverty alleviation; that fail to give women equal rights, education, and economic opportunity—and thereby perpetuate the conditions under which poverty and rapid population growth persist; and that do not discriminate between means of production that are environmentally sound and those that are not.

Of the three principal driving forces, the growing inequality in income between rich and poor stands out in sharpest relief. In 1960, the richest 20 percent of the world's people absorbed 70 percent of global income; by 1989 (the latest year for which comparable figures are available), the wealthy's share had climbed to nearly 83 percent. The poorest 20 percent, meanwhile, saw their share of global income drop from an already meager 2.3 percent to just 1.4 percent. The ratio of the richest fifth's share to the poorest's thus grew from 30 to 1 in 1960 to 59 to 1 in 1989. . . .

This chasm of inequity is a major cause of environmental decline: it fosters overconsumption at the top of the income ladder and persistent poverty at the bottom. By now, ample evidence shows that people at either end of the income spectrum are far more likely than those in the middle to damage the earth's ecological health—the rich because of their high consumption of energy, raw materials, and manufactured goods, and the poor because they must often cut trees, grow crops, or graze cattle in ways harmful to the earth merely to survive from one day to the next.[4]

Families in the western United States, for instance, often use as much as 3,000 liters [800 gallons] of water a day—enough to fill a bathtub twenty times. Overdevelopment of water there has contributed to the depletion of rivers and aquifers, destroyed wetlands and fisheries, and, by creating an illusion of abundance, led to excessive consumption. Meanwhile, nearly one out of every three people in the developing world—some 1.2 billion people in all—lack access to a safe supply of drinking water. This contributes to the spread of debilitating disease and death, and forces women and children to trek many hours a day to collect a few jugs of water to meet their family's most basic needs.[5]

Disparities in food consumption are revealing as well. . . . As many as 700 million people do not eat enough to live and work at their full potential. The average African, for instance, consumes only 87 percent

[4]Alan Thein Durning, *How Much Is Enough? The Consumer Society and the Future of the Earth* (New York: W.W. Norton & Company, 1992); Alan Durning, *Poverty and the Environment: Reversing the Downward Spiral*, Worldwatch Paper 92 (Washington, D.C.: Worldwatch Institute, November 1989).

[5]Sandra Postel, *Last Oasis: Facing Water Scarcity* (New York: W.W. Norton & Company, 1992); 1.2 billion figure from Joseph Christmas and Carel de Rooy, "The Decade and Beyond: At a Glance," *Water International*, September 1991.

of the calories needed for a healthy and productive life. Meanwhile, diets in many rich countries are so laden with animal fat as to cause increased rates of heart disease and cancers. Moreover, the meat-intensive diets of the wealthy usurp a disproportionately large share of the earth's agricultural carrying capacity since producing one kilogram of meat takes several kilograms of grain. If everyone in the world required as much grain for their diet as the average American does, the global harvest would need to be 2.6 times greater than it is today—a highly improbable scenario.[6]

Economic growth—the second driving force—has been fueled in part by the introduction of oil onto the energy scene. Since mid-century, the global economy has expanded fivefold. As much was produced in two-and-a-half months of 1990 as in the entire year of 1950. World trade, moreover, grew even faster: exports of primary commodities and manufactured products rose elevenfold.[7]

The extent to which the overall scale of economic activity damages the earth depends largely on the technologies used and the amount of resources consumed in the process. Electricity generated by burning coal may contribute as much to economic output as an equal amount generated by wind turbines, for example, but burning coal causes far more environmental harm. A similar comparison holds for a ton of paper made from newly cut trees and a ton produced from recycled paper.

Unfortunately, economic growth has most often been of the damaging variety—powered by the extraction and consumption of fossil fuels, water, timber, minerals, and other resources. Between 1950 and 1990, the industrial roundwood harvest doubled, water use tripled, and oil production rose nearly sixfold. Environmental damage increased proportionately.[8]

[6]Number of people without enough food and percentage of necessary calories consumed by the average African from Kevin Cleaver and Gotz Schreiber, *The Population, Agriculture, and Environment Nexus in Sub-Saharan Africa* (Washington, D.C.: World Bank, 1992); fat-laden diets in rich countries from Alan Durning and Holly Brough, *Taking Stock: Animal Farming and the Environment,* Worldwatch Paper 103 (Washington, D.C.: Worldwatch Institute, July 1991); increase in global harvest is a Worldwatch Institute estimate, based on U.S. Department of Agriculture (USDA), *World Grain Database* (unpublished printout) (Washington, D.C.: 1992), and on Population Reference Bureau (PRB), *1990 World Population Data Sheet* (Washington, D.C.: 1990).

[7]Gross world product in 1950 from Herbert R. Block, *The Planetary Product in 1980: A Creative Pause?* (Washington, D.C.: U.S. Department of State, 1981); gross world product in 1990 from International Monetary Fund (IMF), *World Economic Outlook: Interim Assessment* (Washington, D.C.: 1993); increase in value of internationally traded goods from $308 million in 1950 to $3.58 trillion in 1992 (in 1990 dollars) is a Worldwatch Institute estimate, based on IMF, Washington, D.C., unpublished data base; World Bank, Washington, D.C., unpublished data base.

[8]Industrial roundwood from United Nations, *Statistical Yearbook, 1953* (New York: 1954), and from U.N. Food and Agriculture Organization (FAO), *1991 Forest Products Yearbook* (Rome: 1993); water from Postel, op. cit. note 5; oil from American Petroleum Institute, *Basic Petroleum Data Book* (Washington, D.C.: 1992).

Compounding the rises in both poverty and resource consumption 20
related to the worsening of inequality and rapid economic expansion,
population growth has added greatly to pressures on the earth's carrying
capacity. The doubling of world population since 1950 has meant more
or less steady increases in the number of people added to the planet
each year. Whereas births exceeded deaths by 37 million in 1950, the
net population gain in 1993 was 87 million—roughly equal to the
population of Mexico. . . .

Rarely do the driving forces of environmental decline operate in
isolation; more often they entangle, like a spider's web. Where people's
livelihoods depend directly on the renewable resource base around
them, for example, poverty, social inequity, and population growth fuel
a vicious cycle in which environmental decline and worsening poverty
reduce options for escaping these traps. This is plainly evident in the

TOLES copyright The Buffalo News. Reprinted with permission of Universal Press Syndicate. All rights reserved.

African Sahel,[9] where traditional agricultural systems that depended on leaving land fallow for a time to restore its productivity have broken down under population pressures.[10]

On Burkina Faso's Mossi Plateau, for instance, some 60 percent of the arable land is under cultivation in a given year, which means it is not lying idle long enough to rejuvenate. The reduced organic content and moisture-storage capacity of the soil lowers crop productivity and makes farmers more vulnerable to drought. In addition, with firewood in scarce supply in many Sahelian countries, families often use livestock dung for fuel, which also robs the land of nutrients. The result is a lowering of the land's carrying capacity, reduced food security, greater poverty, and continued high population growth.[11]

To take another example, the U.S. government protects domestic sugar producers by keeping sugar prices at three to five times world market levels. Because of the lost market opportunity, low-cost sugarcane growers in the Philippines produce less, putting cane-cutters out of work. The inequitable distribution of cropland in the Philippines combines with rapid population growth to leave the cutters little choice but to migrate into the hills to find land to grow subsistence crops. They clear plots by deforesting the upper watershed, causing increased flooding and soil erosion, which in turn silts up reservoirs and irrigation canals downstream. Poverty deepens, the gap between the rich and poor widens, and the environment deteriorates further.[12]

The Resource Base

The outer limit of the planet's carrying capacity is determined by the total amount of solar energy converted into biochemical energy through plant photosynthesis minus the energy those plants use for their own life processes. This is called the earth's net primary productivity (NPP), and it is the basic food source for all life.

Prior to human impacts, the earth's forests, grasslands, and other 25 terrestrial ecosystems had the potential to produce a net total of some 150 billion tons of organic matter per year. Stanford University biologist Peter Vitousek and his colleagues estimate, however, that humans have destroyed outright about 12 percent of the terrestrial NPP and now directly use or co-opt an additional 27 percent. Thus, one species —*Homo sapiens*—has appropriated nearly 40 percent of the terrestrial

[9]**Sahel:** The usually arid region south of the Sahara Desert.—ED.
[10]IUCN–The World Conservation Union, *The IUCN Sahel Studies 1991* (Gland, Switzerland: 1992).
[11]Ibid.
[12]Maria Concepcion Cruz et al., *Population Growth, Poverty, and Environmental Stress: Frontier Migration in the Philippines and Costa Rica* (Washington, D.C.: World Resources Institute, 1992).

food supply, leaving only 60 percent for the millions of other land-based plants and animals.[13]

It may be tempting to infer that, at 40 percent of NPP, we are still comfortably below the ultimate limit. But this is not the case. We have appropriated the 40 percent that was easiest to acquire. It may be impossible to double our share, yet theoretically that would happen in just sixty years if our share rose in tandem with population growth. And if average resource consumption per person continues to increase, that doubling would occur much sooner.

Perhaps more important, human survival hinges on a host of environmental services provided by natural systems—from forests' regulation of the hydrological cycle to wetlands' filtering of pollutants. As we destroy, alter, or appropriate more of these natural systems for ourselves, these environmental services are compromised. At some point, the likely result is a chain reaction of environmental decline—widespread flooding and erosion brought on by deforestation, for example, or worsened drought and crop losses from desertification, or pervasive aquatic pollution and fisheries losses from wetlands destruction. The simultaneous unfolding of several such scenarios could cause unprecedented human hardship, famine, and disease. Precisely when vital thresholds will be crossed, no one can say. But as Vitousek and his colleagues note, those "who believe that limits to growth are so distant as to be of no consequence for today's decision makers appear unaware of these biological realities."[14]

How have we come to usurp so much of the earth's productive capacity? In our efforts to feed, clothe, house, and otherwise satisfy our ever-growing material desires, we have steadily converted diverse and complex biological systems to more uniform and simple ones that are managed for human benefit. Timber companies cleared primary forests and replaced them with monoculture pine plantations to make pulp and paper. Migrant peasants torched tropical forests in order to plant crops merely to survive. And farmers plowed the prairie grasslands of the U.S. Midwest to plant corn, creating one of the most productive agricultural regions in the world. Although these transformations have allowed more humans to be supported at a higher standard of living, they have come at the expense of natural systems, other plant and animal species, and ecological stability.

Continuing along this course is risky. But the flip side of the problem is equally sobering. What do we do when we have claimed virtually all that we can, yet our population and demands are still growing?

This is precisely the predicament we now face. Opportunities to 30

[13]Peter M. Vitousek et al., "Human Appropriation of the Products of Photosynthesis," *BioScience,* June 1986.
[14]Ibid

expand our use of certain essential resources—including cropland, rangeland, fisheries, water, and forests—are severely limited, and a good share of the resources we have already appropriated, and depend on, are losing productivity. And unlike energy systems, where we can envisage a technically feasible shift from fossil fuels to solar-based sources, there are no identifiable substitutes for these essential biological and water resources. . . .

Redirecting Technology

Advances in technology—which is used broadly here to mean the application of knowledge to an activity—offer at least a partial way out of our predicament. The challenge of finding ways to meet the legitimate needs of our growing population without further destroying the natural resource base certainly ranks among the greatest missions humanity has ever faced. In most cases, "appropriate" technologies will no longer be engineering schemes, techniques, or methods that enable us to claim more of nature's resources, but instead systems that allow us to benefit more from the resources we already have. As long as the resulting gains are directed toward bettering the environment and the lives of the less fortunate instead of toward increased consumption by the rich, such efforts will reduce human impacts on the earth.

The power of technology to help meet human needs was a critical missing piece in the world view of Thomas Malthus, the English curate whose famous 1798 essay postulated that the growth of human population would outstrip the earth's food-producing capabilities. His prediction was a dire one—massive famine, disease, and death. But a stream of agricultural advances combined with the productivity leaps of the Industrial Revolution made the Malthusian nightmare fade for much of the world.

Without question, technological advances have steadily enhanced our capacity to raise living standards. They not only helped boost food production, the main concern of Malthus, they also increased our access to sources of water, energy, timber, and minerals. In many ways, however, technology has proved to be a double-edged sword. Take, for example, the chlorofluorocarbons that at first appeared to be ideal chemicals for so many different uses. It turned out that once they reached the upper atmosphere they began destroying the ozone layer, and thus threatened life on the planet.

Likewise, the irrigation, agricultural chemicals, and high-yielding crop varieties that made the Green Revolution[15] possible also depleted and contaminated water supplies, poisoned wildlife and people, and en-

---

[15]**Green Revolution:** Term referring to the dramatic increases in cereal-grain yields in many developing countries beginning in the 1960s. —ED.

couraged monoculture cropping that reduced agricultural diversity. Huge driftnets boosted fish harvests but contributed to overfishing and the depletion of stocks. And manufacturing processes that rapidly turn timber into pulp and paper have fueled the loss of forests and created mountains of waste paper.

As a society, we have failed to discriminate between technologies 35 that meet our needs in a sustainable way and those that harm the earth. We have let the market largely dictate which technologies move forward, without adjusting for its failure to take proper account of environmental damages. Now that we have exceeded the planet's carrying capacity and are rapidly running down its natural capital, such a correction is urgently needed.

Meeting future food needs, for instance, now depends almost entirely on raising the productivity of land and water resources. Over the last several decades, remarkable gains have been made in boosting cropland productivity. Between 1950 and 1991, world grain production rose 169 percent despite only a 17 percent increase in the area of grain harvested. An impressive 131 percent increase in average grain yield—brought about largely by Green Revolution technologies—allowed production to expand so greatly. If today's grain harvest were being produced at 1950s average yield, we would need at least twice as much land in crops as today—and pressure to turn forests and grasslands into cropland would have increased proportionately.[16]

Whether technological advances continue to raise crop yields fast enough to meet rising demand is, at the moment, an open question. Given the extent of cropland and rangeland degradation and the slowdown in irrigation expansion, it may be difficult to sustain the past pace of yield increases. Indeed, per capita grain production in 1992 was 7 percent lower than the historic peak in 1984. Whether this is a short-term phenomenon or the onset of a longer-term trend will depend on what new crop varieties and technologies reach farmers' fields and if they can overcome the yield-suppressing effects of environmental degradation. Another factor is whether agricultural policies and prices encourage farmers to invest in raising land productivity further.[17]

Currently, yields of the major grain crops are still significantly below their genetic potential, so it is possible that scientists will develop new crop varieties that can boost land productivity. They are working, for example, on a new strain of rice that may offer yield gains within a decade. And they have developed a wheat variety that is resistant to leaf

[16]USDA, op. cit. note 6.
[17]1992 grain production figure from Francis Urban, section leader, Markets and Competition, Economic Research Service, USDA, Washington, D.C., private communication, October 20, 1993; 1984 grain figure from USDA, op. cit. note 6; population figures from U.S. Bureau of the Census, in Francis Urban and Ray Nightingale, *World Population by Country and Region, 1950–1990 and Projections to 2050* (Washington, D.C.: USDA, Economic Research Service, 1993).

rust disease, which could both increase yields and allow wheat to be grown in more humid regions.[18]

Gains from biotechnology may be forthcoming soon as well. According to Gabrielle Persley of the World Bank, rice varieties bioengineered for virus resistance are likely to be in farmers' fields by 1995. Wheat varieties with built-in disease and insect resistance, which could reduce crop losses to pests, are under development. And scientists are genetically engineering maize varieties for insect resistance, although no commercial field applications are expected until sometime after 2000. It remains to be seen whether these and other potential gains materialize and whether they collectively increase yields at the rates needed. The recent cutback in funding for international agricultural research centers, where much of the work on grain crops takes place, is troubling.[19]

Paralleling the need to raise yields, however, is the less recognized 40 challenge of making both existing and future food production systems sustainable. A portion of our current food output is being produced by using land and water unsustainably. Unless this is corrected, food production from these areas will decline at some point.

For instance, in parts of India's Punjab, the nation's breadbasket, the high-yielding rice paddy–wheat rotation that is common requires heavy doses of agricultural chemicals and substantial amounts of irrigation water. A recent study by researchers from the University of Delhi and the World Resources Institute in Washington, D.C., found that in one Punjab district, Ludhiana, groundwater pumping exceeds recharge by one third and water tables are dropping nearly 1 meter per year. Even if water use were reduced to 80 percent of the recommended level, which would cause yields to drop an estimated 8 percent, groundwater levels would still decline by a half-meter per year. Given the importance of the Punjab to India's food production, the authors' conclusion is sobering, to say the least: "Unless production practices are developed that dramatically reduce water use, any paddy production system may be unsustainable in this region."[20]

Indeed, in many agricultural regions—including northern China, southern India (as well as the Punjab), Mexico, the western United

---

[18]Genetic yield potential from Lloyd T. Evans, *Crop Evolution, Adaptation, and Yield* (Cambridge: Cambridge University Press, 1993); new crop strains from Donald O. Mitchell and Merlinda D. Ingco, International Economics Department, *The World Food Outlook: Malthus Must Wait* (Washington, D.C.: World Bank, July 1993 [draft].

[19]Engineering of maize from Gabrielle J. Persley, *Beyond Mendel's Garden: Biotechnology in the Service of World Agriculture* (Wallingford, U.K.: CAB International, 1990); Gabrielle J. Persley, World Bank, Washington, D.C., private communications, July 1993.

[20]R.P.S. Malik and Paul Faeth, "Rice-Wheat Production in Northwest India," in Paul Faeth, ed., *Agricultural Policy and Sustainability: Case Studies from India, Chile, the Philippines, and the United States* (Washington, D.C.: World Resources Institute, 1993).

States, parts of the Middle East, and elsewhere—water may be much more of a constraint to future food production than land, crop yield potential, or most other factors. Developing and distributing technologies and practices that improve water management is critical to sustaining the food production capability we now have, much less increasing it for the future.

Water-short Israel is a front-runner in making its agricultural economy more water-efficient. Its current agricultural output could probably not have been achieved without steady advances in water management—including highly efficient drip irrigation, automated systems that apply water only when crops need it, and the setting of water allocations based on predetermined optimum water applications for each crop. The nation's success is notable: between 1951 and 1990, Israeli farmers reduced the amount of water applied to each hectare of cropland by 36 percent. This allowed the irrigated area to more than triple with only a doubling of irrigation water use.[21]

Whether high-tech, like the Israeli systems, or more traditional, like the vast canal schemes in much of Asia, improvements in irrigation management are critical. At the same time, technologies and methods to raise the productivity of rainfed lands are urgently needed. Particularly in dry regions, where land degradation and drought make soil and water conservation a matter of survival, improvements on many traditional methods could simultaneously raise local food production, reduce hunger, and slow environmental decline.[22]

In the Burkina Faso province of Yatenga, for example, farmers have 45 revived a traditional technique of building simple stone lines across the slopes of their fields to reduce erosion and help store moisture in the soil. With the aid of Oxfam, a U.K.-based development organization, they improved on the earlier technique by constructing the stone walls along contour lines, using a simple water-tube device to help them determine a series of level points. The technique has raised yields by up to 50 percent, and is now being used on more than 8,000 hectares in the province.[23]

Matching the need for sustainable gains in land and water productivity is the need for improvements in the efficiency of wood use and reductions in wood and paper waste in order to reduce pressures on forests and woodlands. A beneficial timber technology is no longer one

[21]Willem Van Tuijl, *Improving Water Use in Agriculture: Experiences in the Middle East and North Africa* (Washington, D.C.: World Bank, 1993).

[22]Postel, op. cit. note 5.

[23]For an overview of some traditional methods and their use, see Chris Reij, *Indigenous Soil and Water Conservation in Africa* (London: International Institute for Environment and Development, 1991); Will Critchley, *Looking after Our Land: Soil and Water Conservation in Dryland Africa* (Oxford: Oxfam, 1991).

that improves logging efficiency—the number of trees cut per hour—but rather one that makes each log harvested go further. Raising the efficiency of forest product manufacturing in the United States, the world's largest wood consumer, roughly to Japanese levels would reduce U.S. timber needs by about a fourth, for instance. Together, available methods of reducing waste, increasing manufacturing efficiency, and recycling more paper could cut U.S. wood consumption in half; a serious effort to produce new wood-saving techniques would reduce it even more.[24]

With the world's paper demand projected to double by the year 2010, there may be good reason to shift production toward "treeless paper"—that made from nonwood pulp. Hemp, bamboo, jute, and kenaf are among the alternative sources of pulp. The fast-growing kenaf plant, for example, produces two to four times more pulp per hectare than southern pine, and the pulp has all of the main qualities needed for making most grades of paper. In China, more than 80 percent of all paper pulp is made from nonwood sources. Treeless paper was manufactured in forty-five countries in 1992, and accounted for 9 percent of the world's paper supply. With proper economic incentives and support for technology and market development, the use of treeless paper could expand greatly.[25]

These are but a few examples of the refocusing of technology that is needed. A key policy instrument for encouraging more sustainable and efficient means of production is the institution of environmental taxes, which would help correct the market's failure to include environmental harm in the pricing of products and activities. In addition, stronger criteria are needed within development institutions and aid agencies to ensure that the projects they fund are ecologically sound and sustainable.

The many past gains from technological advances might make concerns about resource constraints seem anachronistic. But as Dartmouth College professor Donella Meadows and her coauthors caution in their 1992 study *Beyond the Limits,* "the more successfully society puts off its limits through economic and technical adaptations, the more likely it is in the future to run into several of them at the same time." The wiser use of technology can only buy time—and precious time it is—to bring consumption and population growth down to sustainable levels and to distribute resources more equitably.[26] . . .

---

[24]Sandra Postel and John C. Ryan, "Reforming Forestry," in Lester R. Brown, et al., *State of the World 1991* (New York: W. W. Norton & Company, 1991).

[25]Ed Ayres, "Making Paper without Trees," *World Watch,* September/October 1993; 9 percent figure from FAO, *Pulp and Paper Capacities 1992–1997* (Rome: 1993).

[26]Quotation from Donella H. Meadows, Dennis L. Meadows, and Jorgen Randers, *Beyond the Limits* (Post Mills, Vt.: Chelsea Green Publishing Company, 1992).

Lightening the Load

Ship captains pay careful attention to a marking on their vessels called 50 the Plimsoll line. If the water level rises above the Plimsoll line, the boat is too heavy and is in danger of sinking. When that happens, re-arranging items on the ship will not help much. The problem is the to-tal weight, which has surpassed the carrying capacity of the ship.[27]

Economist Herman Daly sometimes uses this analogy to under-score that the scale of human activity can reach a level that the earth's natural systems can no longer support. The ecological equivalent of the Plimsoll line may be the maximum share of the earth's biological re-source base that humans can appropriate before a rapid and cascading deterioration in the planet's life-support systems is set in motion. Given the degree of resource destruction already evident, we may be close to this critical mark. The challenge, then, is to lighten our burden on the planet before "the ship" sinks.

More than 1,600 scientists, including 102 Nobel laureates, under-scored this point in collectively signing a "Warning to Humanity" in late 1992. It states that "No more than one or a few decades remain before the chance to avert the threats we now confront will be lost and the prospects for humanity immeasurably diminished. . . . A new ethic is required—a new attitude towards discharging our responsibility for caring for ourselves and for the earth. . . . This ethic must motivate a great movement, convincing reluctant leaders and reluctant govern-ments and reluctant peoples themselves to effect the needed changes."[28]

A successful global effort to lighten humanity's load on the earth would directly address the three major driving forces of environmental decline—the grossly inequitable distribution of income, resource-consumptive economic growth, and rapid population growth—and would redirect technology and trade to buy time for this great move-ment. Although there is far too much to say about each of these chal-lenges to be comprehensive here, some key points bear noting.

Wealth inequality may be the most intractable problem, since it has existed for millennia. The difference today, however, is that the future. of both rich and poor alike hinges on reducing poverty and thereby eliminating this driving force of global environmental decline. In this way, self-interest joins ethics as a motive for redistributing wealth, and raises the chances that it might be done.

Important actions to narrow the income gap include greatly reduc- 55 ing Third World debt, much talked about in the eighties but still not

[27]This analogy is borrowed from Herman Daly, senior economist, World Bank; Herman E. Daly, "Allocation, Distribution, and Scale: Towards an Economics That Is Efficient, Just, and Sustainable," *Ecological Economics,* December 1992.

[28]Union of Concerned Scientists, "World's Leading Scientists Issue Urgent Warning to Humanity," Washington, D.C., press release, November 18, 1992.

accomplished, and focusing foreign aid, trade, and international lending policies more directly on improving the living standards of the poor. If decision makers consistently asked themselves whether a choice they were about to make would help the poorest of the poor—that 20 percent of the world's people who share only 1.4 percent of the world's income—and acted only if the answer were yes, more people might break out of the poverty trap and have the opportunity to live sustainably.[29]

Especially in poorer countries, much could be gained from greater support for the myriad grass-roots organizations working for a better future. These groups constitute a powerful force for achieving sustainable development in its truest form—through bottom-up action by local people. In an October 1993 address at the World Bank, Kenyan environmentalist Wangari Maathai noted that among the great benefits of the Green Belt Movement, the tree planting campaign she founded, was the understanding it gave people that "no progress can be made when the environment is neglected, polluted, degraded, and overexploited. Many people have also come to appreciate that taking care of the environment is not the responsibility of only the government but of the citizens as well. This awareness is empowering and brings the environment close to the people. Only when this happens do people feel and care for the environment."[30]

A key prescription for reducing the kinds of economic growth that harm the environment is the same as that for making technology and trade more sustainable—internalizing environmental costs. If this is done through the adoption of environmental taxes, governments can avoid imposing heavier taxes overall by lowering income taxes accordingly. In addition, establishing better measures of economic accounting is critical. Since the calculations used to produce the gross national product do not account for the destruction or depletion of natural resources, this popular economic measure is extremely misleading. It tells us we are making progress even as our ecological foundations are crumbling. A better beacon to guide us toward a sustainable path is essential. The United Nations and several individual governments have been working to develop such a measure, but progress has been slow.[31]

[29]External debt in developing countries from IMF, *Annual Report of the Executive Board for the Fiscal Year Ended April 30, 1993* (Washington, D.C.: 1993).

[30]Wangari Maathai, "The Green Belt Movement for Environment & Development," presented at the International Conference on Environmentally Sustainable Development, World Bank, Washington, D.C., October 1, 1993.

[31]United Nations, Statistical Division, *Integrated Environment and Economic Accounting: Handbook of National Accounting,* Studies in Methods (New York: forthcoming); Peter Bartelmus, Officer in Charge of the Environment and Energy Statistics Branch, Statistical Division of the United Nations, New York, private communication, October 21, 1993.

Besides calling on political leaders to effect these changes, individuals in wealthier countries can help lighten humanity's load by voluntarily reducing their personal levels of consumption. By purchasing "greener products" for necessities and reducing discretionary consumption, the top one billion can help create ecological space for the bottom one billion to consume enough for a decent and secure life.

Analyzing Issues and Arguments

1. Reread Sandra Postel's discussion of net primary productivity (NPP) (paras. 24ff), and then explain the concept in your own words: What does it mean? Why is it important?
2. How are the collaborations described by Diane Jukofsky in "Can Marketing Save the Rainforest?" helping to increase the carrying capacity of the tropical regions involved? What potential strains are these programs creating on carrying capacity?
3. What does Postel see as the most critical actions humanity can take to preserve the earth's ability to support us?

Writing about Issues and Arguments

"The future of both rich and poor alike hinges on reducing poverty and thereby eliminating this driving force of global environmental decline" (para. 54). Would William K. Reilly (p. 260) agree with Postel's statement? Write an essay comparing and contrasting the two writers' views of the relationship between poverty and environmental damage. Be sure to consider what both have to say about economic growth, population growth, and technology. Whose analysis do you find more convincing, and why?

JULIAN L. SIMON

Should We Conserve?

Julian L. Simon is a professor of business administration at the University of Maryland, College Park. After graduating from Harvard University in 1953, he served in the navy and then was an advertising copywriter in New York City. He received his M.B.A. and Ph.D. from the University of Chicago and went on to become a professor of economics, marketing, and advertisement at the University of Illinois, Urbana. Simon also has taught at Hebrew University, Jerusalem, and served as a consultant to various public and private organizations. Among his books are *Effort, Opportunity, and Wealth* (1987); *Population Matters: People, Resources, Environment, and Immigration* (1990); *Population and Development in Poor Countries* (1992); and most recently *Scarcity or Abundance: A Debate on the Environment* (1994), coauthored with Norman Myers. Simon's current area of research is population economics. "Should We Conserve?," which comes from his 1981 book *The Ultimate Resource,* reflects his view that market forces will solve scarcity problems.

Should we try to conserve our resources? It depends. Should we avoid all waste? Certainly not. Are the Sierra Club, Friends of the Earth, and other conservationist groups barking up the wrong tree? Yes and no.

We can clarify conservation issues by distinguishing among (1) unique resources, which are one of a kind or close to it and which we value for aesthetic purposes—examples include the Mona Lisa, endangered species of animals, and Muhammad Ali; (2) one-of-a-kind resources that we value as historical artifacts—examples include the U.S. Declaration of Independence, the Dead Sea Scrolls, Abraham Lincoln's first log cabin (if it existed), and perhaps the Mona Lisa; (3) resources that can be reproduced or recycled or substituted for and that we value for their material uses—examples include wood pulp, trees, copper, oil, and food.

This [essay] deals mainly with category (3), resources that we value primarily for the use we make of them. These are the resources whose quantities we can positively influence. That is, these are the resources for which we can calculate whether it is cheaper to conserve them for future use, or use them now and get the services that they give us in some other way in the future. The benefits we get from the resources in the other categories—the Mona Lisa or Lincoln's log cabin—cannot be adequately replaced, and hence the economist cannot determine whether conservation is economically worthwhile. The value of a Mona Lisa or a disappearing breed of snail must be what we as a society decide is the value, a decision upon which market prices may or may not shed some light.

The cost and scarcity of resources in category (3)—energy and extractive materials—is likely to decline continuously in the future.[1] . . . [The question here is] whether as individuals and as a society we should try to use less of these materials than we are willing to pay for. That is, should we make special efforts to refrain from using these natural resources, and hence treat them differently from the consumption of pencils, haircuts, and Hula-Hoops? The answer is that, apart from considerations of national security and international bargaining power, we need not make special efforts to avoid using the resources.

Conservationists perform an invaluable service when they alert us 5 to dangers to our unique treasures, and when they remind us of the values of these treasures to ourselves and to coming generations. But when they move from this role to suggesting that pulp trees or deer should be conserved beyond what we are willing to pay to set aside the trees or the deer's habitat, they are either expressing their own personal aesthetic tastes and religious values, or else they are talking misguided nonsense. And when some famous conservationist tells us that there should be fewer people so that it is easier for him to find a deserted stretch of beach or mountain range or forest, he is simply saying "gimme"—that is, "I want it, and I don't want to share it." . . .

Conservation of Replaceable Resources

Should you save old newspapers rather than throw them away? Sure you should—as long as the price that the recycling center pays is greater than the value to you of your time and energy in saving and hauling them.

Should you conserve energy by turning off lights that are burning needlessly in your house? Of course you should—just as long as the money that you save by so doing is worth the effort of shutting off the light. That is, you should turn out a light if the value of the electrical energy is greater than the cost to you of taking a few steps to the light switch and flicking your wrist. But if you are ten miles away from home and you remember that you left a 100-watt light bulb on, should

---

[1]Simon presents his basis for this claim in chapters 1–3 of *The Ultimate Resource:* "natural resources are not finite in any meaningful economic sense" (p. 17) because as the supply of any resource dwindles, advancing technology will develop new and cheaper ways of producing that resource (for example, mining less-accessible copper ore deposits), or of meeting the needs previously met by that resource (for example, replacing copper with fiber-optic cable), or both.—ED.

you rush back to turn it off? Obviously not; the value of the gasoline spent would be far greater than the electricity saved, even if the light is on for many days. And even if you are on foot and not far away, the value of your time is surely greater to you than the cost of the electricity saved.

The appropriate rule in these cases is that we should conserve and not waste just so far as the benefits of conserving are greater than the costs if we do not conserve. That is, it is rational for us to avoid waste if the value of the resource saved is more than the cost to us of achieving the saving—a matter of pocketbook economics.

A frequent source of confusion is between *physical* conservation and *economic* conservation. For example, some have urged us not to flush our toilets each time we use them, but rather to use other rules of thumb that we need not take up here. The aim is to "save water." But almost all of us would rather pay the cost of obtaining the additional water from groundwater supplies or from cleaning the water; hence, to "save water" by not flushing is not rational economics. It *is* rational economics to systematically replace light bulbs before they burn out, so that all the bulbs can be changed at once; this is not a waste of light-bulb capacity. To do otherwise is to commit yourself to a lower level of material living.

Though a "simpler way of life" has an appeal for some, it can have a surprisingly high economic cost. One student calculated what would happen if U.S. farmers used 1918 agricultural technology instead of contemporary technology, forswearing tractors and fertilizers in order to "save energy" and natural resources: "We'd need 61 million horses and mules . . . it would take 180 million acres of cropland to feed these animals or about one-half of the cropland now in production. We'd need 26 or 27 million additional agricultural workers to achieve 1976 production levels with 1918 technology."[2] 10

Conservation of ordinary resources is not a moral matter but an economic matter, just like all other decisions about production and consumption. It is a misunderstanding of this point that leads us to suggest and do foolish things, actions that—though they have expressive value for us—accomplish nothing, and may even have harmful effects for others. For example, there is no discernible benefit for the food supply of people in poor countries of your not eating meat. In fact, the opposite may be true: heavy meat eating in the United States stimulates grain planting and harvesting in order to feed cattle; this increased capacity represents an increased ability to handle an unexpected massive need for food. As D. Gale Johnson put it,

[2]*Champaign-Urbana News Gazette,* October 16, 1977, p. 52-C.

Suppose that the United States and the other industrial countries had held their direct and indirect per capita use of grain to half of the actual levels for the past several decades. Would this have made more food available to India or Pakistan in 1973 and 1974? The answer is clearly no. The United States, and the other industrial countries as well, would have produced much less grain than has been produced. Reserve stocks would have been much smaller than they have been. If U.S. grain production in 1972 had been 125 million metric tons instead of 200 million or more, it would not have been politically possible to have had 70 million metric tons of grain reserves. . . .

If the industrial countries had had much lower total grain consumption in the past, the institutions required to handle the grain exports to the developing countries in the mid-1960s or in 1972–73 and 1973–74 would not have been able to do so. International trade in grains would have virtually disappeared.[3]

Nor would the research have been done that led to production breakthroughs if industrial countries had consumed less.

Yet experts and laymen alike espouse the "obvious" (though incorrect) short-run view that if we consume less, others in need will have more. Testifying before several Senate subcommittees sitting jointly, Lester Brown said that "it might be wise to reduce consumption of meat a few pounds per capita within affluent, overnourished societies such as the United States."[4] And concerned citizens say, "Millions of people are dying. . . . It sickens me to think of the money spent in America on food that is unnecessary for our basic nutritional needs. Would a sacrifice be so difficult?"[5] And "We . . . serve tens of millions of pets vast quantities of food that could be used to feed millions of starving people in Asia, Africa, and Latin America—if we would only practice birth control for our pets!"[6]

Would it be sound charity to eat less food or eat cheaper food and send the money saved to poor countries? It would indeed be kind for each of us to send money. But why take the money from our food budgets? Why not from our incomes as wholes—that is, while reducing other expenditures as is most convenient, rather than just reducing our expenditures on food? That would make better economic sense (though it might have less ritualistic meaning to us, which could be a persuasive argument for "saving food").

Energy conservation is another favorite target. We are urged not to eat lobsters because it takes 117 times as much energy to catch a lobster

[3]Johnson D. Gale. 1974b. *World Food Problems and Prospects.* Washington, D.C.: Am. Enterprise. pp. 35–37.

[4]Ibid., p. 35, quoting from *Hearings on U.S. and World Food Situation,* 93rd Congress, 1st session, October 1973, p. 103.

[5]Steven Conwin, letter to editor, *New York Times Magazine,* June 30, 1974, p. 20.

[6]*The Humanist,* April 1975, p. 20.

as it does to catch enough herring to yield an equal amount of protein.[7] One of the coauthors of the study that reached this conclusion is Jean Mayer, adviser to presidents, president of Tufts University, and perhaps the best-known student of nutrition in the world (but not a student of energy or economics). Marvelous disputes arise in Washington because everyone is trying to get into the energy-saving act. Any one group's panacea is another group's problem. "Transportation officials are 'outraged' by a Congressional report suggesting that buses, van pools, and car pools may use less energy than mass transit rail systems."[8] And the U.S. Post Office in 1978 issued a postage stamp entitled "Energy Conservation," picturing a light bulb, a gas can, and the sun with an inscrutable face.

Apparently it is an inbred moral intuition that makes us feel that 15 nonconservation is wrong.

> Bishop Edward O'Rourke, head of the Peoria [Illinois] diocese of the Catholic Church, and Bruce Hannon, environmentalist and energy researcher in the UI [University of Illinois] Center for Advanced Computation, attempted to raise the "level of consciousness" of church leaders and laymembers. . . .
>
> One solution they cited for the growing problem is for everyone to lead lives that are simpler, more spiritual, and less resource consuming. . . .
>
> Even buying a tube of toothpaste is energy wasting. . . . The toothpaste is encased in a cardboard box, which must then be put in a paper bag, with a paper sales receipt—all of these products use wood pulp, and all are usually thrown away and destroyed. . . .
>
> "We are custodians and stewards of God's gifts. The more precious the gifts, such as energy, the more urgent the need to protect them," Bishop O'Rourke reminded.[9]

A Louis Harris poll reveals that

> a substantial, 61–23 percent majority thinks it is "morally wrong" for Americans—6 percent of the world's population—to consume an estimated 40 percent of the world's output of energy and raw materials. And, the public indicates it is ready for a number of drastic cutbacks. . . . A 91–7 percent majority is willing to "have one meatless day a week. . . ." A 73–22 percent majority would agree to "wear old clothes, even if they shine, until they wear out. . . ." By 92–5 percent the public reports it would be willing to "reduce the amount of paper towels, bags, tissues, napkins, cups, and other disposables to save energy and to cut pollution."[10]

[7]Study described in *Daily Illini,* October 20, 1977, page unknown.
[8]*New York Times,* October 9, 1977, p. 48.
[9]*Champaign-Urbana News Gazette,* March 15, 1977, p. 2.
[10]In this report of poll results, the first figure represents the majority and the second figure represents the minority. Thus a "61–23 percent majority" means that 61 percent of those surveyed agreed with the statement, 23 percent disagreed, and 16 percent were undecided or did not respond to the question.—ED.

I share this moral impulse. I take a back seat to no one in hating waste—unnecessary lights, avoidable errands, trivial conferences. But I try to restrict my waste fighting to matters where the benefit is worth the cost (though my children have a different view of my behavior). I try to remember not to waste more additional valuable resources in fighting the original waste than the original waste is worth. . . .

After the first spurt of enthusiasm for conservation and recycling, some people began to calculate that the costs of recommended recycling projects can often exceed the savings.

> [A high-school student in Los Angeles] for eighteen weeks . . . collected bottles from a restaurant to raise money for a favorite organization. At the end of that time, he had collected 10,180 pounds of glass, driven 817 miles, consumed 54 gallons of gas . . . and used up 153 man-hours of work. It is difficult to estimate the amount of pollution his car threw into the air.[11]

Why do conservationists think people must be pushed to conserve more than what they "naturally" would? Apparently, they do not believe that people will react rationally to changes in resource availabilities and prices. But the slowdown in growth of electricity consumption since 1973—enough to cause many utilities to drop plans to build new generating plants[12]—should be powerful evidence of consumers' sensitivities to cost and scarcity. Another striking example has been the drop far below the trend in gasoline use in the late 1970s, as gasoline prices rose sharply.

Resources and Future Generations

Conservationists and technologists tend to focus discussion on the fu- 20 ture, and often properly so. They suggest conserving so that there will be "enough" for future generations. We should conserve, they say, even if the value we get from the resource saved is less than what it costs us to achieve the saving.

When we use resources, then, we ought to ask whether our present use is at the expense of future generations. The answer is a straightforward *no*. If the relative prices of natural resources can be expected to be lower for future generations than for us now—and this seems to be a reasonable expectation for most natural resources, as we have seen earlier—this implies that future generations will be faced by no greater economic scarcity than we are, but instead will have just as large or larger supplies of resources to tap, despite our present use of them. Hence our present use of resources, considered in sum, has little

[11] *Champaign-Urbana News Gazette,* March 18, 1973, p. 9.
[12] *Wall Street Journal,* February 7, 1979, p. 38.

if any negative effect upon future generations. And our descendants may well be better off if we use the resources in question right now to build a higher standard of living. So we need make no ethical judgments for our descendants.

Furthermore, the market tends to guard against overuse of materials that may become scarcer in the future. The current price of a material reflects expected future supply and demand as well as current conditions, and therefore current prices make an automatic allowance for future generations. If there is a reasonable basis to expect prices to rise in the future, investors will now buy up oil wells, coal mines, and copper-mining companies; such purchases raise the current prices of oil, coal, and copper, and discourage their use. Paradoxically, normal market speculation "cannot prevent an unduly *low* rate of consumption, which would leave future generations with more reserves than they need—just the opposite of what conservationists worry about!"[13]

But what if the investors are wrong? you may ask. In return I ask you: Are you prepared to believe that your understanding of the matter is better than that of speculators who study the facts full time, who are aware of the information you are aware of, and who earn their livings by not being wrong?

The storage of fresh fruits throughout the year serves as a simple illustration of how markets and businesses ensure a yearlong supply and prevent future scarcity. The example also shows how present price reflects future scarcity, and why it would not make sense to buy oranges in the summer to "conserve" for winter or for future years.

Oranges are harvested in the spring and early summer in various countries such as Italy, Israel, Algeria, and Spain. Naturally the price to consumers is cheapest at harvest time. But fruit dealers also buy at harvest time, and store the fruit in warehouses for later sale. The price throughout the winter is roughly the cost at harvest plus the cost of storage (including the cost of the capital tied up in the oranges). The price in the winter therefore is not much higher than at harvest, and there is no reason for consumers to worry about scarcity.

The force that ensures that prices will not rise precipitously at harvest time is the desire of merchants to make a profit by buying cheap at harvest and selling dear later. And the force that prevents them from pushing the price very high in the winter is the competition of other merchants, who have the same desire. Of course any consumer who worries that winter prices will be unbearably high can stockpile oranges and pay the storage price. Likewise, these forces work to prevent scarcity or a fast price run-up in natural resources. Merchants who be-

[13] Hendrik S. Houthakker, 1976. "The Economics of Nonrenewable Resources." *Beihefte der Konjunkturpolitik* 23: p. 122 (italics added).

lieve—on the basis of a very full investigation, because their economic lives depend upon it—that future scarcity is not yet fully reflected in present prices will buy raw materials now for future resale. They will do our conserving for us, and we will pay them only if they were right. And the argument is even stronger with respect to metals because they do not require a refrigerated warehouse.

The fact that there will be another orange harvest next year does not make the orange situation different from the copper situation discussed earlier. New discoveries of copper, and new technological developments in the mining and use of copper, are also expected to occur, though the timing of the events is less certain with copper than with oranges. But that just means a wider market for speculating merchants. Hence we need not worry that the needs of future generations are being injured by our present consumption patterns. And please notice that orange prices at harvest time, and present copper prices, too, reflect expected population growth. If consumption is expected to rise due to increased population, foresighted merchants will take that into account (and nonforesighted merchants are not able to remain in business for very long).

If the economic situation were different than it really is—if technology were fixed and costs of resources were therefore expected to be higher in the future than now, indicating greater scarcity to come —it might be appropriate to make ethical judgments that would differ from the results that a free market can produce for us. It might then be appropriate to worry that our consumption and fertility (if influenced only by market prices) might have such adverse effects on future generations that a prudent government might intervene to reduce present use of the mineral natural resources. But such intervention is not now necessary or appropriate, because, as Barnett and Morse put it, "By devoting itself to improving the lot of the living . . . each generation . . . transmits a more productive world to those who follow."[14] It does so by accumulating real capital to increase current income, by adding to the stock of useful knowledge, by making its own generation healthier and better educated, and by improving economic institutions. This is why the standard of living has been rising with successive generations.

Because we can expect future generations to be richer than we are, no matter what we do about resources, asking us to refrain from using resources now so that future generations can have them later is like asking the poor to make gifts to the rich.

---

[14]Harold J. Barnett, and Chandler Morse, 1963. *Scarcity and Growth: The Economics of Natural Resource Availability.* Baltimore: Johns Hopkins. p. 249.

Conservation of Animals or People?

Some say that the human population should be stabilized or reduced 30 because it threatens some species of animals. This raises interesting questions. If we assume there is a trade-off between more people and more of species X, then which species should we favor? Buffalo or golden eagles over *Homo sapiens?* If yes, does the same logic hold for rats and cockroaches? And how many people do we want to trade for more buffalo? Should the whole Midwest be made a buffalo preserve, or do we want only to maintain the species just this side of extinction? If the latter, why not just put them in a few big zoos? And do we want to protect malaria-carrying mosquitoes from extinction?

We ought also [to] consider the species of animals whose numbers are increased when the human population increases: chickens, goats, cattle, minks, dogs, cats, and canaries. Is this a justification for increasing our population? (This also is a problem for those who are against killing animals for food or clothing. Without humans to consume these products there would be fewer chickens and minks to be killed.) Which way does one prefer to have it from the viewpoint of animal welfare?

My point: Where costs are not the issue, the decision about what is conserved, and how much, is a matter of tastes and values. Once we recognize this, the arguments are easier to resolve.

Price and Value

The most complex and confusing conservation issues are those that seem as if they are matters of only dollars and cents to some people, but to other people are matters of aesthetics and basic values. Consider the matter of saving old newspapers. Some large institutions save and recycle paper because the money obtained for the waste paper makes the effort profitable. In World War II the price of waste paper rose high enough to make the effort worthwhile for many householders. And now that shredded newspapers can be used as insulation after treatment with fire-retardant chemicals, paper collection is a fund-raising device for community groups such as Boy Scout troops.[15] But nowadays, for most of us the cost of saving and delivering the waste paper seems greater than the amount we would get for it.

Here we must consider, What is the economic meaning of the price paid for waste paper? That price will roughly equal the sum of

---

[15] *Wall Street Journal,* November 3, 1977, p. 1.

what it costs to grow a tree, cut the tree, and then transport and convert the wood to paper. If the cost of growing new trees rises, so will
the cost of paper. But if the cost of growing trees goes down, or if
good substitutes for trees are developed, the price of used and of new
paper, and of wood, will fall. And that is what is happening right now.
The total quantity of growing trees has been increasing, and the newspapers report the successful development of kenaf as a substitute for
paper. . . . So why bother to recycle newspapers?

Environmentalists, however, feel that there is more to be said on 35
this matter. They feel that trees should be saved for reasons other than
the dollars-and-cents value of pulp or lumber. They argue that it is
inherently right to try to avoid cutting down a tree "unnecessarily." I
believe that it is fair to characterize this argument as based on aesthetic or even religious values other than those relating to use by future generations. The environmentalists believe that stands of trees are
unique national or international treasures just as Westminster Abbey is
for Englishmen and as the Mosque of the Golden Dome is for Mus-
lims. Perhaps we can express this by saying that in these cases even the
believer who does not directly use the treasure is willing to pay, in
money or in effort, so that other people—now and in the future—
can enjoy it without paying the full price of creating it. (Additionally,
there is the argument that, even if future generations will be willing
to pay the price, they will be unable to do so if we don't preserve
it for them.) Some people even impute feelings to nature,
to trees or to animals, and they aim to prevent pain to those
feelings. . . .

There is also conservation for the purposes of national security and
international bargaining. It may well make sense for a country to stockpile enough oil and other strategically sensitive resources for months or
even years of consumption. But these political matters are beyond the
scope of this chapter and of the usual discussions of conservation. Furthermore, there is almost no connection between population growth
and such strategic stockpiling. Hence the topic needs no further attention here.

Resources and International Rape

Is there need for ethical judgments to supersede market decisions when
rich countries buy raw materials from poor countries?

The idea that the rich countries are "raping" the poor countries
and "pirating" their bauxite, copper, and oil does not rest on a solid intellectual foundation. These resources have little value for home use in
a country with little industry. But when sold to an industrial country,
the resources provide revenue that can aid in development—and, in

*"And may we continue to be worthy of consuming a
disproportionate share of this planet's resources."*

fact, this revenue may represent a poor country's very best chance of development. What if the "exploiters" stop buying? This is what happened in 1974 in Indonesia.

> Many of those Indonesians who took to the streets only eight months ago to protest alleged Japanese exploitation of their natural resources are now beginning to complain that the Japanese are not exploiting them enough. Because of setbacks in their own economy, Japanese importing companies have had to cut their monthly purchases of 760,000 cubic yards of Indonesian timber by as much as 40 percent. As a result, Indonesian lumber prices have dropped some 60 percent and . . . thirty firms have already gone bankrupt, causing widespread unemployment in . . . timber-dependent areas.[16]

Nor are contemporary poor-country people who sell their resources benefiting at the expense of their own future generations. "Saving" the materials for the poor country's future population runs the grave risk that the resources will drop in relative value in the future, just as coal has become less valuable in the past century; a country that

[16]*Newsweek,* September 30, 1974, p. 52.

hoarded its coal starting a hundred years ago would be a loser on all accounts.

Please remember, too, that the United States and other rich coun- 40 tries export large amounts of primary products that poor countries need, especially food. The primary products that the poorer countries produce enable them to trade for the rich countries' primary products, an exchange from which both parties gain. Of course, nothing in this paragraph suggests that the prices at which rich countries buy these resources from poor countries are "fair" prices. The terms of trade are indeed an ethical matter, but one that is likely to be resolved by the hard facts of supply, demand, market power, and political power.

Analyzing Issues and Arguments

1. "I try to remember not to waste more additional valuable resources in fighting the original waste than the original waste is worth" (para. 17). What criteria does Julian L. Simon use to gauge the worth of the resources he is calling "original waste"? What are his criteria for gauging the worth of "additional valuable resources"? Cite specific passages from the selection to support your answer.

2. On the question of saving water by not flushing our toilets after every use, Simon argues that "almost all of us would rather pay the cost of obtaining the additional water from groundwater supplies or from cleaning the water" (para. 9). On what evidence does he base this statement? What further information would you want to know before agreeing or disagreeing with him?

3. Simon has written much of "Should We Conserve?" in the first-person plural (*we*). In what ways does this choice affect his essay's impact? What group of people does he evidently mean by *we*?

Writing about Issues and Arguments

"Conservation of ordinary resources is not a moral matter but an economic matter" (para. 11). What does Simon mean by this statement? What appear to be his definitions of *moral* and *economic*? What are the behavioral implications of his statement? Write an essay defending or rebutting Simon's position. (You may want to draw on other sources in this book.)

IN THE NEWS

Why Not Tax Our Trash and Our Traffic Jams?

Dianne Dumanoski

The following article ran in Dianne Dumanoski's monthly *Boston Globe* column, "One Earth," on April 1, 1991. Dumanoski is an environment, reporter for the *Globe*. She is currently on leave, coauthoring a book (with scientists Theodora Colborn and J. P. Myers) about the effects of certain toxic environmental chemicals on fetal and reproductive development.

. . . Economist Robert Repetto of the World Resources Institute has two words of advice for states in fiscal crisis: green taxes.

Instead of hiking income taxes, slap a tax on cars traveling at rush hour on congested highways, he suggests. Hong Kong has done that for years, using monitors that read electronic license plates as cars enter the road. It's also done in the Norwegian cities of Oslo and Bergen, in Cambridge, England, and on a Dallas freeway. Besides raising money, the tax reduces traffic congestion and air pollution, and it saves billions of dollars by doing away with the need for more highways, he says.

If trash disposal costs are driving your city or town to bankruptcy, don't raise property taxes, Repetto counsels. Follow the lead of Seattle and make it pay-as-you-throw. Charging households by the pound or barrel for trash raises money while reducing trash and city trash disposal costs.

"You have to tax something," Repetto reasons. For the last decade, the tax debate has focused on "how much," he says, and ignored the equally critical question of "what kind" of taxes. It is a question we ignore at our economic peril.

The idea of taxing pollution and environmentally undesirable behavior   5 is being touted not only by some economists and environmentalists, but is also gaining increasing attention in Washington from both Republicans and Democrats.

A year ago, the House Ways and Means Committee devoted three days to hearings on the question. The Congressional Budget Office and the Environmental Protection Agency have been scrutinizing proposals to combat global warming by taxing carbon dioxide emissions from fossil fuels.

In Repetto's view, however, it is the states struggling with budget deficits and languishing economies that have the most to gain by shifting to green taxes. He is now completing a study on the potential of green taxes for World Resources Institute, an environmental think tank based in Washington, D.C.

Repetto and other economists argue that green taxes not only improve the environment, they are much better for the economy. Their money-making potential, he notes, "is considerable." By his estimate, rush hour taxes on congested highways across the nation could raise tens of billions of dollars.

Yes, that's billions with a "b."

Repetto says green taxes should be particularly attractive to a fiscally be- 10
leaguered state like Massachusetts, because shifting some of the burden from
income and property taxes would lessen the drag on the local economy and
make the state more attractive to business and investors.

The enthusiasm among environmentalists is understandable. Calculated
properly, green taxes could be an efficient way to meet environmental goals,
because they would adjust the price of products to include previously overlooked environmental costs, and let the market do the rest.

"Income taxes are essentially a convenient way to collect money, but they
are not doing much good socially," says Sandra Postel of the Worldwatch Institute. Green taxes do more than raise money, she notes; they discourage
waste and pollution.

In its latest State of the World Report, Postel's research organization recommended shifting 30 percent of the nation's tax base from personal income
to a variety of green taxes, including levies on the carbon dioxide content of
fossil fuels, pesticide sales, paper and paperboard produced from virgin pulp,
and hazardous waste. The package could raise at least $160 billion a year, it
estimated.

How would those proposals affect the average taxpayer?

Postel says lower income taxes would give people more money to spend, 15
but the price of environmentally damaging products would jump because of
the pollution levies, giving so-called green products an edge in the marketplace.

Postel says care should be taken to make sure a shift to green taxes
wouldn't make the tax system regressive, placing a heavier burden on the
poor. A carbon tax, for example, might have this effect because poor families
spend a bigger chunk of their income on gasoline and home heating. Reducing income taxes in the lowest brackets or giving direct payments to those too
poor to pay taxes could correct this problem, she said.

Economist Lawrence Goulder of Stanford University calls the proposal "a
great idea." Most taxes, he explained, fall into two categories: taxes that make
the economy less efficient and taxes that make it work better.

Income and payroll taxes are in this first category, which Goulder calls
"distortionary" taxes, because they have the perverse effect of discouraging
things that are generally good for the economy, such as work, savings, and
investment.

Green taxes, on the other hand, are "corrective" taxes. They correct inefficiencies in the economy by making the price for a product or service,
whether it is fossil fuels or garbage disposal, reflect the social and environmental costs.

Besides the obvious environmental benefits, Goulder says shifting from 20
income taxes to green charges would also reduce the overall drag on the
economy caused by distortionary taxes. He calls this the "double dividend"
earned by green taxes.

Repetto says distortionary taxes are especially damaging to state
economies, because states compete for investors and workers. If a state raises
extra money through income taxes, it makes every dollar earned in the state

worth less to workers and companies and it makes the state less attractive to investors.

But if the state raises additional money through green taxes, "every dollar that's earned in Massachusetts is worth more to investor or worker." That, he says, makes a state more attractive to investors and more competitive with other states.

If green taxes are so great, why aren't they being adopted more quickly and widely? "There's a general perception," Goulder says, "that all taxes are the same and that all taxes are wasteful." So the attitude is "let's not get on board with green taxes or any other taxes."

Secondly, some powerful special interests would be hurt by green taxes, and, Goulder says, these losers "exert a strong political influence."

If Repetto is right, however, Massachusetts could be a winner. It need   25 only to get out in front of what could become a green taxes bandwagon in the next decade.   ∎

Analyzing Issues and Arguments

1. What advantages do green taxes have over income taxes, according to the article?
2. On what economic principles do Robert Repetto and Julian L. Simon appear to agree?

FRANCES CAIRNCROSS

Government and the Economics
of the Environment

Frances Cairncross became the first environmental editor for *The Econo-mist* magazine in London in 1989. She began her career as a writer with the London *Times* in 1967 after earning degrees in history at Oxford and economics at Brown University. She worked for the *Observer* for three years and the *Guardian* for eleven before *The Economist* hired her as Britain editor. With her husband, Hamish McRae, Cairncross has written *Capital City: London as a Financial Centre* (1971) and *The Second Great Crash* (1973); her other books include the first and second *Guardian Guide to the Economy* (1981, 1983). "Government and the Economics of the En-vironment" is from the introduction to her 1991 book *Costing the Earth: The Challenge for Governments, the Opportunities for Business.* This excerpt reflects Cairncross's longtime interest in approaching environmental issues from an economist's standpoint, as well as her belief that effective envi-ronmental protection requires government support.

Environmentalism involves dangerous issues for politicians. [Former British Prime Minister] Margaret Thatcher can hardly have thought through the telling metaphor she used in her speech to the Conserva-tive party conference in October 1988 that marked her transition from Iron Lady to Green Goddess. "No generation has a freehold on the earth," she said. "All we have is a life tenancy—with a full repairing lease." The implications are enormous. For up to now, no generation has carried out its fair share of planetary repairs. Each has ignored the costs that accrue to future generations. To demand that this generation should undertake repairs means making people pay for something that they have previously regarded as free. Yet only government can ulti-mately set the terms of that "full repairing lease."

Environmental policy is inevitably interventionist. Without gov-ernment intervention, the environment cannot be fully protected. That was clearly anticipated over a century ago by John Stuart Mill. "Is there not the earth itself, its forests and waters, above and below the surface?" he asked in his *Principles of Political Economy.* "These are the inheritance of the human race. . . . What rights, and under what conditions, a person shall be allowed to exercise over any portion of this com-mon inheritance cannot be left undecided. No function of government is less optional than the regulation of these things, or more completely involved in the idea of a civilized society."

This intrinsic need for intervention makes environmentalism difficult for political radicals to accept, especially after the 1980s' fashion for deregulation. An eloquent exposition of the free-marketer's case for environmental intervention was made by one of Mrs. Thatcher's closest political allies, Nicholas Ridley, while he was British environment secretary:

> Pollution, like fraud, is something you impose on others against their will so that you can perhaps gain financial advantage. It is an ill for which the operation of the free market provides no automatic cure. Like the prevention of violence and fraud, pollution control is essentially an activity which the State, as protector of the public interest against particular interests, has to regulate and police.[1]

Harder yet for many governments to accept, environmental issues are frequently about justice, too. Allocating rights and determining conditions drags government, willy-nilly, into nasty questions of winners and losers that politicians usually prefer to avoid. The winners and losers may live in the same town. But the gainers may be rich and powerful, the losers poor and weak. The losers may even be foreigners, if one country's environmental damage harms the citizens of another. Or they may be the weakest of the weak: generations yet unborn. "Why should I care about posterity?" Groucho Marx is supposed to have said. "What's posterity ever done for me?" Posterity has no votes; yet caring for the environment is often a matter of changing the habits of today's voters for the benefit of future generations. Heating our homes would cost far more if we used only wind power and solar energy, in order to avoid putting into the atmosphere the carbon dioxide that may well cause global warming. Why should politicians ask us to bear such costs? After all, alarming though the speed of global warming may be in terms of the history of evolution, by the time today's politicians retire, its results will still be barely noticeable.

Even within a country, environmental issues may raise awkward   5 questions of justice and rights which only government can protect. For it is only government that can decide how much society should value the environment, and how that value should be inserted into economic transactions. The market, that mechanism that so marvelously directs human activity to supply human needs, often has no way of putting a proper price on environmental resources. "Free as the air" is all very well, but it means that factories pay nothing to belch smoke from their stacks. It is easy to put a price on a tree as timber. But that price will

[1]Nicholas Ridley, "Policies against Pollution" (London: Centre for Policy Studies, 1989), p. 9.

take no account of its value as a mechanism for preventing soil erosion, or as a home for rare birds or insects, or as a store of carbon dioxide that might otherwise add to the greenhouse gases in the atmosphere.

To talk of trees in the language of economics seems odd to many environmentalists. The very idea that values can be attached to natural beauty is an affront to those who think that it is beyond price. Yet to think of the environment in economic terms is a useful way of understanding environmental problems. In particular, it is a helpful approach for politicians and managers who are familiar with using economic concepts to analyze policy decisions. Some environmentalists have grasped this, and realize that governments and companies may become more concerned with environmental issues if they see them as benefiting their economic interest.

Because the market does not set prices on environmental resources, the economy is skewed in favor of those things that can be developed and marketed and against those that cannot. A developer who wants to put up a factory in a beauty spot can easily calculate the gain in terms of jobs and production. Those who want to protect the beauty spot have no such numbers. The undeveloped spot has no "output" to set against the products of the factory. It is never easy to argue that the gain to those generations who can enjoy its views will be greater, over the years, than the hard cash that the developer thinks can be earned.

Why are environmental goods so often unpriced or underpriced? Sometimes the reason is cultural: in Muslim countries, many of which are dangerously short of water, people have strong religious objections to paying for a gift from God. More often, the reason is that the resource is owned by everybody and therefore by nobody. People take less care of what is theirs than of what is owned collectively; and the ozone layer, the oceans, and the atmosphere are all common property.

This point was made by Joan Robinson, a distinguished British economist, in a famous question: "Why," she asked, "is there litter in the public park, but no litter in my backyard?"[2] In primitive societies, people frequently have long-established customs for ensuring that common property is managed to the maximum benefit of all. Herdsmen accept limits on the number of cattle they can graze on a common field. Yet such traditions are vulnerable. An individual herdsman can always do better by grazing more cattle on the land. Once the common restraint goes, all will be tempted to overgraze until the common field is bare and all are worse off than before. This dilemma was described as "The Tragedy of the Commons" in a famous article by Garret Hardin.[3] In fact, property owned in common is more likely to escape

---

[2]Quoted in John Kay and Aubrey Silberston, "Green Economics," *National Institute Economic Review* (February 1991), p. 50.
[3]Garret Hardin, "The Tragedy of the Commons," *Science,* vol. 162 (1968), pp. 1243–48.

tragedy than property that is accessible to all. That is the position of most environmental resources.

No one owns the sea or the sky; therefore no one charges those who overfish the sea or fill the air with ozone smog. Nobody owns quietness; therefore nobody can set a price on nasty noises. Where no one owns an environmental resource, the market will not give its usual warning signals as that resource is used up. In the early 1970s, some environmentalists fretted terribly about the imminent exhaustion of oil, iron, and copper, which, they rightly pointed out, were nonrenewable. Once all the oil was burned, that was that. They reckoned without the oil-exporting countries, which behaved like any cartel with limited supplies of a product in great demand and jacked up the price. Result: much investment went into energy conservation and into searching for oil in places like the North Sea and Alaska where it would not previously have been profitable.

We will never pump the last barrel of oil. We may well, however, kill the last elephant, for as that mammal becomes more scarce, so the rewards for catching it increase. In fact the true limits to growth are not the earth's stocks of natural resources such as coal, oil, and iron, which are bought and sold at prices that will rise to reflect their increasing scarcity. The limits are the capacity of the environment to deal with waste in all its forms and with the "critical" resources—such as the ozone layer, the carbon cycle, and the Amazon forest—that play no direct part in world commerce but that serve the most basic economic function of all, which is to enable human beings to survive. It is these two kinds of resources, long treated as free goods, that have been most dangerously overexploited.

Making Markets Work

Because the forces of unfettered markets can destroy the environment, environmental lobbyists have wanted to replace markets with government. If private enterprise chops down forests, the argument runs, put the forests in the hands of the state. This extreme faith in the benign green role of the state has faded, thanks in part to growing realization of the scope of environmental catastrophe in the state-run lands of Eastern Europe. Many examples show that bad government policies may make even more of a mess of the environment than the unfettered market.

A better starting point is to look for ways to improve markets. Clear rights of ownership for natural resources may sometimes improve the way they are managed. If ownership of environmental assets is clearly established, then polluters and the polluted will be able to bargain over a reasonable price for allowing pollution to take place. Sometimes such solutions work. If people have fishing rights in a river that they can rent out to others, they will have a strong interest in seeing that their bit of the river is not overfished. They will also be able to bargain with other owners to prevent the whole river from being over-exploited. But often—think of the ozone layer—it is simply not possible to use private enterprise in this way. Establishing ownership is too difficult; the number of polluters and of those affected by pollution is too great for bargaining to be practical.

Another way to improve the working of the market is to make sure consumers and producers pay the true costs of the environmental damage they cause. Markets work best when prices reflect as accurately as possible the costs of production. So the price of a gallon of gas ought to reflect the damage caused by exhaust gases, while the cost of running a bath should incorporate the environmental harm caused by water extraction and sewage disposal. The main ways in which economists urge politicians to pass such information into pricing is through taxation.

But making polluters pay is easier advocated than done. Once a politician pauses and wonders, "Right: but how much?" another set of problems appears. It is impossible to estimate exactly the price that a green government should exact from polluters. If the developer who wanted to build a factory in a beauty spot had wanted, instead, to build it where a housing estate now stands, the price of the site would have reflected the price at which houses are bought and sold. There is a housing market, but there is no beauty market. So if government is to make sure that the beauty spot is properly valued, it has to put a price on loveliness. Economists have thought up ways to do this, such as asking people what they would be willing to pay to keep the spot undeveloped. But none has the real-world quality of the price of a house. Besides, faced with a powerful developer, only a very rash politician would become involved in a fight over the social value of undeveloped land.

Simply because environmental costs are so hard to estimate is no argument for abandoning the effort, for two reasons. First, setting a rough value may be a better basis for policy than none at all. Only by groping for values for environmental resources can governments think sensibly about costs and benefits. Scientists who are alarmed by the prospect of global warming tend to argue that carbon emissions must be halted at any price. Wise governments will first ask what the costs of global warming are likely to be, and then will want an estimate of the costs of slowing the buildup of greenhouse gases. Both figures will be wobbly and widely disputed. But without some grasp of costs and benefits, governments are likely to do either too much or—worse—too little.

Most governments, far from making polluters carry the costs of environmental damage, do precisely the opposite. So a second reason for trying to put values on environmental goods is to discourage such perversity. Many governments subsidize polluting activities. In particular, many third world countries hold down electricity prices. That drives up demand. Generating electricity to supply this demand produces more gases, sulphur dioxide and carbon dioxide, both harmful in different ways. It may mean building more dams for hydropower. It may encourage a country to develop polluting industries.

Such folly is not confined to the poor world. Most rich countries subsidize agriculture. That encourages monoculture—usually more polluting than mixed cropping—and increases the demand for fertilizer and pesticides. America subsidizes the logging of its ancient forests. Britain subsidizes company cars. Germany subsidizes coal mining. Each country has its green madness, often as economically perverse as it is environmentally damaging. Such perversities survive because powerful lobbies back them. Governments, in democracies at least, can rarely do more than their electors want. If this generation of electors is not prepared to foot the bill for that "full repairing lease," governments will find it hard to make them.

To rely exclusively on the force of the market, however ingeniously harnessed, to clean the environment is as naive as relying solely on government intervention. For one thing, markets need information. If polluters are to pay, governments will need to measure pollution. Government will need to punish polluters who cheat. Monitoring, measurement, and enforcement are all jobs that cannot be done voluntarily. They require a legal framework and the sanction of the state.

Governments may sometimes need to make the market work better 20 in other, more subtle ways. If a market does not exist in the first place, giving it green signals will be pointless. The countries of Eastern Europe had elaborate systems of fines and charges to discourage pollution; but, as the fines were rarely collected and the charges were carried by monopolies, pollution simply continued unabated. It is important to worry about creating a market in the first place—getting, say, someone in the Soviet Union to worry about leaks of natural gas or someone in America to care about water lost from pipes—before building elaborate schemes to ensure that polluters carry the full costs of environmental damage.

This is important because a characteristic of many of the activities that most affect the environment—energy supply, the provision of water, transport—is that they are highly regulated by the state. Power lines, sewage works, roads, and airports are frequently monopolies or near-monopolies. It may therefore be difficult to rely on pricing alone, or on market forces harnessed in other ways, to influence the supply of and demand for these services. Raising the price of electricity may encourage consumers to turn off their lights, or it may simply leave them with less cash to spend on other things. Only gradually will it encourage them to buy more efficient central heating or to install double glazing. It may be faster and less painful—and politically easier—if governments also boost conservation in more direct ways. . . .

Many people hope that economic growth can be made environmentally benign. It never truly can. Most economic activity involves using up energy and raw materials; this, in turn, creates waste that the planet has to absorb. Green growth is therefore a chimera. But green*er* growth is possible. The history of technology has been about squeezing more output from the same volume of raw materials. Governments can dramatically reduce the environmental harm done by growth if they create incentives for companies to use raw materials more frugally. That means harnessing the inventive energy of industry.

If effective environmental policies are to be combined with vigorous economic growth, policies must be designed with an eye to their cost-effectiveness. As people grow richer, and want higher environmental standards, the cost of attaining them will rise. Compliance with federal environmental laws and regulations in the United States already costs over $100 billion a year.[4] Almost two-thirds of that bill falls on private business. That has made politicians pause, when lobbied by environmentalists, and wonder who will pick up the tab. At the same time, it is increasingly clear in the richest countries that well-run companies are now reaching a stage where becoming cleaner will cost much more. The first steps in pollution control are inevitably the cheapest. The best companies have already taken most of these. Subsequent measures will cost more with each succeeding step. Diminishing returns will set in.

Plenty remains to be done, of course, to bring the worst companies up to the standards of the best. But further advances in pollution control may involve changing not what companies do, but how individuals behave. To take just one example, for the same number of dollars far more could be achieved to remove nitrous oxides from California's air by changing the cars individuals drive and the ways they drive them than by fitting more exotic bits of machinery to the smokestacks of the state's electricity utilities. . . .

. . . Sound economics and sound environmental policies go hand in hand. Inflation, subsidies, and a failure to charge people the true costs

[4]Project 88—Round II, A Public Policy Study sponsored by Sen. Timothy Wirth and Sen. John Heinz (Washington, D.C., May 1991), p. 1.

of their activities all breed weak economies; they also breed environmental damage. Similarly, sound economics dictates that policies should put as little burden as possible on society to achieve their goal. Environmental policies that harness market forces meet that test. . . .

. . . Beyond the requirements of policy [are] the implications for companies. . . . Only by enlisting the help of companies . . . can governments hope to combine economic growth with good environmental stewardship. Electors will not welcome greener policies if those deliver what they perceive to be a lower standard of living. Government will be able to pursue better environmental policies only if companies find ways to give people the level of comfort to which they have become accustomed, in less environmentally damaging ways. Companies are more likely to help politicians if politicians take their proper responsibilities seriously.

Government must establish environmental priorities and determine what information (as a minimum) needs to be put before the public. It needs to set clear rules and work out how true environmental costs are to be reflected in costs of production. These are not responsibilities for companies. Their role is to respond, energetically and inventively, to the framework that government sets out. The better that framework is designed, and the more imaginatively companies use it, the more electors will support environmental policies.

There is an important lesson here for environmental lobbyists. Many of them feel uncomfortable when companies approach them, as now sometimes happens, asking them to put down their placards, abandon their boycotts, and come into the boardroom with constructive advice. If environmentalists are to campaign effectively for a cleaner world, they need to understand how companies can help. If they talk the language of wealth creation, of incentives, of efficiency, of market opportunities, they are more likely to be listened to by politicians and by managers. To say "We want a green world and to hell with who pays for it" may be good television, but it is ultimately bad politics. By harnessing technology through the deft application of market forces, companies, governments, and environmentalists stand the best chance of jointly building a cleaner environment.

Analyzing Issues and Arguments

1. What changes in belief or behavior does Frances Cairncross advocate? Whom does she evidently hope her argument will convince? Whom does she need to convince in order for her ideas to be put into practice?

2. Think about the actions Cairncross recommends to make markets work (paras. 12ff). In what way(s) are the buyers of rainforest products described in Diane Jukofsky's "Can Marketing Save the Rainforest?" (p. 274) applying Cairncross's ideas?

3. In what respects does Cairncross agree with Julian L. Simon (p. 302) on the issue of assigning economic value to natural resources and environmental damage? In what respects do these two writers disagree? Whose position do you find more persuasive, and why?

Writing about Issues and Arguments

"If environmentalists . . . talk the language of wealth creation, of incentives, of efficiency, of market opportunities, they are more likely to be listened to by politicians and by managers" (para. 28). What position does Dave Foreman (p. 234) take on this idea? Write an essay on effective tactics for environmentalists, using the selections by Cairncross, Foreman, and others in this book as sources.

MAKING CRITICAL CONNECTIONS

1. What common beliefs and goals are shared by Earth First! as Dave Foreman describes it (p. 234), the social ecology movement as Murray Bookchin describes it (p. 244), and the environmental justice movement as Regina Austin and Michael Schill describe it (p. 248; see particularly paras. 15ff)? What criticisms (if any) do these authors offer of each others' environmental movements?

2. "Is there need for ethical judgments to supersede market decisions when rich countries buy raw materials from poor countries?" asks Julian L. Simon in "Should We Conserve?" (p. 302, para. 37). What is his answer? What answers are given elsewhere in this chapter? What is your answer, and why?

3. Compare Frances Cairncross's statements on "green growth" in "Government and the Economics of the Environment" (p. 317) with William K. Reilly's views in "The Green Thumb of Capitalism" (p. 260). On the basis of these two selections and others you have read (for instance, Diane Jukofsky's "Can Marketing Save the Rainforest?" [p. 274] and Sandra Postel's "Carrying Capacity: Earth's Bottom Line" [p. 286]), what position do you think corporations and government should take toward "green growth"? Write an essay explaining and supporting your answer.

4. In "Government and the Economics of the Environment" (p. 317), Cairncross writes: "Scientists who are alarmed by the prospect of global warming tend to argue that carbon emissions must be halted at any price. Wise governments will first ask what the costs of global warming are likely to be, and then will want an estimate of the costs of slowing the buildup of greenhouse gases" (para. 16). Which authors represented in Chapter 3 favor the first of these positions? The second? Which position do you favor, and why? Using Cairncross's essay and those in Chapter 3 as sources, write an essay stating what the U.S. government should do about global warming and explaining why.

5. Reread the questions Murray Bookchin asks about nature in paragraph 5 of "The Problem with Earth First!" (p. 244). What answers to these questions does Bookchin offer? What answers are offered by Dave Foreman in "Earth First!" (p. 234)? By Regina Austin and Michael Schill in "Activists of Color" (p. 248)? By Aldo Leopold in "Toward a Land Ethic" (p. 4)? By Bill McKibben in "The End of Nature" (p. 223)? On the basis of these and other selections you have read in this book, write an essay defining *nature* and explaining why and how it should be protected.

Glossary of Environmental Terms

acid rain: a formation that occurs when sulfur- and nitrogen-based emissions from the burning of **fossil fuels** react with air and water in the atmosphere to form acidic compounds, which drop back to earth as rain or particles. There is some disagreement about the environmental impact of acid rain, but it is generally believed to kill fish in lakes and streams and has been linked to the decline of trees at higher altitudes.

aerosol: (1) a suspension of liquid or solid particles in air or gas; (2) a substance dispensed as an aerosol from a pressurized container.

anthropocentric: possessing the belief that human beings are the central, most important element on earth.

biodegradable: capable of being naturally broken down into simpler elements, typically by microbes and bacteria.

biodiversity: short for *biological diversity;* the variety of different species in a particular area.

biosphere: the entire **ecosystem** of the earth, including all its living things and all the places where they live.

biota: an area's plant and animal life.

biotechnology: technology that makes use of or alters biology, such as the genetic engineering of crops and the use of bacteria to clean up **toxic-waste** sites.

biotic: relating to life.

carbon dioxide (CO_2): a gas produced when **fossil fuels** (coal, oil, and natural gas) and trees burn and when organic matter decays.

carrying capacity: the largest number of any given species that a **habitat** can support indefinitely.

chlorofluorocarbons (CFCs): a class of **hydrocarbon** derivatives; **greenhouse gases** released from air conditioners, refrigerators, and **aerosol** cans; they are thought to contribute to the depletion of the **ozone layer.**

Clean Air Act: federal act, first passed in 1963, that is the major piece of legislation dealing with air pollution; the 1990 amendment addresses **acid rain** controls, more stringent controls on auto emissions, a reduction of the chemicals that contribute to the erosion of the **ozone layer,** and air toxics controls.

clear-cutting: the removal of every tree in a specific area.

climatic noise: several tenths of a degree Celsius warmings and coolings of the earth's temperature over decades; considered normal climate variation.

cogeneration: the process of using steam or heat to generate electricity.

combustible: able to be burned under normal circumstances.

community: the population of living things in a particular **ecoystem.**

conservation: the careful utilization and management of natural resources.

conservationists: individuals dedicated to the careful utilization and management of natural resources.

DDT (dichlorodiphenyltrichloroethane): a chlorinated hydrocarbon type of insecticide, originally thought to pose little risk to humans or any organism not specifically targeted by it. However, it was later learned that DDT stays in an **ecosystem** for a long period of time, which means that it accumulates within the bodies of organisms, threatening the food chain. DDT was banned in the United States in 1972 but is still used in many other countries.

deep ecology: a radical environmental philosophy that believes that nonhuman life has intrinsic value independent of its usefulness to humans, that a substantial decrease in human population is necessary for the well-being of earth, and that the preservation of wilderness is more important than human needs. The term was coined in the early 1970s by the Norwegian philosopher Arne Naess, and it has become the broad philosophical principle underlying the **Earth First!** movement.

degradation: (1) the biological, chemical, or physical breakdown of complex materials into simpler elements; (2) a decline in environmental quality.

desertification: a process by which land that is covered with vegetation is converted to desert; it can be produced by overgrazing, overfarming, deforestation, or prolonged irrigation.

dioxin: a family of 210 chlorine-based compounds that are by-products of incineration and some manufacturing processes; dioxin has been linked to cancer as well as reproductive and developmental disruption.

Earth Day: held on April 22, this annual celebration seeks to promote environmental awareness; first observed in 1970.

Earth First!: a radical environmental organization, cofounded in 1980 by Dave Foreman (p. 234), whose basic principle is that the health of the earth and the preservation of wilderness should take precedence over human welfare. Many Earth First! members advocate acts of sabotage, called "monkeywrenching," in defense of the earth. The organization disbanded in 1990, but several splinter groups remain. (See **deep ecology.**)

ecology: the study of the interactions among organisms and between organisms and their physical environment.

ecosystem: a community of plants and animals living and interacting in a particular physical environment, as well as the chemical and physical factors that influence them (such as rainfall, temperature, sunlight, and nutrients). An ecosystem can be as small as a tidal pool or as large as an ocean.

El Niño: the warming of the eastern tropical Pacific Ocean. (See **La Niña.**)

endangered species: any species of animal or plant that exists in such limited numbers as to be in danger of **extinction.** The U.S. Fish and Wildlife Service and the National Marine Fisheries Service are authorized by the **Endangered Species Act** to list species whose survival is endangered or threatened.

Endangered Species Act (ESA): 1973 federal law establishing guidelines for identifying animal and plant species that are endangered or threatened with **extinction.** Once a species has been listed, it becomes illegal to kill or harm its members, and federal agencies are prohibited from funding or participating in any project that might contribute to its extinction. However, in 1978 Congress formed a panel called the Endangered Species Committee, which is authorized to rule on whether a project's economic benefits outweigh the need to protect a species. The ESA was reauthorized in 1992 and is up for reauthorization again in 1995.

environment: all the physical, chemical, and biological factors that make up the surroundings of an individual or ecological community and influence its form and survival.

environmentalism: (1) a movement to protect the earth and its life forms from harm caused by human activity; (2) as defined by Edward O. Wilson (p. 1), the belief that humans are dependent on the natural world and the other species existing in it and that to survive, humans must sustain the planet in a relatively unaltered state. Wilson contrasts the term with **exemptionalism.**

environmentalist: an advocate of environmentalism.

Environmental Protection Agency (EPA): federal agency established in 1970 to coordinate the various federal activities addressing environmental problems; responsible for developing and enforcing environmental regulations.

erosion: the wearing away of the earth's surface, mainly by water, ice, wind, and gravity.

evolution: the concept that more complex species descended from simpler forms of life, developing gradually over generations as genetic variations were passed down as the result of natural selection processes.

exemptionalism: as defined by Edward O. Wilson (p. 1), the belief that because human beings are superior to other species in intelligence and spirit, they are not bound by the laws of **ecology** that bind other species to the natural world. Wilson contrasts the term with **environmentalism.**

extinction: the disappearance of an entire species because no individual members are alive to reproduce.

fauna: animal life in an area.

flora: plant life in an area.

flow-control laws: laws that require all local garbage to be processed at designated local facilities. In May 1994 the U.S. Supreme Court declared these laws unconstitutional.

fly ash: air emissions resulting from the burning of fuels and incineration.

food chain: the hierarchical feeding sequence of organisms.

fossil fuels: fuels such as coal, oil, and natural gas that are derived from the fossilized remains of plants or animals.

Gaia hypothesis: theory that all life on earth interacts in such a way as to guarantee the earth's self-regulation and continued existence; the hypothesis was developed by British scientist James Lovelock (p. 158) and American biologist Lynn Margulis in the early 1970s. (Gaia was the ancient Greek goddess of the earth.)

geoengineering: the deliberate modification of the environment through technology.

geothermal power: electricity generated from heat and lava below the earth's surface.

global circulation models (GCMs): sophisticated computer models used to predict climatic change.

global warming: a predicted rise in the earth's temperature caused by increased **greenhouse gases** in the atmosphere. (See **greenhouse effect.**)

green: a term loosely used to describe anything or anyone concerned about protecting the environment.

greenhouse gases: gases such as **carbon dioxide, chlorofluorocarbons, methane,** nitrous oxide, **ozone,** and water vapor that contribute to the **greenhouse effect** by trapping heat from the earth.

greenhouse effect: a natural mechanism whereby the earth's atmosphere acts like a greenhouse by letting in heat from the sun and then trapping about 90 percent of it near the planet's surface. Without the greenhouse effect, this heat would dissipate into space, leaving the earth unihabitably cold. (See **global warming.**)

greens: individuals or groups for whom the environment is a major concern. (When capitalized, the term usually refers to a political party that advocates radical environmental reforms.)

green taxes: fines levied against environmentally undesirable behaviors.

habitat: the specific area in which an organism or community of organisms live.

hazardous waste: any waste product that explodes, ignites, reacts strongly with water, is unstable in the presence of heat or shock, corrodes other materials, or is poisonous. (Poisonous waste is also commonly referred to as **toxic waste.**)

heavy metals: metals with a relatively high molecular weight, such as lead, mercury, cadmium, chromium, and zinc; repeated exposure to these metals is associated with a variety of health problems.

humic acid: an acid produced when organic matter **biodegrades.**

herbivores: animals that eat only plants.

hydrocarbons: a class of chemical compounds containing hydrogen and carbon; released during the combustion of fuels, they are a main contributor to air pollution.

hydropower: the use of falling water to generate electricity.

incineration: the process of burning garbage to reduce its volume; most modern incinerators also generate electricity.

La Niña: the sudden, unexplained, and rare cooling of the eastern tropical Pacific Ocean. (See **El Niño.**)

landfill: area where solid waste is buried between layers of earth.

leachate: water that travels through and then escapes from a waste disposal site; contains dissolved and suspended material extracted from the waste and soil.

mass burners: incinerators that burn unseparated waste.

Materials Recovery Facility (MRF): a factory where recyclable materials are sorted.

methane: a **hydrocarbon** gas that results from the decomposition of organic matter; a **greenhouse gas.**

Monitored Retrievable Storage (MRS) facility: place where waste is housed temporarily until a permanent repository is available.

municipal solid waste (MSW): solid waste from households, businesses, and construction sites.

National Environmental Policy Act: 1969 law mandating that federal agencies consider environmental consequences when making policies.

NIMBY: acronym for *not in my backyard;* a derogatory term often used to describe the supposed attitude of individuals and groups who oppose the siting of undesirable facilities (such as incinerators, landfills, prisons, or mental hospitals) in their neighborhoods.

Noah Principle: a theory developed by biologist David Ehrenfeld stating that all species have an equal right to exist and that consequently humans should protect all species.

NPP (Net Primary Productivity): the total amount of the earth's solar energy converted into biochemical energy through plant **photosynthesis,** minus the energy those plants use for their own life processes.

nuclear waste: any solid or liquid waste material containing radioactivity; produced by nuclear power plants, hospitals, research labs, and nuclear weapons plants.

ozone: triatomic oxygen (O_3), a gas in the **stratosphere** that screens out most dangerous ultraviolet radiation; ozone is also found in the atmosphere, where it is a pollutant that irritates the eyes and respiratory tract.

ozone layer: a thin, protective layer of ozone molecules in the **stratosphere** that screens out most dangerous ultraviolet radiation. Many atmospheric scientists believe that the earth's protective ozone layer is being depleted primarily as a result of **chloro-fluorocarbon** (CFC) emissions.

photodegradable: capable of being naturally broken down into smaller elements through exposure to the sun's ultraviolet radiation.

photosynthesis: the process by which green plants and some bacteria use energy from sunlight to manufacture carbohydrates from atmospheric **carbon dioxide** and water and then return oxygen into the atmosphere.

polyvinyl chloride (PVC): a strong plastic that releases hydrochloric acid when it burns.

rainforests: tropical forests covering approximately 7 percent of the earth's surface, in the areas of South and Central America, Southeast Asia, and Central Africa; home to over half of the planet's life forms.

resource recovery plant: See **waste-to-energy power plants.**

scrubber: a pollution-control device that removes harmful particles or gases from emissions generated by combustion; used in incinerators and power plants.

social ecology: a radical environmental movement that argues that environmental problems are the result of humanity's attempt to dominate nature; founded by Murray Bookchin (p. 244).

source reduction: a reduction in the amount of waste that is generated and, consequently, in the amount of waste that must be disposed of or recycled.

species: a group of similar organisms that are capable of successfully interbreeding under natural conditions.

speciesism: the belief that human beings are superior to other species.

strata: layers in the earth's soil.

stratosphere: the second layer of atmosphere above the earth, extending from about 7 to 30 miles above the earth's surface; the **ozone layer** is located in the stratosphere.

Superfund program (Hazardous Substances Superfund): a federal trust fund established by Congress in 1980 and reauthorized in 1986 to clean up the nation's most contaminated hazardous-waste sites.

toxic waste: any waste product that contains chemicals that can cause adverse health effects when they enter or contact the body. In contrast, a hazardous waste is a substance that is dangerous because of its physical properties — it can explode, burn, or react easily with other chemicals. Some substances, like gasoline, can be both toxic and hazardous (toxic to drink but hazardous because it can burn or explode).

troposphere: the layer of the atmosphere closest to the earth.

waste-to-energy power plants (WTEs): incinerators that generate electricity by burning garbage.

wetlands: land areas such as bogs, swamps, and marshes that border freshwater or saltwater and are usually covered or saturated with water.

Suggestions for Further Reading

The sources listed here do not include any of the books or articles from which the main selections, "In the News" pieces, or "Points of View" epigraphs have been excerpted, with the exception of anthologies from which individual essays have been drawn. Many of the general books about environmental issues listed under Chapter 4 may also contain material on topics discussed in the other three chapters. (Cross-references are to page numbers in *The Environmental Predicament* unless otherwise noted.)

Chapter 1

Adler, Jerry, and Mary Hager. "How Much Is a Species Worth?" *National Wildlife* Apr.–May 1992: 4–14. Argues in favor of reauthorizing the Endangered Species Act in its present form and not modifying it to protect ecosystems instead of individual species.

Anderson, H. Michael. "Reforming National-Forest Policy." *Issues in Science and Technology* Winter 1993–94: 40–47. Argues that biological diversity, not timber production, should be the guiding principle when managing U.S. forests.

Baird, Robert M., and Stuart E. Rosenbaum. *Animal Experimentation: The Moral Issues.* Buffalo: Prometheus, 1991. Provides a good overview of opposing viewpoints regarding animal experimentation.

Balkwill, John. "The Owls vs. Loggers Diversion." *Z Magazine* Feb. 1993: 7–9. Argues that the real conflict is between greed and old-growth forests, not between loggers and owls.

Baskin, Yvonne. "There's a New Wildlife Policy in Kenya: Use It or Lose It." *Science* 265 (1994): 733–34. Describes efforts in Kenya to protect wildlife by establishing wildlife businesses, giving rural communities and landowners a direct, financial stake in protecting the animals in a region.

Beans, Bruce E. "The DDT of the 1990s." *New York Times* 22 Sept. 1994: A27. Despite the fact that bald eagles are about to be removed from the endangered species list, the author of this op-ed piece argues that the species is threatened more than ever by development.

Bonner, Raymond. "Crying Wolf over Elephants." *New York Times Magazine* 7 Feb. 1993: 17+. Argues that the threat of killing African elephants to the point of extinction is a scam, used by environmental groups to elicit both sympathy and money for their various causes. (Excerpted and adapted from Bonner's *At the Hand of Man: Peril and Hope for Africa's Wildlife* [New York: Knopf, 1993].)

Breen, Bill. "Why We Need Animal Testing." *Garbage* Apr.–May 1993: 38–45. Argues that the use of animals in medical research is an absolute necessity.

Cohen, Andrew Neal. "Weeding the Garden." *Atlantic* Nov. 1992: 76–86. Discusses the complexity of natural management in a world that continually degrades ecosystems; focuses on the dilemma of whether one species should be exterminated to save another.

Conniff, Richard. "Fuzzy-Wuzzy Thinking about Animal Rights." *Audubon* Nov. 1990: 120–33. Argues that the animal rights movement has elevated ignorance about the natural world almost to the level of a philosophical principle.

Couturier, Lisa. "Going, Going, Gone?" *E Magazine* Mar.–Apr. 1992: 32–37. Argues for the need to keep the Endangered Species Act in place as a means of preserving life's many species.

DiSilvestro, Roger L. *Reclaiming the Last Wild Places: A New Agenda for Biodiversity.* New York: Wiley, 1993. Argues for the importance of biodiversity in terms of overall ecological health and suggests ways to ensure rich biodiversity.

Douglas-Hamilton, Iain, and Oria Douglas-Hamilton. *Battle for the Elephants.* Bergenfield, NJ: Viking, 1992. Describes the successful efforts of Iain Douglas-Hamilton, a British animal scientist, to save the African elephant.

Durbin, Kathie. "From Owls to Eternity." *E Magazine* Mar.–Apr. 1992: 30+. Describes the efforts of a group of scientists to save both the spotted owl and some of the logging economy in the Pacific Northwest.

Easterbrook, Gregg. "The Birds." *New Republic* 26 Mar. 1994: 22–29. Takes issue with the claim that the spotted owl faces extinction. Suggests that this illusion is maintained as a means of protecting forests. (Based on material from Easterbrook's *A Moment on the Earth,* listed in "Suggestions for Further Reading," Chapter 4.)

Elshtain, Jean Bethke. "Why Worry about the Animals?" *Progressive* Mar, 1990: 17–23. Provides a broad, historical overview of the animal rights movement and then wrestles with the dilemma of whether animal research should be allowed, finally deciding that the answer should be no.

Graham, Frank Jr. "Winged Victory." *Audubon* July–Aug. 1994: 36–40. Describes a "success story" for the Endangered Species Act — the "comeback" of the bald eagle and its redesignation as threatened, rather than endangered.

Hauerwas, Stanley, and John Berkman. "The Chief End of All Flesh." *Theology Today* 49 (1992): 196–208. Discusses animal rights from a theological perspective.

Hearne, Vicki. "What's Wrong with Animal Rights: Of Hounds, Horses, and Jeffersonian Happiness." *Harper's* Sept. 1991: 59–65. An animal trainer offers objections to criticisms raised by the animal rights movement.

Keller, Bill. "Even Shorn of Horns, Rhinos of Zimbabwe Face Poacher Calamity." *New York Times* 11 Oct. 1994: C4. Discusses the dramatic failure of Zimbabwe's tactic of dehorning rhinos as a deterrent to poachers.

King, Roger J. H. "Environmental Ethics and the Case for Hunting." *Environmental Ethics* 13.1 (1991): 59–85. Studies hunting from the perspectives of primitivism, feminism, animal liberation, and the land ethic. Finds no justification for hunting within any of these frameworks.

Loos, Ryland. "Friends of the Hunted." *Conservationist* 48.2 (1993): 10–15. Defends hunting, tracing great hunters in history and describing ecological benefits of hunting.

Maxwell, Jessica. "How to Save a Salmon." *Audubon* July–Aug. 1994: 114+. Describes one man's efforts to save the great salmon runs in the Northwest. Specifically addresses the dangers posed by hydroelectric dams.

Meyer, Stephen M. "The Final Act." *New Republic* 15 Aug. 1994: 24–26. Argues that criticisms of the Endangered Species Act are wrongheaded and that the act is our best hope of preserving our national biological heritage.

Middleton, Susan, et al. *Witness: Endangered Species of North America.* San Francisco: Chronicle, 1994. Provides a good overview of the top one hundred species in North America that are currently facing extinction.

Morrison, Adrian R. "What's Wrong with 'Animal Rights.'" *Education Digest* 57.9 (1992): 57–61. Criticizes animal rights advocates who endanger human health by preventing needed medical research.

Phillips, Kathryn. *Tracking the Vanishing Frogs: An Ecological Mystery.* New York: St. Martin's, 1994. Discusses the troubling disappearance of several species of frogs — indicator species whose decline calls into question the overall health of their native ecosystems.

Pothier, Richard. "Animal Tests Saved My Life." *Newsweek* 1 Feb. 1993: 18. An animal rights supporter who received a transplanted heart argues that some animal experimentation is necessary because it saves human lives.

Regan, Tom, and Peter Singer, eds. *Animal Rights and Human Obligations.* 2nd ed. Englewood Cliffs: Prentice, 1989. A volume of essays presenting opposing viewpoints on animal rights; one of the basic texts in this area.

Russow, Lily-Marlene. "Why Do Species Matter?" *Environmental Ethics* 3 (1981): 106–12. After rejecting the three most common arguments in favor of preserving species, a philosopher concludes that we should protect species because individual members of species have value. (Reprinted in Regan and Singer, *Animal Rights,* 266–72.)

Singer, Peter. *Animal Liberation.* 1975. New York: Avon, 1990. A canonical work in the discussion of animal rights.

———, ed. *In Defense of Animals.* New York: Harper, 1985. A collection of essays arguing in favor of animal rights from diverse perspectives. (Singer's preface is on p. 64.)

Speart, Jessica. "Rhino Chainsaw Massacre: Why the Wild Rhino Will Not Survive the Century." *Earth Journal* Jan.–Feb. 1994: 26+. Focuses on the plight of the rhino in Zimbabwe; the animal faces extinction because of the demand for its horns.

Williams, Joy. "The Killing Game." *Best American Essays 1991.* Ed. Joyce Carol Oates and Robert Atwan. Boston: Ticknor, 1991. 251–65. Argues that hunting is immoral and should therefore be made illegal; criticizes the arrogance of hunters.

Wilson, Edward O. *The Diversity of Life.* Cambridge: Belknap–Harvard UP, 1992. A seminal work that presents an eloquent plea for increased understanding of the importance and beauty of biodiversity.

Winkler, Suzanne. "Stopgap Measures." *Atlantic* Jan. 1992: 74–81. Argues against the Endangered Species Act on the grounds that if our goal is to preserve biodiversity, we should focus on protecting diverse ecosystems rather than spending limited funds on heroic measures to save species that are almost extinct. (Appeared in the same issue of the *Atlantic* as "The Butterfly Problem" p. 26, and "The Case for Human Beings," p. 42.)

See also **Joyce, Yoon** in "Suggestions for Further Reading," Chapter 4.

Chapter 2

Adler, Jerry. "It's Not Easy Being Green." *Newsweek* 28 Dec. 1992: 66. Presents pros and cons regarding the construction of an incinerator in East Liverpool, Ohio.

Barnett, Harold C. *Toxic Debts and the Superfund Dilemma*. Chapel Hill: U of North Carolina P, 1994. Examines the reasons behind the failure of Superfund to adequately address hazardous waste sites.

Beers, Allen R., and Thomas J. Getz. "Composting Biosolids Saves $3.2 Million in Landfill Costs." *BioCycle* 33.5 (1992): 42–44. Describes the process by which Anheuser-Busch brewery in New York used composting to save 73,900 cubic yards of landfill.

Bowermaster, Jon. "A Town Called Morrisonville." *Audubon* July–Aug. 1993: 42–51. Discusses Dow Chemical's "buyout" of a Louisiana town — the displacement of residents to avoid the potential dangers of the nearly 3.3 million pounds of toxins the company's plant releases each year into the local air, water, and ground.

Breen, Bill. "Is Recycling Succeeding?" *Garbage* June–July 1993: 36+. Describes the crisis facing recycling efforts, with collections up, markets down, and the public clamoring for more.

Cairncross, Francis. "All That Remains." *Economist* 29 May 1993. An entire issue devoted to the problem of waste disposal, covering such topics as recycling, landfills, and the economic considerations of disposal processes.

Coll, Steve. "Dumping on the Third World." *Washington Post National Weekly Edition* 18–24 Aug. 1994: 9–10. Argues that a restructured global economy has now made it profitable for Western nations to export their garbage and hazardous waste to Eastern European and third world countries.

Fairlie, Simon. "Long Distance, Short Life: Why Big Business Favors Recycling." *Ecologist* Nov.–Dec. 1992: 276–83. Argues that environmental groups that emphasize recycling over reuse, source reduction, and durability of products are playing into the hands of big business, which favors planned obsolescence and industrial expansion.

Garbarine, Rachelle. "Turning an Elizabeth Landfill into a Retail Center." *New York Times* 13 Feb. 1994: sec. 10:9. Discusses the challenges and opportunities that present themselves when land once used for a landfill is slated for another commercial purpose.

Gelbein, Abraham. "To Incinerate or Not to Incinerate?" *Chemtech* 23.7 (1993): 1. Argues for the safety and economic wisdom of incineration but acknowledges the public's mistrust and fear. Given this reality, concludes that the EPA guidelines and a temporary halt to new incinerators make sense.

Goldstein, Nan. "Cocomposting in Tennessee." *BioCycle* 34.11 (1993): 42–48. Describes the process by which a solid waste disposal company undertook composting to extend the life of a landfill in Gatlinburg, Tennessee.

Graham, John D., and March Sadowitz. "Superfund Reform: Reducing Risk through Community Choice." *Issues in Science and Technology* Summer 1994: 35–40. Argues that communities living near Superfund hazardous-waste sites should be allowed to use some cleanup money to address other environmental and public health problems.

Hernandez, Juan Avila. "What Price Nuclear? Waste Siting Controversy Brews on Mescalero Apache Reservation." *E Magazine* July–Aug. 1993: 15–19. Describes a struggle within the Mescalero tribe over a federal proposal to store spent nuclear reactor fuel rods on their reservation. (For other sources on environmental racism, see "Suggestions for Further Reading," Chapter 4.)

Holusha, John. "Recycled Material Is Finding a New and Lucrative Market." *New York Times* 8 Oct. 1994: 1+. Describes how the recent economic recovery has transformed recycling from a gesture to help the environment into a solid business.

Horwitz, Tony. "Inside a 'Dirty MuRF': The Offal Part of the Recycling Boom." *Wall Street Journal* 1 Dec. 1994, eastern ed.: A8. Describes what it's like to work in a materials recovery facility, or MuRF, where recyclables are sorted by a "fast-growing legion of laborers who do the dirty work of keeping America clean."

Kleiner, Art, and Janis Dutton. "Time to Dump Plastics Recycling?" *Garbage* Spring 1994: 44–51. Addresses the economic realities associated with plastics recycling and suggests that an overhaul is needed if such a plan is to become attractive to corporations.

Ladd, Anthony E., and Shirley Laska. "Opposition to Solid Waste Incineration: Pre-implementation Anxieties Surrounding a New Environmental Controversy." *Sociological Inquiry* 61.3 (1991): 229–313. Approaches incineration from a sociological viewpoint, studying the anxieties exhibited in a Louisiana community facing construction of an incinerator.

Lecard, Marc. "Plastic Promises." *Sierra* July–Aug. 1994: 34–35. Points out that much of the plastic collected for recycling will never actually be recycled because the necessary technology is not available. Urges consumers to keep the pressure on the plastics industry to find ways to recycle all the different types of plastics — or else stop making it.

Martin, Justin. "IMBY, Please." *Fortune* 4 Oct. 1993: 13–14. Describes a community in Utah that was very positive about having an incinerator built in its "backyard."

Maxwell, Jessica. "Redressing Plastic Man." *Audubon* Nov.–Dec. 1992: 59–62. Claims it is ironic that so many environmentalists buy outerwear made from plastics and other petroleum-based synthetic fibers.

Misch, Ann. "Chemical Reaction." *World Watch* Mar.–Apr. 1993: 10–17. Presents evidence pointing to serious health problems other than cancer resulting from the chemicals we encounter daily. (Retitled "Better Living through Chemistry?" and excerpted in *Utne Reader* Nov.–Dec. 1993: 90–92.)

Montague, Peter. "Sign of the Times? The Truth about Toxics." *E Magazine* Jul.–Aug. 1993: 54–55. Criticizes the *New York Times* for downplaying the risks of dioxin and other toxic chemicals.

Nixon, Will. "Are We Burying Ourselves in Junk Mail?" *E Magazine* Nov.–Dec. 1993: 30–37. Because so many people shop at home, the direct mail business is booming, creating volumes of junk mail that until recently has not been recyclable.

Poore, Patricia. "Disposable Diapers Are OK." *Garbage* Oct.–Nov. 1992: 27–31. Argues that there is very little difference, environmentally speaking, between cotton and disposable diapers.

Postrel, Virginia I., and Lynn Scarlett. "Talking Trash." *Reason* Aug.–Sept. 1991: 22–31. Argues against mandatory recycling programs and laws requiring the use of recycled or reusable materials.

Quigley, James. "The Rush to Burn: Incinerator Controversies Heat Up." *E Magazine*

Mar.–Apr. 1992: 17–20. Describes how the incinerator industry has begun using expensive, high-profile media campaigns, including prime-time TV ads, to influence voters in communities where incinerator projects are being debated.

Rathje, William. "Rubbish!" *Atlantic* Dec. 1989: 99–109. Expanded into the book of the same name that Rathje coauthored with Cullen Murphy (see p. 93).

Royte, Elizabeth. "Other People's Garbage: The New Politics of Trash, A Case Study." *Harper's* June 1992: 54–60. Describes the community battle that ensued when a desperately poor West Virginia county tried to make a deal to host a gigantic, state-of-the-art landfill that would have purchased out-of-state waste.

Ruben, Barbar. "No Safe Haven: A Community Rallies to Fight a Proposed Rubble Fill and Environmental Discrimination." *Environmental Action Magazine* 25.3 (1993): 27–29. Describes efforts by residents in Havre de Grace, Maryland, to fight a proposed landfill in their area.

Ryan, Megan. "Los Angeles 21, New York 5 . . ." *World Watch* Mar.–Apr. 1993: 18–21. Analyzes why Los Angeles recycles 21 percent of its garbage while New York recycles only 5 percent, arguing that the comparison sheds light on how we need to start looking at garbage — as a resource rather than something to burn or bury.

Savage, George M., et al. "Landfill Mining: Past and Present." *BioCycle* 34.5 (1993): 58–61. Discusses landfill mining, a practice that has begun to gain attention because of declining landfill space in the United States. Landfill mining involves excavating a landfill, retrieving various resources, and selling them.

Schuyler, Nina. "L.A. Moms Fight Back." *Progressive* Aug. 1992: 13. Describes the protest of mothers in Los Angeles against the building of an incinerator next to a high school.

Seidman, Ethan, Bill Breen, and Paul Botts. "An Inside Look at Paper Recycling." *Garbage* Sept.–Oct. 1993: 30–37. Discusses the continued improvement in technology for paper recycling, driven by consumer demand.

Steverson, E. Malone. "Provoking a Firestorm: Waste Incineration." *Environmental Science and Technology* 25(1991): 1808–14. Describes the effects of incineration on the environment.

Steubner, Stephen. "Triumph, Idaho to EPA: Don't Tread on Me." *Garbage* Spring 1994: 13–16. Describes a town's efforts to convince the EPA that the community should not be designated a Superfund hazardous-waste site and that the EPA should change its risk assessment criteria.

Van Gelder, Lindsay. "Saving the Homeplace." *Audubon* Jan.–Feb. 1992: 62+. Describes two women's efforts to strengthen landfill and hazardous-waste legislation in Kentucky.

Van Voorst, Bruce. "Recycling: Stalled at Curbside." *Time* 18 Oct. 1993: 78–80. Describes the economic crisis facing the recycling industry because, while Americans want to recycle their garbage, there is not enough demand for recycled products.

Chapter 3

Baskin, Yvonne. "Forests in the Gas." *Discover* Oct. 1994: 117–21. Argues that the level of carbon dioxide in the atmosphere will double in the next sixty years and reports that efforts are being made to study the ways in which organisms within ecosystems will react.

Beckerman, Wilfred, and Jesse Malkin. "How Much Does Global Warming Matter?"

Public Interest Winter 1994: 3–16. Argues that media coverage has created global warming fears and that attention should be paid to more urgent environmental problems.

Charlson, Robert J., and Tom M. L. Wigley. *Scientific American* Feb. 1994: 48–55. Argues that aerosols must be taken into account when considering global warming levels.

"Cool Costing: Global Warming." *The Economist* 6 Mar. 1993: 84–87. Discusses the projected costs of addressing global warming in terms of the world's gross domestic product.

Denniston, Derek. "Icy Indicators of Global Warming." *World Watch* Jan.–Feb. 1993: 9–11. Discusses the ramifications of and uses for the excess water that will result as rising global temperatures lead to shrinking glaciers.

Global Warming Update: Recent Scientific Findings. Washington, DC: George C. Marshall Inst., 1992. Argues that there are no data to support the notion that humans have caused, or will cause, a dangerous rise in global temperatures.

Gordon, A. H. "Weekdays Warmer than Weekends?" *Nature* (1994): 325–26. Discusses why the global heat signal from human activity is stronger in the middle of the week than on the weekends.

Hamer, Mick. "City Planners against Global Warming." *New Scientist* 24 Jul. 1993: 12–13. Argues that American cities need to be more compact, like those in Europe, so as to reduce carbon dioxide emissions and control global warming.

"Heated Debate." *Dollars & Sense* July–Aug. 1993: 23. Discusses the economic cost of global warming and possible means of solving the problem.

Hecht, Jeff. "Clouds Hold Key to Global Warming Theory." *New Scientist* 22 Jan. (1994): 16. Explains that NASA researchers are considering the viability of using cloud patterns to predict global warming.

Idso, Sherwood. *Carbon Dioxide and Global Change: Earth in Transition.* Tempe: IBR, 1989. Argues that if global warming does occur, it will in fact be beneficial.

Jain, P. C. "Earth-Sun System Energetics and Global Warming." *Climatic Change* 24(1993): 271–72. Argues that increasing the distance between the earth and the sun could offset projected global warming and that the means of producing the energy to create a greater distance might be possible in the future.

Leggett, Jeremy, ed. *Global Warming: The Greenpeace Report.* Oxford: Oxford UP, 1990. A volume of essays that provides an especially good overview of public policy responses to the issue of global warming.

Leutwyler, Kristin. "No Global Warming? CO_2 Readings on Mauna Loa Show Declining Emissions." *Scientific American* Feb. 1994: 24. Readings at a climate observatory in Hawaii indicate a decrease in atmospheric carbon dioxide, but researchers doubt that long-term emissions have slowed.

Linden, Eugene. "Burned by Warming." *Time* 14 Mar. 1994: 79. Discusses the possibility that worsening storms caused by global warming could bankrupt the property and casualty insurance industry.

Lovelock, James. *Gaia: A New Look at Life on Earth.* 1979. Oxford: Oxford UP, 1987. The book in which famous British scientist Lovelock lays out his controversial Gaia hypothesis (see pp. 158, 160, and 207).

MacKenzie, Debora. "Did Northern Forests Stave Off Global Warming?" *New Scientist* 11 Sept. 1993: 6. Argues that the destruction of forests in Eurasia and North America will increase global warming.

McDonald, Kim A. "Scientific Debate Continues to Rage over Rising CO_2, Global Warming." *Chronicle of Higher Education* 39.47 (1993): 14. Argues that most scientists agree that global warming will occur; discrepancies arise as to how quickly temperatures will rise and by how much.

Monastersky, Richard. "Global Warming: Why Is the Planet Feverish?" *Science News*

145(1994): 134. Argues that global warming is due to human rather than natural influences.

———. "Plants and Soils May Worsen Global Warming." *Science News* 143(1993): 100–02. Presents two scientists' findings that suggest a worsening of global warming owing to a boost in levels of carbon dioxide produced by green plants.

Nordhaus, William D. "Expert Opinion on Climatic Change." *American Scientist* 82.1 (1994): 45–51. Addresses two different schools of thought regarding global warming and argues that both global warming and pollution can be successfully combated.

Platt, Anne E. "Local Responses to Global Warming." *World Watch* Mar.–Apr. 1994: 7. Describes measures to control global warming implemented by Portland, Oregon — the first U.S. city to do so.

Powell, Corey S. "Cold Confusion." *Scientific American* Mar. 1994: 22–25. Argues that, based on the study of carbon dioxide in prehistoric ice, there is reason to doubt the relationship between carbon dioxide and global warming.

Redfern, Martin. "Global Warming Cuts No Ice." *New Scientist* 25 Sept. 1993: 16. Argues that there is no real evidence to support the theory that the Antarctic ice sheet is melting in response to global warming.

Roodman, David Malin. "Pioneering Greenhouse Policy." *World Watch* July–Aug. 1993: 7–8. Discusses plans in Denmark and the Netherlands to control global warming.

Root-Bernstein, Robert. "Future Imperfect." *Discover* Nov. 1993: 42–45. Argues that predictions about natural occurrences such as climate changes are necessarily unreliable because of the inaccuracy of data extrapolation.

Ruben, Charles T., and Marc K. Landy. "Global Warming." *Garbage* Feb.–Mar. 1993: 24–29. Argues that public policy about global warming is being shaped by inadequate notions of scientific consensus, the misapplication of hypothetical scenarios, and a false analogy to buying insurance.

Scott, Geoff. "Global Warming: The Controversy Heats Up." *Current Health* 21 Dec. 1993: 6–11. Argues that scientists are arriving at more moderate predictions regarding the effects of global warming.

Singer, S. Fred. "Global Climate Change: Fact and Fiction." *The World & I.* Jul. 1991: 284–91. Argues that despite the increase in greenhouse gases, there is no evidence to support the temperature increases that computer climate models have predicted.

———. "Warming Theories Need Warning Label." *Bulletin of the Atomic Scientists* June 1992: 34–39. Argues that despite the media hype suggesting otherwise, there is no scientific consensus supporting a greenhouse warming threat.

Stouffer, R. J., et al. "Model Assessment of the Role of Natural Variability in Recent Global Warming." *Nature* 367.6464 (1994): 34–36. Traces the rise in global temperature over the last thousand years.

Zimmer, Carl. "The Case of the Missing Carbon." *Discover* Dec. 1993: 38–40. Some scientists suggest that because only half of the carbon dioxide released into the atmosphere remains there (and contributes to global warming), the rest is being absorbed by the oceans.

Chapter 4

Armstrong, Susan J., and Richard G. Botzler, eds. *Environmental Ethics.* New York: McGraw, 1993. Provides a broad overview of different philosophical approaches to the environment.

Berry, Wendell. "Out of Your Car, off Your Horse." *Atlantic* Feb. 1991: 61–63. Offers twenty-seven propositions about global environmental thinking and the sustainability of cities.

Bookchin, Murray. *Remaking Society: Pathways to a Green Future.* Boston: South End, 1990. Probably the best introduction to Bookchin's theory of social ecology (p. 244), which argues that social hierarchy and domination are the roots of our ecological crisis.

Braile, Robert. "Is Racism a Factor in Siting Undesirable Facilities?" *Garbage* Summer 1994: 13+. Reports that new studies question the premise of the environmental justice movement — that a disproportionate share of environmental hazards fall on poor and minority communities. (Expands on Braile's "In the News" piece on p. 258, which reports on one such study.)

————. "'When I Look at Nature, I See a Little Bit of God.'" *Boston Globe Magazine* 24 Apr. 1994: 18–24. Discusses the new ecotheology movement, whose members feel a religious and ethical responsibility to save the environment.

Bramwell, Anna. *Ecology in the 20th Century: A History.* New Haven: Yale UP, 1989. Provides an insightful historical overview of ecology as a discipline and movement.

Brown, Lester R., et al. *State of the World 1994.* New York: Norton, 1994. The Worldwatch Institute's annual overview of global environmental concerns, with articles on such topics as forests, oceans, the power industry, and environmental health risks. Includes Sandra Postel's article (p. 286).

————. *Vital Signs: The Trends That Are Shaping Our Future.* New York: Norton, 1993. Another Worldwatch Institute survey of trends that affect the environment in such areas as food, agricultural resources, energy, and the economy.

Bryant, Bunyan, and Paul Mohai, eds. *Race and the Incidence of Environmental Hazards: A Time for Discourse.* Boulder: Westview, 1992. A collection of articles arguing that people of color are disproportionately exposed to environmental hazards.

Bullard, Robert D., ed. *Unequal Protection: Environmental Justice and Communities of Color.* San Francisco: Sierra Club Books, 1994. A collection of articles analyzing the issue of environmental racism from a variety of perspectives. Includes Regina Austin and Michael Schill's article (p. 248).

Carothers, Andre. "The Green Machine." *New Internationalist* Aug. 1993: 14–16. Discusses the efforts of lobbyists and public relations experts to portray corporations as eco-friendly.

Dashefsky, H. Steven. *Environmental Literacy.* New York: Random, 1993. A glossary of environmental terms and issues.

Davis, John, ed. *The Earth First! Reader: Ten Years of Radical Environmentalism.* Salt Lake City: Gibbs, 1991. A collection of writings by more than forty members of Earth First!, the radical environmental group cofounded by Dave Foreman (p. 234).

Davis, Ruth G. "The Body Shop Plays Hardball." *New York* 19 Sept. 1994: 16+. Describes the retaliatory measures taken by the Body Shop, a giant British cosmetics company, in response to an American journalist's article questioning the company's claims of environmental progressivism and social responsibility. (See **Entine.**)

Diamond, Irene, and Gloria Feman Orenstein, eds. *Reweaving the World: The Emergence of Ecofeminism.* San Francisco: Sierra Club Books, 1990. A collection of essays focusing on ecofeminism, a coming together of the environmental, feminist, and women's spirituality movements.

Durning, Alan Thein. *How Much Is Enough?* New York: Norton, 1992. Argues that

overconsumption among the affluent fifth of humanity must stop if we are to succeed in preserving the environment.

Entine, Jon. "Shattered Image." *Business Ethics* Sept.–Oct. 1994: 23–28. A harsh profile
of the Body Shop, the British cosmetics giant, that disputes its reputation as a socially responsible, environmentally progresssive company. (This article set off an
intense controversy and a drop in stock prices. See **Davis.**)

Easterbrook, Gregg. *A Moment on Earth: The Coming Age of Environmental Optimism.*
New York: Viking, 1994. Argues for moderation in environmental thinking
(what Easterbrook calls "ecorealism") and asserts that we must base our policies
and laws on rational risk assessment rather than media scares.

Fumento, Michael. *Science under Siege.* New York: Morrow, 1993. Argues that many
so-called environmental threats, such as dioxin, pesticides, electromagnetic fields,
and food irradiation, have been exaggerated and even fabricated by activists,
politicians, and the media.

Gordon, Anita, and David Suzuki. *It's a Matter of Survival.* Cambridge: Harvard UP,
1991. Presents a rather dire forecast regarding our ecological condition, arguing that the 1990s will be crucial in determining the planet's prognosis for survival.

Gottlieb, Robert. *Forcing the Spring: The Transformation of the American Environmental
Movement.* Washington, DC: Island P, 1993. A revisionist history of the American
environmental movement. Argues that traditional histories have focused too narrowly on conservation and preservation issues while ignoring a wide range of
early efforts by social and human health activists who did not define themselves as
environmentalists.

Hamilton, Joan. "Babbitt's Retreat." *Sierra* July–Aug. 1994: 53+. Traces many environmentalists' disappointment with Interior Secretary Bruce Babbitt, especially
with his failure to preserve western lands from overgrazing.

Harms, Valerie, et al. *National Audubon Society Almanac of the Environment: The Ecology
of Everyday Life.* New York: Putnam, 1994. An illustrated resource book that addresses a vast array of ecological concerns, with an emphasis on what ordinary
people can do to restore and protect the environment.

Hawken, Paul. *The Ecology of Commerce: A Declaration of Sustainability.* New York:
Harper, 1993. Argues that business is the only vehicle powerful enough to save
the world from its environmental woes; advocates redesigning the market system by making prices reflect the true social and environmental costs of production.

Joyce, Christopher. *Earthly Goods: Medicine-Hunting in the Rainforest.* Boston: Little,
1994. Chronicles the quest by pharmaceutical companies and environmentalists to
find new drugs in the rainforest.

Lerner, Steve. "The Gospel of Green." *Audubon* Jan.–Feb. 1994: 78–81. Describes the
environmental activism of an Episcopal priest.

Meadows, Donella H., Dennis L. Meadows, and Jørgen Randers. *Beyond the Limits:
Confronting Global Collapse, Envisioning a Sustainable Future.* Post Mills, VT:
Chelsea Green, 1992. Argues that the global industrial system has already overshot
some of the earth's vital ecological limits and could collapse by the middle of the
next century unless we make sweeping changes now; a sequel to the authors'
landmark *The Limits of Growth.*

Mowrey, Marc, and Tim Redmond. *Not in Our Backyard: The People and Events That
Have Shaped America's Modern Environmental Movement.* New York: Morrow,
1993. Provides an overview of the grassroots environmental movement.

Myers, Norman, and Julian L. Simon. *Scarcity or Abundance? A Debate on the Environment.* New York: Norton, 1994. Presents opposing views of planetary survival,

with Simon arguing that we continue to experience environmental plenty and Myers warning of ecological degradation.

Pennisi, Elizabeth. "No Man's Land." *Garbage* Spring 1994: 33–39. Describes the North American Wilderness Recovery Project, the brainchild of Earth First! co-founder Dave Foreman (p. 234) that would create a vast system of connected wilderness reserves across the continent.

Plant, Christopher, and Judith Plant, eds. *Green Business: Hope or Hoax? Toward an Authentic Strategy for Restoring the Earth.* Philadelphia: New Society, 1991. A collection of articles that critique "shallow green" consumerism (such as biodegradable plastics and dolphin-safe tuna) while identifying more meaningful strategies for changing the way we do business.

Ray, Dixy Lee, with Lou Guzzo. *Environmental Overkill: Whatever Happened to Common Sense?* Washington, DC: Regnery, 1993. Argues that environmental extremists, scare-mongering journalists, and media-conscious scientists (among others) are hyping ecological threats that don't exist.

Roszak, Theodore. *The Voice of the Earth.* New York: Touchstone, 1992. Introduces the concept of ecopsychology, an offshoot of psychotherapy that explores the relationship between human psychology and the environment.

Shabecoff, Philip. *A Fierce Green Fire: The American Environmental Movement.* New York: Hill and Wang, 1993. A history of the environmental movement that concludes with a prognosis for the future.

Simon, Julian. See **Myers and Simon.**

Snow, Donald. "Wise Use and Public Lands in the West: The Pristine Silence of Leaving It All Alone." *Utne Reader* May–June 1994: 70–77. Insists that the greatest challenge facing the American West is the Wise Use movement, a grassroots conglomeration of organizations and individuals who argue that the government should not protect natural resources.

Stevenson, L. Harold, and Bruce Wyman, eds. *The Facts on File Dictionary of Environmental Science.* New York: Facts on File, 1991. Offers clear definitions and explanations of environmental terms and issues.

Wade, Nicholas, et al., eds. *The New York Times Book of Science Literacy.* Vol 2. *The Environment from Your Backyard to the Ocean Floor.* New York: Times, 1994. A collection of articles on environmental issues that originally appeared in the Science Times section of the *New York Times.*

Wann, David. *BioLogic: Designing with Nature to Protect the Environment.* 1990. Boulder: Johnson, 1994. Proposes an environmental ethic that sees nature as a model for efficient, sustainable energy use, food production, housing, transportation, and recycling of wastes.

Wildavsky, Aaron. *But Is It True? A Citizens' Guide to Health and Safety.* Cambridge: Harvard UP, 1994. Criticizes environmental alarmists on a variety of controversial topics, claiming that the risks associated with certain threats have been exaggerated.

Willers, Bill, ed. *Learning to Listen to the Land.* Washington, DC: Island P, 1991. A collection of essays on environmental topics by such authors as Edward O. Wilson (p. 1), Paul and Anne Ehrlich (p. 13), Barry Commoner (p. 134), James Lovelock (p. 158), Wendell Berry (p. 229), and Dave Foreman (p. 234).

Yoon, Carol Kaesuk. "Drugs from Bugs." *Garbage* Summer 1994: 23–29. Describes efforts by conservationists to harvest medicines from Costa Rica's rainforests.

Ronald Bailey, excerpt from *Eco-Scam*. Copyright © 1993 by Ronald Bailey. From the book, *Eco-Scam: False Prophets of Ecological Apocalypse,* and reprinted with permission of St. Martin's Press, Inc., New York.

Wendell Berry, excerpt from "Conservation is Good Work." From *The Amicus Journal,* Winter 1992. Reprinted with permission.

Murray Bookchin, excerpt from *Defending the Earth: A Dialogue Between Murray Bookchin and Dave Foreman,* edited by Steve Chase (South End Press, 1991). Copyright © 1991 by Murray Bookchin, Dave Foreman, Steve Chase, and David Levine. Reprinted by permission of South End Press.

Daniel B. Botkin, *"Trashing the Planet,"* From the *New York Times Book Review,* 30 September 1990. Copyright © 1990 by The New York Times Company. Reprinted by permission.

Robert Braile, excerpt from "No Pattern of Bias found in Locating Toxic Waste Plants: Study texts findings of racism in sitings." From the *Boston Globe,* 10 May 1994. Reprinted with permission of the author.

Lester R. Brown, Christopher Flavin, and Sandra Postel, excerpt from *Saving the Planet.* Reprinted from *Saving the Planet: How to Shape an Environmentally Sustainable Global Economy* by Lester R. Brown, Christopher Flavin, and Sandra Postel, with the permission of W. W. Norton & Company, Inc. Copyright © 1991 by Worldwatch Institute.

Joseph Bruchac, "The Circle Is the Way to See." From *Story Earth* © 1993 by Inter Press Service. Published by Mercury House, San Francisco, CA and reprinted by permission.

Helen Caldicott, excerpt from *If You Love This Planet.* Reprinted from *If You Love This Planet: A Plan to Heal the Earth* by Helen Caldicott, with the permission of W. W. Norton & Company, Inc. Copyright © 1992 by Helen Caldicott.

Rachel Carson, excerpt from *Silent Spring.* From *Silent Spring* by Rachel Carson. Copyright © 1962 by Rachel L. Carson, renewed 1990 by Roger Christie. Reprinted by permission of Houghton Mifflin Co. All rights reserved.

"Changing the World." From *The Economist,* 26 February 1994. © 1994 The Economist Newspaper Group, Inc. Reprinted with permission.

Christopher Clarke, "Nothing Degrades in a Landfill." From the *Ecology Center Newsletter* (titled *Terrain* after 1992), September 1991. Reprinted with permission of the author.

Carl Cohen, excerpt from "The Case for the Use of Animals in Biomedical Research." From *The New England Journal of Medicine,* Vol. 315, No. 14. Reprinted with permission.

Barry Commoner, excerpt from *Making Peace with the Planet.* From *Making Peace with the Planet* by Barry Commoner. Copyright 1975, 1988, 1989, 1990, 1992 by Barry Commoner. Reprinted by permission of The New Press.

John Deering, cartoon, "So — How does it feel being an endangered species?" *Arkansas Democratic Gazette,* July 1993. Reprinted with permission of the artist.

Dianne Dumanoski, excerpt from "Why not tax our trash and our traffic jams?" From the *Boston Globe,* 1 April 1991. Reprinted courtesy of the *Boston Globe.*

Paul and Anne Ehrlich, preface to "The Rivet Poppers." From *Extinction* by Paul R. Ehrlich and Anne H. Ehrlich. Copyright © 1981 by Paul R. and Anne H. Ehrlich. Reprinted by permission of Random House, Inc.

Dave Foreman, excerpt from "Earth First!" From *Confessions of an Eco-Warrior* by Dave Foreman. Copyright © 1991 by Dave Foreman. Reprinted by permission of Harmony Books, a member of the Crown Publishing Group.

David Foster, excerpt from "Beyond Spotted Owls." From The Associated Press, 15 May 1994. Reprinted with permission of The Associated Press.

John Bellamy Foster, excerpt from "Let Them Eat Pollution." From *Monthly Review,* vol. 44, January 1993. Copyright © 1993 by Monthly Review Inc. Reprinted by permission of Monthly Review Foundation.

Al Gore, excerpt from *Earth in the Balance.* Copyright © 1992 by Senator Al Gore. Reprinted by permission of Houghton Mifflin Co. All rights reserved.

JoAnn C. Gutin, excerpt from "Okay, Okay — Here's Another Look at Plastics." From *E: The Environmental Magazine*, May/June 1994. Excerpted/reprinted by permission from *E: The Environmental Magazine*. Subscription Dept.: P.O. Box 699, Mt. Morris, IL 61054. Subscriptions: $20/year for 6 issues.

Sidney Harris, cartoons: "I can remember when everyone was skeptical about the greenhouse effect," "The Rain Forest: Big City for Animals," "They didn't tell ME what to do with it . . . " © 1993 by Sidney Harris. *From Personal Ads to Cloning Labs,* W. H. Freeman and Co.

David Holmstrom, "Decision on Waste Disposal Raises Environmental Eyebrows." From *The Christian Science Monitor,* 28 June 1994. Reprinted by permission from *The Christian Science Monitor* © 1994 The Christian Science Publishing Society. All rights reserved.

Peter Huber, excerpt from "Biodiversity vs. Bioengineering?" From FORBES Magazine, 26 October 1992. Reprinted by permission of FORBES Magazine © Forbes Inc., 1994.

William Robert Irvin, Letter to the Editor. From *The Atlantic Monthly,* April 1992. Copyright © 1992 William Robert Irvin as first published in *The Atlantic Monthly.*

Diane Jukofsky, "Can Marketing Save the Rainforest?" From *E: The Environmental Magazine,* July/August 1993. Reprinted with permission of the author.

Aaron Katcher and Gregory Wilkins, excerpt from "Dialogue with Animals: Its Nature and Culture." Granted with permission from *"Dialogue with Animals: Its Nature and Culture"; The Biophilia Hypothesis,* edited by Stephen R. Kellert and Edward O. Wilson. Copyright © 1993 by Island Press. Published by Island Press, Washington D.C. and Covelo, California.

Tom Kenworthy, "Administration Moves to Ease Opposition to Biodiversity Act." From the *Washington Post,* 15 June 1994. Copyright © 1994 the *Washington Post.* Reprinted with permission.

Leila L. Kysar, "A Logger's Lament." From *Newsweek,* 22 October 1990. Reprinted with permission.

Aldo Leopold, excerpt from *A Sand County Almanac.* Adapted from *A Sand County Almanac, with Other Essays on Conservation from Round River* by Aldo Leopold. Copyright © 1949, 1953, 1966, renewed 1977, 1981 by Oxford University Press, Inc. Reprinted by permission.

Martin W. Lewis, excerpt from "The Green Threat to Nature," *Harper's,* November 1992. Adapted from *Green Delusions: An Environmentalist Critique of Radical Environmentalism* by Martin L. Lewis (Duke University Press, 1992). Reprinted with permission.

James Lovelock, excerpt from "Rethinking Life on Earth: The Sum: Gaia Takes Flight." From *Earthwatch,* September/October 1992. Reprinted from *Earthwatch* magazine, with permission from James Lovelock. Earthwatch is a nonprofit organization which sponsors scientists and recruits volunteers for field research. Phone: 617-926-8200.

Charles C. Mann and Mark L. Plummer, excerpt from "The Butterfly Problem." Copyright © Charles C. Mann and Mark L. Plummer. First published in the *Atlantic Monthly,* January 1992.

Mary Martin, excerpt from "Truly Fashionable Recycling." From the *Boston Globe,* 2 March 1994. Reprinted with permission of the author.

Charles McCoy, excerpt from "Businesses Are Battling Environmentalism with Its Own Laws." From the *Wall Street Journal,* 28 April 1994. Reprinted by permission of the *Wall Street Journal,* © 1994 Dow Jones & Company, Inc. All Rights Reserved Worldwide.

Bill McKibben, excerpt from "The End of Nature." From *The End of Nature* by Bill McKibben. Copyright © 1989 by Bill McKibben. Reprinted by permission of Random House, Inc.

Donella H. Meadows, "The New World of Plastics — Not New Enough." Granted with permission from *The Global Citizen* by Donella H. Meadows. Copyright © 1991 by Donella H. Meadows. Published by Island Press, Washington D.C. and Covelo, California.

Patrick J. Michaels, excerpt from *Sound and Fury: The Science and Politics of Global Warming* by Patrick J. Michaels. Reprinted with permission from *Sound and Fury* (Cato Institute, 1992).

Will Nixon, book review of *Environmental Overkill.* From *E: The Environmental Magazine,* November/December 1993. Reprinted with permission from *E: The Environmental Magazine.* Subscriptions are $20/year from: E Magazine Subscriptions, P.O. Box 699, Mount Morris, IL 61054-7589/(800) 967-6572.

Michael Oppenheimer and Robert H. Boyle, excerpt from *Dead Heat*. Excerpt used as epigraph from *Dead Heat: The Race Against the Greenhouse Effect* by Michael Oppenheimer and Robert H. Boyle. Copyright © 1990 by Michael Oppenheimer and Robert H. Boyle. Reprinted by permission of BasicBooks, a division of HarperCollins Publishers, Inc.

Thomas Palmer, "The Case for Human Beings." From *Landscape with Reptile* by Thomas Palmer. As published in *Atlantic Monthly*. Copyright © 1992 by Thomas Palmer. Reprinted by permission of Ticknor & Fields/Houghton Mifflin Company. All rights reserved.

Patricia Poore, "America's 'Garbage Crisis.'" Copyright © 1994 by *Harper's Magazine*. All rights reserved. Reproduced from the March issue by special permission.

Sandra Postel, excerpt from "Carrying Capacity: Earth's Bottom Line." Reprinted from *State of the World 1994*: A Worldwatch Institute Report on Progress Toward a Sustainable Society, edited by Lester R. Brown, et al., with the permission of W. W. Norton & Company, Inc. Copyright © 1994 by Worldwatch Institute.

William Rathje and Cullen Murphy, excerpts from *Rubbish! The Archaeology of Garbage* by William Rathje and Cullen Murphy. Copyright © 1992 by William Rathje and Cullen Murphy. Reprinted by permission of HarperCollins Publishers, Inc.

Dixy Lee Ray and Louis R. Guzzo, excerpt from *Trashing the Planet*. From *Trashing the Planet* by Dixy Lee Ray and Louis R. Guzzo. Copyright © 1990 by Regnery Gateway. All Rights Reserved. Reprinted by special permission of Regnery Publishing, Inc., Washington, D.C.

"Recycling: Is It Worth the Effort?" Copyright 1994 by Consumers Union of U.S., Inc., Yonkers, NY 10703-1057. Adapted with permission from CONSUMER REPORTS, February 1994. Although this material originally appeared in CONSUMER REPORTS, the selective adaptation and resulting conclusions presented are those of the author and are not sanctioned or endorsed in any way by Consumers Union, the publisher of CONSUMER REPORTS.

William K. Reilly, excerpt from "The Green Thumb of Capitalism." From *Policy Review*, Fall 1990. Published by the Heritage Foundation. Reprinted with permission.

Matt Ridley and Bobbi S. Low, excerpt from "Can Selfishness Save the Environment?" From *The Atlantic Monthly*, September 1993. Reprinted with permission of Matt Ridley and Bobbi S. Low.

Larry E. Ruff, excerpt from "The Economic Common Sense of Pollution." Reprinted with permission of National Affairs from *The Public Interest*, No. 19 (Spring 1970), pp. 69–85. Copyright © 1970 by National Affairs, Inc.

Kirkpatrick Sale, excerpt from "The Trouble With Earth Day." From *The Nation*, 30 April 1990. Reprinted with permission from *The Nation* magazine. Copyright © The Nation Company, Inc.

Michael Satchell, "Trashing the Reservations." From *U.S. News & World Report*, 11 January 1993. Copyright © January 11, 1993, *U.S. News & World Report*.

David G. Savage, "High Court's Trash Ruling a Blow to Cities." From the *Los Angeles Times*, 3 May 1994. Copyright, 1994, Los Angeles Times. Reprinted by permission.

Keith Schneider, excerpt from "Fetal Harm, Not Cancer, Is Called the Primary Threat from Dioxin." From the *New York Times*, 11 May 1994. Copyright © 1994 by The New York Times Company. Reprinted by permission.

Stephen H. Schneider, excerpt from "The Global Warming Debate Heats Up." From *Global Warming: Are We Entering the Greenhouse Century?* by Stephen H. Schneider. Copyright © 1989 by Stephen H. Schneider. Reprinted with permission of Sierra Club Books.

Julian L. Simon, excerpt from *The Ultimate Resource*. Copyright © 1981 by Princeton University Press. Reprinted with permission of Princeton University Press.

Peter Singer, excerpt from "Ethics and the New Animal Liberation Movement." From *In Defense of Animals*, edited by Peter Singer. Copyright © 1985 by Blackwell Publishers. Reprinted with permission.

Randy Smith, "Developing Nations Top List of Carbon Dioxide Producers." From the Associated Press, 18 April 1994. Reprinted with permission of the Associated Press.

William K. Stevens, "Warming of Deep Sea Is Surprising." From *New York Times*, 10 May 1994. Copyright © 1994 by The New York Times Company. Reprinted by permission.

Mary Tannen, excerpt from "Eco-Yearnings." From *New York Times*, 20 March 1994. Copyright © 1994 by The New York Times Company. Reprinted by permission.

Tom Toles, cartoon, "Land that we loved," Toles, 1994 *The New Republic*. Reprinted with permission of the artist.

Aaron Wildavsky, excerpt from introduction to *The Heated Debate: Greenhouse Predictions Versus Climate Reality* by Robert C. Balling, Jr. (Pacific Research Institute, 1992). Reprinted by permission of Pacific Research Institute for Public Policy, San Francisco, CA.

Edward O. Wilson, excerpt from "Is Humanity Suicidal?" From *New York Times Magazine*, 30 May 1993. Copyright © 1993 by The New York Times Company. Reprinted by permission.

Matt Wuerker, cartoon, "Recycling Center," *Z Magazine*, October 1993. Reprinted with permission of the artist.

Carol Kaesuk Yoon, excerpt from "Rare Butterfly Consigned to Extinction." From *New York Times*, 26 April 1994. Copyright © 1994 by The New York Times Company. Reprinted by permission.

Mary Zepernick, excerpt from "Keeping business in its place." From *Cape Cod Times*, 11 February 1994. Reprinted by permission of the author.

Index of Authors and Titles